The Archaeology of Colonialism

This volume examines human sexuality as an intrinsic element in the interpretation of complex colonial societies. Although archaeological studies of the historic past have explored the dynamics of European colonialism, such work has largely ignored broader issues of sexuality, embodiment, commemoration, reproduction, and sensuality. Recently, however, scholars have begun to recognize these issues as essential components of colonization and imperialism. This book explores a variety of case studies, revealing the multifaceted intersections of colonialism and sexuality. Incorporating work that ranges from Phoenician diasporic communities of the eighth century to Britain's nineteenth-century Australian penal colonies to the contemporary maroon community of Brazil, this volume changes the way we understand the relationship between sexuality and colonial history.

Barbara L. Voss is Associate Professor of Anthropology at Stanford University, where she is also affiliated with the Stanford Archaeology Center, Feminist Studies, and the Center for Comparative Study on Race and Ethnicity. Dr. Voss's field and laboratory research investigates the dynamics and outcomes of transnational cultural encounters in colonial and early industrial North America. She is the author or editor of several books, including, most recently, *The Archaeology of Ethnogenesis: Race, Sexuality, and Identity in Colonial San Francisco; The Archaeology of Chinese Immigrant and Chinese American Communities* (coedited with Bryn Williams); and *Archaeologies of Sexuality* (coedited with Robert A. Schmidt).

Eleanor Conlin Casella is Senior Lecturer in Archaeology at the University of Manchester, where she is also affiliated with the Centre for Research on Socio-Cultural Change. She has directed archaeological projects in Australia, North America, northwest England, and the Scottish Highlands. She is the author or editor of several books, including, most recently, *The Alderley Sandhills Project: An Archaeology of Community Life in (Post)-Industrial England* (coauthored with Sarah Croucher), *The Archaeology of Institutional Confinement, The Archaeology of Plural and Changing Identities* (coedited with Chris Fowler), and *Industrial Archaeology: Future Directions* (coedited with James Symonds).

THE ARCHAEOLOGY OF
COLONIALISM

Intimate Encounters and Sexual Effects

BARBARA L. VOSS
Stanford University

ELEANOR CONLIN CASELLA
University of Manchester

CAMBRIDGE
UNIVERSITY PRESS

CAMBRIDGE UNIVERSITY PRESS
Cambridge, New York, Melbourne, Madrid, Cape Town,
Singapore, São Paulo, Delhi, Tokyo, Mexico City

Cambridge University Press
32 Avenue of the Americas, New York, NY 10013-2473, USA

www.cambridge.org
Information on this title: www.cambridge.org/9781107401266

First published 2012

Printed in the United States of America

A catalog record for this publication is available from the British Library.

Library of Congress Cataloging in Publication data

The archaeology of colonialism : intimate encounters and sexual effects /
[edited by] Barbara L. Voss, Eleanor Conlin Casella.
p.   cm.
Includes bibliographical references and index.
ISBN 978-1-107-00863-2 (hardback) – ISBN 978-1-107-40126-6 (paperback)
1. Sex–Europe–Colonies–History.   2. Europe–Colonies–Race relations–History.   3. Interpersonal
relations–Europe–Colonies–History.   I. Voss, Barbara L., 1967–   II. Casella, Eleanor Conlin.
HQ18.E8A73   2012
306.709171′2–dc22   2011015451

ISBN 978-1-107-00863-2 Hardback
ISBN 978-1-107-40126-6 Paperback

To Meg Conkey, Kent Lightfoot, and Ruth Tringham

CONTENTS

List of Illustrations

List of Tables

List of Contributors

Kira Blaisdell-Sloan received her Ph.D. in anthropology from the University of California–Berkeley in 2006; her Ph.D. thesis was based on two seasons of fieldwork she directed at the indigenous town of Ticamaya, Honduras. In addition to her work on Central American colonial sites, Blaisdell-Sloan has field experience on historic sites in the Bahamas, California, and Louisiana and on pre-Columbian sites in Honduras and Hawaii. Blaisdell-Sloan has taught at Louisiana State University and the University of California–Berkeley, where she is currently employed as the Undergraduate Academic Advisor in History.

Aline Vieira de Carvalho is a Research Fellow at the Public Archaeology in the Environment Research Center (Nepam), University of Campinas, Brazil. She has published articles about historical archaeology, cultural heritage, and public archaeology and a book about Palmares. Currently, she studies the gender relations in Palmares Quilombo.

Eleanor Conlin Casella is Senior Lecturer in Archaeology at the University of Manchester. She is Reviews Editor for *Post-Medieval Archaeology* and a Fellow of the Society of Antiquaries of London. Her publications include *The Alderley Sandhills Project: An Archaeology of Community Life in (Post-)Industrial England* (2010; coauthored with Sarah K. Croucher), *The Archaeology of Institutional Confinement* (2007), and the coedited volumes *Industrial Archaeology: Future Directions* (2005) and *The Archaeology of Plural and Changing Identities* (2005).

Sarah K. Croucher is Assistant Professor of Anthropology; Archaeology; and Feminist, Gender and Sexuality Studies at Wesleyan University, Connecticut, and a Weatherhead Resident Fellow (2010–2011) at the School for Advanced Research. Her dissertation (University of Manchester) won the Society for Historical Archaeology 2008 dissertation prize and is currently being revised for publication. She is the coauthor (with Eleanor Casella) of *The Alderley Sandhills Project: An Archaeology of Community Life in (Post-)Industrial England* (2010) and coeditor (with Lindsay Weiss) of *The Archaeology of Capitalism in Colonial Contexts: Postcolonial Historical Archaeologies* (2011).

SHANNON LEE DAWDY is Associate Professor in Anthropology and the Social Sciences at the University of Chicago. She is the author of *Building the Devil's Empire: French Colonial New Orleans* and coeditor of *Dialogues in Cuban Archaeology*. She is currently directing a multiyear archaeological research project in New Orleans' French Quarter to investigate the economic and ecological conditions of creolization.

ANA DELGADO is Associate Professor of Prehistory and Ancient History in the Humanities Department of Universitat Pompeu Fabra, Barcelona, and member of the Institut Universitari d'Història Jaume Vicens Vives. Since 2003, Delgado has codirected the archaeological project of Cerro del Villar, a Phoenician colony in Malaga. Among her recent publications are "Cultural Contacts in Colonial Settings: The Construction of New Identities in Colonial Phoenician Areas of the Western Mediterranean" (with Meritxell Ferrer) and "Los fenicios en Iberia," in *De Iberia a Hispania*.

MERITXELL FERRER is a Ph.D. candidate at the Institut Universitari d'Història Jaume Vicens Vives and Universitat Pompeu Fabra, Barcelona. She holds a master's in History from the same university and a master's in Museology and Cultural Heritage Management from Universitat de Barcelona. She has been involved in the Cerro del Villar (Universitat Pompeu Fabra), Malaga, project since 2002 and in the Monte Polizzo Project (Stanford University) since 2004. Recent publications include "Cultural Contacts in Colonial Settings" and "Alimentos para los muertos," both coauthored with Ana Delgado.

PEDRO PAULO A. FUNARI is Professor of Historical Archaeology at the University of Campinas, Brazil; Research Associate at Illinois State University and the University of Barcelona, Spain; and former secretary of the World Archaeological Congress. He is coeditor with Martin Hall and Siân Jones of *Historical Archaeology: Back from the Edge* (1999) and with Andrés Zarankin and Emily Stovel of *Global Archaeological Theory* (2005).

RENATA S. GARRAFFONI is a Lecturer at Paraná Federal University (Curitiba, Brazil) and a research associate at State University of Campinas. She is interested in the Roman Empire and has been studying the common people's daily lives and gladiators' fights for several years. She was based at University of Birmingham, United Kingdom, with a British Academy Fellowship from December 2008 to March 2009 to study Roman graffiti from Pompeii, her most recent research project.

MARTIN HALL is Vice Chancellor of the University of Salford. His career has spanned both political change and transformation in South Africa and new directions in archaeology over the past four decades. He has written extensively on South African history, culture, and higher education policy and has served terms as President of the World Archaeological Congress and General Secretary of the South African Archaeological Society.

KATHLEEN L. HULL is Assistant Professor of Anthropology and a Faculty Affiliate of the Sierra Nevada Research Institute at the University of California, Merced. Her research interests include archaeological study of the interaction of demography and culture within small-scale societies. Hull's work on this subject includes *Pestilence and Persistence: Yosemite Indian Demography and Culture in Colonial California* (2009), which takes a broad, comparative approach to the issue of indigenous responses to colonial-era population decline in North America.

ROSEMARY A. JOYCE is the Richard and Rhoda Goldman Distinguished Professor of the Social Sciences at the University of California, Berkeley, where she has been a Professor of Anthropology since 1994. She has directed archaeological fieldwork in Honduras since 1979, in the lower Ulúa Valley, in the Department of Yoro, at Los Naranjos, and, most recently, at the Spanish colonial fort of San Fernando de Omoa. Joyce is the author of four books and coauthor of three others, including the path-breaking work on Honduran archaeology *Cerro Palenque: Power and Identity on the Maya Periphery.*

MIREIA LÓPEZ-BERTRAN holds a Ph.D. in History from at Universitat Pompeu Fabra (Barcelona; 2007); her thesis concerned Phoenician and Punic rituals in the western Mediterranean. She is currently a postdoctoral researcher for the Spanish Ministry of Education and Culture (FECYT) and she carries out her work at the University of Glasgow, where she is Honorary Research Fellow. Her research interests cover rituals, gender, and embodiment in the ancient western Mediterranean. Recent publications include "Practical Movements: Kinetic Rituals in the Ancient Western Mediterraean," in the *Journal of Mediterranean Archaeology* (2011).

DIANA DIPAOLO LOREN has been an Associate Curator at the Peabody Museum of Archaeology and Ethnology, Harvard University, since 1999. Her research interests include materiality, identity, embodiment, and dress in colonial North America. She is the author of *The Archaeology of Clothing and Bodily Adornment in Colonial America* (2010) and *In Contact: Bodies and Spaces in the Sixteenth- and Seventeenth-Century Eastern Woodlands* (2007).

PATRICIA E. RUBERTONE is Professor of Anthropology at Brown University, Providence, Rhode Island. Her research combines archaeology, history, and anthropology to study questions of colonialism, landscape and memory, and representation in the context of European and Native American experiences in southern New England. She is the author of *Grave Undertakings: An Archaeology of Roger Williams and the Narragansett Indians* (2001) and the editor of *Archaeologies of Placemaking: Monuments, Memories, and Engagement in Native North America* (2008).

KAY TARBLE DE SCARAMELLI is Professor in the Departamento de Arqueología, Etnohistoria y Ecología Cultural, Escuela de Antropología, Universidad Central de Venezuela, where she has taught since 1985. A specialist in the archaeology of the Middle Orinoco, she has contributed to the development of the ceramic sequence for the region for both the precontact and postcontact periods. An interest in the impact of colonialism on the indigenous population has led to several publications with her husband, Franz Scaramelli. Other interests include the study of rock art and its role in the construction of the Orinoco landscape.

NICK SHEPHERD is Associate Professor of African Studies and Archaeology at the University of Cape Town. He is joint Editor-in-Chief of the journal *Archaeologies: Journal of the World Archaeological Congress*. He has published widely on questions of archaeology and society in Africa and on questions of public history and heritage. His books include *Desire Lines: Space, Memory and Identity in the Postapartheid City* (2007, with Martin Hall and Noeleen Murray) and *New South African Keywords* (2008, with Steven Robins).

RUSSELL N. SHEPTAK is a Visiting Scholar at the Archaeological Research Facility, University of California, Berkeley. A historical anthropologist, Sheptak conducts research at the Archivo General de Indias (Seville, Spain) and Archivo General de Centroamerica (Guatemala City), from microfilmed collections from the Archivo Eclesiastico de Comayagua, and at archaeological sites throughout Honduras. He currently directs a project to create a finding aid for the microfilmed Archivo General de Centroamerica. He has authored numerous journal articles, the majority in Spanish, about the Honduran past.

BARBARA L. VOSS is Associate Professor of Anthropology at Stanford University. Author of *The Archaeology of Ethnogenesis: Race and Sexuality in Colonial San Francisco* (2008) and coeditor (with Robert Schmidt) of *Archaeologies of Sexuality* (2000), she is a two-time recipient of the Ruth Benedict Prize and winner of the 2008 Gordon R. Willey Prize, both awarded by the American Anthropological Association.

MARY WEISMANTEL is Professor of Anthropology at Northwestern University. She has been writing about gender and sexuality in the Andes of South America for twenty years. Her most recent book, *Cholas and Pishtacos: Tales of Race and Sex in the Andes*, won several prizes. Noteworthy articles include "Moche Sex Pots: Reproduction and Temporality in Ancient South America," *American Anthropologist* (2004); and "Making Kin: Kinship Theory and Zumbagua Adoption," *American Ethnologist* (1995).

LINDSAY WEISS is a Postdoctoral Scholar in the Archaeology Center and Department of Anthropology at Stanford University. Her research focuses on the relationship between colonialism and materiality, the heritage industry, and the history of the South African diamond fields. She has published articles in *American Anthropology* and the *Journal of Social Archaeology* and is the coeditor (with Sarah Croucher) of *The Archaeology of Capitalism in Colonial Contexts: Postcolonial Historical Archaeologies* (2011).

ONE

INTIMATE ENCOUNTERS

An Archaeology of Sexualities
within Colonial Worlds

Eleanor Conlin Casella and Barbara L. Voss

Although archaeological studies of the historic past have long explored the dynamics of European colonialism, broader issues of sexuality, embodiment, commemoration, reproduction, and sensuality have only recently become acknowledged as essential components of the "imperial project." How can we better appreciate the material implications of human sexuality when we come to interpret these complex colonial worlds? Ranging from anticipated and pleasurable, to strategic and even involuntary, these intimate encounters are not merely by-products of colonial projects but are fundamental structures of colonization. This volume offers a unique exploration of this sensitive topic by presenting a series of comparative and contrasting archaeological case studies on the multifaceted intersections of colonialism and sexuality.

DEFINITIONS AND THE POLITICS OF COMPARISON

To appreciate the complexities of this thematic conjuncture, very broad definitions of the key subjects were adopted. Diverse forms of *colonialism* – loosely identified as the process of expansionist settlement and sociocultural replication adopted by various cultural groups through human (pre)history – were contrasted with practices of *imperialism* – which is more often understood as referring to centralized, appropriative, militaristic, and often violent projects of conquest and dispossession. Both colonialism and imperialism can be found in prehistoric and classical examples, as well as in the political, economic, and administrative expansion of Western nation-states over the Early Modern era.

Similarly, our approach to sexuality encompasses the many "tense and tender ties" (Stoler 2001) that bind together political, institutional, economic, emotive, affectionate, and familial aspects of the social lives that unfolded in both metropole and colony. Contributions to this volume have approached *sexuality* as a broad assemblage of socialities and affects – a constellation of embodied and expressive human intimacies – that range from the seductive, pleasurable, and erotic, through the familial, parental, nonnormative and homosocial, and into the involuntary, strategic, and exploitative. Ultimately, we seek to illuminate the *sexual effects*, in their many and diverse material forms, wrought throughout past colonial worlds.

The shift to this focus on sexual effects in colonial contexts is at the core of the comparative project undertaken in this volume. As discussed in greater depth in Chapter 2 (Voss), the historical contingency of both colonialism *and* sexuality poses theoretical and methodological conundrums for comparative study of empire. Yet despite these challenges, recent comparative archaeological research on colonialism has generated new and important perspectives on empire. Significantly, in the 2000s, archaeologists have forged new comparative analyses among prehistoric, classical; and modern empires through projects such as Hall's (2000) *Archaeology and the Modern World* and Gosden's (2004) *Archaeology and Colonialism*, along with multiauthor volumes such as Alcock et al.'s (2001) *Empires* and Stein's (2005) *The Archaeology of Colonial Encounters*. Other archaeologists have turned to the comparative study of modern empires, as in Rothschild's (2003) and Lightfoot's (2005) investigations of the variable impacts of Spanish colonialism versus Dutch and Russian mercantilism, respectively, in North America. Likewise, the multiauthor volume *The Archaeology of Contact in Settler Societies* (Murray 2004) traces the specific material dynamics of settler societies and their effects on indigenous communities in North America, Africa, Australia, and New Zealand.

There are three consistent themes that emerge from these diachronic and synchronic archaeological comparisons of empire. First, archaeology's strength as a discipline is its fine-grained attention to the "on-the-ground" consequences and negotiations of empire, particularly among those who are subject to colonial rule. It is largely through the archaeological record of frontier settlements, mission and military outposts, and mercantile ventures that scholars have been able to trace the ways in which imperial objectives were enacted in practice. Second, archaeological research reveals an internal variability of empire that belies overt, structural conditions. The "differences" that mark colonization are located not only between the colonized and colonizer but also lie within the conflicting interests and differing commitments of those involved in colonial projects. The third finding, which is inseparable from the second, is that indigenous and subaltern responses to colonialism are equally variable: those subject to empire create new social and political worlds that are in negotiation with colonial powers but are far from being determined by them. Similar to Fernando Coronil's (2007) formulation of "imperial effects," these archaeological findings point toward the importance of situated and contextual analysis of empire – in other words, a methodological perspective in which empire is investigated through the experiences of those entangled with colonial projects.

In this volume, we extend this emphasis on the effects of colonialism to ask new questions about sexuality itself. What were the sexual and sensual dynamics of colonial encounters? How can archaeology's interrogation of materiality illuminate the embodied, objectified, spatial, reproductive, and sensual components of the new interactions generated by colonialism? How does colonial use and control of sensuality render sexuality as a strategic marker of social differences within imperial projects? How is it that different, and sometimes contrasting, experiences of sexuality can be generated through colonial encounters – with new sexualities rang-ing from exotic pleasures, creative expressions, and hybrid cultures, to oppressive, ambivalent, and coerced transactions? Finally, how can diachronic and transregional comparisons expand our analysis of the logics and hierarchies of sexuality within colonial contexts?

IMPERIAL INTIMACIES AND COLONIAL ENTANGLEMENTS

The origins of this volume can be traced back to a dedicated symposium theme delivered as part of the Sixth World Archaeology Congress (WAC-6), held in Dublin, Ireland, in July 2008. The symposium theme, "Intimate Encounters, Postcolonial Engagements: Archaeologies of Empire and Sexuality," arose out of our concern that archaeologists have tended to minimize sexuality in their studies of colonial, colonized, and postcolonial societies. Accordingly, we invited participating scholars to reexamine and reimagine archaeological research in ways that confront sex-ual silences in the archaeology of the colonial past and present. In particular, we challenged researchers to consider what archaeology's methodological emphases on place, material culture, and representation could uniquely bring to studies of sexuality and colonialism.

The international dialogue fostered by the WAC-6 symposium both demonstrated the promise of this inquiry and brought to light the challenges facing archaeologists investigating colonial sexualities. We came to realize that this project required a strong cross-disciplinary connection between the archaeology of colonialism and postcolonial studies of gender and sexuality, two bodies of scholarship that have until now only been weakly linked. Compounding this difficulty is the relatively late development of sexuality studies within archaeology, a factor attributed as much to recalcitrant attitudes within the discipline as to the methodological challenges involved (Voss 2008).

To develop more fully our interdisciplinary dialogue into this book, we convened a research project that combined web-based collaboration with a two-day inten-sive working session at Stanford University in the spring of 2009. The contributing authors were recruited from those present at the WAC-6 symposium as well as other scholars whose research interests and experience could uniquely contribute to the project. Dialogues among contributors before and during the Stanford working session began to transform conventional archaeological approaches to colonial sex-ualities.

Contributions to this edited volume explore an important array of new interpretive directions by reassessing and expanding our material appreciations of sexuality and colonization. By emphasizing the unique contributions that an archaeological approach delivers to our broader scholarly understandings of colonial and sexual encounters, the collected chapters all fundamentally consider how an interrogation of *materiality* itself illuminates the embodied, objectified, spatial, reproductive, and sensual dynamics of these new social interactions. Moreover, the sustained dialogue among the authors contributing to this volume has allowed the specific colonial situations under study to be situated within the broader context of diachronic and transregional imperial patterns.

Further, the studies presented here question how different, if sometimes contrasting, experiences of sexuality became generated through the experience of colonial encounter. A central node of investigation is the tense relationship between the oppressive sexual regimes generated by colonial projects and the newer exotic pleasures, creative subjectivities, and affective relationships that are forged within and alongside ambivalent and coerced sexual transactions.

Finally, to better articulate specific case studies within a comparative framework, contributions have considered how a range of other pivotal structural changes classically associated with colonialism – the development of capitalism, the commodification of bodies, the politics of reproduction, the consolidation of state infrastructures, and the emergence of modernity – shaped historically specific vectors of sexual encounters throughout imperial worlds. Ultimately, by adopting this broad comparative approach, contributions to this volume demonstrate how our unique *archaeological* approach expands wider scholarly debates over methodological and epistemological approaches to understanding human sexualities.

TOWARD AN ARCHAEOLOGY OF MATERIAL INTIMACIES

Together, the sixteen case studies published in this volume extend our understanding of how human sexuality – in its many profound and mundane, subtle and explicit, situated and diverse expressions – powerfully shaped both the internal dynamics and the enduring legacy of the imperial project. These case studies are preceded by this introductory chapter and by Chapter 2, "Sexual Effects: Postcolonial and Queer Perspectives on the Archaeology of Sexuality and Empire" (Voss), which outlines the theoretical debates that inform this project.

Although a web of connections and contrasts exist throughout the book, the chapters presented here have been loosely clustered into four overlapping themes: Pleasures and Prohibitions, Engaged Bodies, Commemorations, and Showing and Telling. We have deliberately resisted the tendency to organize the chapters according to region or time period, for we have found that it is precisely the juxtaposition of unfamiliar imperial contexts that can sharply reveal the commonalities and diversities inherent to colonialisms.

The book concludes with a chapter contributed by Martin Hall. Widely recognized as a pioneering scholar in comparative research on colonization, Hall also was among the first archaeologists to directly consider sexuality as a core component of imperial projects (Hall 1995, 2000). Here, he reflects on the particular methodological challenges involved in the archaeology of colonial sexualities and identifies directions for continued development of this area of research.

Pleasures and Prohibitions

Chapters within this initial section explore the contrasting effects of sexual encounters by considering the political, economic, and societal constraints that govern the expression and consequences of sexuality within colonial worlds. They examine how nonnormative sexual relationships were navigated and what types of intimacy, affect, labor, (re)production, and domesticity were maintained through these sexual connections. Together, the chapters within this first cluster illuminate how material culture actively participated in the creation of new sexual relations within past colonial worlds.

"Pleasures and Prohibitions" opens with Chapter 3, contributed by coeditor Eleanor Conlin Casella. By exploring the materiality of Nursery Wards within the female-convict prisons of nineteenth-century colonial Australia, Casella illuminates the painful disruptions of maternal affect within the context of British imperialism. By similarly challenging our traditional models of colonial domestic settlement, Casella's study examines childhood, mothering, and involuntary labor as an embodied "sexual effect" of Britain's policy of imperial transportation and penal servitude. Combining archaeological and archival sources, Casella exposes the profound material dynamics of sexual objectification and maternal idealization that infused these exiled carceral worlds.

In Chapter 4, Lindsay Weiss develops this critique of the heteronormative domestic through her study of intimate masculine household relations in the late-nineteenth-century Diamond Fields of South Africa. Exploring the dynamics of sexual and marriage relations among these African mine workers, Weiss considers the materiality of same-sex domestic space and matrimonial enactments within the segregated space of African worker housing. By considering the material circulations of the intimate male couple, Weiss demonstrates the subversive role of these sexual households within the British colonial context.

Further challenging our traditional perceptions of heterosexual relations, Sarah K. Croucher's study of the clove plantations of nineteenth-century coastal East Africa (Chapter 5) explores the material dynamics of sexual relations within the daily domestic practices of colonial Islamic plantation households. Through her archaeological interpretation of a specific excavation region of the site as the house of an enslaved concubine, Croucher questions our normative assumptions of household constitution, sexual connections, and underlying material relations of exploitation, identity, well-being, and strategic freedom.

The section concludes with Mireia López-Bertran's analysis (Chapter 6) of Punic clay figurines from the Spanish Baleric Islands created over the sixth to second centuries BCE. Her investigation specifically illuminates the diverse gender and sexual identities that may be interpreted from the physical attributes depicted on these anthropomorphic shapes. Drawing from queer theory as a means for transcending the traditional dualities of masculine versus feminine identity, López-Bertran suggests that these clay figurines can be understood as an active ritualization of sexual activities and pleasurable sensations, thereby incorporating a far wider array of intimate encounters and gendered identities than is typically embraced.

Engaged Bodies

The five chapters clustered in the section "Engaged Bodies" focus on the material consequences of demography, reproduction, domestic labor, desire, and the "making" of gender. By considering the dynamics of sexual encounters through an intersection of biological and sociocultural practices, these chapters investigate the embodied aspects of sexuality within colonial contexts. How do these pivotal sexual effects demonstrate the complex relationship between projects of empire and colonized bodies? What corporeal aspects of colonial sexualities can archaeology illuminate?

Chapter 7, contributed by Diana DiPaolo Loren, begins these inquiries through a close analysis of material culture related to the body, especially artifacts of bodily adornment, that were excavated from the Grand Village of Natchez, an eighteenth-century Native American mound and village complex. She argues that differing ideologies of the body between Natchez Indian and French colonists resulted in both the construction of new specific identities and sensory miscommunications. What, Loren asks, is the relationship between desire and fear in colonial sexualities? How do the participants in colonial encounters negotiate the novel choices available to them in clothing and adorning their bodies?

With Kathleen L. Hull's contribution, "Death and Sex" (Chapter 8), the discussion turns to a more explicitly biological concern with the relationship between birth rates and death rates in colonial contexts. Epidemic diseases introduced through colonial projects frequently resulted in catastrophic mortality among indigenous populations; these demographic consequences often preceded the face-to-face colonial encounters that are usually the subject of archaeological inquiry. Hull postulates that survivors of colonial-era epidemics likely engaged in a critical reexamination of sexual taboos and marriage practices as communities sought to rebuild demographically viable populations. Through a long-term diachronic investigation of archaeological and ethnohistoric data from Yosemite Valley, California, Hull finds that sexual choices made by epidemic survivors include population aggregation and a willingness to enter into unions with outsiders. This finding may shed light on the frequent patterns of sexual involvement between native women and male colonists in imperial contexts.

In Chapter 9, Kay Tarble de Scaramelli extends Hull's consideration of the bodily impacts of imperialism through an investigation of the long-term consequences of colonial Jesuit missions in the Middle Orinoco region of northern South America. Evidence of settlement patterns, rock art, and ceramic remains from former residential sites of indigenous people offer a revealing glimpse of their lives as they struggled to confront the challenges of colonialism. Like Hull, Tarble de Scaramelli is concerned with reproduction, particularly the changing relations between indigenous men and women as they enter the Catholic missionary system. Under the colonial regime, some indigenous women were empowered by their productive capacities, both biological and agricultural, and negotiated social mobility through conversion to Catholicism, commodity production, and, in some circumstances, marriage outside their birth community.

Russell N. Sheptak, Kira Blaisdell-Sloan, and Rosemary A. Joyce turn toward the labeling of bodies in their investigation of the Honduran pre-Columbian and colonial town of Ticamaya (Chapter 10). Ticamaya was one important site in the complex development of the "casta system," a Spanish-colonial legal taxonomy that classified bodies according to an ideology of cross-racial reproduction. Through recursive analysis of archaeological and documentary evidence, Sheptak, Blaisdell-Sloan, and Joyce show that that the supposedly immaterial domain of sexuality is indeed material, in both the substantive and the theoretical senses.

The "Engaged Bodies" section concludes with coeditor Barbara L. Voss's study of imperial policies and sexual practices in San Francisco, California (Chapter 11). Voss juxtaposes two historical contexts that are rarely considered together: the Spanish "discovery" and subsequent settlement of the San Francisco Bay region in the late eighteenth century and, 150 years later, the influx of Chinese immigrants to the same region in the mid-nineteenth century following the United States' annexation of California. Through close attention to the spatial organization of bodies, particularly the bodies of male laborers, Voss reveals structural consistencies that bridge colonial and postcolonial historical contexts. In both eras, the intersection of racial segregation with sexual regulation profoundly disrupted heterosexual domesticity and generated new homosocial contexts in which relationships among men became increasingly central to daily life.

Commemorations

This section interrogates the material dynamics between colonial sexualities and memory, demonstrating how ideas of kinship, lineage, affiliation, and belonging are invoked to sustain both families and communities within colonial worlds. Exploring how commemorations provide a material focus for both ancient and contemporary groups, chapters within this section consider the deployment of sexual heritage to acknowledge strategic ancestry, kinships, and public identities.

"Commemorations" begins with Ana Delgado and Meritxell Ferrer's comparative analysis of household deposits and burial practices in Phoenician and Punic diaspora communities in Iberia and Sicily during the eighth and sixth centuries BCE (Chapter 12). Material culture from domestic and funerary contexts of these two colonial settings reveals an everyday life marked by the cohabitation of people of different origins. Delgado and Ferrer's investigation exposes the tensions between the different sexual politics that surrounded the legitimation of colonial power in living practice and in commemoration of the dead.

The concern for commemoration of the dead in colonial contexts continues in Chapter 13, in which Renata S. Garraffoni offers a nuanced reading of the epitaphs found on gladiators' tombstones in the Roman Empire. Comparing epigraphic evidence from Rome and Cordoba, Garraffoni traces the nuanced differences in the commemorative practices used by the gladiators' lovers and spouses to memorialize their deceased loved ones in the colonial metropole and on the frontier. The material culture of the monument prompts a rethinking of violence, sexuality, and Roman identity and brings the voices of mourning women to the forefront in tracing subaltern negotiations of empire.

Chapter 14, by Patricia E. Rubertone, similarly explores the tensions that arise through the sexual politics of monuments in her research on colonialist monuments in the New England region of the United States. There, colonialist monuments and commemorations underrepresented and misrepresented Native women and imposed alien notions of space that discouraged indigenous movement across the commemorative landscape. By attending to Native people's memories and experiences of place, Rubertone reveals how Native women reappropriated colonialist monuments as theaters of action and memory where public performances critiqued colonialism, affirmed cultural knowledge, and challenged their own and their communities' invisibility. Here, Rubertone demonstrates how archaeology, as a hybrid practice, is crucial to decolonizing European Americans' narratives about indigenous gender and sexuality.

The section "Commemorations" concludes with Pedro Paulo A. Funari and Aline Vieira de Carvalho's investigation of the memorialization of *maroon* communities in present-day Brazil (Chapter 15). Populated by escaped slaves, indigenous peoples, foreigners, and other refugees from imperial settlements, *maroons* were communities that formed under colonial conditions yet actively challenged colonial rule. Today, *maroons* have become touchstones for theorizing resistance to colonial structures of power and for rhetorical arguments about pluralism in present-day Brazilian society. Funari and Carvalho pay special attention to the political consequences of interpretations of *maroon* polyandry in this exploration of archaeology and memory.

Showing and Telling

How do we articulate the intimate encounters of colonial sexuality? The chapters in this final section explore both public and private experiences of sexual expressions, erotic materiality, and commodified desires. Emphasizing variations in sociosexual hierarchies, these case studies engage with the material flexibilities of identity, ethnicity, gender, nationalism, and taboo. Questions of ethics infuse these chapters, as the authors consider the politics of exposing the necessary silences of the past. How do colonial objects, spaces, and people become sexualized? What does it mean when we satisfy *our* yearnings for these hidden, yet ever present, subjects?

This section opens with Shannon Lee Dawdy's genealogy of Storyville, New Orleans's early-twentieth-century red light district (Chapter 16). Dawdy traces the link between twenty-first-century tourist desires, twentieth-century legalized prostitution, and New Orleans's colonial past through archaeological case studies of two female-owned hospitality sites (The Rising Sun Hotel and Madame John's Legacy). She demonstrates that from the earliest French-colonial days, the city was gendered in a quite literal fashion. Both white women and women of color possessed the land, the buildings, and the goods that serviced male travelers – soldiers, sailors, hunters, traders, and merchants. Following the Louisiana Purchase, which included New Orleans in the newly annexed territory, to the United States, male adventurers and business travelers built on this history as they imagined themselves taking pleasures from an exotic, feminine city. The contemporary tourist gaze builds on the historic desires of colonial and postcolonial male travelers.

In Chapter 17, Nick Shepherd turns our attention toward the intimacy that arises in relation between an archaeologist and his or her materials – the intimacy involved in the act of knowledge construction. Focusing on two early-twentieth-century encounters involving the South African archaeologist John Goodwin and the indigenous people of the Cape – one group living, the other deceased – Shepherd uncovers the centrality of imagination and desire in the making of archaeological knowledge. His analysis traces the subtle and overt forms of violence that shadow archaeological practice. How do the intimacies of knowledge production create categories of the unshowable, unspeakable, and unthinkable?

The final case study in this volume, Chapter 18, presents Mary Weismantel's engagements with "Obstinate Things," notably the Moche "sex pots" produced on the North Coast of Peru during the first millennium. Despite the overwhelming impact of colonialism and neo-colonialism, these objects obstinately refuse to be completely silenced. Weismantel challenges archaeologists to pay greater attention to sensual and bodily interactions between the archaeologist and the artifacts they study. Moving beyond ahistorical and phenomenological approaches, Weismantel demonstrates the possibilities for embodied archaeological methodologies that are grounded in the political-economic conditions that motivated production of particular objects. Attending to the sensuality of archaeology decolonizes archaeological thinking by decentering logocentric forms of analyses that are themselves a product of Western colonizing processes.

SEXUAL EFFECTS, MATERIALITY, AND COLONIAL WORLDS

Together, these case studies demonstrate that intimate encounters, particularly when viewed through the prism of the colonial past, are far from being by-products, or mere accidents, of the imperial project. Instead, profound social, political, ethical, and economic dynamics shaped, and continue to shape, these sexual expressions. The material legacy and sexual effects of these intimate encounters created powerful signatures within the archaeological record – hidden transcripts we are only now starting to recognize, appreciate, and interpret. Ultimately, by providing an explicitly comparative multiperiod and transregional approach, this edited volume significantly expands our traditional understandings of social archaeology to illuminate the material dynamics of intimacies, of sensualities and bodily experiences, of affects and emotions, and – ultimately – of *sexualities* within past colonial worlds.

ACKNOWLEDGMENTS

A collaborative project such as this owes its success to all those involved. Our first thanks go to the contributing authors, whose multiyear commitment to this inquiry has collectively formed the core of this project. This international body of scholars was deftly coordinated by editorial assistant Guido Pezzarossi, whose careful attention to detail and keen organizational skills were essential to the realization of this project. Rachel Rivera and Megan Kane also assisted with manuscript preparation at key points during the project, and Cathy Hannabach prepared the book index. We also thank the editors, staff, and contractors at Cambridge University Press who shepherded this project from its initial inception through final book production.

We are grateful to several Stanford University departments and programs that provided financial and logistical support for this project: Department of Anthropology, Stanford Archaeology Center, Stanford Humanities Center, Stanford Humanities and Science Dean's Office, Institute for Research in the Social Sciences, Dean of Graduate and Undergraduate Studies, and the Michelle R. Clayman Institute for Gender Research. We especially thank Department of Anthropology staff members Ellen Christensen, Jen Kidwell, Kai Jimenez, Maria Manzanares, Emily Bishop, and Claudia Engel for their assistance with the organization and hosting of the spring

2009 authors' workshop at Stanford University. Essential international travel funding was also provided by grants from the British Academy and from the School of Arts, Histories and Cultures at the University of Manchester.

Barbara Voss thanks Deb Cohler for her steadfast support and timely insights throughout this project. Eleanor Casella thanks Alison Oram for her editorial suggestions and generous patience over the various production stages of this scholarly adventure.

REFERENCES

Alcock, Susan E., Terence N. D'Altroy, Kathleen D. Morrison, and Carla M. Sinopoli, eds. 2001. *Empires: Perspectives from Archaeology and History.* Cambridge: Cambridge University Press.

Coronil, Fernando. 2007. "After Empire: Reflections on Imperialism from the Américas," in Stoler, A. L., C. McGranahan, and P. C. Perdue (eds.), *Imperial Formations.* Santa Fe, NM: School for Advanced Research Press, pp. 241–271.

Gosden, Chris. 2004. *Archaeology and Colonialism: Cultural Contact from 5000 BC to the Present.* Cambridge: Cambridge University Press.

Hall, Martin. 1995. "The Architecture of Patriarchy: Houses, Women, and Slaves in the Eighteenth Century South African Countryside." *Kroeber Anthropological Society Papers* 79: 61–73.

———. 2000. *Archaeology and the Modern World: Colonial Transcripts in South Africa and the Chesapeake.* London: Routledge.

Lightfoot, Kent G. 2005. *Indians, Missionaries, and Merchants: The Legacy of Colonial Encounters on the California Frontiers.* Berkeley and Los Angeles: University of California Press.

Murray, Tim, ed. 2004. *The Archaeology of Contact in Settler Societies.* Cambridge: Cambridge University Press.

Rothschild, Nan A. 2003. *Colonial Encounters in a Native American Landscape: The Spanish and Dutch in North America.* Washington, DC: Smithsonian Books.

Stein, Gil J., ed. 2005. *The Archaeology of Colonial Encounters: Comparative Perspectives.* Santa Fe, NM: School of American Research Press.

Stoler, Ann Laura. 2001. "Tense and Tender Ties: The Politics of Comparison in North American History and (Post) Colonial Studies." *The Journal of American History* 88(3):829–865.

Voss, Barbara L. 2008. "Sexuality Studies in Archaeology." *Annual Review of Anthropology* 37:317–336.

TWO

SEXUAL EFFECTS

Postcolonial and Queer Perspectives on the Archaeology of Sexuality and Empire

Barbara L. Voss

INTRODUCTION

The Archaeology of Colonialism: Intimate Encounters and Sexual Effects seeks to forge a strong connection between two bodies of scholarship that have to date been only weakly linked. The first of these is the increasingly dynamic examination of the sexual politics of empire. With particular emphasis on the European empires of the past two centuries, feminist and postcolonial scholarship has richly demonstrated that sexuality is central to colonial projects. It is now axiomatic that empires produce and rely on "tense and tender ties" (Stoler 2001) that bind together political, institutional, economic, emotive, and familial aspects of social life in both the metropole and the colony.

The second body of scholarship consists of the explosion of archaeological research on colonization, spurred in part by milestone anniversaries such as the 1988 Australian Bicentennial, the 1992 Columbian Quincentennial, and Great Britain's recent commemorations of the 1807 Slave Trade Act. Simultaneously, a growing awareness of archaeology's origins as a colonial, and colonizing, project has generated a new reflexive interest in the relationship between archaeology and empire. Informed by postcolonial and indigenous scholarship, recent archaeological investigations have brought fine-grained attention to the materiality of colonial projects. Increasing, archaeological investigations center on questions of creolization, ethnogenesis, hybridity, and syncretism – themes that point toward the intimate entanglements produced through colonial encounters.

As each of these bodies of scholarship has developed over the past twenty years, there has been little conversation between them. With notable exceptions, archaeologists have rarely examined the archaeological record with attention to the sexual politics of empire. Similarly, although historians, literary scholars, and anthropologists writing about empire call for increasing attention to materiality and micro-scale analysis, they have rarely engaged with the wealth of archaeological studies that provide exactly this body of evidence. The scholars contributing to this volume share a commitment to bridging this gap. While bringing archaeological evidence to bear on the relationship between sexuality and empire, we simultaneously examine the sexual and imperial politics of archaeology.

As discussed in Chapter 1 (Casella and Voss, this volume), terms such as *empire, colonization,* and *sexuality* serve as points of entry for this project rather than its destinations. This might seem like a fine distinction, but it is an important one. Increasingly, researchers have sought to better understand colonial projects by examining empire in comparative perspective. For example, renewed attention to medieval and early modern Islamic, Iberian, Chinese, and Japanese empires (e.g., Stoler et al. 2007) has helped historians "provincialize Europe" (Chakrabarty 2000). Similarly, archaeologists have recently used diachronic comparisons to juxtapose modern empires with classical and pre-Columbian ones (e.g., Alcock et al. 2001; Gosden 2004; Hall 2000; Murray 2004; Stein 2005). Moreover, all colonial projects are internally differentiated – not only between metropole and colony but also between colonies and between colonial institutions and structures. Rather than assuming that empire is stable and consistent, questions of how empires are formed, implemented, contested, and inhabited in particular places and times are central to this book.

Sexuality must also be treated as a variable rather than a constant in comparative studies of empire. Without denying the biological and reproductive aspects of sex, there has been a growing awareness that "sexuality" is a culturally contingent formation (e.g., Foucault 1978; Halperin et al. 1990; Weeks 1981). The connection between sexual practices and social identities, the relationship between gender and sexuality, and the ways that sexuality is (or is not) regulated and policed are all highly variable.

Investigations of empire and sexuality are therefore intrinsically embroiled in "the politics of comparison" (Stoler 2001). I take particular inspiration from Stoler and her colleagues (e.g., Stoler et al. 2007), who have shown that empire itself is a comparative project: "colonialisms' actors and agents critically reflected on analogous governing practices and on those earlier and contemporary contexts from which lessons might be learned" (Stoler 2006: 5). Similarly, sexuality can also be understood as a comparative project that relies on comparisons among bodies and between modernity and tradition, between civilization and the primitive, between norms and perversions, and between acts and identities (Butler 1990; Foucault 1978; Hawley 2001; Muñoz 1999; Sedgwick 1990). Intellectual projects, including this book, are deeply entangled in the politics of such comparisons.

The Archaeology of Colonialism seeks to foster comparative perspectives that draw close attention to the interworkings of empire and sexuality. This chapter provides a conceptual and theoretical foundation for this collaborative project. The argument presented here proceeds in three stages. The first section, "Colonialisms and Imperial Effects," addresses the quandaries that face scholars who engage in broad-scale comparative studies of empire and colonization. After outlining some key aspects of the variability of empire, I turn toward Fernando Coronil's concept of "imperial effects": "to recognize systems of domination by their significance for subjected populations rather than solely by their institutional forms or self-definitions" (Coronil 2007: 243).

The second section, "From Imperial Effects to Sexual Effects," examines sexuality as a historical problem. Reflecting on the perspectives advanced by Raymond Williams, Michel Foucault, David Halperin, and others, I propose that Coronil's emphasis on the *effects* of empire can be applied to comparative research on sexuality – that we may turn our investigations toward "sexual effects." Together, this focus on effects moves us toward an examination of the conjuncture of colonization and sexuality in the lived experiences of the diverse populations that were subject to imperial and sexual hierarchies.

The third section, "Archaeologies of Colonial Sexualities," reviews the history of archaeological scholarship on this topic. Although not always explicitly acknowledged, sexuality has played a central role in archaeological research on colonial contexts. Similarly, archaeology's focus on the material record of daily life challenges many historical assumptions about the sexual politics of empire.

COLONIALISMS AND IMPERIAL EFFECTS

Empire and the Comparative Project

Empire is a slippery and broad term, and any comparative project of colonialism must necessarily grapple with the sheer impossibility of comparison. Empires may be political, military, economic, cultural, religious, or, most often, some combination thereof. They may be territorially contiguous or geographically dispersed; they may involve substantial movements of populations or almost none at all. In some contexts, empire indicates centralization and intentionality – the coordinated and regimented projects orchestrated by an emperor or an imperial government. In other contexts, the term "empire" is more descriptive of the outcomes of social processes than their origins.

Alongside the differences among empires, each empire is internally diverse. Tensions among military, commercial, and religious aims flourish. Different colonizing strategies are deployed in different places and different times. Local responses to empire vary both within and across regions. Indeed, the internal diversity of any colonial project is superseded only by the diversity of the peoples and cultures subject to its rule. Perhaps the core tension of empire is the simultaneous production of difference (national, ethnic, racial, tribal, class, caste, gender, sexual, linguistic, religious, and cultural) and the need to incorporate these differences into a common system of rule (Coronil 2007: 255). Recent comparative historical and archaeological research has shown that there have been as many approaches to negotiating this tension as there have been empires.

Among this variability, there are certain consistencies worth noting. The most salient characteristic of empire is the imposition of an asymmetrical power relationship that reduces local autonomy. Imperialism can be taken broadly to refer to the ideologies and practices associated with the imposition of this external power. Empire generally involves an *expansion* of the spatial scale of governance (territorial, political, economic, religious, or cultural) and an *intensification* of governance to include heightened surveillance and regulation of bodies, relationships, transactions, and movements. The expansion and intensification of empire produces "internal contortions and complexities" (Comaroff 1989: 662) that disrupt the unity of empire. Moreover, empire never develops within a vacant or passive field; the expansion and intensification of empire is met by both internal and external resistance, manipulation, accommodation, revolt, and refusal.

Colonialism most commonly refers to imperial strategies that involve the direct domination by one polity over a population in its own home territory (including, and accounting for, diaspora and genocide – the removal or extermination of a population from its home territory). Comaroff (1989), writing of South Africa, traces three modes of colonialism: a state model, characterized by governmental and military control of a territory; settler colonialism, which seeks to displace or exterminate existing indigenous population with nonindigenous populations; and civilizing colonialism, which uses missions, schools, and other institutions to transform indigenous populations into governable populations. In the nineteenth and twentieth centuries, several "breakaway" settler colonies (for example, the United States, Canada, Australia, and South Africa) became imperial powers in their own right, shifting the relationship between core and periphery in the global political and economic landscape. A particularly common trait of breakaway settler colonies is the formation of "internal colonies" in which subordinate populations are confined and managed within the empire's core territory. Tribal reservations, ethnic and religious ghettos, refugee and detention camps, worker compounds, and free-trade zones all exemplify these "states of exception" (Agamben 2005).

Archaeological research on empire has largely focused on those aspects of colonial projects that involved territorial acquisition and large-scale population movements. This should not detract us from attending to other forms of imperialism not attached to territorial control. Contemporary scholarship on present-day empire has focused particularly on "neo-colonialism" – the rule by force of market as well as by armed forces (Alavi 1964). Increasingly, powerful nations espouse anticolonial ideologies while simultaneously dominating other nations through economic or political subordination (Coronil 2007; Duara 2007). Other scholars trace patterns of recolonization, pointing to ways that newly independent states usurp the self-determination of the people whose interests they purport to represent (Alexander 1997). Archaeological research raises questions about the degree to which these "new" forms of empire are indeed recent permutations. Certainly, archaeological perspectives indicate that market forces and cultural hegemony are ancient, as well as current, strategies of empire.

It is worth asking whether the concept of empire is overused: "Where does empire end and other forms of nonrepresentative or authoritarian polities begin?" (Khalid 2007: 114). The long-term comparative perspective afforded by archaeology brings this question to the fore. It challenges us to address the articulations among empire and other social, economic, and political forms, both past and present.

Postcoloniality and Imperial Effects

The historical shift in the nineteenth and twentieth centuries from territorial colonization toward other forms of imperialism has spurred diverse explorations of "postcoloniality," broadly envisioned. In the most direct sense, postcoloniality addresses the conditions of those in newly independent states who must negotiate the aftermath of colonialism (Gandhi 1998). Initially, postcolonial theory arose through the writings of diasporic scholars reflecting on the colonial legacy of those nations that gained independence from British, French, and Dutch colonial rule following World War II. Edward Said's (1979) *Orientalism*, Frantz Fanon's (1977) and Homi Bhabha's (1984, 1994) explorations of postcolonial identity, and Gayatri Spivak's (1985) attention to the history of the subaltern are foundational texts in this intellectual movement. Postcolonial theory exposes the interconnections between military–economic apparatuses of empire and the production of colonial forms of knowledge (Gandhi 1998). Empires arise not solely out of political ambition or an expanding world economy but also "out of shifting conceptual apparatuses that made certain kinds of actions seem possible, logical, and even inevitable . . . while others were excluded from the realm of possibility" (Cooper and Stoler 1997: vii). Postcoloniality thus conjoins a political stance against imperialism with a critique of imperial modes of knowledge production.

Two core postulates advanced through postcolonial theory are particularly relevant to the projects in this book. The first is that the division between colonizer and colonized cannot be taken for granted; it is an actively constructed, and continually shifting, divide. The arbitrariness of this boundary is continually exposed by the hybrid products of colonization, including mestizaje, syncretism, creolization, and mimicry. These topics have been particularly prominent in archaeological research on empire and colonization, both through the study of households formed through sexual unions between colonizers and colonized and through material culture studies of hybrid objects. Both biologically and metaphorically, hybridity (Young 1995) draws sharp attention to the relationship between sexuality and empire. The second postulate is that the imperial "core" or home front is produced as much through empire as the colonies themselves (Chakrabarty 2000; Coronil 2007; McClintock 1995; Said 1979; Stoler 1992). Archaeological research in the metropole is as relevant to the study of sexuality and empire as research conducted in the imperial periphery.

Postcolonial studies have been soundly criticized even as the insights of postcolonial scholars are applauded (McClintock 1992). Postcolonial theory has tended to homogenize colonial experiences through its focus on the dissolution of late-nineteenth- and early-twentieth-century empires. This has neglected other European empires that preceded Western Europe's Golden Age of Empire (for example, most Spanish, Portuguese, and Russian colonies in the Americas had already gained national independence by the 1850s) as well as the post-independence territorial expansions of breakaway settler colonies such as the United States, Canada, and Australia. The emphasis on recent European empires has also detracted attention from non-European empires (Chinese, Japanese, and Ottoman, for example) that actively competed with European empires for territorial, political, and economic control. For archaeologists, an additional concern is the degree to which postcolonial theory, a body of scholarship developed to address the unique historical conditions of the late twentieth and early twenty-first centuries, can be applied to prehistoric and classical empires.

A second, more pointed critique is that postcolonial studies draw attention away from present-day imperial projects. Not everyone lives in a postcolonial world

(Pagán Jiménez and Rodríguez Ramos 2008), and postcolonial theory's emphasis on knowledge production can draw attention away from the material conditions
of oppression. Anticolonial and decolonization movements are still necessary to
support struggles for self-determination. In former settler colonies, national independence often intensified, rather than ameliorated, subjugation of indigenous
populations. In contexts such as the United States and Australia, indigenous studies
may provide more salient programs for archaeological practice than postcolonial
studies (e.g., Atalay 2006; Liebmann and Rizvi 2008; McNiven and Russell 2005;
Preucel and Cipolla 2008; Watkins 2005). The case studies in this book challenge
the limits of postcolonial theory even as they are inspired by it. Many chapters
work to decolonize archaeology by calling attention to archaeological practices that
perpetuate the racial and sexual legacies of empire. Simultaneously, archaeology's
engagement with the materiality of daily life draws sharp attention to the material conditions of oppression. Archaeology provides new perspectives on how those
caught up in systems and institutions beyond their control not only struggled to
survive but also created meaning and community.

The attention given in this volume to specific locales, communities, and bodies
resonates strongly with the concept of "imperial effects," a term introduced by
Fernando Coronil (2007) in his studies of Latin America. There, Coronil traces a
longue durée of subjugation that began with pre-Columbian empires such as the
Aztecs and Incas, intensified through Spanish and Portuguese colonization, and
continued after formal national independence through British, French, and United
States economic, political, and military control of the region. Additionally, within
national borders, ethnic minorities are subject to internal colonization by local
elites. Imperialism, Coronil writes, has become a commonsense reality in much of
Latin America, even as the forms of empire shift and conceal themselves. Rather than
attempt to define empire, Coronil suggests that scholars of imperialism might better
attend to the *effects* of imperialism. Systems of domination can be best recognized
by their effects on the populations subject to them.

From Imperial Effects to Sexual Effects

Sex as a Historical Problem

For social scientists, sexuality is a particularly fraught aspect of human culture. On
one hand, sexuality is often naturalized and universalized, reduced to biological
functions. It is easy to argue against this essentialist stance by pointing to the infi-
nite variety of sexual identities, practices, relationships, and representations across
cultures and across time. In this regard, sex is often compared with food: everyone needs to eat, but neither nutritional survival nor evolutionary adaptation can
account for the broad diversity in culinary procurement, cultivation, preparation,
tastes, and taboos. Beyond a model of sexual "cuisine," historians and anthropologists have long demonstrated that what counts as sexual, and the configuration
of the sexual, is culturally contingent, including cultural understandings of reproduction (Elliston 1995; Laqueur 1990; Malinowski 1929; Mead 1928; Towle and
Morgan 2002; Weismantel 2004).

For those of us who investigate sexualities in the near and distant past, the cultural contingency of sexuality poses a serious methodological challenge. If the particular organization of diverse acts, anatomies, identities, and social codes into a category of "sexuality" is historically and culturally specific, then the grounds for a comparative analysis of sexuality are unstable. Michel Foucault's (1978) now-famous hypothesis that "sexuality" itself is a modern and Western phenomenon, one that emerged in eighteenth- and nineteenth-century Europe, is perhaps most troublesome to archaeologists. In brief, Foucault argued that the emergence of "sexuality" involved four interrelated elements that are still in process today: first, the consolidation of sexuality as a coherent cultural field; second, a general shift from gender to sexuality in the interpretation of social difference, especially deviance; third, the elaboration of sexual taxonomies; and fourth, the implantation of sexuality in the individual, also sometimes described as the shift from categorization of sexual acts, such as sodomy, to sexual identities, such as the homosexual. Alongside Foucault, historians such as Weeks (1981) and D'Emilio (1983, 1997) have emphasized the rise of industrial capitalism, urbanism, and global-scale military conflicts in the emergence of "sexuality," and anthropological scholarship has decentered the West by paying particular attention to the ways in which sexuality "travels" through colonization, capitalism, migration, and tourism (Boellstorff 2003; Elliston 1995; Manalansan 2003; Mankekar 2004; Sinnott 2004).

Although the proposition that "sexuality" is culturally and historically specific is to some a radical proposition, this analysis is in sympathy with developments in the humanities and social sciences that have called into question other seemingly universal categories of analysis. For example, Raymond Williams's (1977) concept of "structures of feeling" connects the psychological and personal realm of "affect" – mood, mental state, aesthetics, and emotions – with historical and social structures that exceed the realm of individual experience. "We need," Williams (1977: 133) cautions, "on the one hand, to acknowledge (and welcome) the specificity of these elements – specific feelings, specific rhythms – and yet to find ways of recognizing their specific kinds of sociality" that are neither reducible to, nor are outside of, social and historical structures. Similarly, feminist and queer critiques of the universality of sexual identities (heterosexual and homosexual, for example) call attention to the tight relationship between social institutions and what are perceived as individual dispositions (e.g., Boellstorff 2003; Boyd 2003; Butler 1990; Chauncey 1994; Warner 1993). Most recently, the concern with individual identities and affect has expanded into a focus on *affective relationships* – friendships, kinship, camaraderie, and sexual and sensual interconnections (e.g., Casella and Croucher 2010; Gandhi 2006).

What has emerged is a clear commitment to the *historical* quality of the emotional, the affective, the sensual, the sexual, and the interpersonal. If these aspects of social life are formed through the dynamic interplay between social agency and social structure, then they are also historical. The focus on "sexual effects" in this volume is a strategic attempt to leave open a space in which sexuality is not assumed to have an a priori existence independent of its cultural and historical context. For the contributors to this book, the cultural contingency of sexuality provides an opportunity to investigate the articulation of diverse sexualities within and against colonial projects. Just as Coronil's (2007) emphasis on "imperial effects" turns attention toward the experiences of those who are subject to empire, our use of "sexual effects" compels us to ask when and how sexuality emerges in relationship to power dynamics in colonial settings.

Locating Sexuality in Empire

The cultural contingency of sexuality is particularly important to investigations of imperialism. Divergent attitudes toward sexuality, including sexual ideologies, sexual identities, sexual practices, sexual mores, and the formation of sexuality itself, are found throughout colonial contexts. To date, most scholarship on the sexual politics of colonization has focused on modern European empires, especially fifteenth-through nineteenth-century Iberian colonies in the Americas and nineteenth- and twentieth-century British, French, and Dutch empires in Africa and Asia. Three consistent themes from this scholarship are particularly significant for this volume.

The first of these is the tight relationship between sexuality and race. Formulations of racial difference are underpinned by a sexual substructure that promotes or restricts particular reproductive relationships and outcomes. Demography and eugenics, as well as anxieties about miscegenation and celebrations of "hybrid vigor," are all dense imperial nodes in which race and sexuality are deeply intertwined (Davin 1978; Stoler 1995, 2002; Young 1995; Yuval-Davis 1996). In what Gandhi (1998: 11) has termed "the puzzling circulation of desire around the traumatic scene of oppression," racial and ethnic hierarchies incite sexual longing as much as they regulate it.

The second theme is the imperial invention of the distinction between the personal–domestic realms and public–civil society, a process that occurred recursively between metropole and colony. Whether in India (Chakrabarty 1993), Africa (McClintock 1995), or Asia (Stoler 2002), "imperialism cannot be understood without a theory of domestic space" (McClintock 1995: 17). This separation of social life into distinct gendered realms has two implications for investigations of sexuality and empire. First, the separation of domestic and civil society officially relegates sexuality to the private and personal while masking the sexual politics of institutions, governments, and markets. Second, the gendered association of the domestic realm with women and civil society with men heterosexualizes society by barring either gender from being able to negotiate successfully the whole of social life. Marriage and other forms of cross-gender kinship become essential to survival in a society divided into men's and women's realms.

The third theme similarly concerns heterosexualization. A widespread practice of early and late modern European empires was the persecution of indigenous transgendered persons and those who engaged in same-sex sexual relationships. Although these imperial practices are often attributed to Christian missionary activity, other colonial institutions (military, governmental, and economic) were also deeply involved in imposing binary gender systems and heterosexual norms (Blackwood and Wieringa 1999; Casella 2000; Feinberg 1996; Hayes 2001; Roscoe 1998; Sinnott 2004; Trexler 1995; Voss 2008b; Williams 1986). The heterosexual underpinnings of imperial racial hierarchies and domestic–public spheres are more than incidental to colonial rule.

Sexual Violences, Seductive Pleasures

In modern empires, sexuality was used both as a metaphor for imperial power relations and as a means of controlling bodies and communities: "tensions over what colonized people did by night were intimately tied to the daytime structures of colonial domination" (Stoler and Cooper 1997: 27). Imperial sexualities challenge strict divisions between coercion and consent: power is fundamentally coercive, but its campaign is frequently seductive (Gandhi 1998: 14).

The coercive sexual effects of empire are particularly highlighted in Joane Nagel's (2000) concept of "ethnosexual frontiers." Nagel provides a succinct formulation of the sexualized perimeters formed through colonization: an ethnosexual double standard in which dominating groups police "our" women from having sex with "their" men, but "our" men can have sex with "their" women without sanction. Alongside the strategic deployment of sexual violence in colonial contexts, empire itself is metaphorically sexualized as the penetration and domination of feminized primitive lands and peoples by virile and masculine civilizations (Pratt 1992).

One of the core questions examined throughout this volume is whether sexuality is always violently implicated in empire in the manner that Nagel and others describe. The case studies presented in this book indicate that imperial sexual violence may take markedly different forms than the heterosexual penetrations emphasized by Nagel, Pratt, and others. For example, in this volume Weiss (Chapter 4), Casella (Chapter 3), Hull (Chapter 8), Voss (Chapter 11), and Garraffoni (Chapter 13) all trace ways in which colonization led to the profound disruption of heterosexual relationships and related kin networks through disease, captivity, and labor regimes. In contexts such as these, the struggles to build and maintain affective relationships – sexual, sensual, emotive, parental, and familial – become central to subordinate experiences of imperial formations.

Along these lines, many of the chapters in this volume bring new attention to the ways in which sexuality can be a site for the emergence of affective relationships that defy colonial expectations. Writing of Punic diaspora populations in the Mediterranean, López-Bertran (Chapter 6) and Delgado and Ferrer (Chapter 12) identify new articulations of kinship and reproduction that involve novel representations of the body and new attention to sensuality. Casella (Chapter 3), Tarble de Scaramelli (Chapter 9), Loren (Chapter 7), Rubertone (Chapter 14), and Sheptak, Blaisdell-Sloan, and Joyce (Chapter 10) bring new attention to the sexual agency of colonized women whose bodies came under increased scrutiny and regulation. Croucher (Chapter 5), Dawdy (Chapter 16), Weiss (Chapter 4), and Funari and Carvalho (Chapter 15) trace the emergence of new sexual subjectivities and sexual institutions – concubinage, the hospitality industry, male marriages, and polyandry – that offered emotional and economic shelter for those excluded from normative heterosexuality. Further, in many of the chapters in this book, the sensual body – including the archaeologist's body – emerges as a critical site for understanding the lived experiences of those entangled with empire (Loren, Chapter 7; Garraffoni, Chapter 13; Rubertone, Chapter 14; Shepherd, Chapter 17; and Weismantel, Chapter 18).

These archaeological investigations indicate a profound shift in locating sexuality within empire. Amid imperial sexual regulation and exploitation, sexuality emerges in colonial contexts as a "weapon of the weak" (passim Scott 1985). Sexuality is not merely a site where the subaltern can find fleeting pleasure amid the toils of imperial oppression. Strong affective relationships may challenge and destabilize empire by forging emotive, economic, and political bonds that transgress colonial boundaries and stand against imperial oppressions (Gandhi 2006).

THE ARCHAEOLOGY OF COLONIAL SEXUALITIES

Looking back through the history of archaeological research on empire, it becomes apparent that there is a long archaeological tradition of investigating "imperial effects" and "sexual effects." In fact, some of archaeology's earliest studies of sexuality emerged through eighteenth-, nineteenth-, and early-twentieth-century discoveries related to ancient Greek and Roman empires. These inquiries came to have a profound influence on modern concepts of sexuality and on legal and medical sexual regulation. For example, the term *pornography* (literally, whore-writing) was coined in 1850 by German archaeologist C. O. Müller to classify objects and images found at Pompeii; this archaeological term quickly migrated into nineteenth-century law through edicts such as the British Obscene Publications Act of 1857 (Clarke 2003: 11–12). J. J. Winckelmann's studies of classical art (Davis 1996) and John Symonds's *A Problem in Greek Ethics* (1901) were instrumental points of reference for sexologists who formulated current theories of sexual orientation. Other nineteenth-century Europeans turned to the archaeology of ancient Egyptian empires for countercultural models of sexual potency, bisexuality, gender ambiguity, and homoeroticism (Meskell 1998). Renowned twentieth-century American sexologist Alfred Kinsey collected erotic artifacts and collaborated with Larco Hoyle (1965) in analyses of Peruvian "sex pots" (see Weismantel, Chapter 18). Current understandings of "modern" sexuality have been formed in no small part through archaeological encounters with ancient empires.

Since the 1970s, much archaeological research on sexuality has investigated the cultural and historical specificity of sexuality. The earliest examples of this are also found in studies of ancient Greek and Roman Empires. Notably, Brendel's (1970) and Dover's (1978) analyses of erotic representations on ceramic vessels, frescos, and other sources postulated that male–male sexuality in ancient Greece and Rome was not equivalent to 20th-century homosexuality. Dover in particular argued that Greek male–male sexuality was an expression of broader sexual hierarchies between insertive adult male citizens and their subordinate receptive partners. This interpretation has since been expanded into a broader theory termed the "penetrative hypothesis," which posits that sexual congress in imperial Greece and Rome was a zero-sum game. According to this theory, shame accrued to the penetrated and those of lower social status (youths, women, foreigners, and prostitutes) had little or no recourse against the sexual excesses of their social superiors (Richlin 1992; for contrasting views, see Clarke 1998; Davidson 1997; Gleason 1990; Skinner 2005; and Winkler 1990). This stark view of sex as an act that differentiates, rather than unites, its participants has strong parallels with postcolonial analyses of cross-racial sexuality in modern European empires.

Most classical scholarship has concerned itself primarily with sexual relations among Athenian and Roman citizens living in the imperial metropole rather than with the sexual politics of military and economic institutions in the colonies. In recent years, this trend has shifted as new attention to context, ambiguity, and desire is challenging conventional interpretations of classical sexualities. For example, scholars long assumed that black- and red-figured Greek ceramics, dating to approximately 570–470 BCE, were made for use in the male homosocial environment of the Athenian symposium. However, most extant vases with sexual content were actually recovered from Etruscan tombs in central and southern Italy, raising questions about the relationships between sexual representation and interempire commerce (Skinner 2005: 80–81). New scholarship on these painted vessels is notable for attention to the contextual analysis of posture, gesture, and the gaze; these methodologies have been particularly instrumental in identifying overlooked depictions of female homoerotic imagery (Elsner 1996; Frontisi-Ducroux 1996; Rabinowitz 2002).

Continuing the theme of gaze and gesture, Clarke has reexamined sexual representations in ancient Rome to argue that representations of sexuality in empire were not necessarily erotic in intention. For example, images of macrophallic and ithyphallic black men in Pompeiian mosaics may have been intended to ward off the evil eye through humor rather than stimulate sexual desire (Clarke 1996); other sexual representations, such as paintings of lovemaking, were likely acquired to signal the wealth and sophistication of the metropolitan owner (Clarke 1998). Clarke is one of the few scholars to trace the circulation of Roman sexual imagery beyond the metropole into the edges of empire. Mass-produced objects with sexual imagery, such as spintriae (ceramic coin-like objects) and terra-cotta lamps, were circulated throughout Roman colonies in western Europe and raise questions of "sexual acculturation" (Clarke 1998: 243–274). Does the discovery of Roman sexual representations in colonial contexts indicate Roman imposition of sexual regimes on newly conquered territory? Or might colonized Europeans have desired ceramics with sexual imagery because that imagery signaled luxury, wealth, and power associated with their conquerors? Are locally produced sexualized objects in Roman colonies mere copies of imperial sexual imagery, or are they new articulations of sexuality that arose through the intimate encounters of colonialism?

In this book, investigations of classical and prehistoric sexualities turn toward new directions. Chapters contributed by López-Bertran (Chapter 6) and Delgado and Ferrer (Chapter 12) consider the sexual politics of Phoenicia and the spread of the Punic diaspora throughout the Mediterranean. Turning to classical Rome, Garraffoni (Chapter 13) examines the memorials erected by women relatives of gladiators, who occupied ambiguous sexualized positions in the hierarchies of empire. Weismantel (Chapter 18) provides new methodological perspectives on embodiment and the Peruvian "sex pots" that figured so prominently in American sexological research.

Whereas archaeological research on sexuality in classical Greece and Rome began through investigations about male–male sexuality, opposite trends are seen in archaeological studies of modern European empires. Since the 1960s, archaeologists studying Spanish, British, French, Russian, and Dutch colonization have focused on households formed through sexual unions between colonial men and indigenous women. Kathleen Deagan's (1983) landmark research on Spanish-colonial St. Augustine examined domestic interactions between European men and Native American and African women to trace the emergence of distinct creole cultures. Continuing research by Deagan (Deagan 1983, 1995, 2004; Deagan and Cruxent 2002) and others (e.g., Ewen 1991, 1986; South et al. 1988) argues that cross-racial households were sites where Native American and African women served as cultural mediators who profoundly transformed colonial culture (see also Lightfoot et al. 1998; Scott 1991; and Wagner 1998 for examples outside the Spanish empire). The archaeology of interethnic colonial households powerfully demonstrates that even those sexual relationships that conformed to colonial rule were never fully contained by imperial ambitions: the intimate encounters between colonizer and colonized generated far-reaching cultural and political effects. As Deagan (2001: 194) concludes, "it was within these households, and in women's domestic activities, that the social transformation of identity in the imperial colonies began, leading ultimately to the end of empire."

The current explosion of archaeological research on hybridity, creolization, mestizaje, syncretism, and ethnogenesis in colonial contexts further points to the sexual substructures of empire. Sexuality figures prominently in recent comparative research conducted by Lightfoot (2005) and Rothschild (2003) on the long-term consequences of European empires in the Americas. Lightfoot particularly focuses on differences in colonial marriage policies and variations in the frequency of interethnic marriages, whereas Rothschild broadens her analysis to include sexual servitude and sexual coercion along with conjugal sexuality. Both studies demonstrate the material consequences of the sexual politics of empire in shaping the long-term historical outcomes of colonization.

In the past decade, a new wave of scholarship on modern European empires has expanded the archaeology of sexual effects into areas that previously saw little consideration. Beyond interpersonal relationships, archaeological research increasingly attends to the sexual politics of colonial institutions, including missions (Lydon 2005; Voss 2008b), military outposts (Voss 2008a), penal institutions (Casella 2000, 2010), slave plantations (Croucher 2007; Wilkie 2000), and maroon communities (Funari 1999). Questions of desire, longing, and the body provide more flexible entry points into the archaeology of empire and sexuality (Dawdy 2006; Dawdy and Weyhing 2008; Hall 2000; Loren 2008; Schrire 1995), particularly allowing for a consideration of the circulations of desire between people in the past and among archaeological quests for knowledge about the past.

Several chapters in this book forge new connections between domesticity and desire, and between personal relationships and colonial institutions. Tarble de Scaramelli (Chapter 9), Sheptak, Blaisdell-Sloan, and Joyce (Chapter 10), and Delgado and Ferrer (Chapter 12) each return sexuality to the center of archaeological investigations of interethnic colonial households; their research more directly considers the sexual agency of indigenous women who are involved with colonial men. Dawdy (Chapter 16), Croucher (Chapter 5), and Funari and Carvalho (Chapter 15) each expand the interethnic household beyond heterosexual monogamy to investigate prostitution, concubinage, and polyandry as sites of colonial intimate encounters. Loren (Chapter 7) turns our attention toward the cultural production of the clothed body and the cultivation of desire between colonizers and colonized. Voss (Chapter 11) and Weiss (Chapter 4) trace the formation of same-sex households under colonial and postcolonial labor regimes as a process that simultaneously disrupted heterosexual domesticity and fostered same-sex intimacy. Together this research articulates a new synthesis between household archaeology and the archaeology of institutions, through which the conventional figure of the "colonial couple" is expanded into a broader range of colonial intimacies.

CONCLUSION

This chapter has emphasized the conceptual and theoretical issues that inform the comparative project presented in this book. There is, however, one issue that has not been discussed in full: that of the relationship between materiality and sexuality. Sexuality is understood as the most material and bodily realm of social life yet simultaneously is considered to be ephemeral and immaterial, leaving little lasting trace. Archaeologists studying sexuality must grapple with this paradoxical formulation as we seek to interpret the material traces of the archaeological record. Because I have explored my own perspectives on this paradox at length elsewhere (Voss 2000, 2005, 2008c; Voss and Schmidt 2000), I refrain from doing so again here. Instead, I refer the reader to the chapters that follow, in which the contributors to this volume present diverse and novel approaches to investigating sexuality through the archaeological record. Their research demonstrates that it is precisely through our engagement with the materiality of sexuality that archaeology is providing new vantage points on the intimate encounters of empire.

The case studies that follow also demonstrate the political and intellectual necessity for taking sexuality seriously in archaeologies of imperialism. These chapters document and commemorate the devastating ways that sexual violence, coercion, and persecution have affected colonized populations. Simultaneously, they trace the sexual agency, creativity, and persistence enacted by those subject to empire.

What particularly emerges from the comparative perspective offered by this project is a sense of the centrality of affective relationships for those entangled with empire. Rather than idealizing such relationships as ephemeral and fragile shelters from the power dynamics of colonialism, the studies presented here demonstrate that affective ties are materially constituted. These sensual pleasures, sexual gratifications, and emotional bonds are complicated by the oppressive conditions under which these relationships form and by the sometimes exploitative qualities of the relationships themselves. Archaeology has long championed its unique ability to recover the perspectives of those whose experiences of colonialism are omitted from (and distorted by) written history. This book's investigation of sexual effects leads us to an even deeper understanding of the lived experiences of those subject to empire.

REFERENCES

Agamben, Giorgio. 2005. *States of Exception*. Chicago: University of Chicago Press.

Alavi, Hamsa. 1964. "Imperialism Old and New." *Socialist Register* 1:109–126.

Alcock, Susan E., Terence N. D'Altroy, Kathleen D. Morrison, and Carla M. Sinopoli, eds. 2001. *Empires: Perspectives from Archaeology and History*. Cambridge: Cambridge University Press.

Alexander, M. Jacqui. 1997. "Erotic Autonomy as a Politics of Decolonization: An Anatomy of Feminist and State Practice in the Bahamas Tourist Economy," in Alexander, M. J., and C. T. Mohanty, *Feminist Geneaologies, Colonial Legacies, Democratic Futures*. London: Routledge, pp. 63–100.

Atalay, Sonya. 2006. "Indigenous Archaeology as Decolonizing Practice." *American Indian Quarterly* 30(3&4):280–310.

Bhabha, Homi. 1984. "Of Mimicry and Men: The Ambivalence of Colonial Discourse." *October* 28:125–133.

———. 1994. *The Location of Culture*. London: Routledge.

Blackwood, Evelyn, and Saskia E. Wieringa, eds. 1999. *Same-Sex Relations and Female Desires: Transgender Practices across Cultures*. New York: Columbia University Press.

Boellstorff, Tom. 2003. "Dubbing Culture: Indonesian *Gay* and *Lesbi* Subjectivities and Ethnography in an Already Globalized World." *American Ethnologist* 30(2):225–242.

Boyd, Nan Alamilla. 2003. *Wide Open Town: A History of Queer San Francisco to 1965*. Berkeley: University of California Press.

Brendel, O. J. 1970. "The Scope and Temperament of Erotic Art in the Greco-Roman World," in Bowie, T., and C. V. Christenson (eds.), *Studies in Erotic Art*. New York: Basic Books, pp. 3–69.

Butler, Judith. 1990. *Gender Trouble: Feminism and the Subversion of Identity*. New York: Routledge.

Casella, Eleanor Conlin. 2000. "Bulldaggers and Gentle Ladies: Archaeological Approaches to Female Homosexuality in Convict-Era Australia," in Schmidt, R. A., and B. L. Voss (eds.), *Archaeologies of Sexuality*. London: Routledge, pp. 142–159.

———. 2010. "Broads, Studs, and Broken Down Daddies: The Materiality of 'Playing' in the Modern Penitentiary," in Bauer, A., and A. Agabe-Davies (eds.), *Social Archaeologies of Trade and Exchange*. Walnut Creek, CA: Left Coast Press, pp. 165–182.

———, and Sarah K. Croucher. 2010. *The Alderley Sandhills Project: An Archaeology of Community Life in (post)-Industrial England*. Manchester, United Kingdom: Manchester University Press.

Chakrabarty, Dipesh. 1993. "The Difference – Deferral of (A) Colonial Modernity." *History Workshop Journal* 36(1):1–34.

———. 2000. *Provincializing Europe: Postcolonial Thought and Historical Difference*. Princeton, NJ: Princeton University Press.

Chauncey, George. 1994. *Gay New York: Gender, Urban Culture, and the Making of the Gay Male World, 1890–1940*. New York: Basic Books.

Clarke, John R. 1996. "Hypersexual Black Men in Augustan Baths: Ideal Somatotypes and Apotropaic Magic," in Kampen, N. B. (ed.), *Sexuality in Ancient Art: Near East, Egypt, Greece, and Italy*. Cambridge: Cambridge University Press, pp. 184–198.

———. 1998. *Looking at Lovemaking: Constructions of Sexuality in Roman Art, 100 B.C.–A.D. 250*. Berkeley: University of California Press.

———. 2003. *Roman Sex, 100 B.C. to A.D. 250*. New York: Harry N. Abrams.

Comaroff, John L. 1989. "Images of Empire, Contests of Conscience: Models of Colonial Domination in South Africa." *American Ethnologist* 16(4):661–685.

Cooper, Frederick, and Laura Ann Stoler, eds. 1997. *Tensions of Empire: Colonial Cultures in a Bourgeois World*. Berkeley: University of California Press.

Coronil, Fernando. 2007. "After Empire: Reflections on Imperialism from the Américas," in Stoler, A. L., C. McGranahan, and P. C. Perdue (eds.), *Imperial Formations*. Santa Fe, NM: School for Advanced Research Press, pp. 241–271.

Croucher, Sarah K. 2007. "Clove plantations on nineteenth-century Zanzibar: Possibilities for gender archaeology." *Africa Journal of Social Archaeology* 7(3):302–324.

D'Emilio, John. 1983. *Sexual Politics, Sexual Communities: The Making of a Homosexual Minority in the United States 1940–1970*. Chicago: The University of Chicago Press.

———. 1997. "Capitalism and Gay Identity," in Lancaster, R. N., and M. di Leonardo (eds.), *The Gender/Sexuality Reader: Culture, History, Political Economy*. London: Routledge, pp. 169–178.

Davidson, James.1997. *Courtesans and Fishcakes: The Consuming Passions of Classical Athens*. New York: St. Martin's.

Davin, Anna. 1978. "Imperialism and Motherhood." *History Workshop* 5:9–65.

Davis, Whitney. 1996. "Winckelmann's 'Homosexual' Teleologies" in Kampen, N. B. (ed.), *Sexuality in Ancient Art: Near East, Egypt, Greece, and Italy*. Cambridge: Cambridge University Press, pp. 262–276.

Dawdy, Shannon Lee. 2006. "Proper Caresses and Prudent Distance: A How-To Manual from Colonial Louisiana," in Stoler, A. L. (ed.), *Haunted by Empire: Geographies of Intimacy in North American History*. Durham, NC: Duke University Press, pp. 140–162.

———, and Richard Weyhing. 2008. "Beneath the Rising Sun: 'Frenchness' and the Archaeology of Desire." *International Journal of Historical Archaeology* 12(4):370–387.

Deagan, Kathleen. 1983. *Spanish St. Augustine: The Archaeology of a Colonial Creole Community*. New York: Academic Press.

———, ed. 1995. *Puerto Real: The Archaeology of a Sixteenth-Century Spanish Town in Hispaniola*. Gainesville: University Press of Florida.

———. 2001. "Dynamics of Imperial Adjustment in Spanish America: Ideology and Social Integration," in Alcock, S. E., T. N. D'Altroy, K. D. Morrison, and C. M. Sinopoli (eds.), *Empires: Perspectives from Archaeology and History*. Cambridge: Cambridge University Press, pp. 179–194.

———. 2004. "Reconsidering Taíno Social Dynamics after Spanish Conquest: Gender and Class in Culture Contact Studies." *American Antiquity* 69(4):597–626.

———, and José María Cruxent. 2002. *Archaeology at La Isabela: America's First European Town*. New Haven, CT: Yale University Press.

Dover, K. J. 1978. *Greek Homosexuality*. Cambridge, MA: Harvard University Press.

Duara, Prasenjit. 2007. "The Imperialism of 'Free Nations': Japan, Manchukuo, and the History of the Present," in Stoler, A. L., C. McGranahan, and P. C. Perdue (eds.), *Imperial Formations*. Santa Fe, NM: School for Advanced Research Press, pp. 211–239.

Elliston, Deborah. 1995. "Erotic Anthropology: 'Ritualized Homosexuality' in Melanesia and Beyond." *American Ethnologist* 22(4):848–867.

Elsner, John. 1996. "Naturalism and the Erotics of the Gaze: Imitations of Narcissus," in Kampen, N. B. (ed.), *Sexuality in Ancient Art: Near East, Egypt, Greece, and Italy*. Cambridge: Cambridge University Press, pp. 247–261.

Ewen, Charles R. 1991. *From Spaniard to Creole: The Archaeology of Cultural Formation at Puerto Real, Haiti*. Tuscaloosa: University of Alabama Press.

Fanon, Frantz. 1977. *The Wretched of the Earth*. New York: Grove Press.

Feinberg, Leslie. 1996. *Transgender Warriors: Making History from Joan of Arc to RuPaul*. Boston: Beacon Press.

Foucault, Michel. 1978. *The History of Sexuality, Volume I: An Introduction* (R. Hurley, trans.). New York: Random House.

Frontisi-Ducroux, Françoise.1996. "Eros, Desire, and the Gaze," in Kampen, N. B. (ed.), *Sexuality in Ancient Art: Near East, Egypt, Greece, and Italy*. Cambridge: Cambridge University Press, pp. 81–100.

Funari, Pedro Paulo A. 1999. "Maroon, Race, and Gender: Palmares Material Culture and Social Relations in a Runaway Settlement," in Funari, P. P. A., S. Jones, and M. Hall (eds.), *Historical Archaeology: Back from the Edge*. London: Routledge, pp. 308–328.

Gandhi, Leela. 1998. *Postcolonial Theory: A Critical Introduction*. New York: Columbia University Press.

————. 2006. *Affective Communities: Anticolonial Thought, Fin-de-Siècle Radicalism, and the Politics of Friendship*. Durham, NC: Duke University Press.

Gleason, Maud W. 1990. "The Semiotics of Gender: Physiognomy and Self-Fashioning in the Second Century C.E.," in Halperin, D., J. Winkler, and F. Zeitlin (eds.), *Before Sexuality: The Construction of Erotic Experience in the Ancient Greek World*. Princeton, NJ: Princeton University Press, pp. 389–415.

Gosden, Chris. 2004. *Archaeology and Colonialism: Cultural Contact from 5000 BC to the Present*. Cambridge: Cambridge University Press.

Hall, Martin. 2000. *Archaeology and the Modern World: Colonial Transcripts in South Africa and the Chesapeake*. London: Routledge.

Halperin, David M., John J. Winkler, and Froma L. Zeitlin, eds. 1990. *Before Sexuality: The Construction of Erotic Experience in the Ancient Greek World*. Princeton, NJ: Princeton University Press.

Hawley, John C., ed. 2001. *Post-colonial, Queer: Theoretical Intersections*. Albany: State University of New York Press.

Hayes, Jarrod. 2001. "Queer Resistance to (Neo-)colonialism in Algeria," in Hawley, J. C. (ed.) *Post-colonial, Queer: Theoretical Intersections*. Albany: State University of New York Press, pp. 79–97.

Khalid, Adeeb. 2007. "The Soviet Union as an Imperial Formation," in Stoler, A. L., C. McGranahan, and P. C. Perdue (eds.), *Imperial Formations*. Santa Fe, NM: School for Advanced Research Press, pp. 113–139.

Laqueur, Thomas. 1990. *Making Sex: Body and Gender from the Greeks to Freud*. Cambridge, MA: Harvard University Press.

Larco Hoyle, Rafael. 1965. *Checán: Essay on Erotic Elements in Peruvian Art*. Geneva: Nagel.

Liebmann, Matthew, and Uzma Z. Rizvi, eds. 2008. *Archaeology and the Postcolonial Critique*. Lanham, MA: AltaMira Press.

Lightfoot, Kent G. 2005. *Indians, Missionaries, and Merchants: The Legacy of Colonial Encounters on the California Frontiers*. Berkeley and Los Angeles: University of California Press.

————, Antoinette Martinez, and Ann M. Schiff. 1998. "Daily Practice and Material Culture in Pluralistic Social Settings: An Archaeological Study of Culture Change and Persistence from Fort Ross, California." *American Antiquity* 63(2):199–222.

Loren, Diana DiPaolo. 2008. *In Contact: Bodies and Spaces in the Sixteenth- and Seventeenth-Century Eastern Woodlands*. Lanham, MD: Altamira Press.

Lydon, Jane. 2005. "'Watched over by the indefatigable Moravian missionaries': Colonialism and Photography at Ebenezer and Ramahyuck." *La Trobe Journal* 76(Spring):27–48.

Malinowski, B. 1929. *The Sexual Life of Savages in North-Western Melanesia: An Ethnographic Account of Courtship, Marriage, and Family Life among the Natives of the Trobriand Islands, British New Guinea*. New York: Readers League of America, distributed by Eugenics Publishing Company.

Manalansan, Martin F., VI. 2003. *Global Divas: Filipino Gay Men in the Diaspora*. Durham, NC: Duke University Press.

Mankekar, Purnima. 2004. "Dangerous Desires: Television and Erotics in Late Twentieth-Century India." *Journal of Asian Studies* 63(2):403–431.

McClintock, Anne. 1992. "The Angel of Progress: Pitfalls of the Term 'Post-colonialism'." *Social Text* 31/32:84–98.

————. 1995. *Imperial Leather: Race, Gender, and Sexuality in the Colonial Conquest*. New York: Routledge.

McEwan, Bonnie G. 1986. "Domestic Adaptation at Puerto Real, Haiti." *Historical Archaeology* 20:44–49.

McNiven, Ian J., and Lynette Russell. 2005. *Appropriated Pasts: Indigenous Peoples and the Colonial Culture of Archaeology*. Walnut Creek, CA: AltaMira Press.

Mead, Margaret. 1928. *Coming of Age in Samoa*. New York: Morrow.

Meskell, Lynn. 1998. "Consuming Bodies: Cultural Fantasies of Ancient Egypt." *Body and Society* 4(1):63–76.

Muñoz, José Esteban. 1999. *Disidentification: Queers of Color and the Performance of Politics.* Minneapolis: University of Minnesota Press.

Murray, Tim, ed. 2004. *The Archaeology of Contact in Settler Societies.* Cambridge: Cambridge University Press.

Nagel, Joane. 2000. "Ethnicity and Sexuality." *Annual Review of Sociology* 26:107–133.

Pagán Jiménez, Jaime R., and Reniel Rodríguez Ramos. 2008. "Toward the Liberation of Archaeological Praxis in a 'Postcolonial Colony': The Case of Puerto Rico," in Liebmann, M., and U. Z. Rizvi (eds.) *Archaeology and the Postcolonial Critique.* Lanham, MA: AltaMira Press, pp. 53–71.

Pratt, Mary Louise. 1992. *Imperial Eyes: Travel Writing and Transculturation.* London: Routledge.

Preucel, Robert W., and Craig N. Cipolla. 2008. "Indigenous and Postcolonial Archaeologies," in Liebmann, M., and U. Z. Rizvi (eds.) *Archaeology and the Postcolonial Critique.* Lanham, MA: AltaMira Press, pp. 129–140.

Rabinowitz, Nancy Sorkin. 2002. "Excavating Women's Homoeroticism in Ancient Greece: The Evidence from Attic Vase Painting," in Rabinowitz, N. S., and L. Auanger (eds.), *Among Women: From the Homosocial to the Homoerotic in the Ancient World.* Austin: University of Texas Press, pp. 106–166.

Richlin, Amy, ed. 1992. *Pornography and Representation in Greece and Rome.* Oxford: Oxford University Press.

Roscoe, Will. 1998. *Changing Ones: Third and Fourth Genders in Native North America.* New York: St. Martin's Press.

Rothschild, Nan A. 2003. *Colonial Encounters in a Native American Landscape: The Spanish and Dutch in North America.* Washington, DC: Smithsonian Books.

Said, Edward W. 1979. *Orientalism.* New York: Vintage Books.

Schrire, Carmel. 1995. *Digging through Darkness: Chronicles of an Archaeologist.* Charlottesville: University Press of Virginia.

Scott, Elizabeth M. 1991. "A Feminist Approach to Historical Archaeology: Eighteenth-Century Fur Trade Society at Michilimackinac." *Historical Archaeology* 25(4):42–53.

Scott, James C. 1985. *Weapons of the Weak: Everyday Forms of Peasant Resistance.* New Haven, CT: Yale University Press.

Sedgwick, Eve Kosofsky. 1990. *Epistemology of the Closet.* Berkeley and Los Angeles: University of California Press.

Sinnott, Megan. 2004. *Toms and Dees: Transgender Identity and Female Same-Sex Relationships in Thailand.* Honolulu: University of Hawaii Press.

Skinner, Marilyn. 2005. *Sexuality in Greek and Roman Culture.* Oxford: Blackwell.

South, Stanley, Russell K. Skowronek, and Richard E. Johnson, eds. 1988. "Spanish Artifacts from Santa Elena." *Columbia: Anthropology Studies* #7. South Carolina Institute of Archaeology and Anthropology, University of South Carolina.

Spivak, Gayatri. 1985. "Can the Subaltern Speak? Speculations on Widow Sacrifice." *Wedge* 7–8(Winter–Spring):120–30.

Stein, Gil J., ed. 2005. *The Archaeology of Colonial Encounters: Comparative Perspectives.* Santa Fe, NM: School of American Research Press.

Stoler, Ann Laura. 1992. "Sexual Affronts and Racial Frontiers: European Identities and the Cultural Politics of Exclusion in Colonial Southeast Asia." *Comparative Studies in Society and History* 34(3):514–551.

———. 1995. *Race and the Education of Desire: Foucault's History of Sexuality and the Colonial Order of Things.* Durham, NC: Duke University Press.

———. 2001. "Tense and Tender Ties: The Politics of Comparison in North American History and (Post) Colonial Studies." *The Journal of American History* 88(3):829–865.

———. 2002. *Carnal Knowledge and Imperial Power: Race and the Intimate in Colonial Rule.* Berkeley: University of California Press.

———. 2006. "Intimidations of Empire: Predicaments of the Tactile and Unseen," in Stoler, A. L. (ed.), *Haunted by Empire: Geographies of Intimacy in North American History.* Durham, NC: Duke University Press, pp. 1–22.

———, and Frederick Cooper. 1997. "Between Metropole and Colony: Rethinking a Research Agenda," in Cooper, F., and A. L. Stoler (eds.) *Tensions of Empire: Colonial Cultures in a Bourgeois World.* pp. 1–56. Berkeley: University of California Press.

———, Carole McGranahan, and Peter C. Perdue, eds. 2007. *Imperial Formations.* Santa Fe, NM: School for Advanced Research Press.

Symonds, John Addington. 1901. *A Problem in Greek Ethics, Being an Inquiry into the Phenomenon of Sexual Inversion Addressed Especially to Medical Psychologists and Jurists.* London.

Towle, Evan B., and Lynn M Morgan. 2002. "Romancing the Transgender Native: Rethinking the Use of the 'Third Gender' Concept." *GLQ* 8(4):469–497.

Trexler, Richard C. 1995. *Sex and Conquest: Gendered Violence, Political Order, and the European Conquest of the Americas.* Ithaca, NY: Cornell University Press.

Voss, Barbara L. 2000. "Feminisms, queer theories, and the archaeological study of past sexualities." *World Archaeology* 32(2):180–192.

———. 2005. "Sexual Subjects: Identity and Taxonomy in Archaeological Research," in Casella, E. C., and C. Fowler (eds.), *The Archaeology of Plural and Changing Identities: Beyond Identification.* New York: Kulwer Academic/Plenum Publishers, pp. 55–78.

———. 2008a. *The Archaeology of Ethnogenesis: Race and Sexuality in Colonial San Francisco.* Berkeley: University of California Press.

———. 2008b. "Domesticating Imperialism: Sexual Politics and the Archaeology of Empire." *American Anthropologist* 110(2):191–203.

———. 2008c. "Sexuality Studies in Archaeology." *Annual Review of Anthropology* 37:317–336.

———, and Robert A. Schmidt. 2000. "Archaeologies of Sexuality: An Introduction," in Schmidt, R. A., and B. L. Voss (eds.), *Archaeologies of Sexuality.* London: Routledge, pp. 1–32.

Wagner, Mark J. 1998. "Some Think It Impossible to Civilize Them at All: Cultural Change and Continuity among the Early Nineteenth-Century Potawatomi," in Cusick, J. G. (ed.), *Studies in Culture Contact: Interaction, Culture Change, and Archaeology.* Center for Archaeological Investigations, Occasional Paper 25, Southern Illinois University, pp. 430–456.

Warner, Michael, ed. 1993. *Fear of a Queer Planet: Queer Politics and Social Theory.* Minneapolis and London: University of Minnesota Press.

Watkins, Joe. 2005. "Through Wary Eyes: Indigenous Perspectives on Archaeology." *Annual Review of Anthropology* 34:429–449.

Weeks, Jeffrey, 1981. *Sex, Politics, and Society: The Regulation of Sexuality Since 1800.* New York: Longman.

Weismantel, Mary. 2004. "Moche Sex Pots: Reproduction and Temporality in Ancient South America." *American Anthropologist* 106(3):495–505.

Wilkie, Laurie A. 2000. "Magical Passions: Sexuality and African-American Archaeology," in Schmidt, R. A., and B. L. Voss (eds.), *Archaeologies of Sexuality.* London and New York: Routledge, pp. 129–142.

Williams, Raymond. 1977. *Marxism and Literature.* Oxford: Oxford University Press.

Williams, Walter L. 1986. *The Spirit and the Flesh: Sexual Diversity in American Indian Culture.* Boston: Beacon Press.

Winkler, John J. 1990. "Laying Down the Law: The Oversight of Men's Sexual Behavior in Classical Athens," in Halperin, D., J. Winkler, and F. Zeitlin (eds.), *Before Sexuality: The Construction of Erotic Experience in the Ancient Greek World.* Princeton, NJ: Princeton University Press, pp. 171–209.

Young, Robert J. C. 1995. *Colonial Desire: Hybridity in Theory, Culture, and Race.* New York: Routledge.

Yuval-Davis, Nira. 1996. "Women and the Biological Reproduction of 'The Nation'." *Women's Studies International Forum* 19(1/2):17–24.

SECTION I

PLEASURES AND PROHIBITIONS

THREE

LITTLE BASTARD FELONS

Childhood, Affect, and Labour in the Penal Colonies of Nineteenth-Century Australia

Eleanor Conlin Casella

AFFECTIONATE YEARNINGS

In a letter dated February 25, 1848, prison inmate Ellen Cornwall wrote to her husband in Birmingham to explain the fate of their son Henry. At age four, the child had accompanied his convict mother to the British penal colony of Van Diemen's Land (Tasmania), Australia: "the Country did not agree with [our] dear boy. Although he had Medical attendance and everything was done that could be done. But it pleased the lord on the 7th of March to take him to his Heavenly abode out of this vain & wicked world. But my Dear Fredk I shall pass over this scene of sorrow. I only add that it was the greatest trial I ever had. I followed his remains and saw him laid in the Churchyard in the Town" (Casella et al. 2001: 106–107).

How do emotional bonds shape the material worlds of empire? For those entangled within colonial worlds, complex dynamics of personal surveillance, classification, compliance, negotiation, and reformation saturated everyday life. Further, as social categories became increasingly defined and delineated, the 'individual' emerged as a new imperial subject – whether indigenous, settler, creole, visitor, or some complex blend thereof (Gosden 2004; C. Hall 2002; M. Hall 2000; Stoler 2002). As a disciplinary mechanism, this creation of the modern individual (or individualisation) was exacerbated within the stark context of the nineteenth-century Australian penal colonies – outposts of empire explicitly founded to achieve the combined goals of punishment, reformation, and deterrence on the criminal subject (Figure 3.1).

Within this carceral society, all unsanctioned emotional ties developed amongst the imperial exiles proved disruptive to both colonial and criminal discipline. Indeed, historians have demonstrated how such dangerous associations required careful supervision by colonial authorities (Alexander and Anderson 2008; Byrne 1993; Finch 1993; Reid 2007; Ryan 1995). The right to maintain, let alone nurture, relationships of affect – including familial, sexual, domestic, and even friendship – was a negotiated privilege for these imprisoned colonial subjects. Convicts fiercely strove to maintain their affective ties through their material worlds, with various scholars demonstrating how 'Government Women' forged both cross-sex and same-sex romantic relationships that transcended the boundaries of their colonial institutions (Casella 2000; Damousi 1997; Daniels 1998, Reid 2007).

In many cases, modes of unsanctioned relationship intersected, and attempts to maintain adult romantic connections overlapped with anxieties over parenting. In October 1847, a letter was intercepted by the matron of the Cascades Female Factory. Written by inmate M. A. Clark, this rare surviving narrative gently reprimanded her male partner for straying from his domestic responsibilities and requested a material gesture of commitment: "Dear Fred I hope you will be steady till I come out as I intend to keep sober and steady and if you send in a Memorial you can get me out and go to our child in the Orphanage in town, she is in town now. . . . Dear Fred I am suprised [sic] to think you should spend your hard earned Money with that [other] woman old enough to be your Mother. But I hope Dear Fred you know better for the future. Do not forget to write to me and send me some money" (ML 90/8770).

Thus, within this colonial and penal context, affect itself served as a site of critical negotiation. This study explores how the compelling emotional bonds of childhood and parenting, forged through imperial politics of reproduction and production, influenced the material world of the Australian Female Factories. It considers how the Nursery Wards provided ambiguous theatres of conflict within these antipodean British penal colonies. Finally, it explores the influence of sexual objectification, maternal idealization, and disciplinary yearning on the lived experiences of these female imperial exiles.

ON THE VEXING QUESTION OF FEMALE INCARCERATION

Bureaucratic confusion over the nature, purpose, and structure of female imprisonment arose from the gendered origins of the stark phenomena itself. From around 1780, penal incarceration emerged as the dominant mode of state control over its male citizen subjects (Casella 2007). Over the following seventy years, penal philosophies and architectural designs obsessed philanthropic elites, gentlemen politicians, and social reformers of the expanding British Empire. As most famously illustrated by Michel Foucault (1977), this enlightened prison architecture provided a material template for the choreography of subject (re)formation. The recalcitrant male inmate was methodically transformed into a docile body through architecturally enforced solitude and self-regulation. To justify (or indeed, legitimate) the painful logic of this disciplinary process, equal crimes earned meticulously measured doses of equal punishment.

Nevertheless, the specific question of female incarceration created a perpetual anxiety for government administrators. In both Britain and the United States, women's custodial sentences typically occurred within mixed-sex local or state-run prisons. Although initial reforms of the 1780s introduced the internal separation of female wards, such accommodation typically involved shared cells or communal dormitories within penal compounds intended for men (Freedman 1981; Upton

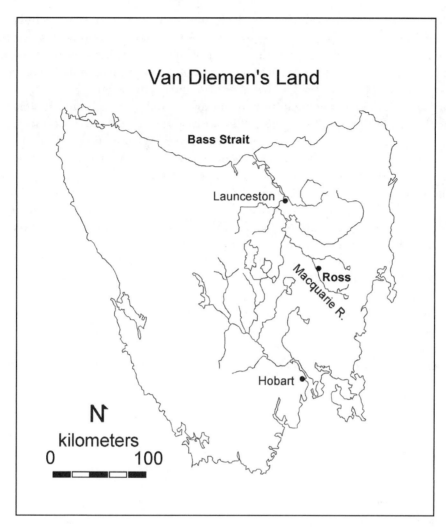

FIGURE 3.1. Map of Tasmania and locations mentioned in text.

1992; Zedner 1991). Some early 'administratively dependent' prisons for women were constructed inside the boundaries of larger male institutional compounds. For example, the first American facility – the Mount Pleasant Female Prison – was established in June 1839 as a satellite of New York's infamous Ossining (or 'Sing-Sing') State Penitentiary (Friedman 1993: 233; Freedman 1981: 48). It remained the only American dedicated female prison until the 1870s.

Within Great Britain, women's custodial sentences were served through a diverse network of mixed-sex local prisons managed by a board of Visiting Justices. By midcentury, a number of these institutions contained separate women's facilities – including, for example, the four-bay wing and matron's quarters at Lincoln Castle (1848) and the female wing, laundry, and washhouse at Oxford Castle (1850) (Brodie et al. 2002: 110). Following administrative reforms in 1850, the House of Correction at Tothill Fields, Westminster (London), catered primarily for women and their dependent children (Zedner 1991: 138). Originally founded in 1618, this obsolete institution provided 240 dark, unheated, and insufficiently ventilated cells for an average population of 430 women. Although penal reformers and civic authorities passionately decried the scandal of women's facilities, in both North America and Europe, the construction of dedicated and purpose-built female prisons would await a second wave of penal reforms during the 1870s.

Britain's disinterest stemmed from an alternative and imperialist agenda for the punishment of women. From 1788, the vast majority of female convicts tried in British courts were sentenced to antipodean penal transportation (Brodie et al. 2002: 134; Oxley 1996: 38–39), a management strategy intended to ameliorate both the stark gender imbalance and lack of domestic labour within colonial Australia (Alford 1984; Damousi 1997; Daniels 1998; Robinson 1993). In other words, women were required (on a rather basic level) for their sexual, reproductive, and productive efforts, with the specific political economy of their incarceration directly linked, as recent historical scholarship has demonstrated, to the broader imperatives of colonial development and administration (Alexander and Anderson 2008). Over 80 years, Great Britain exiled felons to its penal settlements in New South Wales, Van Diemen's Land, and Western Australia. Of the 160,000 convicts transported by the imperial state, approximately 25,000 were female (Robson 1965: 4). Many were mothers, either accompanied in exile by their small children or pregnant as a result of unsanctioned sexual activity within the penal colonies.

Charged with the management of this rapidly growing population of exiles, plus their dependant children, by 1817, Governor Lachlan Macquarie realised that a dedicated institution was essential for their colonial administration and accommodation (Salt 1984). Completed by 1822, his 'Female Factory' (the name an abbreviation of 'Manufactory' or Work House) at Parramatta, New South Wales, therefore provided the first international example of a prison built exclusively and intentionally for female incarceration – established at least two generations before such penal institutions were to appear in either North America or Europe.

Expanding into Queensland and Van Diemen's Land by the late 1820s, these Female Factories were designed as a loose network of probation stations, where upon entry women were assigned to the 'Crime Class,' and incarcerated for a minimum of six months (Casella 2002; Daniels 1998; Heath 1978). While serving this preliminary sentence, the convicts were expected to 'reform' through Christian prayer and mandatory training in acceptably feminine industries, such as textile production, laundry, and sewing. Recalcitrance was punished through lengthy periods of confinement in Solitary Cells, accompanied by severe reduction of food rations. Once they successfully served this probationary period, inmates were promoted into the 'Hiring Class' and awaited assignment to local pastoral properties, completing their convict sentences as unwaged domestic servants for free colonists.

Despite these institutional reforms, colonial administrators continued to struggle with a far more intrinsic ethical dilemma. In every Australian female prison, up to one-third of the human occupants had never committed a crime. For the children of convict women, their exile and incarceration did not reflect an enlightened mode of punishment. It was a mere accident of birth. Yet the very fact of their presence was a physical testimony – a "confession of the flesh" (Foucault 1990 [1978]: 19) – linked explicitly to their mother's sexuality. As austere institutions specifically designed for the punishment, deterrence, and reformation of adult felons, how were these colonial prisons to cope with this noncriminal population of dependant minors?

VULNERABLE SPACES: CHILDHOOD AND THE AUSTRALIAN CONVICT SYSTEM

Children entered Australia's vast penal bureaucracy through three basic routes (Brown 1972; Daniels 1998; Robinson 1993). If aged under five years, children could accompany their convict mothers on the arduous six-month journey aboard a penal transport vessel. Others were born within the Australian female prisons, their convict mothers falling pregnant while on external labour assignment, and returned to imprisonment as punishment for such frequent, yet unsanctioned, sexual activity (Casella 2000; Damousi 1997). Finally, male youths over age nine were transported as convicts themselves, having been sentenced as adults for property crimes committed within Great Britain. These lads could be accommodated at satellite facilities such as Point Puer, a dedicated juvenile compound within the Port Arthur penal settlement on the Tasman Peninsula of Van Diemen's Land (Jackman 2001).

How and where the 'convict babies' were accommodated within the penal system inflamed fierce debates over the nature and reproduction of British imperial subjectivities, as discourses of 'civilization,' class, morality, and religion enmeshed with the harsh realities of substandard clothing, food, and sanitation. Both architectural and archival evidence illuminates how convict mothers collided with the British imperial state over the right to maintain access to their children. The first debates emerged by the 1830s, as numerous inquests in both the New South Wales and Van Diemen's Land colonies linked child deaths to the overcrowded (and supposedly immoral) conditions within the shared dormitories. From 1833, babies were weaned and removed from their mothers at nine months of age, as colonial authorities expressed concern that the children's health would be affected if they continued to associate with criminals (Damousi 1997: 114).

Suspicion over the competence of working-class mothers was not, of course, unique to the convict colonies. Since the advent of the Modern Era, ideologies of proper 'mothering' have inevitably intersected with those of gender, race, citizenship, and power (Finch 1993; Hays 1996; Ladd-Taylor and Umansky 1998; Wilkie 2003). Within this particular clash between ideologies of 'criminality' and 'femininity,' however, corruption extended from the moral to physical realms, with transported convicts portrayed by the Reverend William Ullathorne, Vicar-General of the Australian Colonies, as "filthy, swollen-faced wretches" retaining only "something of the shape of woman in them" as they haunted the streets, abandoned to "stagger with drunkenness, dissoluteness and debauchery." Worse, their children appeared to have acquired their morally dissipated and corrupt characters through maternal contact: "What can I say of such women as mothers, but that their children are cradled in vice, are nursed at the bosom of profanity, and fed with the poison of ungodly lips, and that they drink in iniquity from their parent's example" (Ullathorne 1837: 29).

Thus, to rescue these colonial offspring from such impurities, the colonial state assumed a direct and paternalistic responsibility for the biological welfare of the convicts' children through the establishment of Nursery Wards. Separation of these unique wards from the general Factory compounds was intended as a humane and salubrious improvement on the overcrowded and unsanitary conditions of the inmate dormitories. State intrusion thus produced a systematic alienation of maternal affect. Or, as similarly observed by Kirsty Reid in her recent history of incarceration within the Van Diemen's Land colony: "Rather than creating spaces for the multiplication of home, the colonies were, instead, undermining and subverting familial and domestic order" (2007: 165).

Not surprisingly, these utopian Nursery Wards failed miserably in practice, and desperately high child mortality rates continued to plague the Female Factories. Colonial newspapers blamed the design of the Nurseries, and inmates rallied to defend their reputations as mothers. In 1838, a Convict Department Board of Inquiry was held to investigate the death of Elisabeth Lush, a toddler accommodated within the Cascade Female Factory of Hobart, Van Diemen's Land. In her testimony to the Board, the Nursery overseer Elizabeth Flint (herself a promoted Hiring Class inmate) emphasized the overcrowded conditions of the Nursery. "No less than 13 women and 26 children were housed in two rooms of 47 feet long and 11 1/2 feet wide. The yard was so small, and confined by high walls, that there was no necessary circulation of air" (Damousi 1997: 116).

The other inmates, she vehemently asserted, were not to be blamed for the sickly condition of the Factory children: "The women in my opinion take as much care of the children as free women might." Regardless of the cause, mortality rates continued to be scandalous. Josiah Spode – grandson of the eminent Spode ceramic family of Stoke-on-Trent (England) and Comptroller-General of Convicts for the Van Diemen's Land penal colony – reported to the Colonial Secretary in 1838 that over the first eight years of the Cascade Factory's operation, 208 children had died out of a total of 794 housed there (Archives of Tasmania [AOT] CSO 5/114/2605).

Shamed by damning exposés in the local newspapers, Factory Superintendants were ordered in 1834 to keep the Nurseries "sufficiently clean and thoroughly ventilated" and "always ready for public inspection" (AOT CSO 1/902/19161). Issued by the Comptroller-General of Convicts, these orders further stipulated that on no account were they to "deviate" from the state's instructions. Thus, the colonial state assumed and centralized the displaced role of the "patrichical paterfamilia" (McClintock 1995: 239). Through the medium of the built environment, the colonial bureaucracy simultaneously attempted to cleanse its convict subjects of their illicit sexuality and restore its power as a surrogate paternal authority.

The very institutionalization of care in separated Nursery Wards condemned these exiled children to dangerous vulnerabilities. Throughout the histories of the Female Factories, reports by Visiting Magistrates, Nursery Overseers, and Visiting Ladies' Societies documented frequent incidents of theft from provisions rationed to the Nursery Wards. Food and clothing were the most typical objects stolen. In a May 1838 letter of complaint to the Governor of New South Wales, Mr. John Clapham, Keeper of the Stores for the Parramatta Female Factory, bitterly documented 18 instances of improper use of prison stores over a 60-day period. His entry on April 19 notes: "A Prisoner reported . . . that she did not receive her proper rations for her Child. I told [the Superintendant] I believed her report was not without foundation;

that I knew the Monitor who served out the children's rations was one of the worst women in the Factory and that she had favourites to whom she sold the rations. I told *him* altho I knew this I had no means of preventing it, in fact I dare not interfere. He told me that I must interfere; that it was a cruel thing for the Children to be robbed and me know it" (NLA Heath Collection MS 6131).

Other instances recorded the physical abuse of children kept within the prison Nurseries. During an 1838 judicial inquest into the death of two children within the Cascades Female Factory, Louisa Fuller, a Crime Class inmate, testified that she had seen the mother, Mary Vowles, crying because her baby had been put into the Nursery. At that time Fuller had reassured Vowles that she should not despair at the bruises on the baby's body, because "children will fall about" (Damousi 1997: 114). The jury of fifteen found that the confined state of the nurseries and the absence of proper precaution induced death. The colonial state remained shamefully incompetent in its role as a surrogate parent.

"A MODEL FOR ALL SIMILAR ESTABLISHMENTS IN HER MAJESTY'S COLONIES"[1]

Reforms to the management of convict children culminated in 1846, when the Comptroller-General of Convicts approved establishment of the Ross Female Factory as a special purpose depôt for pregnant and nursing convict women. Located in the rural district of the Northern Midlands, this inland prison site was intended to supply female convict domestic labour to local pastoral properties and provide a healthy bucolic atmosphere for the convict children, thereby alleviating overcrowding in the urban Factories of Hobart and Launceston. In accordance with regulations of the Convict Department, infants at Ross Factory were accommodated with their convict mothers for nutritional purposes until weening was enforced at approximately 9 months of age. Following transfer of their mothers to six months of incarceration – in addition to their original custodial sentence – to the main prison compound, the separated children continued to be accommodated within the Nursery Ward until age 3, when they were transferred to the Queen's Orphan School in Hobart Town, located approximately 69 miles to the south of Ross (Scripps and Clark 1991: 31). By December 31, 1848, muster counts reported that Ross Female Factory incarcerated sixty-two women, twenty-two girls, and twenty boys (AOT CO 282/690/254; Rayner 1980: 30–31).

Funded through the British Academy, archaeological excavations occurred during January 2007 and were supported by the Parks and Wildlife Service, Heritage Tasmania, and the Queen Victoria Museum and Art Gallery. Consisting of an open-area trench of 4 by 8 square metres, the excavations revealed structural remains of the Nursery Ward and adjoining Work Room (Figure 3.2). An assemblage of artefacts was also recovered from deposits that had accumulated in underfloor spaces stratigraphically linked to the Female Factory period of site occupation (Casella 2002: 32, figure 10), and therefore represented activities undertaken within the Nurseries.

Nevertheless, despite extensive archival evidence identifying this region of the Ross Factory as the Nursery Ward, a general absence of obvious 'child'-specific materials (toys, feeding bottles, clothing, etc.) characterised the recovered artefact assemblage. Although initially surprising, the absence itself begged an immediate question: What would constitute a material signature of childhood within this particular archaeological context?

To address the perceived 'invisibility' of children in the archaeological record, scholars have explored the materiality of childhood through sources that range from age-linked burials and iconographic representations of life-cycle rituals, to spatial distributions of objects around households, and ethnoarchaeological evidence of age-linked foraging tasks (see Baxter 2005, 2008; Buchli and Lucas 2001; Joyce 2000; Kamp 2002; Lucy 1994; Sofaer Derevenski 2000). These publications raise important new directions for appreciating childhood as a unique and embodied form of social identity. However, they also presume a degree of parental care and individual agency that cannot be assumed to exist within the stark institutional environment of a prison compound.

What would be the material implications of a childhood dominated by the experience of penal confinement? Recent archaeological studies of noncarceral historic institutions dedicated to the care of children, places such as orphanages or schools (see Beisaw and Gibb 2009), have demonstrated the frequent presence of toy dolls, marbles, rubber balls, writing slates and pencils, toothbrushes, and combs – all objects explicitly related to a process of childhood socialization. Perhaps the absence of such items from the Nursery Ward at the Ross Female Factory was not accidental. Although the absence of obvious 'toys' could be related to the general scarcity of personal belongings within this carceral site, previous archaeological research has critiqued simplistic interpretations of this special category of artefact (see Baxter 2005: 41–53). A 'toy,' in other words, resides in the eye (or grasping little hands) of the beholder. An estimated count of six large ferrous serving spoons were recovered from Nursery-related underfloor deposits, although no archival evidence suggested the preparation of meals within these dormitories. As objects that could be bounced, banged, sucked – but crucially, *not* swallowed – perhaps these kitchen implements served as 'toys' for the infant and toddler residents of the Nurseries?

Regardless of these functional ambiguities, given the specifically *carceral* context of the Nursery Ward, the absence of child-specific artefacts might further suggest an intentional form of delayed socialization, a negation of the materiality of the 'child' within this place of (adult) punishment. By addressing the biological survival of these new colonial subjects, while simultaneously limiting both maternal and material contacts, perhaps the colonial administrators were linking the moment at which the convict child became a social being to their institutional transfer to the Royal Orphan School? Or perhaps the intentional unravelling of emotional bonds between the incarcerated mothers and children provided a significant affective component of the colonial socialization process – the stark act of separation itself generating a story of removal, neglect, and alienated familial ties that became the painful experience of individualisation shared amongst these institutionally raised 'convict babies'?

Ultimately, the invisibility of childhood within this excavated assemblage raises questions on the nature of a *carceral* childhood, where the absences themselves created a unique spatial cartography of power. Developing this line of interpretation

FIGURE 3.2. Area E: Detail of Nursery Ward features, south facing. Ross Factory Archaeology Project, 2007. Photograph by author.

further, perhaps the built environment of the Nursery Wards could be better understood as a landscape of alienation directed toward the criminal mothers, rather than the children confined within its walls. But how would the fabric of these penal Nurseries enable a strategic disruption of maternal affect?

ON THE MATERIALITY OF YEARNING

As previously mentioned, the 2007 excavation season revealed structural remains of the Nursery Ward and adjoining Work Room. Closer analysis of these exposed foundations demonstrated a complicated series of construction, demolition, and modification events, with three primary built phases characterising the architectural evolution of this region of the Ross penal compound (Figure 3.3).

Origins of the Quadrangle (1842)

The Ross quadrangle was originally constructed in 1842 as a road-gang station intended to accommodate a maximum of 220 men. Thus, the eastern and western rooms exposed through archaeological excavation initially functioned as dormitories for male convicts. As extensively discussed in a previous site monograph (Casella 2002), dormitory interiors of this original Ross compound were floored with sandstone flags. An exterior drain system was constructed along the southern wall of the dormitory structure, with the ditch feature exposed during excavations indicating its original location and orientation. A perimeter boundary wall of rough sandstone enclosed the southern rear of the quadrangle compound, its foundations similarly revealed through excavation.

Establishment of the Female Factory (1847)

When recommissioned as Female Factory in 1847, British imperial funds were committed for removal of the original sandstone flags, and their replacement with wooden floorboards (see Casella 2002). Archaeological evidence of this reflooring event appeared as sandstone joist support piers introduced for suspension of the new floorboards. Significantly, this interior modification created an underfloor space where artefacts deposited during the Female Factory period subsequently accumulated. With the arrival of female inmates in January 1848, the excavated eastern and western rooms became reclassified as Nursery Wards. Internally divided into three separate wards, the dormitory structure accommodated a maximum of 50 infants and toddlers.

Over the subsequent six years of institutional operation, separation became the primary mode for both accommodating the children and punishing their mothers. Within the Ross Factory compound, isolation of the Nurseries from the adult inmate wards was carefully enforced through a combination of structural boundaries, procedural regulations, and daily labour routines. A staff duty report completed in October 1848 by Superintendent William Irvine indicated that female convict labour primarily occurred in either the Crime Class Ward, used for needlework and spinning during work hours, or the Laundry Room, located on the eastern side of the compound. As indicated on contemporary architectural plans, the Nursery Ward was isolated from both of these productive regions of the penal compound by a series of separate muster yards, and 9-foot-high wooden fences that subdivided the prison interior into strictly defined functional spaces (AOT PWD 266/1695; Casella 2002: figure 3). Additionally, following weaning and removal of their mother to the Crime Class Ward, Factory children were cared for by assigned "Pass Holders" – promoted Hiring Class inmates – with the daily operation of the Nursery Ward strictly supervised by the Assistant Matron (AOT MM 62/24/10774).

Reinforcing the Factory Regime (1851)

Following series of management scandals, Superintendent Irvine was unceremoniously dismissed and replaced in July 1850 by Dr. Edward Swarbeck Hall, an English surgeon who had previously provided medical service to male convict stations throughout the local area. Described by the Comptroller-General of Convicts as a "thorough disciplinarian" (Scripps & Clark 1991: 49), Hall immediately requisitioned imperial funds for the construction of a new bank of isolated Solitary Cells (excavated during 1997) and a dedicated Work Room, a structure that immediately abutted the southern façade of the Nursery Ward. As a result of his institutional redesign, the original 1842 drain system and perimeter wall were demolished to ground level and covered by the new structure (see Figure 3.3).

A thoroughly disciplinary space, the new Work Room was intentionally positioned to provide labouring inmates with a view dominated by the new block of Solitary

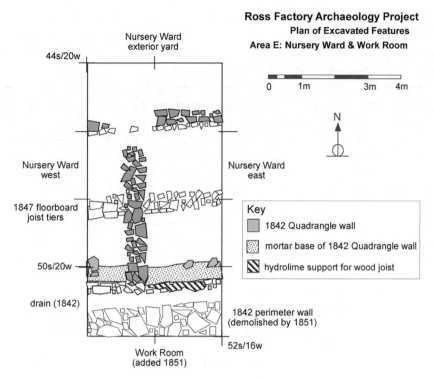

FIGURE 3.3. Area E: Plan of excavated features, including details of building phases. Ross Factory Archaeology Project, 2007. Drawn by author.

Cells and the elevated prison Chapel – the architectural choice, in other words, between Salvation and Damnation. Additionally, it not only shared a conjoined wall with the Nurseries but also retained the structural isolation of these two penitential zones. Following completion of the Work Rooms in 1851, the primary access route across the prison compound required female convicts to be marched twice daily past the Nursery Wards, their views and access into these sensitive yards physically blocked by a 9-foot-high timber fence. Inside the Work Room, the women laboured in ten-hour shifts to achieve their daily targets for knitting, spinning, washing, and sewing, as specified in an itemized "Revised Scale of Task Work" issued by the Comptroller-General of Convicts (AOT CO 280/699/268, p. 162).

While working – burdened with the knowledge of the Nurseries on the opposite side of the adjoining wall – perhaps they were able to hear noises through the single-course of shoddy masonry that separated them from their children? Allowed no official contact with their infants, these women inhabited an institutional landscape designed to engender a painful yearning for the affectionate bonds of motherhood. Anxieties created by these mundane separations were further inflamed by childhood mortality rates, with sixty-two children succumbing to maladies variously recorded as diarrhoea, catarrh, marasmus (malnutrition), or simply "debilitas" (Scripps and Clark 1991: 31). By 1855, a final posttransportation colonial inquest determined that Factory infant deaths were due to a combination of mismanagement and neglect (Brown 1972: 65).

Australian historian Joy Damousi has written on the paradox of convict motherhood, noting that while the colonial state attempted to 'feminise' convicts through
enforced productive labour, maternity – a crucial part of nineteenth-century femininity – was denied to them. This exclusion, she argues, "worked as an effective form
of disciplinary action for it punished women not only by the torture of the mind or
an inscription on the body, but through the power of emotional yearning created
by absence" (Damousi 1997: 119).

Colonial authorities themselves explicitly acknowledged the disciplinary value of
physical separation; in 1841, Mrs. Slea, Matron at the Cascades Factory, insisted the
"only inducement to conduct themselves well in assignment, I consider to be the
hope of being permitted to see their children" (AOT CSO 22/50).

Thus, the presence of the Nurseries within the Ross Female Factory revealed a
basic contradiction to the efficient operation of a British penal system designed for
the colonial reformation of criminal subjects. Did the Nurseries architecturally represent a form of state *welfare* for the children, or state *punishment* for the mothers?
Perhaps they offered a means for ideological displacement – punishing the tart for
her illicit encounter, while avoiding direct reference to the terrible generative practices themselves. Or as observed by Michel Foucault, from the dawn of the Modern
Era, calling sex by its name became increasingly difficult and costly: "According to
the new pastoral, sex must not be named imprudently, but its aspects, its correlations,
and its effects must be pursued down to their slenderest ramifications" (Foucault
1990 [1978]: 19).

Thus, through the strategic disruption of family, the colonial prison not only disciplined but desexualized the female convict. The intended effect "was to encourage
dependency on the institution and increase the likelihood that inmates would inter-
nalize the reformatory's teachings about how women like themselves should behave"
(Rafter 1990: 169).

SOME MISCHIEF STILL

> For Satan always finds some mischief still for idle hands to do.
>   Isaac Watts, English politician (died 1748)

Despite the intended separation of carceral regions, archaeological excavations suggested a more ambiguous set of functional activities within the excavated Nursery
rooms. Although no immediately 'childhood' associated artefacts were recovered,
excavations did reveal a substantial number of sewing-related artefacts from stratigraphic contexts associated with the underfloor deposits. These materials included
bone, ferrous metal, and shell buttons; copper-alloy sewing pins; thimbles and fas-
teners; and (surprisingly) part of a bone lacework bobbin.

The assemblage also included three cloth bale seals, stamped into lead. Offering
a mode of material accounting for the international sale and distribution of textiles,
the stamped lead bale seal was clamped over a 'bale,' or finished and weighed
measure, of woven cloth, thereby ensuring it as a verified unit of sale (Figure 3.4).
Clamped by a strap around the bolt of woven cloth, and into the cloth itself, the bale
seal hindered the pilfering of off-cuts and thereby ensured a secure transmission of
these manufactured commodities across the British Empire.

FIGURE 3.4. Detail of cloth bale monument, Municipal Museum De Lakenhal, Leiden (Netherlands), 1640. Until 1874, the building served as the regional Clothmaker's Hall. Photograph by author, December 2008.

Of the three lead artefacts recovered from the Ross Female Factory, two were corroded. The third displayed a detailed insignia, one that directly echoed a decorative freize carved over the doorway of the Commissariat Store (1836), one of the early historic sandstone buildings located within the central crossroads of the Ross township (Figure 3.5). Previous historical research indicated that the structure fell under the jurisdiction of the Royal Army Ordnance Corps, or that division of His Majesty's army charged with provisioning the imperial convicts (Scripps 1996: 5).

As a component of their labour regime, female convicts were charged with producing uniforms for distribution to inmates through the penal colony, and sewing a prescriptive range of clothing items for sale to the general population. The Matron was charged with the duty of cutting out the cloth from set patterns to ensure no wastage of valuable imported textiles (Scripps and Clark 1991: 22). Uniforms issued to male convicts tended to consist of a jacket and trousers constructed of shoddy wool, a fabric that may have been colonially produced on a local scale for sale to the Convict Department but – as suggested by the registry of commercial imports listed within the 1849 colonial "Almanack" – far more likely bulk-imported as manufactured inexpensive 'woollens' from England (Wood 1849). Additionally, female uniforms consisted of a combination of shoddy wool and calico or flannel (Table 3.1). Further, hospital garments and dressings, clothes for the Nursery children, and clothing for general sale were all constructed of calico, flannel, or muslin (Brand 1990: 250; Scripps and Clark 1991: 18). As either cotton- or wool-based manufactured textiles, these various fabrics were likely to have originated in the industrial northwest of England – that region of the British Empire that commanded the mass-production of commercial textiles from the mid-eighteenth

Table 3.1. Uniform issued to female factory
inmates after 1845

Quantity	Item	Fabric
1	Jacket	Grey wool
1 pair	Stockings	Grey wool
1 pair	Shoes	Leather
1	Cap	Calico or flannel
1	Shift	Calico or flannel
1	Handkerchief	Calico or flannel
1	Petticoat (skirt)	Grey wool
1	Apron	Calico or flannel

Source: "Regulations of the Probationary Establishments for Female Convicts in Van Diemen's Land, 1 July 1845" (reprinted in Brand 1990: 250).

through early twentieth century. Thus, as imperial commodities, they were likely to have been bulk imported to the prison colony as bales of cloth and provisioned to the Ross Female Factory via the local unit of the Royal Army Ordnance Corp.

Did the presence of these unique artefacts within underfloor deposits merely indicate that prison authorities stored valuable work-related materials within the Nursery Ward at times when the infant population was low? Or perhaps, given the presence of sewing-related artefacts, the underfloor assemblage suggested a degree of circumvention of the strict separation between the Nurseries and adjoining Work Rooms? While temporarily accommodated with their infants before enforced weening, convict mothers were not required to undertake official task-work duties. Thus, the presence of textile-related artefacts could materially indicate an unofficial negotiation of penal guidelines, despite the rigid orders and guidelines issued by the Comptroller-General of Convicts. Were breast-feeding mothers relegated to task work during their time within the Nursery Ward, with this labour requirement itself representing a local violation of official colonial regulations?

Alternatively, perhaps Crime Class inmates – specifically the mothers who had been returned to the general population following weening of their babies – were quietly permitted to complete their mandatory task-work duties while in the company of their infants within the Nursery Ward and thereby enjoy a limited degree of maternal contact, nurture brief periods of affectionate connection, and ultimately engender some form of childhood socialisation on their offspring. Certainly, archival evidence can be found to suggest such deviations from official regulations occurred more often than desired by authorities of the Convict Department.

'A DISTURBANCE': THE DISCIPLINARY REGIME UNRAVELS

Given the threats and dangers inherent to the Nursery Wards, these ambiguous spaces became emotive theatres of conflict within the carceral landscapes of the colonial Female Factories. As hinted in the archaeological evidence, convict women did not easily relinquish access to their children. In May 1849, the Visiting Magistrate investigated formal complaints by Constable Taylor, a lesser employee of the Ross

FIGURE 3.5. Excavated lead bale seal, Ross Factory Archaeology Project, 2007. Insert: Detail of Commissariat Store (1836), Church Street, Ross. Photographs by author.

Female Factory. His subsequent report documented details of a distressing public altercation within the Nursery Yards. As an indulgence to the better behaved, Superintendent William Irvine had occasionally permitted mothers in the Crime Class to see their children on Sundays after church services. Perhaps as a result of such limited contact, on one particular Sunday in early 1849: "At the [time] for returning the child of Bridget Hines to the nursery, [Hines] was reluctant to part with it – [Constable] Taylor endeavoured to remove it by force" (AOT MM 62/26/11946).

This altercation then led to a spectacular public disturbance, and Mr. Imrie (the Assistant Superintendant) was called forth to enforce order on the rioting women. Arriving at the scene unfolding in the Nursery Ward, Mr. Imrie found Constable Taylor to be "unnecessarily violent" toward both inmate Hines and her baby. The Visiting Magistrate's report judged Taylor to be "a very passionate as well as jealous man" and determined that "Taylor was disconcerted and certainly misconducted himself." The circumstances were believed to justify Mr. Imrie's use of swear words and threats toward his Constable in front of the audience of convict mothers. As a result of this public 'disturbance,' Superintendent Irvine was reprimanded for his questionable breach of official regulations toward the Nursery Wards.

CONCLUSIONS

By way of conclusion, two suggestions can be interpreted from this dramatic incident. First, inmate mothers actively resisted their separation from their children. Although the maternal process of childhood socialisation was officially limited as a disciplinary strategy, female convicts were well aware of the threats inherent in allowing the state to assume the role of surrogate parent. The Nursery Wards therefore provided a central arena of conflict within the carceral worlds of the Female Factories, a space where the ability to nurture affectionate familial ties became a fiercely guarded right.

Second, despite the officially enforced policies of disrupted maternal affect, enacted through architectural isolation, procedural regulations, and daily labour routines, the complete cultivation of disciplinary yearning appears to have been locally, and mostly quietly, negotiated throughout the everyday operation of these colonial prisons. Both archival and archaeological evidence suggests a degree of collusion by Factory authorities, with convict mothers allowed access to their children during both recreational and labouring periods of the penal regime. And rather than passively submit to a disciplinary regulation of their emotional ties, inmates co-opted the Nursery Wards for public protest against the appropriative surrogacy of the colonial state.

This chapter has explored conflicts over the painful process of 'individualisation' that saturated everyday life within the Australian penal colonies. Forged through imperial politics of reproduction, socialisation, and sexual regulation, the affective ties of childhood and parenting served as a critical site of disruption, not only linking female convicts to their infants but also challenging the power of the imperial state over its exiled subjects.

NOTE

1. AOT MM 62/29/14958.

REFERENCES

Alexander, J., and C. Anderson. 2008. "Politics, Penality and (Post-)Colonialism: An Introduction." *Cultural and Social History* 5(4):391–394.

Alford, K. 1984. *Production or Reproduction: An Economic History of Women in Australia.* Melbourne: Oxford University Press.

AOT (Archives of Tasmania) CO 280/699/268, p. 162. Revised Scale of Task Work, 29 December 1849.

AOT CO 282/690/254. Report from J. S. Hampton, Comptroller-General of Convicts, to W. Denison, Lieutenant-Governor of Van Diemen's Land, 1849.

AOT CSO 5/114/2605. Letter from Josiah Spode, Comptroller-General of Convicts, to Colonial Secretary, 1838.

AOT CSO 1/902/19161. Instructions for the Medical Officer Attending the Female House of Correction, 1834.

AOT CSO 22/50. Report and Evidence of a Committee Enquiring into Female Convict Discipline, 1841–1843.

AOT MM 62/24/10774. Duties of the Staff at the Ross Female Factory. Report by Dr. W. Irvine to Comptroller-General Hampton, October 1848.

AOT MM 62/26/11946. Case of Constable Taylor. Report by Visiting Magistrate to Comptroller-General Hampton, May 1849.

AOT MM 62/29/14958. Extracts from the Visitor's Book, Ross Female Factory, 1851.

AOT PWD 266/1695. Plan of the Female House of Correction, Ross. 1848.

Baxter, J. 2005. *The Archaeology of Childhood.* Lanham, MD: AltaMira Press.

———. 2008. "The Archaeology of Childhood." *Annual Review of Anthropology* 37:159–175.

Beisaw, A. M., and J. G. Gibb. 2009. *The Archaeology of Institutional Life.* Tuscaloosa: University of Alabama Press.

Brand, I. 1990. *The Convict Probation System: Van Diemen's Land 1839–1854.* Hobart, Australia: Blubber Head Press.

Brodie, A., J. Croom, and J. O. Davies. 2002. *English Prisons.* Swindon, United Kingdom: English Heritage.

Brown, J. 1972. *Poverty Is Not a Crime: Social Services in Tasmania 1803–1900.* Hobart, Australia: Blubber Head Press.

Buchli, V., and G. Lucas 2001. "The Archaeology of Alienation: A Late Twentieth-Century British Council House," in Buchli, V., and G. Lucas (eds.), *Archaeologies of the Contemporary Past.* London: Routledge, pp. 158–167.

Byrne, P. 1993. *Criminal Law and the Colonial Subject.* Cambridge: Cambridge University Press.

Casella, E. C. 2000. "'Doing Trade': A Sexual Economy of 19th Century Australian Female Convict Prisons." *World Archaeology* 32(2):209–221.

———. 2002. *Archaeology of the Ross Female Factory.* Records of the Queen Victoria Museum, Number 108. Launceston, Australia: Queen Victoria Museum and Art Gallery.

———. 2007. *The Archaeology of Institutional Confinement.* Gainesville: University Press of Florida.

———, E. Cornwall, and L. Frost. 2001. "'your unfortunate and undutiful wife.'" In Frost, L., and H. Maxwell-Stewart (eds.), *Chain Letters.* Melbourne: Melbourne University Press, pp. 105–115.

Damousi, J. 1997. *Depraved and Disorderly.* Cambridge: Cambridge University Press.

Daniels, K. 1998. *Convict Women.* Sydney: Allen & Unwin.

Finch, L. 1993 *The Classing Gaze.* Sydney: Allen & Unwin.

Foucault, M. 1977. *Discipline and Punish.* London: Penguin.

———. 1990 [1978]. *The History of Sexuality, Volume 1.* New York: Vintage Books.

Freedman, E. 1981. *'Their Sisters' Keepers': Women's Prison Reform in America 1830–1930.* Ann Arbor: University of Michigan Press.

Friedman, L. 1993. *Crime and Punishment in American History.* New York: HarperCollins.

Gosden, C. 2004. *Archaeology and Colonialism.* Cambridge: Cambridge University Press.

Hall, C. 2002. *Civilizing Subjects.* Cambridge: Polity Press.

Hall, M. 2000. *Archaeology and the Modern World.* London: Routledge.

Hays, S. 1996. *The Cultural Contradictions of Motherhood.* New Haven, CT: Yale University Press.

Heath, L. M. 1978. *The Female Convict Factories of New South Wales and Van Diemen's Land.* Unpublished master's thesis, Department of History, Australian National University.

Jackman, G. 2001. "'Get Thee to Church': Hard Work, Godliness and Tourism at Australia's First Rural Reformatory." *Australasian Historical Archaeology* 19:6–13.

Joyce, R. 2000. "Girling the Girl and Boying the Boy: The Production of Adulthood in Ancient Mesoamerica." *World Archaeology* 31(3):472–483.

Kamp, K. 2002. *Children in the Prehistoric Puebloan Southwest.* Salt Lake City: University of Utah Press.

Ladd-Taylor, M., and L. Umansky. 1998. *"Bad" Mothers: The Politics of Blame in Twentieth-Century America.* New York: New York University Press.

Lucy, S. 1994. "Children in Early Medieval Cemeteries." *Archaeological Review of Cambridge* 13(2):21–34.

McClintock, A. 1995 *Imperial Leather.* New York: Routledge.

Mitchell Library of Sydney (ML) Tasmanian Papers, No. 90, 8770. 29 October 1847. Letter and attachments from A. B. Jones, Superintendent of the Cascades Female Factory to J. S. Hampton, Comptroller-General of Convicts.

National Library of Australia, Canberra (NLA), L. M. Heath Collection. Archives and Manuscripts Office, MS 6131.

Oxley, D. 1996. *Convict Maids.* Cambridge: Cambridge University Press.

Rafter, N. 1990. *Partial Justice,* 2nd ed. New Bruswick, NJ: Transaction Publishers.

Rayner, T. 1980. Historical Survey of the Ross Female Factory Site, Tasmania. Unpublished report prepared for the Parks & Wildlife Service of Tasmania, Australia.

Reid, K. 2007. *Gender, Crime and Empire*. Manchester, United Kingdom: Manchester University Press.

Robinson, P. 1993. *The Women of Botany Bay*. Ringwood, Australia: Penguin Books Australia.

Robson, L. L. 1965. *The Convict Settlers of Australia*. Melbourne: Melbourne University Press.

Ryan, L. 1995. "From Stridency to Silence: The Policing of Convict Women, 1803–1853," in Kirkby, D. (ed.), *Sex, Power and Justice*. Melbourne: Oxford University Press, pp. 70–85.

Salt, A. 1984. *These Outcast Women: The Parramatta Female Factory 1821–1848*. Sydney: Hale and Iremonger.

Scripps, L. 1996. The Military at Ross. Unpublished report prepared for the Tasmanian Wool Centre of Ross, Tasmania.

Scripps, L., and J. Clark. 1991. The Ross Female Factory, Tasmania. Unpublished report prepared for the Parks & Wildlife Service of Tasmania, Australia.

Sofaer Derevenski, J. 2000. *Children and Material Culture*. London: Routledge.

Stoler, A. 2002. *Carnal Knowledge and Imperial Power*. Berkeley: University of California Press.

Ullathorne, W. 1837. *The Catholic Mission in Australasia*. Liverpool: Rockliff & Duckworth.

Upton, D. 1992. "The City as Material Culture," in Yentsch, A., and M. Beaudry (eds.), *The Art and Mystery of Historical Archaeology*. Boca Raton, FL: CRC Press, pp. 51–72.

Wilkie, L. 2003, *The Archaeology of Mothering*. New York: Routledge.

Wood, J. 1849. *The Tasmanian Royal Kalendar, colonial register, and almanack*. Launceston, Australia: Henry Dowling.

Zedner, L. 1991. *Women, Crime and Custody in Victorian England*. Oxford: Clarendon Press.

FOUR

THE CURRENCY OF INTIMACY

Transformations of the Domestic Sphere on the Late-Nineteenth-Century Diamond Fields

Lindsay Weiss

INTRODUCTION

Historical archaeology is always a story about some manner of production and reproduction. Its sites consist of factories, mills, bunker houses, and plantations – spaces where people come together to create more and more things – and, in the process, such sites carve out spaces for the concretions of race, gender, ethnicity, class, and domesticity. Somewhere in all of this, people continually made each other too: reproduction, at its most biologically essential, did not pause for the onset of industrialization, colonization, or nationalism, even as it was often radically rescripted by these same processes. To consider the materiality and artifact record of these sorts of intimate solidarities, affective ties such as motherhood, sexual attraction, burgeoning masculinities, carnal encounters, or the attrition of marital ties in the colonies can often present a tremendous challenge to the archaeologist, particularly because the trails of such enactments are often ephemeral. The presumption of ephemerality in itself, however, arouses some archaeological suspicion, because it raises the question of what concepts (such as gender or reproduction) could possibly mean outside of their colonial housing (Voss 2000); prison-house currencies (Casella 2000); gendered prohibitions according to monastic, missionary, or prison spatialities (Gilchrist 1994); privileged parceling according to factory hierarchy (Hardesty 1998); or integration with spiritual practice (Meskell 1999). Intimacy, sex, and reproduction can only ever occur in, on, and for something – existing within a mesh of what Anna Tsing might include in what she calls 'frictions' (Tsing 2005), those encounters with existing infrastructures, the contingencies of physical conditions and the particular ordering of things at any one historical moment, which often collectively redirect global engendering, in 'queer' sorts of directions.

The various historically normative categories for procreative and sensual gratification or the extent to which these behaviors could be collapsed with gender or the institution of marriage have always been predicated on the contingencies of historical conditions and the mesh of biopower that any one couple find themselves within. In the colonial context, these proscriptive mores surrounding sex and marriage often came to take on a life of their own, and these institutions were really functioning at a rupture from what might otherwise be read as an uninterrupted historical ontology tracing back to a Christian European genealogy (Povinelli 2007; Taylor 2007). This disjuncture between metropolitan prescriptions for intimacy and love (and all of the subtle injunctions and political forms they mobilized) and how these relationships came to manifest themselves, indicates a good deal about what was at stake, politically, in settler colonies. As Beth Povinelli claims, it is,

> the *intimate couple* [that] is a key transfer point between, on the one hand, liberal imaginaries of contractual economics, politics and sociality, and, on the other, liberal forms of power in the contemporary world. Love, as an intimate event, secures the self-evident good of social institutions, social distributions of life and death, and social responsibilities for these institutions and distributions. If you want to locate the hegemonic home of liberal logics and aspirations, look to love in settler colonies. (Povinelli 2006: 17)

This chapter is an attempt to foreground the intimate couple as it was stretched and reformulated on the Diamond Fields during the implementation of segregated worker housing, one of the first large-scale official segregations of its kind in colonial South Africa. Many of the key events on the late-nineteenth-century Diamond Fields occurred within the sphere of the biopolitical, operating through the workings of the body, intimacy, and domesticity. The colonial architects attempted to distribute the self-evident good of certain practices of intimate love for some and to suspend these same practices for others. The inherent ambivalence of the hegemonic discourse of colonial intimacy (Bhabha 1990), however, can be revealed through a closer discussion of the archaeological evidence indicating how this discourse was invoked and deployed by diamond rushers along multiple contradictory registers.

Tracing the material culture of the Diamond Fields, from the late 1860s to corporate monopolization in the 1880s, offers a critical vantage on how centrally the trope of love and matrimony figured into the political forces at work in this colonial outpost. Specifically, the materiality of intimate enactments reveals key contradictions between intimacy as an actually occurring event, on one hand, and as it was prescribed at this same historical moment, on the other. Such subtle contradictions are arguably at the core of a more central and pervasive dilemma of colonial rule: the indecipherable character of the intimate, the domestic or familial context within the colonial political structure. As Ann Stoler argues, "affections and attachments – familial and otherwise – were often impervious to the meddling priorities of a supposedly 'rational' and reasoned state. Efforts to redirect those sentiments – or cancel them out – revealed 'epistemological worries'" (Stoler 2008: 3).

AT HOME IN THE PUBLIC

In the early days of the late-nineteenth-century diamond rush, sexuality and intimate enactments, by architectural and environmental necessity, unfolded largely outside of the domestic proprieties of the conventional Victorian domicile. Reproduction,

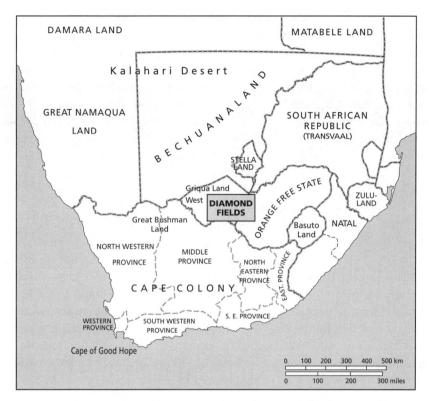

FIGURE 4.1. Locality of the Diamond Fields, adapted from "Sketch Map of South Africa showing British Possessions." *Scottish Geographical Magazine*, Volume I, 1885.

the rearing of children, and family life more generally had to be undertaken within transient, roadside social contexts and was thus exposed to what contemporaneous discourse described as a somewhat unsavory public audience. Direct evidence for this sort of establishment comes from a rural canteen and hotel that I excavated, a site called the Half-Way House Hotel, a venue notable in the written records only for having "better entertainment than any other hotel on the fields" (Macleod et al. 1872: 176).

Rural hotels, according to travelogues, were surrounded with rotting animal carcasses, filled with flies and fleas, and catered to gamblers, illegal traders, and frontier transients moving about the fields (see Figure 4.1). Child rearing and the forging of settler domesticity in this context would have prompted just such 'epistemological worries' referenced by Stoler, worries about how domesticity was transplanting into the colonies, particularly as it was doing so in a manner that was beginning to blur metropolitan divides between intimacy and the public sphere, colonizer and colonized, and ultimately the distinction between family business and illegal business. In light of this, it is important to understand the relationship between the archaeological remains of sites such as the hotel in contrast to the sort of housing that was subsequently implemented on the late Diamond Fields. The early hotel assemblage reflected the early public culture of the fields and reveals a surprising presence of children's toys and tea sets, as well as ceramic tableware with the sorts of transfer-printed patterns emulative of the Victorian home. All of this was in contrast to written records that suggest a predominance of utilitarian settings of enameled tin wares for rush-camp establishments (Lawrence 2000: 134). The assemblage at the hotel was redolent of the aspirational décor of a traditional Victorian home, producing the remnants of molded porcelain bric-a-brac (eloquently described by Paul Mullins as "daydreaming commodities"; Mullins 2001: 76), fragments of Parian ware indicating either the presence of potted plants or butter molds, Staffordshire wares with images of cherubs garlanding feminine classical cameos, and dainty gilt tea cups and saucers, all collectively indicating the canteen and hotel's enmeshment in the etiquettes and accoutrements of the advertised "English home."

Such claims to domesticity in the context of a ramshackle outpost tent for a transient public represented an emergent set of practices that ran against metropolitan standards of bourgeois privacy and propriety. As this form of imagining a transient public on the fields came to be associated with the inscrutable and increasingly problematic illegal diamond trade, these sites became even more charged locations.

However, the central provocation of spaces like the Half should be understood through the precise sorts of impositions that the spatial and material restrictions imposed on what was, for the late Victorian colonial era, a rigidly patrolled separation between public and private. Particularly relevant to consider in the context of a hotel is the heart of domestic intimacy, or the space delineated as the private bedroom. For countless travelers, spaces being claimed as private rooms were, in fact, little more than rectangular plots divided by relatively flimsy galvanized iron sheets, or, more frequently, strips of baize fabric draped over strings (Payton 1872: 127), partitioning materials that all too frequently failed to block out the noises and glimpses of neighboring members of the transient public. These fleeting bedrooms could be thought of as a microcosm of the constantly shifting tented landscape of the fields themselves, honeycombing the treacherous terrain of the central diggings, in which travelers described wandering among the hundreds of glowing tents at night and witnessing "novel sights and grotesque scenes . . . showing shadows on the wall" (Matthews 1887: 99). It is no small point of social practice to underscore that in such hotels, the act of sleeping had become public – particularly when weather conditions and the contingencies of travel frequently forced people to sleep on the floor or on tables under animal skins in an arrangement locally referred to as "shake-downs" (Payton 1872: 127). The same holds true for the very foundations of the hotel; the presence of tent pegs denoted insubstantial walls of canvas incapable of completely sealing off the interior from the notorious dust and flies coating the diggings.

Thus, although the archaeological evidence indicates that the motifs and types of artifacts recovered at the hotel far surpassed the most expedient material culture in favor of a home-style and genteel Victorian table service, at the same time, it is also important to emphasize that this was also an extremely unstable sort of domesticity, and, on the grander colonial landscape, this haphazard sort of enactment also marked a blurring of formal colonial strictures regarding public trade and less formal colonial strictures regarding domestic propriety on the part of settlers. This jumbled approach to décor was a fairly typical aspect of the transitory mind-set of members of "get rich quick" communities (Hardesty 2005: 82), yet the variety of patterns and colors as well as the absence of serving vessels suggest a somewhat unsystematic atmosphere for the Victorian meal service.[1]

The procurement of an atmosphere of domestic comfort at this hotel must have been continually compromised with a mixture of low and informal material culture that was inextricable from the general informality that pervaded the sociality of the camp. Faunal remains indicating locally procured game, unimproved sheep species, as well as animal pelts also indicate a hotel service that was improvisational and a cuisine dependent on local trade and hunting rather than the comforts of the "English Home" (Voigt 2007). The fast-paced and chaotic environment of this road-side establishment (needy travelers obtaining meals and service at all hours of day and night) is evident in the ceramic tableware assemblage, which consists of more than twenty transfer-print patterns for the early decade of the hotel interspersed with a variety of lowly "spongeware" patterns, and intermixed with gilt refined indus-trial wares (see Figures 4.2 and 4.3), collectively indicating a blended tablescape. Interestingly, one of the most well-represented designs on the transfer-print wares was the "Orange Blossom" decal, which was produced by the Scotia Pottery 1863–1865, opened by Edward Bodley after the death of his wife (Godden 1964: 82). In Victorian culture, orange blossoms were intimately associated with marriage as a result of the custom of tying orange blossoms into the bridal veil; this was popu-larized by Queen Victoria's marriage to King Albert in the mid-nineteenth century (Gernsheim 1981: 33). In one instance, the classical motifs on the transfer-printed plates adorn the female figure in laurel wreaths and consisted of cameos depicting neoclassical women in profile. As with so much of the material culture of the Vic-torian era, the tableware at the hotel seemed to center around the image of "[t]he 'perfect lady' [which] was commercially apotheosized through her identification with distant, historical ideals. Swathed in robes, barefoot, and crowned with laurel wreathes, [she] . . . presented an aggrandized portrait of feminine power" (Loeb 1994: 10).

The fragmentary nature of these gestures to the English home marks a captivating intersection with the unorthodox approach on the part of the hotel staff toward Victorian rituals of courtship and marriage. Scanty archival records document the proprietor's assistants (claiming to be on a "matrimonial bent") having regularly sent away for the Matrimonial News – a popular late-nineteenth-century mail-order bride catalog (Enss 2005). This hotel worker claimed to have "fallen in love with one of them; at least with one side of her face, and was writing to Germany to say that if the other side came up to sample she may come out and he will marry her" (Warren 1902: 318). This "stretching" of the formalities of domestic and matrimonial ritual, the commercial and almost transactional framing of the courtship ritual, at the time when courtship was coded as the most highly personal and intimate pursuit, that of matrimonial love, colludes with the hotel's irreverent claims to domestic propriety in the midst of so much materiality and physical circumstances undermining the suitability of these claims. The vigilantly patrolled boundaries associated with the Victorian tropes of privacy, domesticity, and marriage seem to have been obviated in the fantastic imagination of the proprietors, who went to the effort of purchasing romantic and pastoral transfer-printed tableware, serving dishes, and even porcelain

FIGURE 4.2. Top: classical transfer-print pattern from early Half-Way House Hotel. Bottom: detail from another transfer-print.

figurines, while at the same time proudly advertising the arrival of the most basic amenities such as doors and showers, years after the inception of the hotel.

Elite travelogues, with their sneering accounts of dishes served in sauces of "house-flies," did not miss the inadequacies of the hotel's home-style service, however

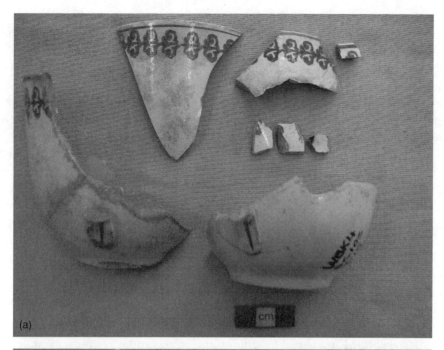

FIGURE 4.3. Top: spongeware cup from Half-Way House. Bottom: gilt "clover leaf" teacups.

(Boyle 1873:110). Importantly, the fine-tuned niceties of orthodox Victorian domesticity were thought achievable, by some, according to an unorthodox set of techniques, much in the same sense that the larger impetus toward wealth at the Diamond Fields emerged from a very unorthodox set of views about labor and love. Significantly, the qualities of the material assemblage of the early hotel indicated a broader spirit at work on the fields, in which there was a quality of the gamble, through which the *means* to domesticity, to intimate relationships, had become transitory and less meaningful than their ultimate attainment (and the promise of untold wealth and happiness that accompanied the fantasy of this attainment). Thus, privacy was privacy, whether through proper walls or through improvisational and flimsy materials. Marriage was marriage, whether through advertisements or conducted through proper familial relations and the complex rituals of engagement. This was all inextricable from the emergent collective belief among some rushers that wealth was wealth, whether through labor, informal market exchanges, or theft.

These speculative affects, gleaned from the material record and the reminiscences of these superfluous men who had come to forge such speculative spaces, suggests a radical reconsideration of how new ideas and practices of intimacy were tightly enmeshed within the tensions of legibility and domestic respectability that enshrouded and even promulgated illicit diamond trade. Within the penal landscapes of the compounds that were built a mere decade after the inception of the fields (a landscape reestablishing boundaries between domestic privacy and communal life), there persisted a certain subversion of the orthodoxies of intimacy via the very material and architectural instruments of the biopolitical-colonial project. Ultimately, the mesh of institutional controls and carceral spaces also came to be construed according to a very different imaginary, according to which an emergent set of practices and aspirations, again, worked to stretch the normative concepts of intimacy and love.

All of these early spaces gave way – as a result of the amalgamation of the mines and the incorporation of worker housing – to a complete spatial and material bifurcation of sexual practices. A new dual injunction emerged that presaged the apartheid landscape: to produce marital intimacy (if you were a European mine worker) and to retain a permanent sort of nonreproductive bachelorhood (if you were an African mine worker). This is not an intrinsically startling dynamic of colonial encounters or the greater imperial agenda of cheap labor, except that when we examine the materialities enshrouding these sexual practices, we see that desire, intimacy, love, and masculinity took on their own circulation and, in the process, rescripted what might otherwise have marked a very recognizable colonial narrative.

MINE MARRIAGES: COMPOUNDING DESIRE

> We will no more be able to "find" the intimate within the close confines of a dwelling-place than we can investigate a world-system solely through a map of the wall.
>
> (Voss, Chapter 11, this volume)

In the mid-1880s, as the mines increasingly came under the ownership of consolidated companies, worker villages and closed compounds were implemented in response to the transient culture of the labor supply and the perception of mass diamond theft. These mining housing schemes marked "the translation of power into built form" (Home 2000: 322), yet the historical documentation of South Africa's economic and social transformations have often marginalized the central role of built space (Demissie 1998: 446) and especially the relationship that these sorts of disciplinarian spaces held to preceding landscapes. The reallocations of intimacy and sexuality as emergent from within these built spaces has been similarly neglected, often dismissed as "a temporary aberration," rather than marking what was an intensely "subversive and destabilizing" aspect of the lives of those men who were forced to fulfill the terms of their labor contract under prisonlike conditions (Spurlin 2001: 190). Here I hope to supplement existing discussions of these intimate exchanges and practices of laborers through the prism of the built form and material flows, forms and flows that were often reappropriated and subverted from the original context of their biopolitical deployment, eventuating radical new worlds within ostensibly "total" institutions.

European housing for contracted mine overseers came to consist of a model suburban estate called Kenilworth, a stately tree-lined suburb in close proximity to the mines and affording workers (de facto overseers) subsidized rents and "a range of social and welfare facilities" (Harries 1993: 73), in the process, lending a sense of domestic privacy and conferring the full architectural theater of bourgeois niceties and practices, as imagined by its creator, Cecil Rhodes of the De Beers company (Bozzoli 1981: 79). The workers' village was built at a remove from the urban agglomeration of the diggings to implement "general isolation." Bungalow-style cottages with verandas adorned by wrought-iron Broekie lace ("panty lace") were separated from the public streets by private gardens. The spaces of public congregation were being rescripted according to metropolitan grids of gentility, and clubhouses and recreational facilities were drawn up around the imagery of procreative, leafy suburban life (Jackson 2005; Rall 2002: 28–29). Such elements introduced to the laborers' lives a spatial and material bedding for an emergent "rhetoric of privacy" (Povinelli 2006: 198).

These bungalow-style cottages, gardens, clubhouses, recreational facilities, churches, schoolhouses, and libraries had very few unscripted public spaces – absolutely no stores, bars, or public meeting spaces aside from the centrally run club (Williams 1905: 475). This regridding of the workers' off-hours attempted to institute a new set of emotional bonds that to some extent displaced the incipient workers' alliances, demonstrated by the worker strikes that occurred just before the imposition of worker housing. Substituted in the place of these organized social networks was the more intimate nexus of the family life and the practices of bourgeois culture, wherein allegiances and social networking came largely to circulate around family life and reproduction.

At a dramatic contrast were the worker compounds termed "bachelor barracks" (Rex 1974), the housing complex that Rhodes modeled after Brazilian slave barracks and implemented exclusively for the African workers in 1886 (Turrell 1982: 57; Figure 4.4).

These compounds, of course, were antithetical to the social imaginary behind Kenilworth. Workers were forced to stay on the premises for the duration of their contract (up to six months), and during this time, they were prohibited conjugal visits. Labor compounds in South Africa have been widely documented to have been the sites of same-sex relationships. Most interviews and archival records cover the relationships as they formed in worker compounds on the gold mines, and this chapter assumes the extremely likely precedence of such same-sex relationships on the closed compounds of De Beers (implemented just over a decade earlier; Moodie and Ndatshe 1994: 76). Information about these same-sex relationships comes through interviews recorded by oral historians and were described as being conducted according to an informal set of compound rules and practices (*mteto*) that ultimately gave these relationships the form and rituals associated with marriages at this time (Harries 1990: 323, Moodie et al. 1988).[2] These relationships were described as involving a scenario in which an experienced miner would adopt a newly arrived miner (younger) as his wife.

Mine marriages became highly ritualized in the early to mid-twentieth century, although they were generally monogamous (often described as a way to avoid the unsafe and expensive option of female sex workers), involved "thigh sex" in which the younger wife could not reciprocate, and these unions typically lasted until the wife either chose to return home or felt himself ready to acquire his own wife (Moodie 1988).[3] Broadly, they were part of a reconfiguration of the disciplining built space and regimes of the compound, in which drab repetitiveness and the absence of private spaces "declared . . . that the work relationship overrode any other social ties" (Home 2000: 327). Provocatively, it was the very environment that was to reconfigure intimate social and sexual life in an entirely nonreproductive context that rendered this enactment of connubial-style sexual relations a profoundly destabilizing set of practices. The system of taking on young men as wives (*nkhontxana*) afforded an array of domestic services (the younger wife being expected to cook and wash clothing) and intimate pleasures, producing a "monogamous and affectionate" marriage (Forman 2002: 13). The husband provided, in return, an introduction to the overwhelming system of the compound, something invariably undertaken through the mode of the gift. As Harries relates, "[o]ne of the husband's first acts was to take the young novitiate to the concession store on mine property and buy for him clothes, soap and other everyday necessities" (Harries 1990: 328). Because wives provided physical care and emotional support associated with marriage, they came to be considered deserving recipients of such gifts as dresses, trousers, colorful blankets (Niehaus 2002: 84) and even bicycles. As one miner expressed in an interview, "you spend all your money buying clothes and giving money to your wife [who lives far from the mines]. That's somehow a loss of money . . . she does not even wash your vest" (Moodie et al. 1988: 234).

The solace provided in these ritualized and coded intimacies were repeatedly described as being about more than sexual pleasure; they offered an assuaging of psychological brittleness that emerged in the wake of these extended periods of totally rote and dehumanizing schedules and spaces (Moodie et al. 1988: 232). These men were not only proposing sexual intimacy; they were proposing *love*, even as it was melancholically described as being a sort of love "only for the mines" (ibid.). As one Mpondo informant related,

> I felt very lonely for all the long period without meeting a woman. . . . I need[ed] someone to be with me. . . . I proposed love to him in the compound – called on him in our spare time. . . . I loved that boy very much. (ibid.)

Materiality was pivotal to these relationships; miners would pay *lobola*[4] for their wives, sacrificing a goat in the process to solidify the marriage practices (Junod

FIGURE 4.4. Photograph of De Beers Compound 1919. (Homer L. Shantz, Smithsonian African Expedition).

1962; Niehaus 2002). Miners often had female wives at home, further marking these mine relationships as a bodily and ritual circumscription of the pathologizing thrust of colonial legislation (which had banned both the traditional African marital practice of polygyny and *lobola* in the late nineteenth century) (Mamdani 1996: 91–92). One Witbank coal miner's love for his mine wife was so intense that upon learning of an infidelity, he took his own life (Niehaus 2002: 85). Notably, this tragic act was profoundly circumscribed by the material accoutrements of his beloved, "the distraught husband took his wife's clothes, shredded them and put the remnants in a bag. He then hung the bag from the rafters and placed the noose around his own neck" (ibid.).

Even as the heteronormative style of these relationships gestured toward a certain marital orthodoxy, it was, unquestionably, also subverting this institution in its legislatively prescribed form according to the twentieth-century colonial government. As Niehaus describes: "same sex intimacy . . . was a deliberate strategy by senior migrants to realize masculine personhood, intimacy, romance and the comforts of home" (Niehaus 2002: 94), but these enactments were also stretching the terms for what it meant to be married more broadly. The architecture of the compounds would seem to exclude the possibility of just such tender marital ties, literally designed in the fashion of the bachelor boarding house and canteen. The spartan restrictions imposed on items provided on compound kiosks gave mine managers the conceit of arbitrating the so-called material necessities of the miners' lives for the duration of their contracts. Yet mine purchases marked a radical material challenge to the sets of practices and behaviors that were ostensibly being dispensed according to the Victorian mores of labor managers.

To illustrate, the seemingly trivial or ephemeral commodity of soap has long been theorized as being at the forefront of a set of items broadly proposed as performing a sort of "commodity racism" on the part of Victorian culture in Africa (Burke 1996; McClintock 1995: 33). According to this line of argument, soap marked the pinnacle of the imposition of Victorian standards of hygiene and propriety on the African body – indeed, the act of smearing ochre and fat on the body had long been a source of repulsion expressed within European travelogues (Boonzaier 2000: 59). In the compounds, however, and especially in the context of sex, soap participated in quite a different set of daily rituals. Rather than solely marking the promise of salvation or colonial regimes of domestic hygiene, it became a part of the intimate assemblage provided by husbands to their mine wives, and it came to be an integral part of the ritual of washing off the genitals and thighs before and after intracrural sex (Forman 2002: 11). As such, even as soap ostensibly denoted care for the body as proscribed by the institutional planners, it was also integral to washing away the harshness of solitary labor as well as the colonial suspension of family life and personal pleasures. These gifts provided by husbands to wives were as much about "payment" and status within the oppressive "total institution" of the compound as they were about establishing a zone of sexual and personal intimacy. Thus, illicit markets for such purchases as makeup, lotions, razors, expensive dresses, nail polish, and even rings flourished, because such items were lavished on married men in the construction of what Niehaus terms romance and the "comforts of home" (Niehaus 2002: 86). In what sense were these items – this soap, or these blankets, in fact, imposing any sort of hegemonic behavioral repertoire? As one Tsonga informant related, young men on the mines might regard potential husbands as vehicles for various commodities and "wish they were so-and-so's wife, for the sake of security, for the acquisition of property . . . and for the fun itself" (Moodie 1988: 235). In the proper marriage, it was possible to actualize a set of desires that far exceeded the ostensible state of laborer, for, "the *inkotshane* [wife, or *nkhontxana*] is well fed and paid, presents and luxuries are lavished upon him [sic]" (ibid.). The commodities and wages of the compound system were transfigured into what Eleanor Casella aptly terms "valuable tokens of enticed desire and illicit sexual expression" (Casella 2000: 220).

These materialities, and the space of the compound more generally, marked their own sort of dense transfer-point of power, where the very moment of incarceration became a moment of other freedoms, as came to be enacted through these small exchanges and items (Casella, Chapter 3, this volume). So, even as Zackie Achmat (1993) argues, "the compound regime partially freed the male body through its enslavement, creating a network of new pleasures and desires: sex" (p. 106), these emancipatory carnalities also came to inscribe themselves into a variety of commodity forms and spatial demarcations that similarly enfleshed and encoded the intimacy of these relations. Even without the ability to obtain the desired accoutrements of femininity, wives would engage in a material bricolage to enhance their new gender, "they would get pieces of clothing material and they would sew it together so that it appeared like real breasts. They would then attach it to other strings that make it look almost like a bra so that at the evening dancing 'she' would dance with the 'husband'" (Moodie 1988: 235).

Critically, when these people left the mines and returned to their various heterosexual marriages (Epprecht 1998: 49), without any sense of irreparable "break"
within their sexual identities, new genealogies of intimacy inexorably trailed in their
wake, which came to undermine European concepts of the traditional domestic
subjectivity (Achmat 1993: 106). Mining companies, alert to the potential scandal
of "unnatural vice" in their compounds, attempted to minimize the significance of
these marriages, either claiming they were largely an import of the "Mozambiquan
workers" of VaThonga or Shangaan origin, or, alternately, distracting the public with
campaigns against female sex workers (Epprecht 1998: 50). Importantly, however,
"this was long after it was privately well known in official and missionary circles that
many other ethnic groups were implicated and indeed that a common vocabulary
concerning male–male sex had developed over a whole vast region as far away as
Malawi" (ibid.).

This circumscription of African homosexuality persisted and was actively constructed in the language of the apartheid regime; even among anthropologists,
"silence and timidity extended across the middle decades of the twentieth century"
(ibid.). It was not until the late 1990s that queer anthropology destabilized what
had amounted to a largely functionalist or heterosexist interpretation of male–male
desire in institutional settings (Achmat 1993), exploring the "complexities and conflict within same sex subcultures" (Epprecht 1998: 63). This discursive ambivalence,
the delay in adequately accounting for the political and social tensions inherent in
the mode of inquiry by which information could even be obtained on these practices, coincides with a broader lag in construing intimate enactments as profound
sites of refiguring the terms of political constraint and political freedom (Povinelli
2006).

To begin to think about flesh and matter, objects and fabrics, with an eye to
carnality and intimacy, allows us to construe intimate encounters, in modern and
colonial South Africa, as more than merely the sum total or response to their
discursive representation, architectural confinement, or relational positioning to
some imagined heteronormative paradigm. It allows us to understand the dynamic
interplay of materiality, commodity, flesh, and intimacy as these "things" and "bodies"
collectively epitomized and refigured prevailing conceptualizations of freedom, constraint, and desire. It would seem, as Appadurai suggested in *The Social Life of Things*,
that commodity fetishism is something always meta-fetishized as well (Appadurai
1986: 50).

Even as commodities and indeed spaces were enacted against the transgressive
practices of the early Diamond Fields, they were consistently vulnerable to the artful
play of intimate enactments, always capricious sources of profit and expenditure.
The informal blending of the domestic home, the stretching of the traditional
rituals of marriage, and the familial atmosphere that had camouflaged a tented
landscape of illicit trade and unpredictable encounters on the early Diamond Fields
continued to subvert the translation of power into built form, even in the wake of
corporate consolidation. Corporate attempts to distribute racially the differential
spaces for "home" or "marriage" on the fields illustrate the impossibility of such an
imagined project, as well as the impossibility of outmaneuvering the complex and
ever-shifting tournaments of value within which people were blending these spatial

restrictions and material limitations into everyday economic and intimate transactions. As Appadurai reminds us, from the Kula ring to the futures exchange, the circulation of commodities are always and already about a certain "agonistic, romantic, individualistic and gamelike ethos" (ibid.: 50) where relationships, reputations, and even love, can hang in the balance.

The failure to circumscribe space or the "work" of the commodities that were sold to African miners, the inability to extricate the imaginary of luxuries and romance from what were repeatedly (and ineffectually) confined to "basic necessities," is a failure that reveals the ceaseless drive of the speculative culture inspired by the Diamond Fields, one that arguably exceeded the alienation of laborers. This was a speculative drive that was simultaneously economic and sexual, and ultimately one that transformed the lives of those superfluous men who rushed to the fields. Just as Gawa shells allowed a person's fame to travel far beyond what would have been possible physically, the seemingly mundane act of a miner purchasing soap within the drab and repetitive concrete landscape of the compound, was, in fact, an act enabling an extension of intimate personhood (Munn 1986). The perils of overdetermined objects and spaces is in evidence here (see also Dawdy, Chapter 16, this volume). Even while ostensibly participating in the unfurling biopolitical project of the colonial imperialists and the alienation of labor conditions, such purchases, and their regifting within the context of a marriage, came to be about summoning an imaginary of domestic love and a sort of intimate autonomy.

The impossibility of squaring historical things and spaces from either the colonizer's or colonized's perspective mirrors the tension elucidated in the work of Said and Bhabha, a tension between a synchronic colonial vision and the necessarily more complicated deployment of this vision in real histories. Within the literature of commodity exchange, colonial Africa has frequently been theorized as a liminal space with regard to these sorts of manifestations, in which commodity values would supposedly undergo an ever-advancing set of exposures in which "exchange" performed the work of empire-building (Comaroff and Comaroff 2006; McClintock 1995). In light of this framing, it always emerges as something of a surprise that, in fact, this was not a unidirectional process and, "insofar as the commodity conveniently gave imperialists the Midas touch, it did so by turning whatever they touched into an object of exchange . . . but . . . the commodity was, in the end, nobody's lackey" (Richards 1990: 151–152). It is important to understand how fundamentally material objects (and their circulation) marked out the shadowy edges of a frontier, through which exchange, economy, intimacy, and the ensuing imaginary of personal freedom constantly exceeded colonial or metropolitan prescriptions.

The compound, and the constant circumvention of its directive for extended bachelorhood for Africans, marked an exceptionally heightened arena for the deployment of such tensions. For instance, another ubiquitous commodity, blankets, came to transform the bachelor-style public rooms – for when they were hung around one's bed (referred to on the Witbank mines as *madia dia*; Niehaus 2002: 84), they came to enable the zone where husbands and wives could go about creating a private emotionally restorative world.

What had been restricted from the miners for the duration of their labor contract was the possibility of biological reproduction. They had been housed in an

environment that materially summoned and ordered their lives as bachelor laborers, not fathers, not husbands, and yet, in a radical move, intimacy, and even love,
indeed all of the affective pleasures normatively linked with a marriage, were invoked
by these same miners and flourished in a stretching of traditional marital practices.
Through a complex constellation of seemingly banal material items – blankets,
bangles, soap, dresses – grew a collective enactment, a refiguration, of the obvious
material failings of their living conditions. This was something continually and powerfully enacted – both before and after the segregated landscape of the Diamond
Fields ostensibly came to racially separate domestic practices.

CONCLUSION

The speculative culture of the diamond rush prompted a heady and complex transformation of the material settings for marriage and domesticity. Those who lived at
the diamond diggings came to imagine the possibilities for, and to enact an array of,
new intimacies that were interwoven with the material and emotional demands of the
public life of the camp. The archaeological perspective on such heterotopic spaces
indicates that the speculative culture at rush sites came to substitute the suitability of
intimate relationships, sex, and marital arrangements with an expediency and informality that impelled the radical reinscribing of domestic practice in the following
decade of company-worker housing. Closed compounds, however, became the sites
of radical new intimacies that co-opted and transformed what might otherwise have
been construed as the very tokens of disciplinarity into the new orthodoxies of labor
courtship, mine marriage, and long-distance marriages. The material culture of the
Diamond Fields was inextricable from these dense "transfer-points" of power (Foucault 1978:103; Stoler 2008: 63), complexly subverting even as they upheld the
instruments of colonial disciplinarity.

This process occurred on either side of the racial divide. Within the early roadside
canteens and hotels, as they hastily co-opted and stretched the traditional signatures
and bric-a-brac of connubial domesticity, as well as within the context of mine
marriages on the worker compounds, the constraining and liberating aspects of
traditional marriage were navigated through the mesh of material facades, tokens
of love, and emblems of matrimony and desire. The laboratory of the Diamond Fields
propelled new modes of intimacy and carnal freedoms that were carried across the
South African landscape and continued to disrupt (and assimilate) traditional forms
of intimacy, marriage, and love in twentieth-century South Africa, where same-sex
relationships continued simultaneously to occupy the doubled space of the highest
constitutional–legal force as well as profound social misrecognition and disavowal.

As Povinelli (2006) suggested, the taking up of liberal logics as the self-evident
good of love in settler colonies was something that was often, at one point, part
of the distribution of life and death and, at other points, the radical subversion
of these same biopolitical logics. The matter of these various circulations of love
and marriage was that all their various "mattering forths" perpetually stretched
the normative assumptions surrounding the liberal institutions of courtship and
procreative marriage. Intimacy, as such, was not merely enacted in the flesh, being
patrolled by the disciplinary space; it continually reforged and redistributed these

very carceral spaces and even their equipments – producing ephemeral assemblages of intimacy.

Marriage, as such, was never simplistically about the colonially stipulated binaries of "either" heterosexual or homosexual, courtship or mail order, polygyny or monogomy, procreation or production; marriage was a constantly mutating intimate engagement. Gathering in its wake new cartographies of desire, exchanges, and goods, marriage had become a line of flight from the inhuman demands of the market and colonist; it marked a space in which couples could perform intimate contestations of their political circumscriptions and navigate the increasingly divided colonial landscape with desires for and fantasies of intimacy and freedom.

NOTES

1. The absence of tureens indicates a familiar and less structured meal service likely served straight from the kitchen. By contrast, the representations of tureens at the hotel dramatically increases in the wake of segregated worker housing, indicating a substantive transformation of the formerly intimate ambience of the hotel.

2. These oral histories were supplemented by the 1907 Taberer Report and the writings of Junod, both describing same-sex marriages as they related to gender-segregated mining conditions (Murray and Roscoe 1998: 178). Before the implementation of colonial criminal labor systems, same-sex relationships were not criminally punished, as Moshesh's testimony in 1883 revealed (West and Green 1997: 13).

3. Interviews describing these marriages as limited to "thigh sex" has been critiqued as perpetuating a profoundly heteronormative bias on the historical reading of same-sex relationships, and descriptions were doubtlessly laden with substitutions, euphemisms, and other concessions to the perceived prudery of their interlocutors. The illegality of sodomy under apartheid systematically may have prevented the discussion of certain forms of sexual relationships on the mines, as well as those same-sex relationships that endured in townships and locations (Spurlin 2001: 191–195).

4. Lobola is a traditional southern African payment for a bride, typically paid in cattle.

REFERENCES

Achmat, Z. 1993. "Apostles of Civilized Vice: Immoral Practices and Unnatural Vice in South African Prisons and Compounds, 1890–1920." *Social Dynamics* 19:92–110.

Appadurai, A. 1986. *The Social Life of Things: Commodities in Cultural Perspective.* Cambridge: Cambridge University Press.

Bhabha, H. 1990. "The Third Space," in Rutherford, J. (ed.), *Identity, Community, Culture, Difference.* London: Lawrence & Wishart, pp. 207–221.

Boonzaier, E. 2000. *The Cape Herders: A History of the Khoikhoi of Southern Africa.* Cape Town: D. Philip; Athens: Ohio University Press.

Boyle, F. 1873. *To the Cape for Diamonds.* London: Simon and Hall.

Bozzoli, B. 1981. *The Political Nature of a Ruling Class: Capital and Ideology in South Africa, 1890–1933.* London: Routledge.

Burke, T. 1996. *Lifebuoy Men, Lux Women: Commodification, Consumption, and Cleanliness in Modern Zimbabwe.* Durham, NC: Duke University Press.

Casella, E. 2000. "'Doing trade': A Sexual Economy of Nineteenth-Century Australian Female Convict Prisons." *World Archaeology* 32:209–221.

Comaroff, J., and J. Comaroff. 2006. "Beasts, Banknotes and the Colour of Money in Colonial South Africa." *Archaeological Dialogues* 12:107–132.

Demissie, F. 1998. "In the Shadow of the Gold Mines: Migrancy and Mine Housing in South Africa. *Housing Studies* 13:445–469.

Enss, C. 2005. *Hearts West: True Stories of Mail-Order Brides on the Frontier.* Guilford, CT: TwoDot.

Epprecht, M. 2008. *Heterosexual Africa? The History of an Idea from the Age of Exploration to the Age of AIDS.* New African Histories Series. Athens: Ohio University Press.

Forman, R. G. 2002. "Randy on the Rand: Portuguese African Labour and the Discourse on 'Unnatural Vice' in the Transvaal in the Early Twentieth Century." *Journal of the History of Sexuality* 11:570–609.

Foucault, M. 1978. *The History of Sexuality.* New York: Pantheon Books.

Gernsheim, Alison 1981. *Victorian & Edwardian Fashion: A Photographic Survey.* London: Constable.

Gilchrist, R. 1994. *Gender and Material Culture: The Archaeology of Religious Women.* New York: Routledge.

Godden, Geoffrey A. 1964. *Encyclopaedia of British Pottery and Porcelain Marks.* London: Herbert Jenkins.

Hardesty, D. 2005. "Mining Rushes and Landscape Learning in the Modern World," in Rockman, M., and J. Steele (eds.), *Colonization of Unfamiliar Landscapes.* New York: Routledge, pp. 81–96.

Hardesty, D. L. 1998. "Power and the Industrial Mining Community in the American West," in Knapp, A. B., V. C. Piggot, and E. W. Herbert (eds.), *Social Approaches to an Industrial Past.* London: Routledge, pp. 81–96.

Harries, P. 1990. "Symbols and Sexuality: Culture and Identity on the Early Witwatersrand Gold Mines." *Gender & History* 2:318–336.

———. 1993. *Work, Culture, and Identity: Migrant Laborers in Mozambique and South Africa, c. 1860–1910.* Portsmouth, NH: Heinemann.

Home, R. K. 2000. "From Barrack Compounds to the Single-Family House: Planning Worker Housing in Colonial Natal and Northern Rhodesia." *Planning Perspectives* 15:327–347.

Jackson, S. 2005. "Cape Colonial Architecture, Town Planning, and the Crafting of Modern Space in South Africa." *Africa Today* 51:33–54.

Junod, H. A. 1962. *The Life of a South African Tribe.* New York

Lawrence, S. 2000. *Dolly's Creek.* Carlton South, Australia: Melbourne University Press.

Loeb, Lori Anne. 1994. *Consuming Angels: Advertising and Victorian Women.* Oxford: Oxford University Press.

Macleod, N., N. Macleod, J. M. F. Ludlow, and A. Lang. 1872. *Good Words.* London: J. Strahan and Co.

Mamdani, M. 1996. *Citizen and Subject: Contemporary Africa and the Legacy of Late Colonialism.* Princeton, NJ: Princeton University Press.

Matthews, J. W. 1887. *Ingwadi Yami.* Johannesburg: Africana Book Society.

McClintock, A. 1995. *Imperial Leather: Race, Gender, and Sexuality in the Colonial Conquest.* New York: Routledge.

Meskell, L. 1999. *Archaeologies of Social Life: Age, Sex, Class etcetera in Ancient Egypt. Social Archaeology.* Malden, MA: Blackwell.

Moodie, T. D., V. Ndashe, and B. Sibuyi. 1988. "Migrancy and Male Sexuality on the South African Gold Mines." *Journal of Southern African Studies* 14:228–256.

Moodie, T. D., and V. Ndatshe. 1994. *Going for Gold: Men, Mines, and Migration.* Berkeley: University of California Press.

Mullins, P. 2001. "Racializing the Parlor: Race and Victorian Bric-Brac Consumption," in Orser, C. (ed.), *Race and Archaeology of Identity.* Philadelphia: University of Pennsylvania Press, pp. 158–76.

Munn, N. D. 1986. *The Fame of Gawa.* Cambridge: Cambridge University Press.

Niehaus, I. 2002. "Renegotiating Masculinity in the South African Lowveld: Narratives of Male–Male Sex in Labour Compounds and in Prisons." *African Studies* 61:77–98.

Payton, C. A., Sir. 1872. *The Diamond Diggings of South Africa: A Personal and Practical Account.* London: Horace Cox.

Povinelli, E. 2007. "Can Sex Be a Minor Form of Spitting?" Available at http://www.ssrc.org/blogs/immanent_frame/2007/12/13/can-sex-be-a-minor-form-of-spitting.

Povinelli, E. A. 2006. *The Empire of Love: Toward a Theory of Intimacy, Genealogy, and Carnality.* Public Planet Books series. Durham, NC; London: Duke University Press.

Rall, M. 2002. *Petticoat Pioneers: The History of the Pioneer Women Who Lived on the Diamond Fields in the Early Years.* Kimberley, South Africa: Kimberley Africana Library.

Rex, J. 1974. "The Compound, the Reserve and the Urban Location." *South African Labour Bulletin* 1:4–17.

Richards, T. 1990. *The Commodity Culture of Victorian England: Advertising and Spectacle, 1851–1914.* Stanford, CA: Stanford University Press.

Spurlin, W. 2001. "Broadening Postcolonial Studies/Decolonizing Queer Studies," in Hawley, J. (ed.), *Post-Colonial Queer: Theoretical Intersections.* Albany, New York: SUNY Press, pp. 185–205.

Stoler, A. L. 2008. *Along the Archival Grain: Thinking through Colonial Ontologies.* Princeton, NJ: Princeton University Press.

Taylor, C. 2007. *A Secular Age.* Cambridge, MA; London: Belknap.

Tsing, A. L. 2005. *Friction: An Ethnography of Global Connection.* Princeton, NJ: Princeton University Press.

Turrell, R. V. 1982. "Kimberley: Labour and Compounds, 1871–1888," in Marks, S., and R. Rathbone (eds.), *Industrialisation and Social Change in South Africa.* London: Longman Group, pp. 45–76.

Voigt, Elizabeth 2007. *Country Fare at Wildebeestkuil, Northern Cape.* Unpublished faunal report. Kimberley, South Africa: McGregor Museum.

Voss, B. L. 2000. "Colonial Sex: Archaeology, Structured Space, and Sexuality in Alta California's Spanish-Colonial Missions," in Schmidt, R. A., and B. L. Voss (eds.), *Archaeologies of Sexuality.* London: Routledge, pp. 35–61.

Warren, C., Sir. 1902. *On the Veldt in the Seventies.* London: Isbister & Co.

Williams, G. F. 1905. *The Diamond Mines of South Africa* [new edition]. New York: B.F. Buck.

FIVE

"A CONCUBINE IS STILL A SLAVE"

Sexual Relations and Omani Colonial Identities in Nineteenth-Century East Africa

Sarah K. Croucher

INTRODUCTION

Concubinage, in which women were enslaved for the purpose of sexual relations with their male owners outside the institution of marriage, was an integral part of nineteenth-century Islamic colonial Zanzibari society.[1] Initially, I aimed to identify concubinage within the archaeology of a nineteenth-century Zanzibari clove plantation, but archaeological materials did not simply proclaim their connections to sexuality. It is no easy task for an archaeologist to identify material traces of the many women who were enslaved to be forced into sexual relations and/or for reproduction. The interpretations presented here thus draw both on archaeological evidence and on my conversations about former plantation residents with contemporary Zanzibaris, in the process of which I was confronted with the historical reality of concubinage. I have also had to grapple with the politics and ethics of writing a scholarly paper that examines the subjectivities of enslaved women who were forced into sexual relations with their owners, an oppressive relationship that paradoxically may have offered a route to their greatest potential material well-being and eventual freedom.

Both of these topics have yet to be discussed by archaeologists working along the East African "Swahili" coast, where historical and archaeological analyses of houses are generally interpreted as structured by Islamic gender dichotomies (Donley-Reid 1990; Fleisher and LaViolette 2007; Horton and Middleton 2000; Sheriff 1995a, 1995b). The most recent scholarship, focused on urban Zanzibar, has blurred such strict dichotomies by examining the intersections of class and gender within East African house space (Myers 1997). Separate from these materially focused studies, historians of gender on the East African coast have shown that sexual relations between husbands and wives and masters and concubines were an important aspect through which women mediated ethnic and class relations (Fair 1996; McCurdy 2006). This chapter draws together these two strands of scholarship. Focusing on the material remains of nineteenth-century rural clove plantations on Zanzibar, I explore the way in which sexual relations were embedded in spatial practices of households.

My interpretations rest on the theoretical foundation that the routine use of space is a primary means through which social actors understand and perform their identities (Bourdieu 1977, 2000). The production of identity is widely recognized to be a performative act (Butler 1993), rooted in embodied forms through the body and through symbolic relations with material culture (Casella and Fowler 2005; Meskell and Joyce 2003). In African contexts, archaeologists have long recognized the importance of the relationship among spatial practices, the materiality of buildings, and the construction of identities across a range of structuralist and poststructuralist theoretical positions (Fewster 2006; Huffman 1984). Feminist ethnoarchaeological studies have shown the deep relationship between the everyday spatial practice and the understandings of gendered identities within domestic contexts, specifically regarding the degree of women's permanence and power within the household (Christie 2006; Lyons 1998; Moore 1986). In the Zanzibari colonial context, such dimensions of practice theory are complicated by the diversity of newly arrived colonial immigrants, who would not all have shared the same habituated understandings of plantation buildings. Architecture would have had polyvalent social meanings as new social relations and subjectivities were forged through the material structuring of new routines of quotidian life and new identities based on sexual relations.

OMANI COLONIALISM AND CLOVE PLANTATIONS

The roots of nineteenth-century Zanzibari society lie within Africa and wider Indian Ocean cultures. Before colonial rule, the islands of Zanzibar (Unguja and Pemba) were culturally part of the Swahili coast, a region stretching along the coastal strip of East Africa from present-day Somalia to Mozambique (Horton and Middleton 2000). The peoples of this region were joined together in cultural practices around Islamic urban centers, the earliest of which date to approximately the ninth century CE (Horton 1996) and which show clear ceramic continuities with earlier Iron Age sites of East Africa (Chami 1998). Although Swahili towns were African in origin, they were also strongly mercantile and had deep economic and cultural ties with the wider Indian Ocean world (LaViolette 2008).

During the fifteenth century CE, the coast came loosely under Portuguese colonial rule, although the cultural impact of this colonial period seems to have been isolated to particular trading forts. However, the presence of the Portuguese led the indigenous rulers of Mombasa to invite the Sultanate of Oman to aid them in ousting Portuguese rule in the late seventeenth century. As a result, Omanis became increasingly involved in the East African coast, largely in the growing caravan trade in ivory and enslaved persons running inland through present-day mainland Tanzania (Sheriff 1987). By the early nineteenth century, the Omani Sultanate was nominally in control of a booming mercantile capitalist trading system, fed through the growing urban center of Zanzibar Stone Town.

The wealth generated by this capitalist trade led to a new form of Omani colonial rule; greater numbers of Omani men emigrated to East Africa, made money in trading, and then invested in agricultural capitalism. A new cash crop, the clove tree, began to be planted on the islands by Arab elites in the nineteenth century. Clove plantations were run by Omani merchants with enslaved agricultural labor. Large household groups, which following traditional norms of African and Islamic slavery were regularly formed of a mixture of enslaved and free, remained crucial to the social status of Arab elites on the island (Cooper 1979, 1981). Alongside enslaved agricultural and menial laborers, many women from mainland Africa were enslaved as concubines in East African households. Islamic law allowed men to have up to four legal wives and unlimited numbers of concubines. Concubinage was widespread, and the wealthiest Omani colonial households may have included hundreds of concubines (Reute 1998 [1886]). Concubined women were in a particular form of enslavement based on their sexual relations but concomitantly had the potential for freedom and more material wealth than peers who were enslaved to work as laborers (Cooper 1977; Fair 2001; Glassman 1995; McCurdy 2006; Romero Curtin 1983).

Throughout this period of Omani colonialism, the majority of the Zanzibari population consisted of enslaved persons or recently manumitted slaves, along with Omani Arabs, Indian and other Arab immigrants from Yemen (these latter two groups largely lived in urban areas on the islands), and indigenous Swahili residents (Cooper 1977; Fair 2001; Middleton 1992). Central to the formation of new identities in this colonial situation were women's sexual practices sanctioned within relationships of marriage or concubinage. The children of concubined women were given ethnic status equal to that of other children of their father. The children of both types of relationships provided a new generation of free Zanzibaris, who drew together the varied cultural heritage of their parents. New forms of distinctly Zanzibari identities were formed from the merging of these ethnic identities and religious practices and from the tensions between modern mercantilist capitalism and traditional Islamic cultural practices.

PLANTATION ARCHAEOLOGY

The material data in this chapter is based on fieldwork investigating the remains of the clove plantations that dominated much of the rural landscape of Pemba and of northern Unguja by the end of the nineteenth century (see Figure 5.1). My fieldwork projects integrated recording oral histories of plantation life along with archaeological surface survey, as well as excavation at a single plantation site. Most sites were identified to our team through the accounts of local residents, which meant that at all stages of the process, the material data was intertwined with local social memories of plantations. Out of sixty-four sites recorded, only three were associated with enslaved laborers, possibly reflecting the ephemerality of enslaved housing and social distantiation by descendants of enslaved laborers. The presence of enslaved laborers on plantations was discussed widely by many Zanzibaris, but almost no one mentioned any direct heritage to persons identified as such. Forgetting specific locales of enslaved laborers' dwellings may therefore be part of a larger process of historical representation.

More than a third of sites were identified by local residents as having been the households of plantation owners. These were varied in their architectural form;

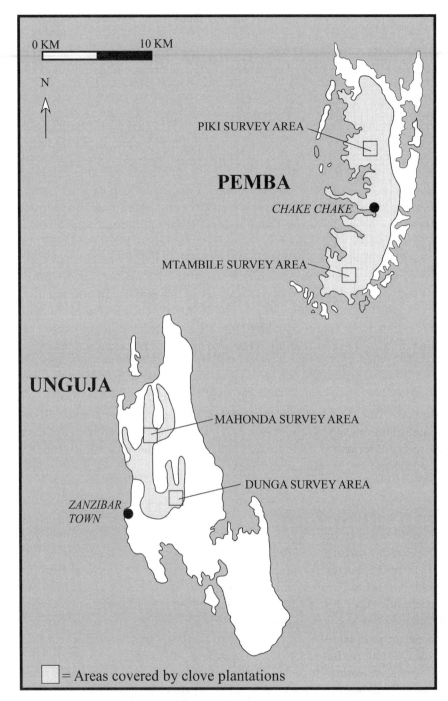

FIGURE 5.1. Map of the islands of Zanzibar showing areas covered by clove plantations and archaeological survey areas (after Sheriff 1987:52).

although many were built of stone, many were built of wattle and daub, leaving visible archaeological remains of mounds of earth and associated artifact scatters, but remaining highly visible in local social memories. Excavations were undertaken at one of these large stone plantation owners' homes – Mgoli, in the Piki survey

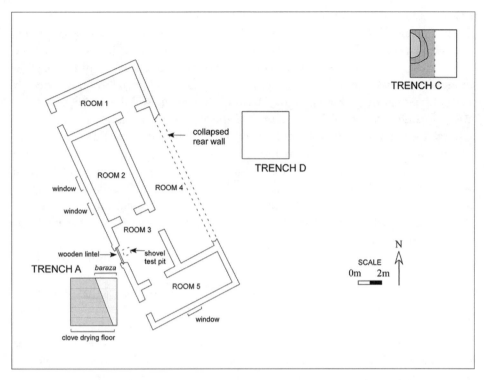

FIGURE 5.2. Plan of the site of Mgoli, showing the stone house and trench locations.

region. In this area, such homes had been built of stone, demonstrating through purely material terms the relative wealth of the plantation owner at Mgoli. Perhaps more significant in this regard are the vivid social memories of the planter. This man, Abdalla bin Jabir, was described as having migrated to Pemba in the mid-nineteenth century to establish Mgoli. His social worth was partly measured by the fact that he had brought with him many enslaved laborers, whom he immediately put to work to clear the land and plant clove trees. It was also mentioned that Abdalla bin Jabir had at least one wife and more than one woman in a relationship of concubinage. The social fact that women who had been held in such relationships of enslavement, defined through sexual relations, was a common feature of discussions of nineteenth-century plantation life. In formal interviews, interviewees were clear that all women taken as concubines originated from mainland Africa, although they disagreed on whether these women had lived in a manner more comparable to free wives or had performed the majority of household labor.[2] Outside of formal interviews, as we worked at the site of Mgoli and chatted to local visitors about the site, it was casually mentioned that women who were in relationships of concubinage were present at the site during the nineteenth century, just as enslaved laborers had been. Even if there was no specific memory of these women, and none were remembered by names or had self-identified descendants, they formed a solid part of the local memories of the social histories of plantations.

Dominating the site of Mgoli was a five-room, stone house (see Figure 5.2), which would have served as the main plantation home. It was a single story in height and broadly followed the stylistic conventions of the houses of Omani elites living in urban Zanzibar (Sheriff 1995b). The walls were finished with a plain white plaster on interior and exterior, with the only adornments being occasional large plaster niches inset into walls of interior rooms – probably for displaying items – and simple plaster arches above the windows and doorway to the front of the building. A carved wooden lintel was also in place above the front door, and probably an elaborately carved "Zanzibar door," signaling the status of the owner, would have been in place (Aldrick 1990). Abutting the front wall of the house was a *baraza*, a small bench built of stone that would have run most of the length of the building, functioning primarily as a public male space, in line with social norms governing the use of space in nineteenth-century Zanzibar. A clove-drying floor made of compacted rubble stretched away to the front, easily visible for those seated on the *baraza*. This space would have been one in which the plantation owner and his male peers could have observed the work of enslaved laborers in the public arena of the plantation at harvest time (Croucher 2007b).

In contrast to this public space would have been the more private area of the household to the rear (the eastern side of the stone house; see Figure 5.2). Histories of architectural space on Zanzibar and the East African coast suggest that a courtyard or open space would have been located here, acting as the locus for cooking activities and other daily practical tasks of the household (Myers 1997). Reconstructing this space precisely at Mgoli is difficult, because the rear wall had collapsed; it was impossible to tell whether there had been a rear doorway from the stone house. However, excavations in Trench D located the remnants of a trash pit, as evidenced by a clear cut into the clay soil and large amounts of domestic debris, including lenses of ash suggesting occasional burning of trash, a practice that would fit exactly with the way trash pits are used alongside contemporary house yards on Zanzibar. It is reasonable to use this to support the argument that domestic work, largely carried out by the wives, concubines, or enslaved laborers of Abdalla bin Jabir, would have taken place in this area.

From these observations, the archaeological evidence seems to mesh with the historical argument that the houses of nineteenth-century East Africa were divided into public/male realms of activity toward the front of the house, contrasting with private/female realms of activity located to the rear of the house. However, additional archaeological data allowed for the expansion of this picture, along with regular commentary from local visitors providing suggestions for further potential interpretations of the meaning of the evidence: further to the east of Trench D, where the kitchen and yard space of the main house were located, another structure was visible in Trench C (see Figure 5.2 for the location of trenches). This was a little more than 20 meters from the main house, still within the private yard of the main stone house. In Trench C were the remains of a wall constructed of a large proportion of lime mortar and rubble mixed with a smaller amount of mud, combined into a compact building material known locally as *chokaa* (see Figure 5.3 for a detailed plan of this trench). Although the trench only cut across the corner of the building, making it difficult to discern the precise dimensions and features of the building, the quality of the building materials strongly mitigate against this being a simple outbuilding, because these were normally constructed of far more flimsy materials (Myers 1997). Therefore, the building may have been a single or multiroomed dwelling but appears to have been where one or more members of the

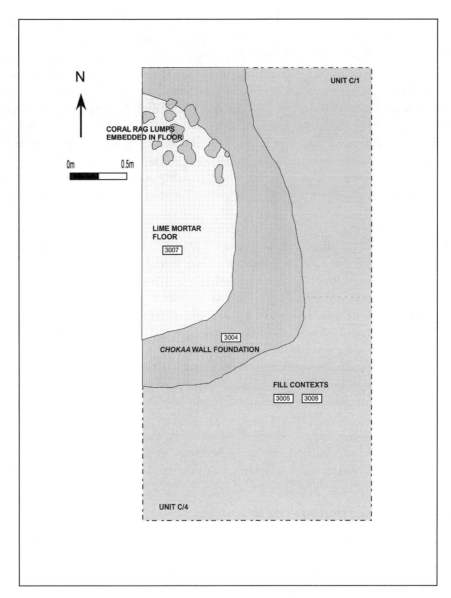

FIGURE 5.3. Archaeological plan of Trench C showing lime mortar (*chokaa*) house foundation.

plantation household – not enslaved field laborers – would have resided, moving within the private "female" domestic area of the house courtyard to provide access between the two structures. According to the conventions of Islamic architectural practice on the coast, guests were restricted from entering such private areas of the household (Donley-Reid 1990; Fleisher and LaViolette 2007; Sheriff 1995b).

ARTIFACTS, IDENTITIES, AND PRACTICES

Building on the architectural evidence, I now turn to the artifacts excavated from Trench C. The majority of these may have been deposited as a single fill event at the time of the building's construction. These consisted primarily of mid-nineteenth-century ceramics and other domestic debris. Intriguingly, however, the number of jewelry components found in this context (sixteen in total) was much higher than the number recovered from the trash pit in Trench D (only seven in total), despite the much higher concentration of debris in the trash pit.

Along with fifteen glass and shell beads, one of the finds in Trench C included a small copper alloy earring made of fine small loops of metal joined together with a hinge at the top (see Figure 5.4). These types of jewelry components were recalled by older women to have been worn by nonelite women as everyday adornment. Brass jewelry such as that found in Trench C was apparently popular with women unable to afford gold earrings and nose rings, with one woman claiming that "brass jewelry like rings and earrings" was commonly owned by "local Pembans" – that is, non-Arab and Indian immigrants.[3]

Little else distinguished material found in Trench D and Trench C, suggesting homogeneity in the use of locally produced and imported ceramics and the foodways of the two buildings. Oral histories recorded as a part of this project suggested residents of a building that was part of the same plantation household as the stone house would have all shared the same meals, probably from the same shared dishes.[4]

Combined archaeological and oral historical evidence therefore raises some interesting points about the identification and practices of those living within the Mgoli plantation household. The buildings suggest that Abdalla bin Jabir headed a large household, and oral histories argued that women who were concubines would certainly have been present. Beads and the brass earring within Trench C also seem to hint, in relation to old women's accounts of jewelry use, that a lady residing in this building may have been finely adorned but had worn the kinds of jewelry that were common for non-Arab Zanzibari women – precisely the kind of status that a woman enslaved as a concubine might have had.

ARCHITECTURAL HISTORIES OF ZANZIBAR

Another line of scholarship that aids the interpretation of the Trench C building is architectural histories of Zanzibar. Particularly informative is the work of the historical geographer Garth Myers (1997, 2003) on Ng'ambo, or the "other side," of Zanzibar Stone Town. Although this cannot be directly extrapolated to the plantation context, his examination of the relationship between urban houses and Zanzibari social structure provides a framework to begin to interpret the Trench C house.

Previous analyses of East African domestic coastal architecture focused on a gradient of privacy between public and private, in which "public" equated to male activities and "private" to female. This division is argued to match Islamic practices structuring the seclusion of women, with a clear separation of gendered public and private activities (Donley-Reid 1990; Ghaidan 1975; Sheriff 1995b). Structuring the meaning of Zanzibar housing, Myers (1997) argues, were complex social rules of *uwezo* (power) and *desturi* (custom). Residents of urban Zanzibar had the capacity in particular to build materials in accordance with their social power, and, in turn, houses were also an important signifier of social status. The most expensive and difficult to procure of building materials was stone, and stone-built houses can be

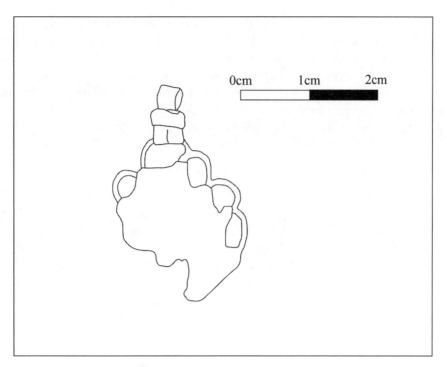

FIGURE 5.4. Copper alloy earring, Trench C, context 3005. Small conjoined metal hoops with hinge at top.

regarded to have expressed a high level of power in terms of the wealth required to purchase the stone and the labor required to build the house.

No simple dichotomy between the elite stone-built houses and those of Zanzibaris with lower status existed, however. As one ran down the social scale, the proportion of stone in walls lessened, foundations became less solid, walls became thinner, and numbers of rooms decreased. The lime mortar and rubble house foundation of the Trench C house at Mgoli would have required economic power for the purchase of materials and skilled labor, suggesting a high level of social power embodied by the structure and those who lived within it (Myers 1997: 254). From survey data, it can be surmised that the majority of plantation owners were living in the same types of structures as the majority of urban Zanzibaris: their houses may have contained a little coral rag stone and lime plaster, but the lack of indications of these materials at sites recorded as plantation owners' homes suggests that they were mostly constructed of wattle and daub. This fits with the few historical recordings of rural architecture on the islands in the early twentieth century (Craster 1913; Croucher 2007b; Lyne 2001 [1905]: 21).

Turning back to Trench C, I have already suggested that the location of this building within the domestic yard space of the main plantation house suggests it was the home of a person or persons who were integral to the plantation household as a social unit. The nineteenth century on Zanzibar was a period during which the social status and rights of enslaved laborers sharply decreased (Cooper 1977: 180; Glassman 1995). Given that "*permanence* of structure [in terms of the amount of stone and lime mortar used in construction] was the most visible symbol of social power"

(Myers 1997: 253, emphasis in original), it seems deeply unlikely that enslaved laborers at Mgoli would have been able to have the status required to inhabit such a structure. When the fact that most plantation owners lived in wattle and daub houses is added, as well as that the little that is known of enslaved laborers' dwellings in the nineteenth century suggests they lived scattered within the plantation in wattle and daub houses (Cooper 1977: 163; Romero Curtin 1983: 866), it seems increasingly impossible to argue for a nonelite resident of a home built of lime mortar.

SEXUALITY AND SOCIETY IN COLONIAL ZANZIBAR

Women enslaved as concubines would, however, have had precisely the kind of relational status within the plantation household to inhabit such a structure. Social divisions among nineteenth-century East Africans were not simply between enslaved and free; several distinctions existed between the level of social integration an enslaved person existed within Zanzibari society. Enslaved laborers on plantations were low on the gradation, classified as *washenzi* ("unacculturated" or "barbarian" first-generation slaves) or *wazalia* (second-generation slaves with slightly higher rights; Glassman 1991: 290). Great social upheavals marked nineteenth-century Zanzibar, with immigrant numbers greatly outweighing the indigenous population, new strictures of colonial rule, and a society increasingly shaped by capitalist ideas. Within the capitalist economy, opportunities existed to increase wealth and social standing. Such possibilities were mostly open to male Arab and Indian immigrants. Although these opportunities were decreasing during the nineteenth century, some degree of possibility remained open for enslaved men to rise in social standing by working hard and developing a relationship with their owner (Cooper 1977: 211, 1979; Glassman 1991; 1995; McCurdy 2006: 445). Over time these men could even rise to positions in which they bought and sold other enslaved persons, living largely outside the supervision of their owners (Cooper 1977: 188; Romero 1986). For women, the social opportunities were very different. Omani colonial rule has been argued to have increased Islamic practices of patriarchy and the seclusion of women (Askew 1999: 91). Although evidence exists that freeborn women on Zanzibar retained a degree of power, sometimes even owning plantations (Croucher 2007b, in preparation), it is also apparent that women were increasingly being closed out of public life (Fair 2001). For enslaved women, this separation from the wider East African business sphere was particularly marked. "Dominant male consensus" prevented women from taking advantage of routes to higher social prestige available to enslaved men (Glassman 1991: 292).

Studies by historians provide further background to understanding the place of women within relations of concubinage. Along the caravan routes of East Africa, many women were apparently enslaved for this purpose (McCurdy 2006: 445), often taken at a young age (Cooper 1977: 196; Reute 1998 [1886]: 4). Concubined women, called *masuria* (sing., *suria*) in Kiswahili, may have performed domestic tasks within the household, including cooking, cleaning, washing, and the raising of their children (Fair 1996: 149). The picture of their degree of participation in such tasks remains unclear, with some accounts suggesting that they did few of the household chores (Romero Curtin 1983: 873; Reute 1998 [1886]). This muddy picture of the precise practices of household labor as divided between free wives, women who were in relationships of concubinage to their owner, and enslaved field laborers concurs with the divergent views presented in oral histories I recorded. However, in many nineteenth-century coastal households, cooking may have been the one task in which both concubines and free wives participated (Romero Curtin 1983: 873). Food preparation may have been socially charged, because mealtimes were recorded in one account as having been the moment at which social distinctions between wives and concubines were most clearly articulated through seating arrangements, even as household members sat and ate together communally (Reute 1998 [1886]: 22).

An interesting counterpoint to spatial distinctions is the continuity in styles of local ceramics, which follow forms dating back several centuries as found all along the East African coast, despite the massive influx of immigrants and the ease with which ceramics could have been made alternatively (Croucher 2007a; Croucher and Wynne Jones 2006). Domestic tasks such as food production – given the wide range of social norms of immigrant women who came from a range of mainland African communities, from other locales on the East African coast and from Oman – may have been an important way in which women negotiated social difference within households.

The primary reason that concubines were in plantation households was for sexual relations with the men who owned them. Historical accounts of the nineteenth and twentieth centuries make it clear that lessons about sexuality were common for most girls (although differing by social status) at puberty. A female initiation ritual, called *unyago*, spread from mainland East Africa to the coast during the course of the nineteenth century, partially brought by Manyema women known for their sexual attractiveness (Fair 1996; McCurdy 2006). *Unyago* initiation lessons taught girls about proper sexual relations in different social contexts (Caplan 1976; Fair 1996; 2004; Romero Curtin 1983; McCurdy 2006). Girls were taught "how to achieve sexual satisfaction for themselves and their partners" (Fair 1996: 152), learning that sexual relations were to be a source of pleasure both for the men with whom they had intercourse and for themselves. The initiation was carried out by instructors who had already been through this same initiation process, building strong bonds between new communities of women, based on sexual knowledge, providing a degree of social stability between women who had frequently been displaced by enslavement (McCurdy 2006: 454). Sexual practices learned by women during *unyago* initiations have been argued to have served as a means of social power for women. Young girls who were to be in positions of concubinage were taught to be the purveyors of sexual pleasure to the men who controlled them (McCurdy 2006: 460). It was understood that these women might, through affectionate relations, gain a particular degree of power over their master, for it was widely believed that "the special concubine, not the wife, most often captured the heart of the master" (Romero Curtin 1983: 876) and lessons of *unyago* initiation taught women to take advantage of their sexual prowess for material gains (Caplan 1976: 28).

I want to be wary here of potentially painting a picture of nineteenth-century Zanzibar in which women who were enslaved as concubines happily took advantage of men via sexual relations and became wealthy in the process. The children born of concubines were considered full and legitimate children of their fathers within nineteenth-century Zanzibari society and held social status equal to children of freeborn wives (Cooper 1977: 198; Fair 2001; Reute 1998 [1886]). After giving birth, concubines became legally free, although still dependent on the father of their child for their material well-being. However, until this point, they remained under full conditions of enslavement, a point commented on by female enslaved laborers on the mainland coast in the song quoted in this chapter's title (Glassman 1995: 90). Even upon achieving freedom, they were still identified by others as concubines, making the idea of this subject position one not only of legal enslavement but of a continued expected relationship of sexual subordination by an enslaved or formerly enslaved woman and the man who had been able to purchase her. This status was recognized through comments in oral history interviews arguing that concubines were "just bought" and that they "didn't get the same rights" as wives and could be taken into the control of sons upon the death of the man who had them in a relationship of concubinage.[5] We can therefore see the complexities of the dialectical relationship between sexual relations under enslavement being the route to the production of a kind of freedom, contingent upon knowledge of sexual practices and the ability to bear children.

In contrast to the open sexuality taught by *unyago* initiation, freeborn Arab women, including the daughters of concubines, underwent a different set of lessons at puberty in which they were instructed to be chaste in their sexual relationships and practices (Fair 1996: 147). For elite urban women "sexual purity and restraint" was a key marker of their identity in contrast to lower-status women (Fair 1996: 153). For the women at Mgoli during the nineteenth century, the type of female initiation they had gone through and their actual sexual relations and practices may have been a key way of demarcating different social classes within the core of the plantation household.

SEXUALITY AND THE PLANTATION HOUSEHOLD

The various strands of evidence from oral and documentary history concerning the place of concubines within plantation households makes a strong argument that the lime mortar house in Trench C was that of a woman held in relations of concubinage to the owner of Mgoli. All of the other plantation houses recorded appeared to be single buildings, and, although few descriptions exist in general, no historical sources I have come across thus far discuss such a pairing of buildings. This house could represent the gains of one woman's social standing within a plantation household, demonstrating that through affective abilities of sexual relations, it was possible for a woman enslaved as a concubine to gain material wealth in the relative context of Zanzibari society. The woman living in the Trench C house may have been legally free through childbirth, with a child or children straddling both social worlds, but she would also have been tied into the household through relations of domination, with her only route to better living conditions through this peculiar type of sexual enslavement and through knowing how to effectively pleasure her master as learned from her peers through initiation.

The space between the stone house and the Trench C house, as the location for domestic practices, would have been an area in which concubines and freeborn wives were in regular contact through their own work or the supervision of tasks such as cooking. In historical and anthropological studies of Islamic and non-Islamic African households in which polygamy and concubinage were practiced, comparable domestic spaces are argued to have been a key location for the negotiation of social relations and tensions (Lyons 1998; Mack 1992; Robson 2006). However, it should be noted that studies of colonial African domesticity have cautioned against taking domestic practices as the single defining location of women's identities (Hansen 1992: 6). At Mgoli, the importance of this space in interpreting the material relations of sexuality is confined to a small group – the free wife or wives and the concubine(s) of this single household. All of these women were involved in the production of a new elite Zanzibari colonial identity, one in which they and their children could participate in varying degrees, separated by sexual identities, gender, and enslavement (see Casella, Chapter 3 of this volume, for further discussion on the complexities of motherhood and captivity in archaeology).

Identifying remains associated with a concubined woman at Mgoli provides a significant step in understanding colonial Zanzibari society in new ways. The location and construction of the Trench C house also allows for interpretations of the tensions embedded within the subject position of women enslaved for the purposes of sexual relations and childbearing. A lime mortar house was a clear marker of a high social status, in terms relative to other Zanzibaris. The occupants of the Trench C house would have clearly demonstrated social power above that of the majority of wattle-and-daub-house dwellers, including other plantation owners (Croucher 2007b), cementing the idea that the children of this plantation household were part of an elite segment of Zanzibar society. But for the initial resident of the Trench C house, such social power related to a very specific kind of subject position, one which emphasized shared relations and knowledge with other women of enslaved classes and the power of affective relations of sexual pleasure with a rich plantation owner elaborated so successfully as to have a house built. It demonstrates the attainment of the use of sexual relationships to gain wealth, as per some of the teachings of *unyago* initiation.

Daily practices in the space between the stone house and the Trench C house would have engaged relationships between women who had children of equal status, who performed the same daily tasks, and who had access to the same material wealth. What separated them most may have been the manner in which they participated in sexual relationships with the same man – for a concubine, these practices may have run the gamut from open seduction of the master, partly for her own pleasure, in the "private" space to the rear of the main stone house, to deeply coercive sexual acts between a man and a woman he had enslaved. Movement around the buildings may have emphasized the differences between these women. According to the social norms of the time, an elite Arab woman would not have engaged in any kind of sexual activity in this area, which was public to other members of a household. In contrast, concubines might be taking advantage of the "liminal domestic space" in which a man could "escape the constraints of public expectations and gendered prescriptions of behavior" (McCurdy 2006: 459). Ties forged through initiation lessons and rituals might also have aided enslaved women of the household in forming social bonds that excluded freeborn wives. The Trench C house may have been a continual reminder of the importance of sexual practices within the household, perhaps a point of jealousy for wives, and of social standing, of a sort, for a concubine. It was literally the material inscription of the status of concubinage, relating simultaneously to a high material status and relegation as an outsider to the elite stone Omani architecture of the plantation owner's house. Adding in the dimension of sexuality to the interpretation of the plantation household shows some of the complex material negotiations of relational identities that were taking place in colonial Zanzibari society, allowing interpretations of space that go beyond the intersection of gender and status alone.

CONCLUSIONS

The study of sexuality in African colonial history is a topic of increasing scrutiny (Comaroff and Comaroff 1992; Hansen 1992; McClintock 1995). As studies such as this progress, it is imperative to be mindful of projecting back feminist subjectivities from Western academia straightforwardly to the subjects under study (Mahmood 2004). Exploring sexuality in colonial Zanzibar moves the picture beyond exotic images of women in harems "trammeled by the iconography of the veil" (McClintock 1995: 31) and beyond a simple binary of increasingly secluded women within the private space of the house. Nonetheless, caution must be exercised in understanding the power relations of the *chokaa* house at Mgoli. This chapter has centered on enslaved women who routinely entered into sexual relations with men who were not of their choosing, but part of lessons from *unyago* initiations encouraged women to gain sexual satisfaction from these relations. Even in viewing the attainment of living in a lime mortar house as one way in which enslaved women were able to access routes of social power, it is difficult to understand the complex subjectivities of domination and resistance that may have been involved for both concubines and freeborn wives.

Sexual identities were a crucial part of the relational practices and complex intersections of colonial identities in nineteenth-century East Africa, with the performances of *unyago* initiation in particular serving to "demarcate boundaries of acceptable forms of sexuality as well as class" (Fair 1996: 153). These did not only exist in performances – the subtleties of architectural construction and the use of space sustained day to day lived experiences of these identities. In understanding colonial lives, archaeologists are drawn to households with the knowledge that social lives and social and cultural change were both enacted at the micro-scale of quotidian life within households (King 2006: 299; Tringham 1992). The social and cultural relationships that formed the basis of wider Zanzibari colonial identities, which in turn formed the basis of larger political units, were continuously produced and reproduced within households (Hendon 2004; King 2006).

For historians the study of colonial sexualities is always limited by the source material available (Arondekar 2005). In the East African context, this has resulted in histories of gender and sexuality beginning largely from the early twentieth century and focusing mostly on urban areas. In contrast, the combination of archaeology and oral histories as presented here has been able to move the study of colonial East Africa out of the urban context and outside the views of European visitors who wrote accounts on which many historical discussions are based. By understanding that sexual identities were a crucial part of the social lives of Zanzibari society, it is possible to see how these were materially manifest at a plantation site. Making this interpretive move pushes discussions of domestic space in colonial Zanzibar beyond gender and status alone. A gradient of privacy according to gender, mediated by status, likely did exist within the Mgoli household. However, within the "private" and "female" inner space between the stone and lime mortar houses, spatial practice and meaning also helped to structure and inscribe differences within the broad category of women's identities around sexual practices.

Within the growing field of African historical archaeology (e.g., Reid and Lane 2004), those exploring the archaeology of colonialism have yet to address the centrality of sexual relations and identities (although see Weiss, Chapter 4 of this volume). Yet historians and anthropologists of colonial Africa increasingly stress the importance of sexuality (e.g., Benson and Chadya 2005; Stoler 1989). In this chapter, I have drawn dimensions of sexual relations and identities into my interpretations, demonstrating how important addressing the archaeology of concubinage is for at least one context of colonial archaeology in Africa.

Notes

1. The quotation in the title is taken from Glassman (1995: 90) and refers to a song recorded to have been sung by enslaved women on the Tanzanian mainland in the late nineteenth century.
2. Croucher 2006: Appendix K (2005 Oral History Interviews), interviews 5, 6, 7, and 9.
3. Croucher 2006: Appendix K (2005 Oral History Interviews), interviews 4, 7, 8, and 9.
4. Croucher 2006: Appendix K (2005 Oral History Interviews), interviews 1, 5, 6, 7, 8, and 9.
5. Croucher 2006: Appendix K (2005 Oral History Interviews), interview 7.

References

Aldrick, J. 1990. "The Nineteenth-Century Carved Wooden Doors of the East African Coast." *Azania* 25:1–27.

Arondekar, Anjali. 2005. "Without a Trace: Sexuality and the Colonial Archive." *Journal of the History of Sexuality* 14(1/2):10–27.

Askew, Kelly M. 1999. "Female Circles and Male Lines: Gender Dynamics along the Swahili Coast." *Africa Today* 46(3/4):67–102.

Benson, Koni, and Joyce M. Chadya. 2005. "*Ukubhinya*: Gender and Sexual Violence in Bulawayo, Colonial Zimbabwe, 1946–1956." *Journal of Southern African Studies* 31(3):587–610.

Bourdieu, Pierre. 1977. *Outline of a Theory of Practice*. Cambridge Studies in Social and Cultural Anthropology. Cambridge: Cambridge University Press.

———. 2000. "The Berber House or the World Revisited," in Thomas, J. (ed.), *Interpretive Archaeology: A Reader*. Social Science Information series. London and New York: Leicester University Press, pp. 150–170.

Brode, Heinrich. 2000. *Tippu Tip: The Story of His Career in Zanzibar and Central Africa, Narrated from His Own Accounts* (H. Havelock, trans.). Zanzibar: The Gallery Publications.

Butler, Judith. 1993. *Bodies That Matter: On the Discursive Limits of "Sex."* New York: Routledge.

Caplan, Pat. 1976. "Boys' Circumcision and Girls' Puberty Rites among the Swahili of Mafia Island, Tanzania." *Africa: Journal of the International African Institute* 46(1):21–33.

Casella, Eleanor Conlin, and Chris Fowler. 2005. "Beyond Identification: An Introduction," in Casella, E. C., and C. Fowler (eds.), *The Archaeology of Plural and Changing Identities*. New York: Springer, pp. 1–8.

Chami, Felix. 1998. "A Review of Swahili Archaeology." *African Archaeological Review* 15 (3):199–218.

Comaroff, Jean, and John L. Comaroff. 1992. "Home-Made Hegemony: Modernity, Domesticity, and Colonialism in South Africa," in Hansen, K. T. (ed.), *African Encounters with Domesticity*. New Brunswick, New Jersey: Rutgers University Press, pp. 37–74.

Cooper, Frederick. 1977. *Plantation Slavery on the East Coast of Africa*. New Haven: Yale University Press.

———. 1979. "The Problem of Slavery in African Studies." *The Journal of African History* 20(1):103–125.

———. 1981. "Islam and Cultural Hegemony: The Ideology of Slaveowners on the East African Coast." In Lovejoy, P. E. (ed.), *The Ideology of Slavery in Africa*. London: Sage, pp. 271–307.

Craster, John Evelyn Edmund. 1913. *Pemba, the Spice Island of Zanzibar*. London: T. Fisher Unwin.

Croucher, Sarah K. 2007a. "Clove Plantations on Nineteenth-Century Zanzibar: Possibilities for Gender Archaeology in Africa." *Journal of Social Archaeology* 7(3):302–324.

———. 2007b. "Facing Many Ways: Approaches to the Archaeological Landscapes of the East African Coast." In Hicks, D., L. McAtackney, and G. Fairclough (eds.), *Envisioning Landscape: Situations and Standpoints in Archaeology and Heritage*. Walnut Creek, CA: Left Coast Press, pp. 55–74.

———. In preparation. *Capitalism and Cloves: A Critique of Historical Archaeology*. New York: Springer.

———, and Stephanie Wynne-Jones. 2006. "People, Not Pots: Locally Produced Ceramics and Identity on the 19th Century East African Coast." *International Journal of African Historical Studies* 39(1):107–124.

Donley-Reid, Linda. 1990. "A Structuring Structure: The Swahili House," in Kent, S. (ed.), *Domestic Architecture and the Use of Space*. Cambridge, UK: Cambridge University Press, pp. 63–73.

Fair, Laura. 1996. "Identity, Difference, and Dance: Female Initiation in Zanzibar, 1890 to 1930." *Frontiers: A Journal of Women Studies* 17(3):146–172.

———. 2001. *Pastimes and Politics: Culture, Community, and Identity in Post-Abolition Urban Zanzibar, 1890–1945, Eastern African Studies*. Athens: Ohio University Press.

———. 2004. "Remaking Fashion in the Paris of the Indian Ocean: Dress, Performance, and the Cultural Construction of a Cosmopolitan Zanzibari Identity," in Allman, J., (ed.), *Fashioning Africa: Power and the Politics of Dress, African Expressive Cultures*. Bloomington and Indianapolis: Indiana University Press, pp. 13–30.

Fewster, Kathryn J. 2006. "The Potential of Analogy in Post-Processual Archaeologies: A Case Study from Basimane Ward, Serowe, Botswana." *Journal of the Royal Anthropological Institute (New Series)* 12(1):61–87.

Fleisher, Jeffrey B., and Adria LaViolette. 2007. "The Changing Power of Swahili Houses, Fourteenth to Nineteenth Centuries A.D.," in Beck, R. A. J. (ed.), *The Durable House: House Society Models in Archaeology*. Carbondale: Center for Archaeological Investigations, Southern Illinois University Carbondale.

Glassman, Jonathon. 1991. "The Bonsman's New Clothes: The Contradictory Consciousness of Slave Resistance on the Swahili Coast." *Journal of African History* 32:277–312.

———. 1995. *Feasts and Riot: Revelry, Rebellion and Popular Consciousness on The Swahili Coast, 1856–1888*. Portsmouth, NH, and London: Heinemann/James Currey.

Hansen, Karen Tranberg, 1992. "Introduction: Domesticity in Africa," in Hansen, K. T. (ed.), *African Encounters with Domesticity*. New Brunswick, NJ: Rutgers University Press, pp .1–33.

Hendon, Julia A. 2004. "Living and Working at Home: The Social Archaeology of Household Production and Social Relations," in Meskell, L., and R. Preucel (eds.), *A Companion to Social Archaeology*. Malden, MA: Blackwell, pp. 272–287.

Horton, Mark. 1996. *Shanga: The Archaeology of a Muslim Trading Community on the Coast of East Africa*. London: British Institute in Eastern Africa.

———, and John Middleton. 2000. *The Swahili: The Social Landscape of a Mercantile Society*. Malden, MA: Blackwell.

Huffman, Thomas N. 1984. "Expressive Space in the Zimbabwe Culture." *Man (New Series)* 19(4):593–612.

King, Julia A. 2006. "Household Archaeology, Identities and Biographies," in Hicks, D., and M. C. Beaudry (eds.), *The Cambridge Companion to Historical Archaeology*. New York: Cambridge University Press, pp. 293–313.

LaViolette, Adrian. 2008. "Swahili cosmopolitanism in Africa and the Indian Ocean World, A.D. 600–1500." *Archaeologies* 4(1):24–49.

Lyne, Robert Nunez. 2001 [1905]. *Zanzibar in Contemporary Times: A Short History of the Southern East Africa in the Nineteenth Century*. Zanzibar: Gallery Publications.

Lyons, Diane. 1998. "Witchcraft, Gender, Power and Intimate Relations in Mura Compounds in Déla, Northern Cameroon." *World Archaeology* 29(3):344–362.

Mack, Beverly B. 1992. "Harem Domesticity in Kano, Nigeria," in Hansen, K. T. (ed.), *African Encounters with Domesticity*. New Brunswick, New Jersey: Rutgers University Press, pp. 75–97.

Mahmood, Saba. 2005. *Politics of Piety: The Islamic Revival and the Feminist Subject*. Princeton, NJ: Princeton University Press.

McClintock, Anne. 1995. *Imperial Leather: Race, Gender and Sexuality in Colonial Contest*. New York: Routledge.

McCurdy, Sheryl. 2006. "Fashioning Sexuality: Desire, Manyema Ethnicity, and the Creation of the *Kanga*, ca. 1880–1900." *International Journal of African Historical Studies* 39(3):441–469.

Meskell, Lynn, and Rosemary A. Joyce. 2003. *Embodied Lives: Figuring Ancient Maya and Egyptian Experience*. London: Routledge.

Middleton, John. 1992. *The World of the Swahili*. New Haven, CT: Yale University Press.

Moore, Henrietta L. 1986. *Space, Text and Gender: An Anthropological Study of the Marakwet of Kenya*. Cambridge: Cambridge University Press.

Myers, Garth Andrew. 1997. "Sticks and Stones: Colonialism and Zanzibari Housing." *Africa* 67(2):252–272.

———. 2003. *Verandahs of Power: Colonialism and Space in Urban Africa*. Space, Place and Society series (J. R. Short, ed.). Syracuse, NY: Syracuse University Press.

Reid, Andrew, and Paul J. Lane. 2004. "African Historical Archaeologies: An Introductory Consideration of Scope and Potential," in Reid, A. M., and P. J. Lane (eds.), *African Historical Archaeologies*. New York: Kluwer Academic/Plenum Publishers, pp. 1–32.

Reute, Emily (born Salme, Princess of Oman and Zanzibar). 1998 [1886]. *Memoirs of an Arabian Princess from Zanzibar*. Zanzibar: Gallery Publications.

Robson, Elsbeth. 2006. "The 'Kitchen' as Women's Space in Rural Hausaland, Northern Nigeria." *Gender, Place and Culture* 13(6):669–676.

Romero Curtin, Patricia. 1983. "Laboratory for the Oral History of Slavery: The Island of Lamu on the Kenya Coast." *The American Historical Review* 88(4):858–882.

Romero, Patricia W. 1986. "'Where have all the slaves gone?' Emancipation and Post-Emancipation in Lamu, Kenya." *Journal of African History* 27(3):497–512.

Schmidt, Robert A., and Barbara L. Voss, eds. 2000. *Archaeologies of Sexuality*. New York: Routledge.

Sheriff, Abdul. 1987. *Slaves, Spices and Ivory in Zanzibar*. Athens: Ohio University Press.

———. 1995a. "Introduction," in Sheriff, Abdul (ed.), *The History and Conservation of Zanzibar Stone Town*. Athens: Ohio University Press (in Association with the Department of Archives, Museums and Antiquities, Zanzibar), pp. 1–7.

———. 1995b. "An Outline History of Zanzibar Stone Town," in Sheriff, Abdul (ed.), *The History and Conservation of Zanzibar Stone Town*. Athens: Ohio University Press (in Association with the Department of Archives, Museums and Antiquities, Zanzibar), pp. 8–29.

Stoler, Ann L. 1989. "Making Empire Respectable: The Politics of Race and Sexual Morality in 20th Century Colonial Cultures." *American Ethnologist* 16(4):643–660.

Tringham, Ruth. 1992. "Engendered Places in Prehistory." *Gender, Place and Culture* 1(2): 169–202.

SIX

THE POLITICS OF REPRODUCTION, RITUALS, AND SEX IN PUNIC EIVISSA

Mireia López-Bertran

INTRODUCTION

Clay human figurines may be thought of as material culture with diverse dimensions because they are considered representations of a given reality. They betray the ways that people perceive both themselves and others. However, the methods and approaches available to us for the interpretation of such figurines vary widely. Although the most common approach is to study their functionality in relation to their iconography, this strategy establishes single explanations and rules out many other possible interpretations. In this chapter, it is my intention to study clay figurines from a corporeal and embodied point of view to shed light on questions of reproduction, sex, and gender in Punic society of the sixth to the second centuries BCE. Following the main goals of this volume, figurines materialize the important role of intimate encounters in cultural contact situations.

To this end, I concentrate on a group of figurines recovered from the sanctuary of Illa Plana on the island Eivissa (also known as Ibiza), of the Baleric Islands of modern Spain (Figure 6.1; Almagro Gorbea 1980; Aubet 1969; Ferron and Aubet 1974; Hachuel and Marí 1988; San Nicolás 1987; Tarradell and Font 1975). First, I connect the figurines with their political and social context by concentrating on the politics of reproduction in Punic societies, especially on the island of Eivissa. Second, I consider the role of sex as a ritual performance. I intend to argue that the figurines ritualize sexual activities. Finally, I analyze the attribution of gender to the figurines within established scholarly discourse to expose traditional assumptions regarding gender as based primarily on a bipolar model of heterosexual representation. I suggest other interpretive possibilities beyond this duality, taking into account queer theory approaches, in accordance with the themes of this volume.

I would like to thank Barbara Voss and Eleanor Casella for inviting me to participate in this project. I also thank Mary Weismantel for her insightful comments and suggestions on my chapter. Finally, I am in debt to Jordi H. Fernández, director of the Museu Arqueològic d'Eivissa i Formentera, for providing illustrations of the figurines.

THE PUNIC WESTERN MEDITERRANEAN AND THE ISLAND OF EIVISSA

The Historical Context

Punic and *Punic identity* are not easily defined terms. Punic derives from a Latin word (*Poenus*), which refers to the descendants of the Phoenicians (see Delgado and Ferrer, Chapter 12, this volume) who settled on the western Mediterranean and the Atlantic coast of Iberia and North Africa. In most cases, the term *Punic* implies a chronological distinction between the earlier Phoenicians in the eighth to sixth centuries BCE, and the Punic presence, which ranges from the fifth to the first century BCE. However, this chronological and geographic definition hides a complex reality.

As a Latin term, the word Punic signifies an outsider's (i.e., Roman) perception of this group, who were seen as the "Other" in the context of the general political scene of the period. Punic is a term attested only in literary sources, and it is likely that the people defined as Punic never referred to themselves by this term (Prag 2006: 30). Furthermore, it is often used as a synonym for Carthaginian. Carthage (present-day Tunisia) was the most important of the Phoenician colonies. From the sixth century BCE, Carthage initiated an economic expansion in the western Mediterranean, creating a web of settlements in Sardinia, Sicily, Eivissa, North Africa, and the southern Iberian Peninsula (Lancel 1995).

Although there is a common assumption that *Punic* and *Carthaginian* are interchangeable concepts, some scholars have suggested that they are not synonymous (see Van Dommelen and Gómez Bellard 2008). The reason for this assumption lies in the so-called imperial politics of the city of Carthage. Carthage, as a military power that invaded other areas, primarily for agricultural reasons, would have disseminated Carthaginian culture throughout the territories of the Mediterranean. Consequently, the Punic world has been traditionally defined in terms of the colonial influences of Carthage.

Furthermore, this stereotype of a merged Carthaginian culture is at odds with the currently known archaeological data because the existence of indigenous populations alongside the former Phoenician settlers created multifaceted situations. Therefore, the Punic label is used to characterize a great variety of political and cultural contexts, across a wide geographic expanse, and encompassing a diversity of material culture (Van Dommelen and Gómez Bellard 2008: 5). Under the Punic label, we find cultural traditions and material culture that reflect Carthaginian influence integrated with local traditions and customs. Thus, the archaeological data requires us to qualify the concept of military conquest as well as the idea of Carthage as an empire.

Assuming that an empire seeks "the imposition of an asymmetrical power relationship that reduces local autonomy" (Voss, Chapter 2, this volume), the relationship between the Punic people and the Carthaginians would be considered anything but an empire. We might define Carthage as an empire from the second century BCE on, beginning with the Second Punic War, but, again, this label would be supported more by the ancient Greek and Roman written sources than by the archaeological data. Once we assume that the Carthaginian presence in the western Mediterranean

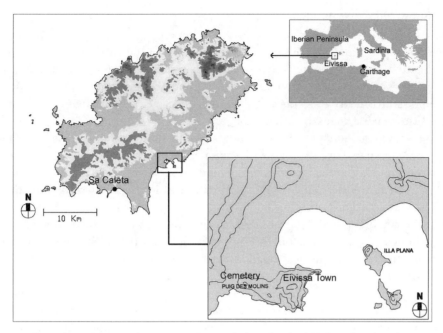

FIGURE 6.1. Map of the Mediterranean Sea and the island of Eivissa showing the sites discussed in the text.

is best explained in terms of cultural influence, rather than using militaristic or colonialist concepts, we might find the words *hegemonic* and *connectivity* the most useful in referring to this cultural phenomenon (Whittaker 1978). As other scholars have asserted, "Carthage, both the urban authorities and elites, no doubt played a key role in forging and facilitating these connections but we insist on substantial regional autonomy in the shaping of the Punic landscapes" (Van Dommelen and Gómez Bellard 2008: 237–238).

Within an awareness of this panorama, it has been suggested that Punic peoples are a combination of local populations from different western Mediterranean areas integrated with arrivals from North African communities, mainly from Carthage. Thus, it is more appropriate to describe this world as Punic rather than part of a "Carthaginian Empire" (Van Dommelen and Gómez Bellard 2008: 12 and 238). Consequently, the use of the term Punic cannot denote ethnic or political identities, but can only be used as an archaeological or historical category.

Punic Eivissa

The Phoenicians settlers, allegedly from southern Spain, first set foot on the island of Eivissa (Figure 6.1) in the mid-seventh century BCE and established two small settlements on the eastern coast of the island, one at Sa Caleta (Ramon 2007) and the other at the town of Eivissa. By the end of the seventh century BCE, Sa Caleta was abandoned, and all inhabitants seem to have concentrated in the town of Eivissa.

This settlement is not well known but a sanctuary, Illa Plana, and the cemetery, Puig des Molins, have been extensively studied. The cemetery provides us with fresh evidence about the inhabitants of the island and about their funerary rituals around the time that the shrine of Illa Plana was in use. The earliest inhabitants of Eivissa maintained close connections with the Phoenician settlements in Andalusia (southern Spain) and with indigenous settlements on the eastern coast of Spain. The island has been characterized as an important port of call on the main shipping routes across the Western Mediterranean (Gómez Bellard 2008: 47). But, from the mid-sixth century BCE the island developed closer contacts with the central Mediterranean, particularly with Carthage.

How do we conceptualize these foundations and subsequent movements of people? Some scholars have suggested that these movements cannot properly be seen as colonial and imperial situations in the modern sense of the term but rather that in the ancient Mediterranean, we should expect a situation in which "mobility is high and communities are interdependent but independent" (Osborne 2008: 282, 284).The colonial paradigm, in contrast, asserts the existence of a degree of political or military control by people of foreign origin and the subsequent economic exploitation and asymmetrical relationships between the indigenous groups and the newcomers (van Dommelen 1998: 16; Lyons and Papadopoulos 2002: 12; see general discussion in Vives-Ferrándiz 2008: 290). For instance, Voss (this volume, Chapter 2) points out that "colonization most commonly refers to imperial strategies that involve the direct domination by one polity over a population in their own territory," a point of view that understands colonialism as a process triggering local tension and conflict (González-Ruibal 2008: 287).

Keeping in mind the foregoing clarification of the concept of Punic, *Punic* Eivissa was as much a cultural situation as a political or military one; movements of people also require attention and explanation. From the sixth century BCE on, the material culture of Eivissa attests to the arrival of people with traditions connected to the central Mediterranean, a process that can be better understood in terms of sustained migrations and movements, such as traders or settlers, rather than a colonial process *sensu stricto*. As Vives-Ferrándiz (2008: 289) has pointed out regarding the colonial nature of the movements of Phoenician traders and settlers along the Western Mediterranean, what is key "is not just the contact itself but the subsequent phenomena of continued and sustained interaction, and therefore the underlying forces and the motivations and conflicts of the people involved." In this case study, such motivations are addressed through the material culture of the Illa Plana rituals associated with the politics of reproduction and its related sexual performances.

The Shrine of Illa Plana and the Figurines

Although today Illa Plana is part of the larger island, during the first millennium BCE the coastline was somewhat different, with the shrine located on an island in the middle of Eivissa bay, not far from the harbor (Figure 6.1). Illa Plana has been defined as a sacralized natural site because no architectural structures have been recorded, although a votive well has been found. It contained the figurines addressed here and is dated between the end of the sixth century BCE to the end of the fifth century BCE, so, it is believed to have been in use for a century.

FIGURE 6.2. Illa Plana bell-shape figurines with painted decoration. Museu Arqueològic d'Eivissa i Formentera.

The site was first excavated at the beginning of the twentieth century, and there are no reliable stratigraphic references relating the figurines to their archaeological context (Hachuel and Marí 1988: 21). In addition, other figurines were found outside of the well, including molded and hand-built figurines. These additional artifacts are regarded as Phoenician objects, dated between the end of the seventh century to the mid-sixth century BCE (Hachuel and Marí 1988: 57). Despite the presence of these Phoenician objects, scholars propose that Illa Plana only functioned as a well-defined shrine during the Punic period and not during the earlier period of the sparse Phoenician presence.

From the point of view of their production, there are two groups of figurines, the mold-made figurines, found outside the well, and the so-called wheel-made figurines, recovered from inside the well. There are thirty-one wheel-made figurines, all produced using the same technique. The body and head were modeled using the potter's wheel, and then the most significant parts of the body – the eyes, mouth, genitalia, and arms – were added later. This was done by making incisions and perforations and then attaching clay fragments representing arms and, especially, penises and breasts. This supports the idea that each figurine represents different postures and actions and, thus, different performances.

A morphological classification of the wheel-made figurines has also been suggested (Table 6.1). The first morphological group is a bell-shape type. They may represent praying supplicants, suggested by the position of the hands with palms open, as if asking for something or praying. Some of these figures hold Punic oil lamps. Many still preserve painted decoration, mainly red sashes on the head and on the body, which may represent clothing, head decorations, or other adornments (Figure 6.2). The second morphological group is the cylindrical terra-cottas, less significant in terms of the number of pieces recovered. Finally, the ovoid-type figurines represent a third morphological group. Some of this group are described as "bird-headed" (Figure 6.3) and others as "African" (Figure 6.4) because of their

Table 6.1. Physical and typological description of the figurines

Museum number inventory	Typology	Genitalia and breasts	Decoration
1684	Bell shape	Vulva and breasts	Red sashes on head and body
1674	Bell shape	Vulva and breasts	Red sashes on head and body
2513	Bell shape	Penis	Red sashes on head and body
1679	Bell shape	Penis	Red sashes on head and body
8003	Bell shape	Penis	Red sashes on head and body
2512	Bell shape	Vulva and breasts	
1670	Bell shape	Vulva and breasts	
1685	Bell shape	Penis	
8499	Bell shape	Vulva	
8500	Bell shape	Penis	
s.n.	Bell shape	Penis	
1686	Bell shape	Penis	
8498	Bell shape	Penis and breasts	
8496	Bell shape	Penis	
31234	Bell shape	Penis	
1671	Bell shape	Penis and breasts	Oil lamp on the head and the left hand
			Red sashes on the body
1672	Bell shape	Penis	Oil lamp on the head
			Red sashes on the body
8497	Bell shape	Penis	Oil lamp on the head and on the hand
			Red sashes on the body
1681	Cylindrical	Vulva and breasts	Incised bracelet on the left hand
1673	Cylindrical	Penis and breasts	Oil lamps on two hands and on the head
1683	Cylindrical	Penis	
8005	Ovoid shape	Penis and breasts	Bird-headed and necklace
8004	Ovoid shape	Penis and breasts	Bird-headed and necklace
1682	Ovoid shape	Penis	Bird-headed and necklace
1680	Ovoid shape	Penis	Bird-headed and necklace
31237	Ovoid shape	Penis and breasts	Bird-headed and necklace
8495	Ovoid shape	Penis	Bird-headed, necklace and clay sheet on the head
s/n	Ovoid shape	Penis	Bird-headed and necklace
1687	Ovoid shape	Penis and breasts	Necklace and clay sheet on the head
8494	Ovoid shape	Penis and breasts	Necklace and ribbon on the head
31235	Ovoid shape	Penis and breasts	Clay sheet on the head

physical appearance, particularly the predominant lips (Hachuel and Marí 1988: 37–41). They are generally around 20 centimeters long. It is important to note that these figurines do not represent gods or goddesses but rather people attending the sanctuary and performing ritual activities. Interpreting figurines as representations of people rather than as representations of divine beings increases the importance of considering the sensory and bodily features of material culture.

FIGURE 6.3. Illa Plana ovoid, bird-headed figurines. Museu Arqueològic d'Eivissa i Formentera.

FIGURE 6.4. Illa Plana ovoid figurine. Museu Arqueològic d'Eivissa i Formentera.

ILLA PLANA AND THE POLITICS OF REPRODUCTION

Framing Illa Plana in the political context of Eivissa island is useful for an understanding of these figurines in connection with demography and the politics of reproduction. As we have already seen, the Phoenicians created two sites from scratch: Sa Caleta, abandoned around 650 BCE, and the town of Eivissa, created around 600 BCE. Keeping in mind that the island was first settled in the final centuries of the third millenium BCE (Costa and Benito 2000: 222–227), it is not entirely clear whether the Phoenicians encountered an uninhabited island (Gómez Bellard 1995) or there were indigenous groups living there. Whatever the case, the available data is poor and gives the impression of largely uninhabited areas on the island of Eivissa, with at most a minimal number of indigenous people who did not affect the activities of the newcomers, which were mainly composed of young immigrant families (Gómez Bellard 2008: 47).

Until the end of the sixth century BCE, the only settled area of the island was the immediate vicinity of Eivissa city. However, an important cultural change is recorded during the second half of the sixth century into the beginning of the fifth century BCE. Funerary practices shift from cremation practices to inhumation burials, and changes in pottery reveal the cultural influence of, and connection with, the city of Carthage. Survey studies have shown that from the fifth century on, the island was progressively occupied by a number of small rural settlements (Gómez Bellard et al. 2011). It is likely significant that the shrine of Illa Plana is also dated to this period.

The appearance of new cultural practices and materials during this period has traditionally been attributed to the arrival of people from the Central Mediterranean, especially from Carthage and the island of Sardinia. Indeed, the type of figurines found in Illa Plana are also recorded in Carthage, Sardinia and Sicily. In addition, population growth on the island may also have been driven by the politics of reproduction in the local population as well, which would explain the extensive occupation of inland areas of the island (Gómez Bellard 2008: 68–72). In fact, the most intense period of use of the Puig des Molins cemetery is precisely during the fifth century BCE.

The figurines of Illa Plana date from the end of the sixth century BCE to the end of the fifth century BCE, coinciding precisely with the recorded population increase. Not coincidentally, the corporealities of the figurines shed light onto this issue. On the one hand, figurines provide useful indications of the arrival of migrants. This theory is often supported by interpretation of some of the figurines of Illa Plana as "African" (Figure 6.4). A critique of this ethnic designation, however, is that prominent lips do not necessarily represent Africans, as modern categories of race may not be directly imposed on the past. From a corporeal perspective, I propose that prominent lips could also highlight the role of the mouth as a significant sensory organ. Whatever populations these figurines may represent, I analyze how they reinforce the idea of a complex, heterogeneous Eivissa population with diverse body politics and gender categories.

On the other hand, whatever may have been the reasons behind the population increase on Eivissa, the figurines would have clearly reinforced the connection between fertility and reproduction through the representation of big genitalia. In this sense, the figurines might be indicating how important sexual relationships were for increasing the population on an almost uninhabited island. Thus, it is a reasonable suggestion that the figurines represent young and fertile people with high sexual power.

The role of fertility is also clear for the Phoenician period of the shrine. As previously noted, clay figurines were found outside of the votive well, representing the goddess Astarte and the god Bes. Both deities have fertility features, and Bes, in particular, is considered a protector god for women in labor (Hachuel and Marí 1988: 69).

However we may imagine the devotees at the shrine, they shared an interest in reproducing themselves as the genitalia materialize. In this sense, the array of rituals performed at the shrine was essential to maintaining group values and to achieve a sense of belonging in a new land. Unfortunately, we do not know whether these rituals, and the politics of reproduction that the rituals involved, were connected to households, families, or other groups or communities.

SEX AS RITUAL PERFORMANCE

Representations of large genitalia have been selected as key evidence for interpreting these figurines, both masculine and feminine, as fertility votives. However, focusing solely on fertility obscures other interpretations. As other scholars have pointed out, the overemphasis on a concern for personal fecundity derives from the influence of Christian ideas in explaining religious phenomena in antiquity. In fact, such overemphasis directs attention away from other possible interpretations of sexual practices taking place during ritual performances (Meskell and Joyce 2003: 116). Western contemporary conceptions of the body usually connect sexual practices with privacy and the interior space of the house in private life (Voss 2008: 42). Indeed, sexuality, like many other cultural features, is socially constructed (as all the chapters of this volume demonstrate). We should be aware that sex as an intimate encounter, practiced exclusively among two people, may not have occurred in Punic society or in specific rituals. Sexual intercourse during rituals might be one of the multiple activities of which a ritual was constituted, and it may have involved many people.

I argue that the explicit genitalia of many of the figurines (see Table 6.1) can be alternatively interpreted as revealing the presence of ritualized sex activities. In using the term *ritualization*, I define rituals by practices, that is, what people actually did, and minimize the generic and universal features usually attached to rituals. By focusing on practices, we can take into account to what extent, and in what ways, rituals differ from other daily practices (Bell 1992: 74). In this case study, the representation of genitalia would be a form of ritualization in that it emphasizes the role of sex by inscribing the practice in material culture. So, in other words, the practice of sex would have logically fitted in to ritual performances and, consequently, would be represented in the figurines.

The posture of figurines touching their genitalia might be associated not only with fertility but also with sexual contact. In fact, the scarce number of feminine figurines (see Table 6.1) in comparison with masculine and bird-headed figurines (discussed subsequently) sheds light not only on the practice of homosexuality but also on the practice of masturbation, as suggested by the figurines touching penises.

Sexual intercourse might be accompanied by a comprehensive sensory exploitation, and this is materialized through the overrepresentation of physical sense organs – the eyes, ears, nose, mouth, and hands. Let us examine, then, how the idea of sensory exploitation was inscribed in material culture through not only the representation of sense organs but also the presence of masks and necklaces, and how this sensory explotation can be related to the achievement of altered states of consciousness. Anthropological studies have shown that singing, music, percussion activities, praying, or inhaling incense or other substances are ways to achieve altered states of consciousness (Pollack-Eltz 2004), and these activities can be identified in the figurines of Illa Plana.

Some figurines are represented with a large, open mouth, as if they were singing, chanting, praying, or lamenting. Indeed, the human voice is perhaps the most ancient musical instrument. Sight and smell appear to be other senses significant in these ritual practices, and are represented by open eyes and big noses. Eyes would be essential not only to see the performances carried out in rituals involving figurines but also to provide a means for symbolic vision. Equally, smell was clearly considered an essential sense in ancient ritual because it was related to hygienic practices and the search of pleasant odors attested by the widespread practice of burning perfumes or oils during a ritual (Classen 1993: 7). This is well illustrated at Illa Plana by figurines holding oil lamps (Figure 6.2a). Furthermore, smoke would have been regarded as the means through which the practices of ritual materialized a connection among the figurines, the participants, and the otherwordly beings (Meskell and Joyce 2003). Hearing seems to have also been significant: ears are faithfully represented, indicating the importance attributed to music and sounds in ritual performance. Sound and music were necessary to make contact with divinities and to receive their messages (Lawson *et al.* 1998: 124).

I argue that the presence of masks and necklaces may also be related to the achievement of altered states of consciousness. Necklaces associated with Illa Plana figurines that have a small box attached as a pendant (Figure 6.3) have been interpreted as containers for psychoactive substances. In most cases, necklaces are also related to the use of masks. Some scholars suggest that masks are a way of transforming perception and personhood to create liminal states (Mitchell 2006: 393).

Although the exploitation of the senses through ritual is well demonstrated by all the Illa Plana figurines, the "bird-headed" terra-cottas present an especially expressive combination of features and materials. These bird-headed forms are the only figurines that exhibit masks and necklaces together. Interestingly, these figurines also touch their genitalia. This reinforces the suggestion that the figurines might represent special characters who embody their role not only through gender and decoration but also through the use of special substances and sexual acts to achieve altered states of consciousness.

Figurines and Performances

Human figurines can be interpreted not only as representations of people but also as figurines in motion (Bailey 2005; Meskell 2007), that is, as material culture that actually plays a role in ritual performances. On one hand, human terra-cottas represent not only the bodies of people who visit the shrine and perform rituals, that is, are objects showing what Joyce defines as iconicity; they also provide relevant information about the activities and practices of their creators and users, or are what Joyce terms indexical objects (Joyce 2007: 102). On the other hand, they are not simply decorative objects but materials with which people performed activities, so when they are used and moved by people, they can be understood not as mere objects but as materials undergoing a process of transformation. Thus, objects can also be apprehended at a tactile level, and to take a sensory reading of them is a useful methodology for making them speak (Weismantel, Chapter 18, this volume).

Terra-cottas play an active role in ritual performances as people hold, talk to, and move them. Recall that the Illa Plana terra-cottas are only 20 centimeters long, so they would be easy to hold and manipulate interactively. Although I assume all the figurines would have been used in some kind of interaction with and among devotees at a ritual, only one group show clearly how figurines represent active objects in performing a ritual. Four specific figurines (see Figure 6.2a) are represented as holding oil lamps in their hands and arms or on their heads. It seems likely that these figurines were multifunctional: they not only represent people but were also used to burn oils or other substances in the context of the ritual performances. Indeed, cremation is repeatedly recorded in ritual practices in Phoenician and Punic ritual contexts (López-Bertran 2007), so the representations of oil lamps may be connected to that practice and the sensory explotation of the smell. Therefore, I maintain that these terra-cottas themselves participated in rituals through their use as oil lamps. Equally, it is also feasible that the other figurines were used as characters performing sexual activities.

From this perspective, the term *performance* acquires a more nuanced and complex meaning. For these performances, there might be an active audience, an important role played by actual, physical bodies, and the presence of materials in motion (here, the figurines) (Inomata and Coben 2006: 15). Thus, the figurines of Illa Plana stress the performative features of rituals.

ENGENDERING THE FIGURINES

Beyond the Dual-Gender Division

Traditional studies on Punic human figurines of the Western Mediterranean have usually attributed gender through a bipolar model of heterosexual differentiation (men–women, feminine–masculine) based on the representation of genitalia on the figurines (a penis for male, a vulva for female). Within this model, those figurines that do not have explicitly represented sexual organs are defined as undetermined. Scholars usually assume that all figurines would have originally shown genitalia but that in some cases, the genitalia was not preserved. In any case, alternative possibilities regarding the existence of more than two genders are not considered.

By defining the figurines in terms of this bipolar distinction between masculinity and femininity, scholars have essentially engendered even the undetermined figurines by assuming they fit into one of these two categories. It goes without saying that there is no convincing argument for this assumption. In many cases, the figurines with ornamentation and jewelry have been exclusively labeled as female, betraying a sexist assumption of contemporary criteria of (some) Western body decoration traditions. These interpretations assume a conception of the body that demands analysis. From this perspective, the body is defined as a feminine arena, so that there is a link among bodies, senses, and women. They are seen as passive elements and ruled by the mind, which is associated with men (Davis 1997: 5). However, such interpretations are not in keeping with the fact that some masculine figurines have ornamentation, as is clearly shown in Illa Plana figurines.

The absence of sex markers is as significant as their presence, which is why I emphasize the need to look beyond a simplistic dual division between male and female. In fact, in other cultural milieus, figurines without explicit representations of genitalia may be considered asexual, or at least as sexually ambiguous (Assante 2006: 183; Dobres 2000; Garcia-Ventura and López Bertran 2010: 744-746; Picazo 2000: 33).

The presence of breasts has been another traditional indicator used to ascribe gender to figurines, drawing a direct association between women and breasts. Again, however, this relationship might be misleading because there are a number of Illa Plana masculine figurines with breasts. Thus, at Illa Plana, the association between masculine figurines and breasts severs the traditional relationship between female breasts and fertility, opening up new gender categories (see Table 6.1 and Figure 6.4). Moreover, these male figurines suggest that Punic culture may define masculinity differently from modern Western assumptions about masculinity. Consequently, masculine figurines might also be connected with fertility, and breasts may not have always been a feminine marker.

Therefore, the data and material culture from Illa Plana show a heterogenous situation in which the bipolarity of genders is blurred and other gender categories may appear. Among the thirty-one figurines from Illa Plana, a traditional gender division would result in a greater number of masculine figurines: twenty-five male to six female (Hachuel and Marí 1988: 75). Interestingly however, the ovoid-type figurines, specifically the bird-headed forms, might represent a third gender category, a hybrid one that can be defined as transgender (Figure 6.3). This suggestion is based on the physical appearance of these forms. They are bird-headed and yet have explicit representations of both penises and breasts (seven pieces). Thus, these figures in particular are especially relevant materials with which to explore topics related to bodies, ritual, and gender identities.

Hybrid Beings and Gender as a Performance

The first question that has arisen when approaching the study of this type of figurine is, are they to be seen as humans wearing a bird-type mask, or are they considered fantastic beings, mixing human and animal features? I argue that this difference is meaningless because the use of a mask is a way of embodying hybrid beings. Wearing a mask is a way of embedding the fantastic realm into real life, creating a new category of person. Such new persons have transformative and performative capacities (Merrill 2004: 16). From this perspective, these figurines embody features of personhood which are alien to the conception of individual identity found in many contemporary Western societies: dividuality and partiability (Fowler 2004). These latter two concepts refer to the idea that human identities are created through the relations they maintain – not only with other people but also with other beings and materials.

Bird-headed figurines share an animal and a human personhood, showing a relational and dividual identity. The dividuality and partiability of groups attending the Illa Plana shrine is demonstrated not only in the use of bird masks but also in ornamentation of the body. These elements further extend the constructed hybridity of the body. For example, some figurines exhibit both a necklace and a clay base on top of the head, interpreted as remains of a hat. Both these elements reinforce the role of this hybrid personhood in connecting the human and the animal. The creation of these new beings is embodied primarily in the head of the figure. The head and the face are the most significant body parts in this context, because most of the senses are located there, and hence the head can represent sensory manipulation or alteration in ritual (Merrill 2004: 29; Meskell and Joyce 2003: 32; Schildkrout 2004: 319–320). Consequently, faces transformed by masks are a powerful means through which to build feelings and practices in ritual performances related to sex and fertility practices. The involvement of sex and the presence of masks in rituals might be related to rites of passage because body decorations have been interpreted as material culture that constructs issues of the transformation of identity (Stig Sørensen 1991: 136).

Furthermore, personhood is created not only through bodies and their relations with other beings and materials but also through gender. The relational nature of personhood and of gender results in unstable identities. Assuming the insights provided by theories of performativity (Butler 1993), figures having penises and wearing masks may not necessarily represent a male gender but rather a new gender based on the hybridity between human and nonhuman. In these figurines, I regard gender as a performance. Gender is like fancy dress, revealing the idea of an intrinsic and internal sex identity as false (Butler 1993). Thus, the figurines illustrate that gender is not a natural or biological construction but a cultural one. Through performance, that is, through the action of wearing masks, necklaces, and hats, a new personhood and a new gender is created. By the same logic, big penises have nothing essential to do with masculinity. Anatomical sex is not equivalent to gender (Voss 2008: 36).

What is the role of these transgender beings in the ritual practices carried out in Illa Plana? I argue that they, together with the so-called African figurines, are ritual specialists, embodying this role through their gender and decoration. They may serve in this function for various reasons – for example, as a head of family, or for reasons of age or status. They might have an important role in the demographic politics of the island as well. Furthermore, these characters may also achieve a more intense altered state of consciousness via the psychoactive substances hidden inside their necklaces than other participants. As many ethnographic studies show (see, for instance, the example of Native American two-spirits in North America; (Voss 2008: 39), ritual specialists, such as shamans, are men who manifest other sexual features, going beyond the bipolar heterosexual scheme to create another gender.

I have used the term *ritual specialist* rather than *priest* because the latter term has contemporary Western connotations (López-Bertran 2011). The danger in projecting the concept of priests onto antiquity is that we risk imposing a modern interpretation onto an ancient ritual. Priests are essential to many current religions, especially monotheistic faiths such as Christianity, because they rule and lead the performances of the ritual. The participants are usually a passive audience following instructions. Acknowledging that Illa Plana ritual entailed performance, actions, and ritual practices, I would define the presence of individuals with a specialized role from a different perspective. In fact, if we look for priests who are full-time workers, leaders, and directors of ritual, there were likely no priests in Illa Plana.

Interpreting the figurines from a queer point of view undermines the traditional argument that the higher number of masculine figurines indicate a greater presence of men in Illa Plana (Hachuel and Marí 1988). Instead, this interpretation presents a panorama in which other gender categories also play a role in performances. Within this panorama of genders, female gender is as significant as any other gender. Although there is little representation of women (six out of thirty-one) in the figurines, their bodies construct the same ritual practices as male, or transgender. The corporealities of female figurines are the same as other figurines: they assume the same posture, with hands open in prayer, and exhibit the same apparel-like, red fringe decoration on the body and head (Figure 6.2a and 6.2b). Furthermore, from a sensory point of view, the eyes and mouth are as prominent as for the other figurines (López-Bertran 2007). This recognition of females in Illa Plana rituals is especially notable as the Greco-Roman literary sources allege that the Phoenicians and the Punic forbade the entrance of women in temples and shrines (Van Berchem 1967: 87 and 90). However, archaeological evidence indicates that women seem to have played the role of highly specialized participants in religious rituals related to musical activities (Garcia-Ventura and López-Bertran, 2009 a and b). In all, studying material culture from an embodied point of view clarifies the presence of women in religious rituals and reveals the biases of some ancient literary sources.

Rituals provide an excellent arena to study the ways in which genders are culturally constructed. At Illa Plana, we can identify at least three genders created through performances, gestures, and body decoration. At the same time, gender defines the ritual identity of individuals, as demonstrated by the bird-headed/transgender figurines. Because they have a different gender, they may assume the role of ritual specialists. This role is embodied not only through gender but also through decoration (see Loren, Chapter 7, this volume, for a discussion of the ways that body decorations embody intimate and gender relationships).

To Sum Up

By exploring several dimensions of clay figurines from the Illa Plana shrine on the island of Eivissa, I have shown how material culture allows multifaceted perspectives – not only in the present but also in the past.

I have focused on three features of the figurines: reproduction, sex, and gender, as they relate to the performance of rituals. First, I suggest figurines may have been connected to the politics of reproduction on Eivissa because they are dated to a period of expansion and an increase in birth rate. This increase may be attributed not only to local inhabitants but also to the arrival of immigrants. Both share a desire to increase their communities as the representations of genitalia show. Second, sex relationships might be ritual performances carried out not only by people but also between the figurines themselves. Sex might be one of multiple activities in a ritual, together with the burning of oil or incense, singing, and dancing. In addition, altered states of consciousness would be essential elements of ritual, especially as represented by the bird-headed/transgender figures, proposed as ritual specialists. Third, the terra-cottas demonstrate the existence of several genders – masculine, feminine, and the so-called bird-headed or transgender.

In all, the figurines from Illa Plana represent useful materials to assess issues of sexuality when attempting to reconstruct cultural milieus in antiquity. Although the context analyzed here is not considered an imperial or colonial situation, this analysis demonstrates how figurines might reveal people with different body and gender politics sharing rituals and a sacred place.

REFERENCES

Almagro Gorbea, J. M. 1980. *Corpus de las terracotas de Ibiza.* Madrid: Bibliotheca Praehistorica Hispana, XVIII.

Assante, J. 2006. "Undressing the Nude: Problems in Analyzing Nudity in Ancient Art, with an Old Babylonian Case Study," in Schroer, S. (ed.), *Images and Gender: Contributions to the Hermeneutics of Reading Ancient Art.* Orbis Biblicus et Orientalis 220. Freiburg and Göttingen: Academic Press Fribourg, Vandenhoeck & Ruprecht Göttingen, pp. 177–207.

Aubet, M. E. 1969. "Los depósitos votivos de la Illa Plana (Eivissa) y Bithia (Cerdeña)," *Estudia Arqueológica 3.* Santiago de Compostela: Universidad de Santiago de Compostela.

Bailey, D. W. 2005. *Prehistoric Figurines. Representation and Corporeality in the Neolithic.* London: Routledge.

Bell, C. 1992. *Ritual Theory, Ritual Practice.* Oxford: Oxford University Press.

Butler, J. 1993. *Bodies That Matter. On the Discursive Limits of "Sex."* New York: Routledge.

Classen, C. 1993. *Worlds of Sense. Exploring the Senses in History and across Cultures.* London: Routledge.

Costa, B., and Benito, N. 2000. "El poblament de les Illes Pitiüses durant la Prehistòria. Estat actual de la investigació," in Guerrero, V. and Gornés, S. (eds.), *Colonització humana en ambients insulars. Interacció amb el medi i adaptació cultural.* Palma: Univeristat de les Illes Balears, pp. 215–317.

Davis, K. 1997. "Embody-ing Theory: Beyond Modernist and Postmodernist Readings of the Body," in Davis, K. (ed.) *Embodied Practices. Feminist Perspectives on the Body.* London: Sage Publications, pp. 1–26.

Dobres, M. A. 2000. "Scrutizing the Interpreters: Feminist Perspectives on the Study and Interpretation of Ancient Female and "Goddess" Imagery," in *Diosas. Imágenes femeninas del Mediterráneo de la prehistoria al mundo romano.* Barcelona: Museu d'Història de la Ciutat de Barcelona, pp. 36–46.

Ferron, J., and Aubet, M. E. 1974. *Orants de Carthage.* Collection Cahiers de Byrsa, Série Monographies, I, Paris: Geuthner.

Fowler, C. 2004. *The Archaeology of Personhood. An Anthropological Approach.* London: Routledge.

Garcia-Ventura, A., and López-Bertran, M. 2009a. "Music and Sounds in Punic Ibiza (Balearic Islands, Spain)," in Ozkan Aygun, C. (ed.), *Proceedings of the XI Symposium on Mediterranean Archaeology,* Istanbul Technical University, April 24 and 29, 2007, British Archeological Report International Series 1900, pp. 12–17.

———. and López-Bertran, M. 2009b. "Embodying Musical Performances in the Ancient Mediterranean." *Archeomusicological Review of the Ancient Near East* I:39–45.

———. and López-Bertran, M. 2010. "Embodying some Tell-Asmar Figurines," in Matthiae, P., Pinnock, F. Nigro, L., Marchetti, N. (eds.), *Proceedings of the 6th International Congress on the Archaeology of the Ancient Near East*, Università di Roma "Sapienza," May 5 and 10, 2008, Wiesbaden: Harrassowitz Verlag, pp. 739–749.

Gómez Bellard, C. 1995. "The First Colonization of Ibiza and Formentera (Balearic Islands, Spain): Some More Islands out of Stream?." *World Archaeology* 26:442–455.

———. 2008. "Ibiza: The Making of New Landscapes," in Van Dommelen, P., and C. Gómez Bellard (eds.), *Rural Landscapes of the Punic World*. Monographs in Mediterranean Archaeology 11. London: Equinox, pp. 44–75.

Gómez Bellard, C., Díes Cusí, E., and Marí i Costa, V. 2011. *Tres paisajes ibicencos: un estudio arqueológico*. Saguntum Extra n° 10. València: Universitat de València.

González-Ruibal, A. 2008. "Discussion and Debate. Postpolitical Colonialism. *Journal of Mediterranean Archaeology* 21(2):285–288.

Hachuel, E., and Marí, V. 1988. *El Santuario de la Illa Plana. Una propuesta de análisis*, Treballs del Museu Arqueològic d'Eivissa i Formentera, 18. Eivissa: Museu Arqueològic d'Eivissa.

Inomata, T., and Coben, S. L. 2006. "Overture: An Invitation to the Archeological Theater," in Inomata, T., and Coben, S. L. (eds.), *Archeology of Performance. Theaters of Power, Community and Politics*. Oxford: Altamira Press, pp. 11–44.

Joyce, R. A. 2007. "Figurines, Meaning and Meaning-Making in Early Mesoamerica," Renfrew, C. and I. Morley (eds.), *Image and Imagination: A Global Prehistory of Figurative Representation*. McDonald Institute Monographs. Cambridge: Cambridge University Press, pp. 101–110.

Lancel, S. 1995. *Carthage. A History*. Oxford: Blackwell.

Lawson, G., Scarre, C., Cross, I., and Hills, C.1998. "Mounds, Megaliths, Music and Mind: Some Thoughts on the Acoustical Properties and Purposes of Archaeological Spaces." *Archaeological Review from Cambridge* 15(1):111–134.

López-Bertran, M. 2007. *Ritualizando cuerpos y paisajes: un análisis antropológico de los ritos fenicio-púnicos*. Ph.D. dissertation, Universitat Pompeu Fabra, Barcelona. Available at http://www.tesisenred.net/TDX-0513108–170353.

———. 2011. "Where are the priests? Constructing ritual mastery in Punic shrines", in Chaniotis, A. (ed.), *Ritual Dynamics in the Ancient Mediterranean: Agency, Emotion, Gender, Representation*. Stuttgart: Steiner Verlag, pp. 43–60.

Lyons, C. L., and Papadopoulos, J. K. 2002. "Archaeology and colonialism," in Lyons, C. L., and Papadopoulos, J. K. (eds.), *The Archaeology of Colonialism*. Los Angeles: Getty Research Institute, pp. 1–23.

Merrill, M. S. 2004. "Masks, Metaphor and Transformation: The Communication of Belief in Ritual Performance." *Journal of Ritual Studies* 18(1):16–33.

Meskell, L. 2007. "Refiguring the Corpus at Çatalhöyük," in Renfrew, C., and I. Morley (eds.), *Image and Imagination. A Global Prehistory of Figurative Representation*. McDonald Institute Monographs. Cambridge: Cambridge University Press, pp. 137–149.

Meskell, L., and Joyce, R. A. 2003. *Embodied Lives. Figuring Ancient Maya and Egyptian Experience*. London: Routledge.

Mitchell, J. P. 2006. "Performance," in Tilley, C., Keane, W. Kuechler-Fogden, S. Rowlands, M. and Spyer, P. (eds.), *Handbook of Material Culture*. London: Sage, pp. 384–401.

Osborne, R. 2008. "Discussion and Debate. Colonial Cancer." *Journal of Mediterranean Archaeology* 21(2):281–284.

Picazo, M. 2000. "Imaginary Goddesses or Real Women: Female Representations in the Ancient Mediterranean," in *Diosas. Imágenes femeninas del Mediterráneo de la prehistoria al mundo romano*. Barcelona: Museu d'Història de la Ciutat de Barcelona, pp. 22–34.

Pollack-Eltz, A. 2004. "Ecstatic Worship," in Salamone, F. A. (ed.), *Encyclopedia of Religious Rites, Rituals and Festivals*. Routledge Encyclopedias of Religion and Society. London: Routledge, pp. 22–25.

Prag, J. 2006. "*Poenus planes est* – but who were the 'Punickes?'. " *Papers of the British School at Rome* 74:1–30.

Ramon, J. 2007. *Excavaciones arqueológicas en el asentamiento fenicio de Sa Caleta (Ibiza).* Cuadernos de Arqueología Mediterránea 16. Barcelona: Edicions Bellaterra.

San Nicolás, M. P. 1987. *Las terracotas figuradas de la Ibiza púnica.* Rome: Consiglio Nazionale delle Ricerche.

Schildkrout, E. 2004. "Inscribing the body." *Annual Review of Anthropology* 33:319–344.

Stig Sørensen, M. L. 2000. *Gender Archaeology.* Cambridge: Polity Press.

Tarradell, M., and Font, M. 1975. *Eivissa Cartaginesa.* Barcelona: Curial.

Van Berchem, D. 1967. "Sanctuaries d'Hercule-Melqart. Contribution à l'ètude de l'expansion phénicienne en Mediterranèe." *Syria* XLIV:73–109.

Van Dommelen, P. 1998. *On Colonial Grounds. A Comparative Study of Colonialism and Rural Settlement in First Millennium BCE West Central Sardinia.* Archaeological Studies Leiden University 2. Leiden: University of Leiden.

Van Dommelen, P., and C. Gómez-Bellard. 2008. "Defining the Punic World and Its Rural Contexts," in Van Dommelen, P., and C. Gómez-Bellard (eds.), *Rural Landscapes of the Punic World.* Monographs in Mediterranean Archaeology 11. London: Equinox, pp. 1–21.

Vives-Ferrándiz, J. 2008. "Discussion and Debate. Response: Re-negotiating the Encounter." *Journal of Mediterranean Archaeology* 21(2):289–295.

Voss, B. L. 2008. "Las políticas sexuales de imperio en la Américas españolas: perspectivas arqueológicas del San Francisco colonial," in Ruiz, A. (ed.), *Desencuentros culturales: una mirada desde la cultura material de las Américas.* Cuadernos de Arqueología Mediterránea 17. Barcelona: Edicions Bellaterra, pp. 31–49.

Whittaker, C. 1978. "Carthaginian imperialism in the fifth and the fourth centuries," in Garnsey, P., and C. Whittaker (eds.), *Imperialism in the Ancient World,* Cambridge: Cambridge University Press, pp. 59–90.

Section II

Engaged Bodies

SEVEN

FEAR, DESIRE, AND MATERIAL STRATEGIES IN COLONIAL LOUISIANA

Diana DiPaolo Loren

INTRODUCTION

The history of intimate relations in eighteenth-century Louisiana is a familiar colonial story. Through historical documents we learn of the commonplace nature of interracial and interethnic sexual relations in the colony, the frustrations of missionaries regarding the lack of legitimate Christian marriage, concerns regarding Native American and African concubines, and the very real threat (at least in the eyes of colonial officials and missionaries) of French men leaving behind their cultural traditions and their spiritual selves to "go native." Numerous academic publications have emphasized the complex nature of colonial *métissage* and an increasing number of authors continue to draw out the lived experiences of women and their mixed-race children in these entanglements (e.g., Hodes 1997; Spear 1999, 2003, 2009; Stoler 2001). Spear (1999, 2003) and Dawdy (2006) have used historical documents to detail some of the intimate relations that existed between the Native American and French occupants of colonial Louisiana. Drawing from this same body of literature, Usner (2003: 22) notes that "intimate border crossing" was common in the colony, especially because young Native American women could freely engage in sexual relations before marriage without social sanction. Additionally, Hodes (1997: 39) highlights the sexual and material aspects of intimate encounters, indicating that Native American women may have sought out relationships with French men to allow themselves access to more European-manufactured goods, thus enabling them to gain status within their communities. These contemporary writings that examine eighteenth-century documents reveal the central role of sex and intimate relationships in the Louisiana colony: sexual attractions of unfamiliar bodies, policing of those desires, maintenance of social hierarchies and skin color, and material

My deep gratitude to El Casella and Barb Voss for their inclusion of my work in this volume, their thoughtful comments, and good humor throughout the process. I am indebted to the insight on this topic given to me by the other scholars who participated in the Intimate Encounters workshop held at Stanford University in 2009.

strategies used in dressing one's body in this context of colonization, desire, and fear.

Given that intimate border crossings were so ordinary, part of the everyday rhythm of life in French Louisiana, here I explore archaeological and archival perspectives of intimate relations in French Colonial Louisiana. What do these sources have to say about the ways in which intimate relations were materialized? When viewed together, how to they provide insight on colonial conceptualizations and constructions of desire? My study focuses on Natchez dress and adornment. Natchez people incorporated aspects of Native American- and European-manufactured material culture into their dressing practices. Although these practices allowed Natchez people to create new colonial identities that would enable further intimate border crossings, these dressing practices created a colonial body that was so sensorially different from European bodies that it was simultaneously feared and desired by French colonizers.

In this chapter, I examine material culture related to the body and bodily adornment excavated from the Grand Village of the Natchez, an eighteenth-century Natchez Indian mound and village complex also known as the Fatherland Site located in present-day Mississippi (Figure 7.1). Elsewhere, I have discussed the promulgation of Christian doctrines in relation to notions of nakedness and practices of dressing (Loren 2001, 2007, 2008). My focus here is not on nakedness but rather the ways in which Natchez Indian people chose to cover and adorn their bodies with combinations of familiar and nonfamiliar material goods. In this investigation, I explore body movement, the ways that material culture became part of colonial bodies, and the sensory impact those bodies had in the creation of colonial fear and desire.

MATERIALIZING COLONIAL BODIES

My interest on colonial intimate relations and material culture focuses on the body: the corporeal space in which identity was created, materialized, sexualized, and embodied. During the Enlightenment, most Europeans claimed moral, bodily, and cultural superiority over the Native American and African bodies (Chaplin 2003: 9, 14; Orser 2007). The body was at the center of most colonial narratives as it was fundamental to most imperial projects; it marked where you fit within colonial hierarchies and categories, and policing sexual relationships allowed for the maintenance of social boundaries (Chaplin 1997: 233; see also Chaplin 2003; Lindman and Tarter 2001: 2; Pagden 1982; Spear 2009). Social hierarchies brought to the New World from the Old were inscribed with early modern notions of race and embodiment, which privileged mind over body. These conceptualizations of race also asserted that individuals had the capacity (or not) to be civilized through engagement of the mind (Pagden 1982; Sala-Molins 2006). This same philosophical reasoning also allowed for practices of enslavement, branding, and other corporeal punishments (Lindman and Tarter 2001: 4). Most colonial narratives contain thick descriptions of other peoples encountered during colonial entanglements and an assessment regarding their capacity to be civilized. Not only were gender and skin color subject to imperial scrutiny, but so were the actions that these bodies took – how they dressed, moved, acted, engaged, and danced – especially in relation to

FIGURE 7.1. Location of the Grand Village of the Natchez/Fatherland site, Adams County, Mississippi.

European colonial officials, priests, and authors. Thus, European narratives about colonized peoples generally agree that colonial bodies were contested spaces, places of uncertainty and anxiety that needed to be watched and controlled.

All activities regarding clothing and adornment are anchored by the body and in this way, body and dress are inseparable. It is through the body that one experiences the world, forms and performs identity, and mediates social exchanges (Butler 1990; Merleau-Ponty 1989). In this conceptualization and exploration of the sensuality of colonial bodies and the intersection of body and object, I draw from two theoretical perspectives: the first being recent work on materiality within the discipline of anthropology and second, the concept of embodiment from the work of French philosopher Maurice Merleau-Ponty.

Recent research on materiality has brought renewed interest to the study of objects – not as object-based narratives but rather in explicating the convergence of "situated experiences of material life, the constitution of the object world, and concomitantly its shaping of human experience" (Meskell 2004: 249; see also Keane 2005; Miller 2005). Broadly theorized, materiality constitutes our physical engagement with the world – how an individual both shapes objects and uses objects to shape identity – as well as the role that objects play in constituting identities

(Gosden and Knowles 2001; Joyce 2005, 2007; Meskell 2004a; Miller 2005). In most materialist approaches, objects are given as much interpretive weight as those of subjects; and in some cases, to the point that objects are understood as having agency separate from those of the subjects with which they are connected (see Pinney 2005). This is not to say that objects are sentient; rather this approach seeks to recover the lives objects lead away from people and how objects constrain and influence the lives of the people with whom they come in contact (Miller 2005; Pinney 2005).

While objects do lead lives away from subjects, when objects and subjects meaningfully intersect and become entangled in daily life, one's identity or sense of self is constructed at this intersection of object and self. This general definition of materiality is complementary to those espoused in embodiment literature, and this alignment supports the argument that identity is created through the movement, action, and interaction of one's body in a specific social and physical landscape (Merleau-Ponty 1989; see also Butler 1990; Enwhistle 2000; Joyce 2005, 2007; Meskell 1999). Merleau-Ponty (1989: 5) argues that bodies "are what give us our expression in the world, the visible form of our intentions"; thus, the ways we think about the world that surrounds our bodies are based and grounded on the experiences of our bodies in that world. In this way, bodily praxis is situated in a discourse of appropriate bodily action, and bodily experience is given meaning through that discourse (see Moore 1994: 58–63); that is, experiences of the body can only be understood in the context – the time and space – in which that body exists. This dual understanding of embodiment and materiality is key to understanding the lived experience of social actors and how material culture constituted different identities. Moreover, this dual focus cites bodily experience as culturally specific, moving far from the often-cited critique that embodiment and phenomenological approaches treat bodily experience as universal (cf. Grosz 1994: 86–111; see also Joyce 2007).

When considering the body in the colonial world, attention must be given to how material culture of clothing and adornment shaped and constituted bodily experiences. In all societies, bodies are "dressed" in some way, and everywhere dress and adornment play "symbolic, communicative and aesthetic roles" (Wilson 2003: 3; see also Eicher and Roach-Higgins 1992; Eicher 1995; Greenblatt 1984; Joyce 2005, 2007; Loren 2001, Loren 2010; Meskell 1999; Shannon 1996; Voss 2008; Weiner 1985; Weiner and Schneider 1989). More than just material culture that lived on the surface of the physical body, the embodiment of colonial identities was constituted with clothing and adornment (Deagan 2002; Loren 2001, 2007, 2010). Dress was such a powerful medium that in colonial contexts of control, definition, and redefinition, dress and presentation of the body needed to be monitored and challenged (Loren 2010; Shannon 1996; Voss 2008; White 2003). In colonial Louisiana, these imperial concerns centered on how the dress of noblemen, servants, soldiers, Jesuit priests, Native American and African peoples aligned with sumptuary laws and cultural expectations of dress (for example, the extent to which a body was clothed or unclothed and the color and appropriateness of clothing in specific contexts) (Roche 1994: 6; White 2003).

From an archaeological perspective, attention has been placed on the material culture of clothing and adornment with relation to issues of manufacture, consumerism, and trade (see, for example, White 2005). Objects of clothing and adornment in practices of dressing, however, were more varied and creative than imagined by the manufacturers and suppliers of those items. Dressing and adorning one's body was not only about visual impact but also about how one's body moved through colonial spaces (Loren 2008, 2010). Sounds and music were an inherent aspect of many seventeenth- and eighteenth-century Native American ceremonies (Loren 2008). For example, French planter Antoine Simone Le Page du Pratz (1975: 363–384) described several ceremonies he witnessed while he lived alongside the Natchez in the first decades of the eighteenth century, including the Feast of Corn and the funeral of a Natchez nobleman, Tattooed Serpent. Religious and ceremonial regalia often incorporated bells, tinkling cones, and other items that would jangle during dances and songs (Figure 7.2). With these thoughts in mind, I turn to some of the history of French and Natchez Indian relations gleaned from the historical record.

NARRATIVES ON NATCHEZ AND FRENCH BODILY AND MATERIAL RELATIONS

Located along the east bank of the Mississippi River in what is now southwestern Mississippi, the Grand Village of the Natchez was occupied between 1682 and 1729 (Neitzel 1965). The Grand Village, a large mound and village complex with a large central plaza, was the main ceremonial center for the tribe, which also included five Natchez districts: Flour, Jenzenaque, White Apple, Grigra, and Tiou (Neitzel 1965). The Natchez had occupied this area of the American Southeast for several centuries before French exploration in the late seventeenth century (Neitzel 1965; Usner 1992). Mobile, the capital of the colony, was established in 1702, after several decades of exploration in the Lower Mississippi Valley. Soon after, more households, posts, and concessions (plantations) were established along the Mississippi River. In the Natchez area, work began on Fort Rosalie in 1716. In 1723, less than 200 French settlers lived in the community, and by 1729, the area's population comprised more than 400 French, 280 enslaved Africans, and approximately 2,000 Natchez (Liebersohn 2001: 49).

Interactions between the French and Natchez were, as in many colonial situations, fraught with violence, which culminated in the 1729 movement against the French now known as the Natchez Massacre in which most of the French inhabitants of Fort Rosalie were killed (Sayre 2005: 204). Ensuing violence between the French and the Natchez resulted in the dispersal of the Natchez from their homelands. Many Natchez refugees joined other tribes, including the Chickasaws, Creeks, and Cherokees. Today, people of Natchez descent live among the Creek and Cherokee Indians, yet there is no organized Natchez tribe with federal or state recognition (Barnett 2007; National Park Service 2008).

Anxieties regarding fear and desire seep from numerous archival accounts, with most accounts agreeing on the notion that the bodies of Natchez men, women, and children were visually, spiritually, and sexually different from their own. Historical documents often linger on the commonplace nature of interracial sexual relations, as opposed to intermarriage (ordained in a church) as was hoped by religious and government officials (see Hackett 1934, vol. 1: 247, 255; Mississippi Provincial Archives, French Dominion [MPAFD], 1929: 27–28, 56–58, 72, 169,

226–227; MPAFD, 1984: 73). The growth of the colony was initially dependent on intermarriage. In 1699, Pierre Le Moyne d'Iberville, a naval captain in New France, encouraged "the French who will settle in this country to marry Indian girls" (cited in Spears 2009: 1). However, by 1735, Louis XIV had outlawed intermarriage, arguing that it was detrimental not only to the growth of the colony but also to the doctrine of Christianity to have European men "liv[ing] in extreme debauchery with the Indian women" (Spear 2003: 19). In the form of letters and other correspondence, priests and colonial officials lamented the numerous sexual relationships occurring between Natchez women and French men living at Fort Rosalie, fearing that these interactions would degrade the morality and civility of the growing colony (Dawdy 2006; Spear 1999, 2003, 2009; Usner 2003: 22). Antoine Le Page du Pratz's *Histoire de la Louisiane*, published in three volumes in Paris in 1758, provides a different perspective. Le Page du Pratz ran a concession near the Natchez between 1720 and 1728, establishing close social relations with his Natchez neighbors. These intimate relations no doubt influenced the way he described the Natchez and their world. Additionally, another intimate relationship may have had an impact on his writing; Le Page du Pratz had a long-standing relationship with a Chitimatcha Indian woman. Similar to other French men in the colony, du Pratz fostered a desire for Native American bodies (Dawdy 2006: 154). Colonial authors were fascinated by the ways in which Natchez peoples, especially women, adorned their bodies. For example, Le Page du Pratz (1975: 137) described the dress of Natchez women: "From their belts to their knees hang many strings from the same cord [ribbon] which are attached claws of birds or prey like eagles, tiercelets, buzzards, etc., which when these girls walk make a kind of clicking, which pleases them." Natchez men also adorned themselves with ear pendants, rattles, and bells so that their movements were amplified (Swanton 1911: 127). French engineer Dumont de Montigny noted that "their tresses are ordinarily laced by way of ornament with strings of blue, white, green, or black beads [made of glass]" (Swanton 1911: 51). Natchez men were also described as being similarly adorned with ear pendants, rattles, glass beads, and bells; their fashions were described as foppish and effeminate (Swanton 1911: 127).

Adorned Native American bodies invaded the senses of French authors. These writers were startled with the ways in which Natchez bodies were displayed and moved, and particularly the sounds that emanated from their bodies. To the French, these sights and sounds displayed a freedom of body presentation and movement that was markedly different from the ways the French moved within the colonial world (Spear 1999, 2009). It is in these thick descriptions that French authors produced colonial desires, a taste for the exotic and erotic to be found in the bodies of Natchez people. Conversion to Christianity dictated the covering of flesh as well as the limitation of physical movements and expression to de-eroticize one's body (Delâge, 1993: 201–202; see also Loren, 2001, 2007). Although only a handful of Jesuit and Capuchin priests lived in the Natchez region, the overwhelming majority of French settlers were schooled in these beliefs about the body. So much so that they were startled with the knowledge of the ways in which Natchez bodies were displayed and moved, which signaled to the French unrestrained sexuality (Spear 1999, 2009).

FIGURE 7.2. Communal Dance. Reproduced from Antoine Simon Le Page du Pratz, *Histoire de la Louisiane*, 1758.

For the Natchez, the use of material culture in the embodiment of their identities was more multivocal than these accounts suggest. The answer to how the Natchez materialized their intimate relations with the French is found in the archaeological record and along the margins of historical writings. Ethnohistorical accounts that emphasize nudity, tattoos, and overt sexuality also suggest that the Natchez were quite strategic in their acquisition and use of clothing, particularly French styles. Le Petit noted in 1730 that of those French spared during the Natchez Massacre included French women and "a Tailor and a Carpenter, who were able to serve their wants. . . . The least miserable were those who knew how to sew, because they kept them busy making shirts, dresses, etc." (Father le Petit 1730: 165–167). These accounts indicate how the Natchez people chose to adorn their bodies with specific European-manufactured goods that embodied not only to their intimate relations with the French but also their agency in those engagements.

MATERIAL RELATIONS AT THE GRAND VILLAGE OF THE NATCHEZ

Presentation of the body through dress and adornment offers one of the most visual manifestations of one's identity and self. Artifacts associated with clothing and personal adornment, such as buckles, bracelets, beads, Jesuit rings, and thimbles, although admittedly rare finds at most historical-period sites, are informative about the practices of dressing and the ways in which identities were constituted in relation to official dictates, local conditions, and personal beliefs (Beaudry 2006; Deagan 2002; Loren 2010; Loren and Beaudry 2006). The objects of dress and adornment that resonate in this case study of the material culture of intimate relations are glass beads. Although glass beads may not seem to be an item that would suggest intimacy or sexuality, they were animated in distinct ways against the skin that captured the attention of many colonial peoples.

Initially arriving in North America from their production sites in Italy, Amsterdam, and other areas of Europe as some of the first items to be traded with Native Americans, glass beads soon became one of the most common items related to clothing and adornment produced in Europe for consumption in North America and other parts of the globe during the colonial period. Glass beads were produced in a multitude of colors and forms: seed (very small), standard beads (from medium to very large), blown wire-wound or drawn, pressed and molded, etched, in almost every conceivable color or color combination. As an item of commodity and meaning, glass beads have reached almost an iconic status within material studies in historical archaeology. Quimby (1966) detailed the occurrence of glass beads on early colonial-period sites throughout the Great Lakes. Kidd and Kidd's (1970) typology of glass beads brought new understandings of glass construction and composition to archaeological analysis, and Karklins (1985, 1992), Hamell (1983), Phillips (1998), and Turgeon (2001, 2004, 2006) have discussed glass bead usage and meanings for Native Americans in Canada and the Eastern Woodlands. This prior research on the chronology and sourcing of glass beads has provided a strong baseline for current discussions of the use and meaning of glass beads in Native American contexts, particularly on the emphasis placed on the use of different bead forms (i.e., seed versus necklace beads) and the color of beads in different Native American and African American contexts (Hamell 1983; Thomas 2002; Wilkie 1995, 1997).

In the archaeological record, glass beads are usually recovered as single objects (rather than as the component of an object) and interpretations of the social use of glass beads tend to rely on the analysis of this material according to chronology. Archaeological publications that examine how glass beads were animated in practices of clothing and adornment by looking at the location of beads in relation to human body have provided detail on these practices (e.g., 2007, 2010). Additionally, ethnographic collections provide numerous examples of how glass beads were sewn on clothing, woven into belts, embroidered on bags, worn as necklaces and earrings, woven into hair, and hung from cradle boards (Karklins 1992: 12–13; Neitzel 1965: 88–89).

I draw inspiration from Laurier Turgeon's work to explore the eroticism of glass beads from the perspective of embodiment. In his writing, Turgeon eloquently argues how material culture placed on the body becomes part of one's body: "Food and clothing are integrated into or put onto the body and thereby transform it . . . a piece of clothing is more than a sign, or a representation of something, it is an essence in itself. This material association between biological (the body) and cultural domains is what makes alimentary and vestimentary practices so efficient for the affirmation of individual and collective identities" (Turgeon 2006: 108).

Turgeon (2004: 35–36) argues that glass beads were a particularly important aspect of colonial dress because of the associations between beads and bodies, particularly because beads were often likened to eyes or light. More so, glass beads create small clinking sound that appears to emanate from the body itself during dance, performance, or just movement (Turgeon 2004: 37). The clinking is richly described by French authors, as well as the cool smoothness of glass against the skin and the ability of glass beads to capture light and color. These qualities of glass when worn on the body became the body that was deeply desired.

Historical accounts of Natchez uses of glass resonate here. For example, Jesuit Father le Petit, missionary among the Natchez, discussed the extent to which they valued glass and placed it as an object of reverence within their main temple building (Swanton 1911:269). Glass was also an important material used in adorning the body. For example, the "Luxembourg Memoir" states that "Their greatest adornment consists of bead necklaces of different colors, with which they load the neck and the ears" (Swanton 1911: 55; Figure 7.3). Intimate relations were established as a means to acquire glass beads. In an eighteenth-century account, French Lieutenant Henri Joutel described Native American women trading sexual favors (although these interactions may have in fact been coerced or forced) for "needles, knives, and particularly strings of beads" (cited in Spears 2009: 27). As this and other quotations suggest, desire went both ways. Glass beads were desired by the Natchez to be worn about their bodies, and Europeans were fixated by the ways that Natchez women (and men) wore glass beads in particularly sumptuous and sexual ways, free of restraint.

Archaeological investigations at the Grand Village of the Natchez were conducted in 1930, 1962, and 1972 (Neitzel 1965, 1983). Moreau Chambers excavated several burials from Mound C at the site in the 1930s, and these excavations were later published by Neitzel as part of the site report on his own excavations at the site in 1962 (Neitzel 1965: 40–47). In the 1970s, Neitzel returned to the site to conduct excavations on the mounds, including several domestic structures and the large plaza area (Neitzel 1983).

Overall, the material assemblage from the site shares similarities with other colonial sites in the region in that Native American-manufactured material was often found in combination with European-manufactured items in domestic and burial contexts. The difference, however, is a matter of degree. With the exception of items of dress and adornment, European-manufactured items occur in much fewer numbers than many other Native American sites in the Lower Mississippi Valley (Neitzel 1983: 107–117). For example, at the nearby Trudeau site, European-manufactured ceramics and other material often equal the numbers of Native American-manufactured items (Brain 1988).

In my analysis, I draw from Neitzel's published research on Natchez burials. Netizel's research was conducted in the larger arena of mid-twentieth century North American archaeological practice, which emphasized burial contexts and the excavation of burials over domestic contexts (see Shepherd, Chapter 17, this volume). In the over twenty years since the passage of the Native American Graves Protection and Repatriation Act, North American archaeological practice has refocused its gaze on the sensitivities that accompany the interpretation of different contexts and especially material recovered from burial contexts. My use of burial data in this chapter by no means intends to further a colonial vision of the past but rather is intended to provide a sense of how individuals were lovingly cared for by their families and communities at the time of death.

Artifacts related to clothing and adornment recovered from burial and nonburial contexts at the Fatherland site include a shell ear pin, four cupreous metal buckles (two of which were shoe buckles), fifty-one tinkler cones, two religious medals, four signet rings, two brass band rings, a bear incisor pendant, two bone beads, brass coils used as earrings, five brass buttons, numerous hawk bells, and thousands of different varieties of glass beads (Neitzel 1965: 49–51, 1983: 106–117). The limited numbers of religious items present in this assemblage lead us to consider what impact (if at all) efforts of conversion had among the Natchez. Historical documents suggest that these efforts were less than successful among the Natchez, but in these efforts, crucifixes and other religious paraphernalia were distributed among Native American populations in efforts to convert the unconverted. In this case, clearly the possession of Christian symbols (saint medals, crucifixes, etc.) does not always signify that the owner was on the path to conversion because such an object could have been symbolically mobilized in other ways. The basis of most interactions between the Natchez and their neighbors was not religious; rather, these entanglements were social, economic, and sexual. Given this, another form of material culture likely materially manifested these relationships. In the context of French colonial Louisiana, I suggest that the one form of material culture mobilized in this fashion was glass beads.

Glass beads of all varieties were recovered from burials and in nonburial contexts at the Grand Village (Neitzel 1965: 51). In almost every instance, they were worn in combination with both Native American- and European-manufactured material, suggesting the importance of this category of material in lived experiences of Natchez peoples. Varieties recovered from nonburial contexts at the Grand Village include

FIGURE 7.3. Indian bride with fan, and young Indian woman with a paddle, Jean-François-Benjamin Dumont de Montigny, *Poême en vers touchant l'établissement de la province de la Loüisiane....* (ca. 1742). Courtesy of the Bibliothèque Nationale de France.

drawn tubular and wire-wound glass beads commonly found on mid-eighteenth-century sites in the colonial American Southeast including blue, white, and green medium-sized glass beads; polychrome beads; dark amber to black, flattened spherical beads; porcelain beads; medium red opaque; drawn, tubular white and blue glass beads; and raspberry beads (Neitzel 1965: 51, Neitzel 1983: 109–110). Unlike nonburial contexts, the majority of glass beads recovered from burials were medium-sized blue or white beads worn as necklaces (Table 7.1). No data exist regarding the sex of the individuals in the burials; the only distinction made was between adult and child burials. Although this limitation prohibits an analysis of glass beads based on sex, it is important to note that in most of the adult burials, blue and white glass beads were found around the neck and near the head of the individual suggesting that Natchez adults (both men and women) wore beads around their neck, woven into their hair, and/or in their ears. An exception to this pattern is found in Burial 15, in which an individual was buried wearing a wool frock coat with metal buttons. A box was laid on the chest of the individual and contained four iron buckles, brass coil springs (used as earrings), brass tinklers, a silver bell, brass buttons, red pigment (for painting the skin), a variety of glass beads, including oval white and blue striped beads and spherical and oval, white and black beads (Neitzel 1965: 43). Although

Table 7.1. Burials excavated at Mound C, Fatherland Site (compiled from Neitzel 1965)

Burial	Location of glass beads	Other items of dress and adornment
Burial 1: unknown	Blue glass beads under jaw	
Burial 3: adult	Blue glass beads near neck	
	Blue glass beads around ear	Shell earpin and brass hawk bells at right ear
		Brass button near torso
Burial 4: adult	Five strands of glass beads blue and white glass beads at neck Blue and white beads near the ears	Thimble and two religious medallions found at neck with beads
Burial 7: two adults	No glass beads	Iron and copper c-bracelets on arm, two brass rings on fingers
		Wire coils at ears
Burial 8: adult	Four strands of medium- to large-blue glass beads, five purple beads and one blue-striped white tubular bead at neck	
Burial 9: adult	Strings of alternating medium blue and large dark blue glass beads with white stripes around neck	Silver bell
Burial 11: unknown	White glass beads nearby	
Burial 12: child	Medium-sized blue glass beads	
Burial 14: child	Small blue and white glass beads	Twenty brass hawk bells and remnants of fur
Burial 15: adult		Individual buried wearing wool frock coat with metal buttons; a box laid on the chest of the individual contained four iron buckles, brass coil springs (used as earrings), brass tinklers, silver bell, brass buttons, red pigment (for painting), oval white and blue striped glass beads, oval and spherical white and black glass beads
Burial 17: adult	Blue glass beads lay near jaw (preserved as necklace with string intact)	Two brass bells near head
Burial 19: adult	Two strands of white glass beads and one strand of alternating white, pink, and blue striped glass beads near the neck	Seven Jesuit rings lay near the head; quartz crystal
Burial 20: adult	String of green glass beads near neck	

blue and white glass beads were recovered from the two child burials, the location of the glass beads within the burials was not noted.

Shell beads, and in fact shell artifacts in general, are almost completely absent from the site and their absence is striking in this context as glass beads are often found in combination with shell beads in most Native American sites in the colonial Eastern Woodlands (see Loren 2007). This replacement of shell beads with glass beads was highly unusual in Native North America and highlights variability of indigenous engagements with introduced material culture.

One could argue that glass beads were just objects of adornment, baubles acquired by the Natchez to incorporate into their dressing practices. If identity is constituted using material culture, then items of adornment never just sit on the surface of the body as these items are as important to the body as clothing itself in the process of embodying and performing identities. Historical and archaeological data indicate that Natchez people actively sought to acquire glass beads. Glass beads then became so integral to dress that shell beads were forgotten altogether. What was is about the material of glass that captured the imagination and desires of the Natchez in their practices of adornment? I suggest that it was both the sound and color of glass, so strikingly different than shell, which evoked the desire and imagination of Natchez people. There is little archaeological or historical evidence to suggest that Natchez people wore or made beaded clothing; rather, the labor invested to beads was limited to stringing them into necklaces of distinct color combinations to be worn about the face of Natchez adults to capture light and color that would reflect back on their skin and clink together in daily movement.

French officer Diron d'Artaguiette noted that Native American women were "mistresses of their own bodies (to use their own expression)" (cited in Spears 2009: 29). The ways in which Natchez people wore glass beads were unfamiliar to the French but captured their imagination and desires. Glass beads were evocative of the changing sexual relationships within Natchez and French communities – new understandings of bodies, identities, and sexuality. These relationships brought about the feelings of fear and desire found in colonial narratives but, at the same time, were indicative of changing identities of gender, sexuality, prestige, and perhaps even childhood that were formed through the new fashion of wearing glass beads about one's person.

CONCLUSIONS

Glass beads manufactured in Venice and Amsterdam were brought to the Natchez through the hands of their French neighbors. More than simply adornment, glass beads became part of their bodies in life and in death (Turgeon 2004, 2006). Although there is no information on why the color blue or the location of blue beads near the face were so important to the Natchez, this pattern found in burial contexts suggests that the Natchez did find meaning in these combinations. Glass beads were the materialization of intimate relations with the French, relations that that had reshaped their community and sense of self. It is no coincidence that glass beads were the items that were chosen so frequently among other kinds of European-manufactured items, including other items of clothing and adornment. The properties of glass – color, sound, and translucence – were meaningful to the

Natchez in the ways they viewed and adorned their own bodies in relation to French bodies. Glass beads were more than just simple adornment, because they were used to evoke other memories and associations meaningful to constructing early colonial identities. To wear glass beads was to transform the body, to physically embody new understandings of self that were actualized through their intimate associations with the French. The French did not share these same fashions of adornment with glass beads; it was too far from what sumptuary laws and social practice dictated regarding how they held and performed their bodies. These sartorial differences were at the heart of the creation for the desire for Natchez bodies – beaded, adorned, resonating in seductive ways that were strongly heard in colonial narratives.

Just before the 1729 uprising, a Natchez elder discussed how many in the community were at odds with the material and social entanglements of French and Natchez worlds. These transformations of identity constituted with European-manufactured material culture had come at a cost: "The wares of the French yield pleasure to the youth; but in effect, to what purpose is all this, but to debauch the young women, and taint the blood of the nation, and make them vain and idle? The young men are in the same case; and the married must work themselves to death to maintain their families and please their children" (Le Page du Pratz 1975: 76).

Beaded bodies were both feared and desired by the French. Artifacts worn on the body became part of colonial bodies, the materialization of intimate relations between the Natchez and their French neighbors – a relationship that could be seen, heard, and longed for. The embodiment of glass beads in constructions of identity was one of sensory miscommunication because French and Natchez cultural understandings about the colonial body were, at least initially, contradictory. Yet acts of adornment indicate the active manipulation of glass beads by Natchez peoples who mobilized glass beads to transform their bodies and embody their intimate relationships with others in life and death.

REFERENCES

Barnett, Jim. 2007. "The Natchez Indians." *Mississippi History Now*. Available at http:// mshistory.k12.ms.us/index.php?id=4.

Beaudry, M. C. 2006. *Findings: The Material Culture of Needlework and Sewing.* New Haven, CT: Yale University Press.

Brain, Jeffrey P. 1988. *Tunica Archaeology, Papers of the Peabody Museum of Archaeology and Ethnography, Volume 78.* Cambridge, MA: Harvard University Press.

Butler, Judith. 1990. *Gender Trouble: Feminism and the Subversion of Identity.* London: Routledge Press.

Chaplin, Joyce E. 1997. "Natural Philosophy and an Early Racial Idiom in North America: Comparing English and Indian Bodies." *The William and Mary Quarterly* 54(1): 229–252.

————. 2003. *Subject Matter: Technology, the Body, and Science on the Anglo-American Frontier, 1500–1676.* Cambridge, MA: Harvard University Press.

Dawdy, Shannon Lee. 2006. "Proper Caresses and Prudent Distance: A How-To Manual from Colonial Louisiana," in Stoler, Ann Laura (ed.), *Haunted by Empire: Geographies of Intimacy in North American History.* Durham, NC: Duke University Press, pp. 140–162.

Deagan, Kathleen. 2002. *Artifacts of the Spanish Colonies of Florida and the Caribbean 1500–1800, Volume 2: Personal Portable Possessions.* Washington, DC: Smithsonian Institution Press.

Delâge, Denis. 1993. *Bitter Feast: Amerindians and Europeans in Northeastern North America, 1600–1664.* Vancouver, Canada: University of British Columbia Press.

Eicher, Joanne B. 1995. *Dress and Ethnicity: Change across Space and Time.* Oxford: Berg.

Eicher, Joanne B., and Mary Ellen Roach-Higgins. 1992. "Definition and Classification of Dress: Implications for Analysis of Gender Roles," in Barnes, Ruth, and Joanne B. Eicher (eds.), *Dress and Gender: Making and Meaning*. Oxford: Berg Press, pp. 9–28.

Entwistle, Joanne. 2000. *The Fashioned Body: Fashion, Dress, and Modern Social Theory*. Cambridge: Polity Press.

Father le Petit. 1730. "Letter from Father le Petit, Missionary, to Father d'Avaugour, Procurator of the Missions in North America, July 12, 1730," in Thwaites, Reuben Gold (ed.), *The Jesuit Relations and Allied Documents*, Vol. LXVIII.

Gosden, Chris, and Chantel Knowles. 2001. *Collecting Colonialism: Material Culture and Colonial Change*. Oxford: Berg.

Greenblatt, Stephen. 1984. *Renaissance Self-Fashioning: From More to Shakespeare*. Chicago: University of Chicago Press.

Grosz, E. 1994. *Volatile Bodies: Toward Corporeal Feminism*. Bloomington: Indiana University Press.

Hackett, Charles Wilson. 1934. *Pichardo's Treatise on the Limits of Louisiana and Texas (5 volumes)*. Austin: University of Texas Press.

Hamell, George R. 1983. "Trading and Metaphors: The Magic of Beads," in Hayes, Charles F., III, (ed.), *Proceedings of the 1982 Glass Trade Bead Conference*, Rochester, NY: Rochester Museum and Science Center Research Record, pp. 5–28.

Hodes, Martha. 1997. *White Women, Black Men: Illicit Sex in the Nineteenth-Century South*.

Joyce, Rosemary A. 2005. "Archaeology of the Body." *Annual Review of Anthropology* 34:139–158.

———. 2007. "Embodied Subjectivity: Gender, Femininity, Masculinity, and Sexuality," in Meskell, Lynn, and Robert W. Pruecel (eds.), *A Companion to Social Archaeology*. Oxford: Blackwell, pp. 82–95.

Karklins, Karlis. 1985. *Glass Beads: The Nineteenth-Century Levin Catalogue and Venetian Bead Book and Guide to Description of Glass Beads*. Studies in Archaeology, Architecture, and History. Ottawa, Canada: Environment Parks Canada.

———. 1992. *Trade Ornament Usage among the Native Peoples of Canada: A Source Book*. Ottawa: Environment Parks Canada.

Keane, W. 2005. Signs Are Not The Garb of Meaning: On the Social Analysis of Material Things, in *Materiality*, D. Miller (ed.). Durham, NC: Duke University Press, pp. 182–205.

Kidd. Kenneth A., and Martha A. Kidd. 1970. "A Classification System for Glass Beads for the Use of Field Archaeologists." *Canadian Historic Sites: Occasional Papers in Archaeology and History* 1:45–89.

Le Page du Pratz, A. S. 1758. *L'Histoire de la Louisiane*. Available at http://darkwing.uoregon.edu/~gsayre/LPDP.html.

Le Page du Pratz, A. S. 1975. *The History of Louisiana* (English reprint of the 1774 original edition). Baton Rouge: Louisiana State University Press.

Liebersohn, Harry. 2001. *Aristocratic Encounters: European Travelers and North American Indians*. Cambridge: Cambridge University Press.

Lindman, Janet Moore, and Michele Lise Tarter. 2001. "The earthly frame, a minute Fabrick, a Centre of Wonders," in Lindman, Janet M., and Michele L. Tarter (eds.), *A Centre of Wonders: The Body in Early America*. Ithaca: Cornell University Press, pp. 1–9.

Loren, Diana DiPaolo. 2001. "Social Skins: Orthodoxies and Practices of Dressing in the Early Colonial Lower Mississippi Valley." *Journal of Social Archaeology* 1(2):172–189.

———. 2007 *In Contact: Bodies and Landscapes in the 16th and 17th-Century Eastern Woodlands*. Walnut Creek: Altamira Press.

———. 2008 "Beyond the Visual: Considering the Archaeology of Colonial Sounds." *International Journal of Historical Archaeology* 12(4):360–369.

———. 2010. *The Archaeology of Clothing and Bodily Adornment in Colonial America*. Gainesville: University Press of Florida.

———, and Mary C. Beaudry. 2006. "Becoming American: Small Things Remembered," in Silliman, Stephen W., and Martin Hall (eds.), *Historical Archaeology*. Oxford: Blackwell Press, pp. 251–271.

Merleau-Ponty, Maurice. 1989. *Phenomenology of Perception.* London: Routledge.

Meskell, Lynn. 1999. *Archaeologies of Social Life: Age, Sex, Class et cetera in Ancient Egypt.* Oxford: Blackwell.

———. 2004. "Divine Things," in DeMarrais, E., C. Gosden, and C. Renfrew (eds.), *Rethinking Materiality: The Engagement of the Mind with the Material World.* London: Oxbow Books, pp. 249–259.

Miller, D. 2005. *Materiality.* Durham, NC: Duke University Press.

Mississippi Provincial Archives, French Dominion [MPAFD]. 1929. *Volume 2, 1701–1729* (D. Rowland and A. G. Saunders, trans. and ed.). Jackson: Mississippi Department of Archives and History.

———. 1984. *Volume 4, 1729–1748* (D. Rowland and A. G. Saunders, trans. and ed.; Patricia K. Galloway, ed.). Baton Rouge: Louisiana State University Press.

Moore, Henrietta L. 1994. *A Passion for Difference: Essays in Anthropology and Gender.* Cambridge: Polity Press.

National Park Service. 2008. "Grand Village of the Natchez Indians." Available at http://www.nps.gov/history/NR/travel/mounds/gra.htm.

Neitzel, Robert S. 1983. *The Grand Village of the Natchez Revisited: Excavations of the Fatherland Site, Adams County, Mississippi, 1972.* Archaeological Report No. 12. Jackson: Mississippi Department of Archives and History.

———. 1965. *Archaeology of the Fatherland Site: The Grand Village of the Natchez,* Volume 51, Part 1. New York: Anthropological Papers of the American Museum of Natural History.

Orser, Charles E. 2007. *The Archaeology of Race and Racialization in Historic America.* Gainesville: University of Florida Press.

Pagden, Anthony. 1982. *The Fall of Natural Man: The American Indian and the Origins of Comparative Ethnology.* Cambridge: Cambridge University Press.

Phillips, Ruth B. 1998. *Trading Identities: The Souvenir in Native North American Art from the Northeast, 1700–1900.* Seattle: University of Washington Press.

Pinney, C. 2005. "Things Happen: Or, From Which Moment Does That Object Come?" in Miller, D. (ed.), *Materiality.* Durham, NC: Duke University Press, pp. 182–205.

Quimby, George I. 1966. *Indian Culture and European Trade Goods.* Madison: University of Wisconsin Press.

Roche, Daniel. 1994. *The Culture of Clothing: Dress and fashion in the "ancien régime."* Cambridge: Cambridge University Press.

Sala-Molins, Louis. 2006. *Dark Side of the Light: Slavery and the French Enlightenment.* Duluth: University of Minnesota Press.

Sayre, G. M. 2005. *The Indian Chief as Tragic Hero: Native Resistance and the Literatures of America, from Moctezuma to Tecumseh.* Chapel Hill: University of North Carolina Press

Shannon, Timothy J. 1996. "Dressing for Success on the Mohawk Frontier: Hendrick, William Johnson, and the Indian Fashion." *William and Mary Quarterly* 53:13–42.

Spear. Jennifer M. 2009. *Race, Sex, and Social Order in Early New Orleans.* Baltimore: John Hopkins University Press.

———. 2003. "Colonial Intimacies: Legislating Sex in French Louisiana." *The William and Mary Quarterly* 60: 75–98. Available at http://www.historycooperative.org/journals/wm/60.1/spear.html.

———. 1999. "'They Need Wives': Métissage and the Regulation of Sexuality in French Louisiana, 1699–1730," in Hodes, Martha (ed.), *Sex, Love, Race: Crossing Boundaries in North American History.* New York: New York University Press, pp. 35–59.

Stoler, Ann Laura. 2001. "Tense and Tender Ties: The Politics of Comparison in North American History and Colonial Studies," *The Journal of American History* 88(3):829–865.

Swanton, J. R. 1911. *Indian Tribes of the Lower Mississippi Valley and Adjacent Coast of Mexico.* Washington, DC: Bureau of American Ethnology Bulletin 43, Smithsonian Institution.

Thomas, Brian W. 2002. "Struggling with the Past: Some Views of African American Identity." *International Journal of Historical Archaeology* 6(2):143–151.

Turgeon, Laurier. 2006. "The Cartier Voyages to Canada (1534–1542) and the Beginnings of French Colonialism in North America," in Rothstein, Marian (ed.), *Charting Change in France around 1540*. Mount Carmel, PA: Susquehanna University Press, pp. 97–118.

———. 2004. "Beads, Bodies and Regimes of Value: From France to North America, c. 1500–c. 1650," in Murray, Tim (ed.), *The Archaeology of Contact in Settler Societies*. Cambridge: Cambridge University Press, pp. 19–47.

———. 2001. "French Beads in France and Northeastern North America during the Sixteenth Century." *Historical Archaeology* 35(4):58–82.

Usner, D. H. 1992. *Indians, Settlers and Slaves in a Frontier Exchange Economy: The Lower Mississippi Valley before 1783*. Chapel Hill: University of North Carolina Press.

———. 2003. *American Indians in the Lower Mississippi Valley: Social and Economic Histories*. Lincoln: University of Nebraska Press.

Voss, Barbara L. 2008. " 'Poor people in silk shirts': Dress and Ethnogenesis in Spanish-Colonial San Francisco." *Journal of Social Archaeology* 8(3):404–432.

Weiner, A. 1985. "Inalienable Wealth." *American Ethnologist* 12:210–217.

———, and J. Schneider (eds.). 1989. *Cloth and Human Experience*. Washington, DC: Smithsonian Institution Press.

White, Carolyn. 2005. *American Artifacts of Personal Adornment, 1680–1820: A Guide to Identification and Interpretation*. Walnut Creek, CA: Altamira Press.

White, Sophie. 2003. "'Wearing three or four handkerchiefs around his collar, and elsewhere about him': Slave's Constructions of Masculinity and Ethnicity in French Colonial New Orleans." *Gender and History* 15(3):528–549.

Wilkie, Laurie A. 1995. "Magic and Empowerment on the Plantation: An Archaeological Consideration of African-American worldview." *Southeastern Archaeology* 14(2):136–157.

———. 1997. "Secret and Sacred: Contextualizing the Artifacts of African-American Magic and Religion." *Historical Archaeology* 31(4):81–106.

Wilson, E. 2003. *Adorned in Dreams: Fashion and Modernity*. New Brunswick: Rutgers University Press.

EIGHT

DEATH AND SEX

Procreation in the Wake of Fatal Epidemics within Indigenous Communities

Kathleen L. Hull

Engagement of indigenous people in the enterprise of European colonialism in the Americas is usually conceived as part of a process that transpired wholly within the sphere of direct interaction between native and nonnative people. Yet anthropological focus on economic relationships with fur traders, native labor in the fields and mines of a world system, or voluntary or forced participation of indigenous people in religious missions may overlook potentially profound social effects elsewhere. Native social change initiated by the colonial venture also occurred within traditional indigenous communities located in areas at great distances from colonists and in situations that entailed little or no direct interaction with Europeans. In addition, the changes in these settings involved not only economic, political, or ideological shifts but also likely encompassed diverse social interactions within groups, including challenges to, or changes in, the intimate relationships and sexual practices of indigenous people.

Such shifts may be anticipated, in part, because of native catastrophic depopulation brought about by down-the-line transmission of introduced Old World diseases and resultant fatal epidemics. That is, sexual practices may have been altered to respond to the reproductive priorities supported by such liaisons. Still, the renegotiation of sexual roles, mores, and practices within native communities of the colonial hinterland remains unexplored, even as the sexual and reproductive consequences of colonialism in institutional settings or across landscapes that were physically or socially dominated by European interlopers have been at least initially examined by anthropological archaeologists, especially with respect to intermarriage (e.g., Deagan 1983; Lightfoot et al. 1998; Voss 2008; Woodhouse-Beyer 1999). Given the scale of population decline within native communities during the colonial era and, especially, the initiation of such processes in areas beyond the view of literate observers, it is important for archaeologists to turn their attention to this arena of the colonial "encounter" as well and explore the social and cultural consequences that such events may have precipitated. To understand the subsequent course of native cultural resistance or change expressed in sexual encounters with European people, we must first appreciate the challenges already faced and modifications already underway within these communities before face-to-face interaction.

To initiate such discussion, this analysis draws on archaeological research from interior California and thus begins with a brief review of the cultural context of indigenous life and procreation in colonial North America. The specific issue of sexual consequences in the wake of fatal epidemics is then considered in terms of anthropological expectations and general analytical needs in approaching the question of sexual relations engaged in for the purpose of procreation, with particular emphasis on small-scale foraging societies. Finally, these expectations are assessed through an archaeological case study of the Awahnichi, who experienced substantial disease-induced population decline approximately fifty years before face-to-face engagement with nonnative people in their traditional territory in the Yosemite region of California's Sierra Nevada. As this study illustrates, many traditional practices that structured intimate relationships between native men and women were resistant to change, despite significant demographic and social challenges. Ethnohistoric data, however, also suggest that certain adjustments in marriage practices, at least, may have been made in light of the new reality of colonial-era life. As a result, this case study provides some perspective on choices made by native people in more traditional colonial settings and the potential consequences of forced change in such practices within institutional colonial contexts in other times or places, with repercussions for both biological and social survival.

This study articulates well with the notion of "affective relationships" adopted elsewhere in this volume (see Voss, Chapter 2, this volume) because it is theoretically informed in part by my recent efforts to reconceptualize the demography of small-scale societies as the objectification of intimate practice and personal relations rather than as the outcome of macroeconomic processes (Hull 2011). Similarly, my understanding of culture change rooted in such routine acts draws on Bourdieu's (1977) concepts of practice and habitus. Unlike some other contributors to this volume (e.g., Croucher, Chapter 5, this volume), however, my focus is on practice in which physiological bodies are the material consequence rather than the materiality of iterative performance common to most archaeological applications of Bourdieu (1977). Thus, this study remains attentive to the role of perception (see Hull 2005) in the potential to reconceive sexual unions in practice. The application of somewhat unconventional archaeological methodology to reconstruct indigenous demographic change brings new understanding to concrete acts of social reproduction.

THE COLONIAL CONTEXT OF NATIVE AMERICAN REPRODUCTION

The geography of colonial-era indigenous North America and the social context of biological reproduction therein encompasses diverse people and traditions, from small-scale, residentially mobile hunting and gathering societies typical of many groups who lived west of the Rocky Mountains to large-scale, hierarchical societies of the Southeast who practiced agriculture and resided in permanent villages. Just as economic and social organization varied, so, too, did customs pertaining to individual behavior and intimate relations. As a result, few general statements regarding practices germane to biological reproduction can be offered, other than to note that both social and biological factors likely worked together to keep populations in check in all such societies because there is little or no archaeological evidence for significant population growth or environmental degradation tied to overpopulation in the decades leading up to colonial encounters. Therefore, the introduction of lethal pathogens within indigenous communities in the decades and centuries following the Columbian landfall – occurring in some areas as early as the mid-1500s and in others delayed until the late 1700s – would have posed significant challenges to the social and biological viability of many native groups.

This was true even in native California, despite the fact that the aboriginal population is estimated to have exceeded 133,000 individuals (Cook 1978: 91). At the time Spanish missionaries established the first permanent European colonial outpost on the California coast in 1776, the landscape of native life included peoples speaking diverse languages who largely maintained their community identity at the level of the village cluster (or "tribelet") rather than within larger, more abstract integrative units based on geography, language, customs, or some combination of such features. In addition, there were often additional divisions within tribelets that structured social relations, including marriage customs. Thus, sexual practices germane to procreation and group sustainability were defined at a local level, and interactions between groups simultaneously created a web of social and economic relationships that stretched well beyond any one tribelet.

The Awahnichi were one such group (Figure 8.1), taking their name from Awahnee, the valley known today as Yosemite. Although it is difficult to define the full suite of Awahnichi cultural practices before the influence or infiltration of nonnative people in the central Sierra Nevada, an unusually rich combination of ethnographic and ethnohistoric data paint a picture of life for several hundred native people inhabiting approximately fifteen small villages in Yosemite Valley. For the group as a whole, two moieties were recognized and exogamous marriage between individuals of these two divisions was the custom (Levy 1978; Perlot 1985: 232). Marriage appears to have been entered into freely by both men and women, although there is evidence that marriage was sometimes used a means to forge alliances or seen as a partnership underwriting the economic security made possible for both parties through the division of domestic labor (Bunnell 1990: 260; Clark 1907: 52; Perlot 1985: 232) rather than simply as an expression of emotional or physical attraction. In any case, procreation seems to have been at least one aim of marriage by the mid-1800s, if not before, and Perlot (1985: 232) notes that decisions on the timing of unions and number of wives took reproductive success into account. Ethnohistoric data also suggest possible preference for the birth of children in the spring or summer – which, in turn, could indicate some regulation of sexual intercourse even within marriage – although this might be a postcontact phenomenon (Perlot 1985: 230). Data on sexual unions outside of marriage is less clear, although it is likely that both consensual and nonconsensual unions occurred.

In the scope of North American colonial encounters, the Awahnichi represent remarkably late influence of both epidemic disease and nonnative lifeways. Physical incursion into their traditional territory did not occur until the early 1850s, spurred

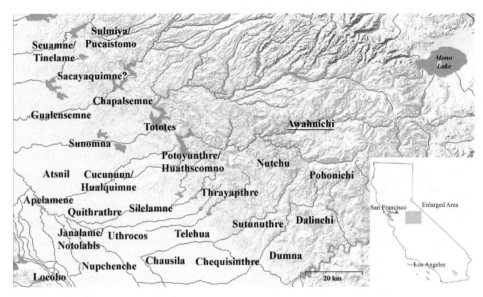

FIGURE 8.1. Contact-era native communities of the Yosemite region and adjoining areas to the west (adapted from Milliken 2006).

by the influx of miners into the neighboring foothills to the west during the Gold Rush. Still, native oral history recorded in 1851 indicates that the intrusion of non-native disease arrived as much as 60 years earlier in the form of a fatal epidemic that resulted in significant local population loss. Given the timing and geography of colonial occupation within California, the introduction of nonnative disease among the Awahnichi represents down-the-line transmission of disease into the mountains, because the nearest Spanish mission was located more than 250 kilometers to the west at San Francisco Bay. Unlike many other areas of North America, then, the consequences of lethal pathogens were dealt with by the Awahnichi in an environment free from the physical, economic, or religious entanglements typical of many other areas. Still the distant effects of the colonial presence made life during the early to mid-1800s a time of social turmoil that ultimately came to encompass additional threats to survival and economic entanglements with nonnative people typical of other regions of the continent.

DEMOGRAPHIC CATASTROPHE AND SEXUAL CONSEQUENCES

Catastrophic mortality due to introduced Old World diseases was often one of the first effects of European colonization on many indigenous peoples of the Americas. Study of the timing and magnitude of colonial-era native population decline due to fatal epidemics has been the focus of both historical and archaeological research for more than fifty years and, more recently, the subject of often intense debate (e.g., Dobyns 1966, 1983, 1991; Henige 1998, 2008; Hull 2009; Livi-Bacci 2006; Ramenofsky 1987, 1990; Ramenofsky et al. 2003; Thornton 1987, 1997, 2000; Ubelaker 1992, 2000). Although estimates of relative decline vary, native mortality exceeding 90 percent of the total continental population has been suggested due to successive fatal epidemics, including exposure to pathogens such as smallpox, measles, and influenza (e.g., Dobyns 1983; Ramenofsky 1987). At a minimum, epidemiological information indicates mortality of at least 25 percent within a population subject to a virgin-soil outbreak of an introduced disease such smallpox (e.g., Bianchine and Russo 1995; Ramenofsky 1987, 1993, 1996; Ramenofsky et al. 2003). In addition, historical and archaeological data reveal that such fatal pathogens may have been introduced into some native populations many years or even decades in advance of face-to-face contact between native and nonnative people (e.g., Dobyns 1983; Hull 2009; Ramenofsky 1987). Therefore, significant cultural changes may have been well underway or already firmly established in practice by the time of physical incursion of Europeans into traditional native territories.

Regardless of the specific timing or even the exact magnitude of virgin-soil epidemics and likely subsequent waves of Old World diseases, the scale of mortality within many affected groups was probably sufficient to result in profound biological, cultural, and psychological consequences for the survivors, as indicated by both archaeological and ethnohistoric data from throughout the Americas. Unlike colonial institutional settings, however, native decision making in wake of fatal epidemics oftentimes played out in an environment free from the direct involvement of colonists. Therefore, these contexts reflect internal choice rather than external dictate and may reveal deeply held beliefs about sexual intimacy, including those practices particularly resistant to change. Potential cultural consequences of colonial-era catastrophic depopulation included population aggregation, emigration, creolization and ethnogenesis, changes in external relations, decreased diversity in cultural practices, despecialization, and simplification of social structure (Hull 2009). These choices, in turn, likely necessitated a renegotiation, or at least a critical examination, of many related beliefs and practices, such as sexual taboos, reproductive and non-reproductive sexual activity, and marriage customs, as individuals sought to rebuild biologically viable communities or create new social groups. Such adjustments may have been particularly acute when individuals of different cultural traditions came together to forge such communities.

Archaeological assessment of these colonial-era processes is challenging both in terms of recognizing the timing and magnitude of such demographic events and in determining the cultural consequences, especially with respect to intimate relations. Fine-grained temporal data may be lacking, and preservation of human remains most suitable for establishing the broadest suite of demographic parameters may be poor. Such analysis also necessitates a solid understanding of the demographic and social circumstances in the decades, centuries, and millennia leading up to the time nonnative disease struck, so that the prior experience and, perhaps, "preadaptation" of groups to significant oscillations in population size can be taken into account in interpretation. That is, a long-term view of native life, rather than simply knowledge of the colonial era, is required to assess whether and how cultural practices may have changed (e.g., Lightfoot 1995). For an agent-based approach relevant to intimate relations, it is also useful to have some means to assess the cultural consequences of decision making and more clearly reveal the communal and personal stakes in any given situation. Fortunately, the quantitative aspect of demographic data allows for use of computer simulations that enhance such interpretation (e.g., Gaines and Gaines 1997).

With these analytical goals and strategies in mind, a useful starting point for assessment of changing intimate relations in the wake of colonial-era epidemics is anthropological demography in general, with particular focus on marriage practices. In contemporary demographic analyses, "marriage" is convenient shorthand for sexual activity for the purpose of procreation. Although useful for the quantitative approach of demographers who often must rely on civic records, conflating reproductive sexual activity and the social institution of marriage is clearly problematic for an anthropological analysis. Such shorthand mislabels or ignores myriad practices with implications for biological reproduction, including nonconsensual sex and sexual activity outside of marriage for the purpose of procreation. In addition, it also overlooks the fact that some marriage partners may have been infertile, but marriages nonetheless were maintained. Thus, the discussion here attempts to go beyond the literal confines of marriage, although given the relative paucity of ethnohistoric or ethnographic data on the significance of premarital or extramarital sexual activity to biological reproduction within Native American groups, a focus on marriage may not be entirely misplaced. This is especially true with respect to the Awahnichi, given ethnohistoric information on marriage practices and the apparent significance of procreation to such unions.

Envisioned in the simplest terms, the biological viability of a closed population depends on a positive balance between fertility and mortality, although age-specific – rather than simply overall – fertility and mortality are important to this equation. Studies of extant small-scale foraging societies have demonstrated that population growth rates reflecting this balance are extremely low (see Hull 2009: 140–144). What we know of long-term human history from archaeology further supports the fact that population growth rates were likely modest in most times and places. Thus, fertility and mortality were evidently in relative equilibrium in many such populations, and colonial-era catastrophic mortality would have had a devastating short-term – and perhaps even long-term – effect. Although high mortality in virgin-soil conditions would be limited to a relatively brief, intense spike, the effect would be spread across individuals of all ages. That is, death would not be limited to just the very young and old, as is typical in normal circumstances, but would also encompass individuals of childbearing age if an epidemic was not a second or subsequent wave of a pathogen to which the adult population had already acquired immunity. Therefore, lethal epidemics had negative consequences for native population stability or growth both in terms of mortality and fertility, because short-term reproductive capacity was also undermined.

From a purely mathematical perspective, swift regeneration of a population to predisease size would only occur as a result of augmentation of the population through immigration (i.e., opening a closed population) or through increased fertility. In the latter case, fertility would need to exceed greatly that prevailing before depopulation, at least in the short-term. If low growth within a group before substantial depopulation had been maintained through a high-fertility and high-mortality regime – that is, reproductive capacity was already pushed to the limit – then achievement of even greater fertility might prove especially challenging or impossible.

If, however, low growth was the product of a low-fertility and low-mortality regime, then significant enhancement of reproductive capacity through either biological or cultural means might be possible. In fact, exceptionally high fertility might be anticipated in either type of population in the short-term if women had lost unweaned children to disease and female fecundity improved in the resulting absence of lactation amenorrhea. In either scenario (i.e., high or low fertility before catastrophic depopulation), mortality rates would have to return to predisease conditions or better, and decline in mortality for women of childbearing age would be particularly important. In the longer term, population recovery would be facilitated by improved survival of the young, recognized by demographers via increasing expectation of life at birth. This is so because girls born in the wake of fatal epidemics would need to survive to reproductive age to contribute to population rebound. It is not enough to have high fertility and low mortality of adult women in the short term if this is accompanied by continued high mortality of infants and prepubescent girls, as would prevail with subsequent waves of a fatal disease. In light of these observations, the social value of female children might increase in the wake of depopulation (see Tarble de Scaramelli, Chapter 9, this volume), but the social and sexual "burden" to women in such circumstances also would be significant. Furthermore, there might be lasting social implications for the role of women within society as a result of this, at first temporary, measure (see Meyers 1978), even as the biological significance of individual female reproductive capacity declined with population rebound.

Age-specific and overall fertility rates within a population depend on biological and cultural factors operating simultaneously at either the individual or group level. For example, female fecundity is affected by health, nutrition, and lactation, and the total number of fecund females within a population directly affects maximum population growth given the reproductive capacity of humans. Exposure to deadly pathogens would not only reduce the number of fecund women through death but also might compromise the reproductive health of those women of childbearing age who survived. Cultural influences on individual and group fertility rates include age at first marriage or other social sanction of initiation of sexual activity for females, postpartum and other reasons for periodic or prolonged sexual abstinence, and proscriptions on remarriage after the death of a spouse. In addition, cultural practices such as endogamy, exogamy, and rules defining incestuous relationships influence the available pool of potential sexual partners. In the aftermath of catastrophic depopulation, some or all of these practices might be significant inhibitors to population viability, so changes in practices with direct bearing on sexual relations and concomitant societal norms might be instituted. Therefore, the cultural rather than biological factors facilitating increased fertility will be further considered here.

Age at first marriage or participation in sexual activity with the potential to result in offspring affects the reproductive potential of women over the course of a lifetime. Fecund females marrying or otherwise engaging in coitus at a younger age have the potential to produce more offspring, whereas those fecund women initiating such activity at an older age will have proportionally fewer children during their lives if societal norms for postpartum sexual behavior, breast-feeding, parity-dependent fertility, or other practices pertain equally to all women. The ability to remarry after the death of a spouse is critical for the same reason, because widowhood effectively cuts short the reproductive potential of younger wives, in particular, if proscriptions on reproductive sexual activity outside of marriage existed for widows. Thus, in the wake of catastrophic depopulation, we might anticipate that younger age at marriage or other reproductive sexual activity of females, at least, would be tolerated or even encouraged if additional postpubescent females were sexually available via such means – that is, if predisease practices did not already encompass all females of childbearing age. Although not related to procreation, male sexual liaisons with younger girls might also be tolerated by the community or engaged in without sanction if male mortality due to disease was significantly less than female mortality. Similarly, female remarriage or remarriage to a partner other than one previously sanctioned (e.g., levirate, sororate, or, in stratified societies, persons of the same social status) might be permitted among the survivors. Such shifts in either age at marriage or potential to remarry might be favored if population rebound was deemed important to individuals, households, or the group; if women needed the social or economic security that a marital relationship with a man might bring; or if surviving men were simply in need of a wife for either domestic responsibilities or intimate relations.

In addition to those changes that would maximize the fertility of individual females by lengthening the span of sexual activity over a lifetime, increased fertility could also be encouraged via other means that allowed marriages under conditions in which building sexual unions would otherwise be difficult or impossible. In this case, previously existing rules defining appropriate partners might be ignored, relaxed, or permanently altered, including changing proscriptions on endogamy, exogamy, polygamy, or incest (for the purposes of this discussion, the latter is limited to sexual relations potentially resulting in offspring; see Leavitt 2007: 409). Catastrophic mortality within small-scale societies would clearly undermine endogamous marriage and might lead survivors to look elsewhere for willing or unwilling mates. Among the Iroquoian-speaking peoples of interior northeastern North America, for example, incorporation of women from neighboring groups was apparently an intentional strategy to rebuild decimated populations (Snow 1996; see also Stewart 2001). Catastrophic depopulation might also undermine exogamous marriage practices, if such unions were based on individual affiliation with a smaller social unit within a population such as a moiety. In fact, exogamy might be a particular challenge under the latter conditions, even more so than endogamy, because the potential pool of partners would be especially small. Conversely, if exogamous relations extended to neighboring groups, especially those relatively unaffected by epidemic disease, population rebound might not be quite so difficult. Polygamy would facilitate population rebound in those cases in which adult male mortality exceeded female mortality or female fecundity was adversely affected by disease (i.e., infertility of an existing wife), whereas polygamy might also be instituted in some societies if progenitor of certain male lines was deemed especially important by individuals or the group. Given the ubiquity of incest taboos cross-culturally, it is unlikely that incest proscriptions based on close genetic relationships would be ignored (cf. Leavitt 2007) even under the dire prospects of colonial-era native population decline. Still, it is possible that taboos on marriage between certain surviving affines – previously considered incestuous – might be lifted.

Finally, if population recovery at the household or group level was sought, proscriptions on periodic sexual abstinence within or beyond marriage might also be eased or abolished. In addition, parity-dependent fertility might no longer be relevant, because couples would opt to maximize fertility rather than seek an optimum family size. Thus, sexual activity for the purpose of procreation might be engaged in more frequently or at times not previously permitted, at least until conception was confirmed. Given that many surviving women of childbearing age might have lost unweaned infants to disease, however, increased sexual activity in the immediate aftermath of epidemics would probably result in higher than average reproductive success if disease had not compromised fertility. This is so because lactation amenorrhea would no longer be a factor adversely affecting fecundity. A related option might be to decrease birth spacing to facilitate quicker rebound, if the connection between breast-feeding and fecundity was recognized.

Whether altered by shifts in marriage practices, definitions of identity facilitating unions, or frequency of sexual activity (especially coitus), this review suggests that the landscape of intimate relations in the aftermath of catastrophic depopulation likely entailed a challenge to or radical rethinking of traditional beliefs and even the mythical or practical rationale underlying such beliefs. The social and sexual burden to women would be especially significant, because the means to population recovery lay in their bodies and their care. Although women might be more valued within communities under such circumstances, it is also possible that younger girls would be expected to engage in sexual relations for the purpose of procreation or that women of childbearing age would be threatened with sexual aggression by men outside of the community if attempts were made to enhance individual or group fertility through capture of mates. As detailed above, possible options included (1) earlier age at first marriage or participation in reproductive sexual activity, in general, by females; (2) enabling remarriage, including remarriage to those not previously identified as appropriate spouses; (3) allowing marriage with outsiders other than those previously sanctioned; (4) polygamy; (5) changes in incest taboos; and (6) abandonment of proscriptions on sexual abstinence. Any or all of these solutions might have been envisioned as necessary short-term remedies, without any intent for permanent change. Therefore, underlying beliefs may have gone relatively unchallenged. Once instituted, however, it is possible that practices could not be reversed or were not reversed before direct encounters with colonists, possibly leading to social instability as erosion of these traditional practices became institutionalized. In addition, such shifts may have secondary effects in precipitating subsequent sexual relations with Europeans. For example, the breakdown of endogamous marriage or moiety exogamy might have facilitated later intermarriage with nonnative men. Conversely, rigid adherence to other sexual proscriptions by the survivors of epidemics such as age at first marriage might have actually necessitated unions with colonists or other outsiders. Thus, the sexual politics of some colonial settings may have had their roots in significant demographic events that often preceded such encounters. Finally, as noted earlier, cultural adjustments rooted in demographic recovery may have placed native women in more limited domestic or sexual roles that persisted or were reinforced within traditional colonial settings into which native people were later incorporated.

AWAHNICHI CASE STUDY

Ethnohistoric, archaeological, and dendrochronological evidence indicate that a fatal epidemic decimated the Awahnichi of Yosemite Valley in the late 1790s (Hull 2009). This event was recounted in 1851 by Chief Tenaya, who described a "black sickness" that so reduced the native population that survivors temporarily relocated to the territory of Paiute people living east of Yosemite at Mono Lake (Bunnell 1990, Figure 8.1). Tenaya's father was one of the survivors, and Tenaya himself had been born of a Paiute mother during the self-imposed exile of the Awahnichi from their traditional territory. Eventually, Tenaya led his people back to their ancestral home in the western Sierra Nevada and ultimately forged a new community that came to encompass both Awahnichi descendants and others (Hull 2009). Tree-ring dating of conifer stands in Yosemite Valley documents the temporary cessation of aboriginal burning during the absence of native occupation, and archaeological investigations have both confirmed the timing of this event and demonstrated the relative magnitude of colonial-era population decline.

Archaeological study of this colonial-era demographic event was based on a temporally unbiased random sample of archaeological sites within Yosemite Valley (Hull 2009). This sampling provided in a long-term population profile spanning the past 5,500 years of use in the region, based on two proxy measures of population developed from archaeological data. The first proxy was based on debitage frequency through time, and the other was subsite frequency, a measure of habitation site frequency adjusted for site size. Nearly three thousand obsidian hydration dates supporting the temporal placement of population proxies were derived using a temperature-dependent rate for Casa Diablo obsidian (Hull 2001), the most common lithic material used by the native inhabitants of Yosemite Valley for the manufacture of flaked stone tools. Correspondence of proxy data with models of resource use for abundant (i.e., lithic) versus limited (i.e., land) resources, careful consideration of formation processes potentially affecting the relationship of each proxy measure to population size, and strong positive covariation of the two indices provided confidence in the population trends revealed (Hull 2009, 2011). The debitage proxy data, which are more sensitive to population change than subsite frequency (see Hull 2009), indicated that the Awahnichi population declined at least 25 percent as a result of the "black sickness," which struck in the 1790s (Figure 8.2). Although not as substantial as that posited elsewhere in the Americas on the basis of ethnohistoric data (e.g., Dobyns 1983) or indicated by general epidemiological studies (e.g., Ramenofsky 1987; Ramenofsky et al. 2003), this loss of life was nonetheless devastating, because the initial population was relatively small at the time disease struck. In fact, the Awahnichi may have numbered no more than three hundred individuals in the mid-1700s and, thus, the population declined to approximately two hundred people as a result of exposure to one or more lethal pathogens.

Spanning several millennia, the long-term population data revealed that this small size was due to a previous significant population decline that occurred between 500 and 1350 CE. This decline brought about a population nadir that had no equal in the previous four thousand years of occupation, and the Awahnichi had managed only very slow population growth from this nadir in the two centuries before the

infiltration of nonnative disease. In contrast, significant population rebound – perhaps as much as 100 percent – occurred after the colonial-era population decima-
tion, with such recovery likely facilitated first by intermarriage with neighboring
Mono Paiute people and, later, by immigration of and intermarriage with native
people from elsewhere (Hull 2009).

Although changing sexual practices may also have contributed to colonial-era population recovery, the long-term view of native demography suggests that marriage
or other practices potentially affecting biological reproduction were particularly
resistant to reformation even in times of apparent demographic crisis. This is indicated especially by the slow recovery following the decline around 1350 CE, which
suggests that no dramatic efforts were made to spur population growth through any
available means, including changes in sexual unions. That is, fertility was similar to
that evident in earlier times, despite the demographic crisis that such a small population may have presented. The likely contribution of immigrants to population
rebound during the colonial era makes it difficult to determine to what extent this
recovery was facilitated by changes in sexual practices such as earlier age at first
marriage or abandonment of sexual abstinence. However, the very incorporation
of outsiders into the population revealed by both ethnohistoric and archaeological data – including the appearance of one form of serrated projectile point with
antecedents in California's Central Valley (Hull 2004, 2009) – suggests the potential
for changes in marriage practices at least with respect to spouse selection, unlike
during the pre-colonial era.

Additional assessment of possible changes in Awahnichi social practices with direct
bearing on procreation during the colonial era was facilitated by more detailed
examination of the demographic data beyond population growth rates (Hull 2009).
The long-term population profile revealed that the Awahnichi experienced low
growth typical of small foraging societies throughout their history. In fact, the population growth rate was near zero for most of the past 5,500 years and never exceeded
0.001619 (i.e., 1.6 persons per 1,000 individuals per year) except when spurred by
immigration such as that following colonial-era population loss. Quantitative analysis
of female fertility underlying such low growth was possible given the mathematical
relationship between population growth rate, gross reproduction rate (number of
daughters per woman in the absence of mortality), probability of survival from birth
to the average age of childbearing for females, and an estimate of the average length
of a generation. Using estimates of expectation of life at birth ranging from eighteen
to thirty years derived from cross-cultural ethnographic data, analysis indicated that
Awahnichi women likely gave birth to four to six children over the course of their
lives (i.e., total fertility rate of four to six).

Based in part on these estimates, analysis further indicated only a 30 to 47 percent chance of survival to childbearing age for those cohorts of Awahnichi women
affected by the colonial-era epidemic. Thus, the potential pool of reproductive
females was severely compromised, and the older women among the survivors may
not have had the reproductive capacity in their remaining childbearing years to
reestablish families of the size typical before the epidemic. In fact, the radical drop
in expectation of life at birth that accompanied the epidemic suggested that the
"capacity to maintain post-disease population size – let alone recover to pre-disease

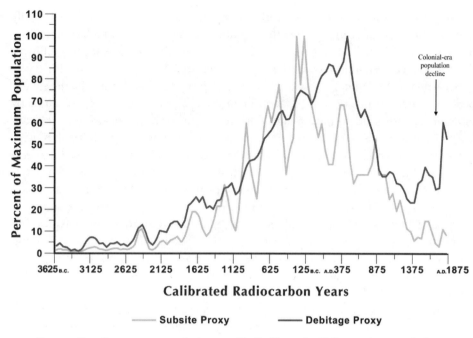

FIGURE 8.2. Long-term population profile for Yosemite Valley native population.

population size – would have been virtually impossible . . . [and] augmentation of the Yosemite Indian population from outside was necessary to maintain a viable population" (Hull 2009: 146). Population recovery would have been further exacerbated if all of the surviving women of childbearing age were not considered suitable partners – that is, if cultural proscriptions on first age at marriage, remarriage, or other practices existed and were maintained in the wake of disease. However, the data suggested that similar poor survivorship for females of reproductive age had likely prevailed at various times between 550 and 1325 CE, and thus, the colonial-era situation was not unique. Therefore, during the colonial era the Awahnichi were facing challenges and decisions that their ancestors had also faced.

Given the small initial population size at the time disease struck and resulting dire circumstances in the wake of fatal disease, computer simulations suggest that intermarriage (or access to fecund females and resulting offspring via other means) may have been the only viable option for swift population recovery or, even, population viability. Such simulations determine demographic outcomes under different rules for marriage, given a known or postulated schedule of age-specific fertility, mortality, and population age structure. Although age-specific fertility and mortality figures could not be developed for the Awahnichi based on the archaeological methods employed, simulations suggested that a group of three hundred individuals with the midrange fertility, midrange mortality, and low growth typical of the precolonial Awahnichi would probably have been viable for less than five hundred years following catastrophic depopulation if few or no restrictions on unions existed. If cultural proscriptions such as exogamy existed, however, the simulations indicated that population viability would be even shorter lived. Thus, abandonment of exogamy would help the situation. Conversely, simulations suggested that easing incest restrictions would have relatively little impact, although the simulations did not specifically address the issue of affines rather than genetic relatives. Minor stochastic fluctuations in vital rates typical of small populations would add even greater instability to the colonial-era situation (see Gaines and Gaines 1997).

Because the Awahnichi chose to relocate and intermarry with their Paiute neighbors, we might conclude that female fertility was already pushed to the limit by biological conditions, cultural means, or both. Conversely, the decision to relocate might have been based on their commitment to (or inability to perceive alteratives to) existing marriage practices that effectively kept fertility in check. Comparison of the Awahnichi with other historic preindustrial populations and modern hunter-gatherers allows general assessment of these two alternatives. Analysis indicated that the Awahnichi maintained low growth under normal (i.e., nonepidemic) conditions because of a midrange fertility and mortality regime. Moreover, given the typical fertility rates – below the total fertility rate identified even within some extant foraging groups or historical preindustrial societies – it appeared that significantly greater fertility was possible for the Awahnichi, if biological factors undermining fecundity did not intervene. Importantly, the relative stability in expectation of life at birth over the 5,500-year span further suggested that low growth was maintained, in part, through cultural proscriptions on marriage and perhaps other sexual unions with reproductive potential. It may be that the Awahnichi were unconcerned with population recovery – a mind-set perhaps more typical of decision making driven by macroeconomic imperatives than affective relationships – or else the decision to relocate reflected a desire by survivors to maintain traditional marriage or other practices pertaining to procreation, despite the potentially adverse consequences for long-term population survival that such a decision entailed. In either case, these practices were so important or so embedded in practice that survivors opted for temporary exile and intermarriage with others, with this latter practice perhaps representing the only cultural "concession" to the predicament in which they found themselves. Although they may have been unwilling to compromise their beliefs and were reluctant to abandon traditional ways, ethnographic data from the early twentieth century also suggest that beliefs such as moiety exogamy were held onto more in thought than rigidly adhered to in practice (e.g., Gifford 1926).

CONCLUSION

Although it is difficult to quantitatively or even qualitatively assess changes in intimate relations with archaeological data, anthropological demography suggests a host of potential modifications in procreative sexual practices that could have followed from catastrophic depopulation within indigenous communities in North America and elsewhere during the colonial era. These include allowing earlier age at first marriage, remarriage, marriage to outsiders, and polygamy, as well as possible changes in incest taboos or abandonment of proscriptions on periodic sexual abstinence or initiation of female sexual activity following puberty. Under conditions of severely reduced population, changes in practices relevant to sexual unions in the wake of epidemics could have had a potentially profound impact on the pace of population recovery, whereas reconfiguring incest taboos might have had little to no significance. Agent-based demographic modeling of small-scale societies has demonstrated both the vulnerability of such populations to demographic shocks as well as the importance of different marriage practices to long-term biological viability. Further application of such methods can augment archaeological data and thus contribute substantially to more thorough consideration of demographic, social, and sexual consequences of indirect colonial "encounters" in the hinterlands.

Given the long-term perspective on native demography provided by the Awahnichi case study, however, it appears that the more radical of these cultural solutions to substantial population loss may not have been instituted. Population aggregation and intermarriage with outsiders were the first (and perhaps only) choice, and this may or may not have even necessitated a redefinition of sexual roles or group identities, depending on the nature of existing intergroup relations. This case may be particularly extreme, however, given the small size of the initial population. That is, even radical shifts might not have accomplished the goal of population recovery for the Awahnichi. In a less extreme situation, such as that prevailing with a somewhat higher initial population, internal adjustments such as younger age at first marriage or changes in remarriage might have been sufficient to allow recovery, although certain groups also raided other native communities for mates. The long-term view of Awahnichi demography also suggests that population recovery was not a sufficiently high priority in either the colonial era or in earlier times to warrant a realignment of priorities. That is, unlike colonists who often viewed their own low population as a problem to be solved and native bodies as commodities to be used, produced, or least maintained for the service of others, no such imperative is evident among the Awahnichi. Instead, social reproduction via the maintenance of cultural traditions was as much, if not more, important than biological reproduction to indigenous people. At the same time, the willingness of both native men and women to enter into unions with outsiders may be especially enlightening in understanding the subsequent involvement of native women, in particular, in sexual relationships with nonnative men in many regions of the Americas.

REFERENCES

Bianchine, Peter J., and Thomas A. Russo. 1995. "The Role of Epidemic Infectious Diseases in the Discovery of America," in Settipane, Guy A. (ed.), *Columbus and the New World: medical implications*. Providence, RI: Oceanside Publications, pp. 11–18.

Bourdieu, Pierre. 1977. *Outline of a Theory of Practice*. Cambridge Studies in Social and Cultural Anthropology. Cambridge: Cambridge University Press.

Bunnell, Lafayette H. 1990. *Discovery of the Yosemite, and the Indian War of 1851, Which Led to That Event*. Yosemite National Park, CA: Yosemite Association. Reprint of fourth edition, originally published 1911, Los Angeles: G. W. Gerlicher.

Clark, Galen. 1907. *Indians of the Yosemite Valley and Vicinity*. Yosemite Valley, CA: Galen Clark. Reprinted 1987, Walnut Creek, CA: Diablo Books.

Cook, Sherburne F. 1978. "Historical Demography," in Heizer, Robert F. (ed.), *California. Handbook of North American Indians, Vol. 8* (William C. Sturtevant, general ed.). Washington, DC: Smithsonian Institution, pp. 91–98.

Deagan, Kathleen A. 1983. *Spanish St. Augustine: The Archaeology of a Colonial Creole Community*. New York: Academic Press.

Dobyns, Henry F. 1966. "An Appraisal of Techniques for Estimating Aboriginal Population with a New Hemispheric Estimate." *Current Anthropology* 7(4):395–415.

_____. 1983. *Their Number Become Thinned: Native American Population Dynamics in Eastern North America.* Knoxville: University of Tennessee Press.

_____. 1991. "New Native World: Links between Demographic and Cultural Changes," in Thomas, David Hurst (ed.), *Columbian Consequences, Volume 3: The Spanish Borderlands in Pan-American Perspective.* Washington, DC: Smithsonian Institution Press, pp. 541–560.

Gaines, Sylvia W., and Warren M. Gaines. 1997. "Simulating Success or Failure: Another Look at Small-Population Dynamics." *American Antiquity* 62(4):683–697.

Gifford, Edward Winslow. 1926. "Miwok Lineages and the Political Unit in Aboriginal California." *American Anthropologist* 28(2):389–401.

Henige, David. 1998. *Numbers from Nowhere: The American Indian Contact Population Debate.* Norman: University of Oklahoma Press.

_____. 2008. "Recent Work and Prospects in American Indian Contact Population." *History Compass* 6(1):183–206.

Hull, Kathleen L. 2001. "Reasserting the Utility of Obsidian Hydration Dating: A Temperature-Dependent Empirical Approach to Practical Temporal Resolution with Archaeological Obsidians." *Journal of Archaeological Science* 28:1025–1040.

_____. 2004. "Emergent Cultural Traditions in the Central Sierra Nevada Foothills." *Society for California Archaeology Proceedings* 17:113–118.

_____. 2005. "Process, Perception, and Practice: Time Perspectivism in Yosemite Native Demography." *Journal of Anthropological Archaeology* 24:354–377.

_____. 2009. *Pestilence and Persistence: Yosemite Indian Demography and Culture in Colonial California.* Berkeley: University of California Press.

_____. 2011. "Thinking Small: Hunter-Gatherer Demography and Culture Change," in Sassaman, Kenneth E. and Donald H. Holly (eds.), *Hunter-Gatherer Archaeology as Historical Process.* Tucson: University of Arizona Press, pp. 34–54.

Leavitt, Gregory. 2007. "The Incest Taboo?: A Reconsideration of Westermarck." *Anthropological Theory* 7(4):393–419.

Levy, Richard. 1978. "Eastern Miwok," in Heizer, Robert F. (ed.), *California. Handbook of North American Indians, Vol. 8* (William C. Sturtevant, general ed.). Washington, DC: Smithsonian Institution, pp. 398–413.

Lightfoot, Kent G. 1995. "Culture Contact Studies: Redefining the Relationship between Prehistoric and Historical Archaeology." *American Antiquity* 60(2):199–217.

_____, Antoinette Martinez, and Ann M. Schiff. 1998. "Daily Practice and Material Culture in Pluralistic Social Settings: An Archaeological Study of Culture Change and Persistence from Fort Ross, California." *American Antiquity* 63:199–222.

Livi-Bacci, Massimo. 2006. "The Depopulation of Hispanic America after the Conquest." *Population and Development Review* 32(2):1–34.

Meyers, Carol. 1978. "The Roots of Restriction: Women in Early Israel." *The Biblical Archaeologist* 41(3):91–103.

Milliken, Randall. 2006. *The Central California Ethnographic Community Distribution Model, version 2.0, with Special Attention to the San Francisco Bay Area.* Report submitted to California Department of Transportation, District 4, Oakland. Davis, CA: Far Western Anthropological Research Group.

Perlot, Jean-Nicolas 1985. *Gold Seeker: Adventures of a Belgian Argonaut during the Gold Rush Years.* New Haven, CT: Yale University Press.

Ramenofsky, Ann F. 1987. *Vectors of Death.* Albuquerque: University of New Mexico Press.

_____. 1990. "Loss of Innocence: Explanations of Differential Persistence in the Sixteenth-Century Southeast," in *Columbian Consequences, Volume 2: Archaeological and Historical Perspectives on the Spanish Borderlands East,* Thomas, David Hurst (ed.), pp. 31–48. Washington, DC: Smithsonian Institution Press.

_____. 1993. "Diseases of the Americas, 1492–1700," in Kiple, Kenneth F. (ed.), *The Cambridge World History of Human Disease.* Cambridge: Cambridge University Press, pp. 317–327.

———. 1996. "The Problem of Introduced Infectious Diseases in New Mexico: A.D. 1540–1680." *Journal of Anthropological Research* 52:161–184.

———, Alicia K. Wilbur, and Anne C. Stone. 2003. "Native American Disease History: Past, Present and Future Directions." *World Archaeology* 35(3):241–257.

Snow, Dean R. 1996. "Mohawk Demography and the Effects of Exogenous Epidemics on American Indian Populations." *Journal of Anthropological Archaeology* 15:160–182.

Stewart, Frank Henderson 2001. "Hidatsa," in DeMallie, Raymond J. (ed.), *Plains, Handbook of North American Indians, Vol. 13, part 1* (William C. Sturtevant, general ed.). Washington, DC: Smithsonian Institution Press, pp. 329–348.

Thornton, Russell. 1987. *American Indian Holocaust and Survival: A Population History since 1492*. Norman: University of Oklahoma Press.

———. 1997. "Aboriginal North American Population and Rates of Decline, ca. A.D. 1500–1900." *Current Anthropology* 38(2): 310–315.

———. 2000. "Population History of Native North Americans," in *A Population History of North America*, Haines, Michael R., and Richard H. Steckel (eds.), pp. 9–50. Cambridge: Cambridge University Press.

Ubelaker, Douglas H. 1992. "North American Indian Population Size: Changing Perspectives," in Verano, John W., and Douglas H. Ubelaker (eds.), *Disease and Demography in the Americas*. Washington, DC: Smithsonian Institution Press, pp. 169–176.

———. 2000. "Patterns of Disease in Early North American Populations," in Verano, John W., and Douglas H. Ubelaker (eds.), *A Population History of North America*. Cambridge: Cambridge University Press, pp. 51–97.

Voss, Barbara L. 2008. "Gender, Race, and Labor in the Archaeology of the Spanish Colonial Americas." *Current Anthropology* 49(5):861–875.

Woodhouse-Beyer, Katharine. 1999. "*Artels* and Identities: Gender, Power and Russian America," in Sweely, Tracy L. (ed.), *Manifesting Power: Gender and the Interpretation of Power in Archaeology*. London: Routledge, pp. 129–154.

NINE

EFFECTS OF EMPIRE

Gendered Transformations on the Orinoco Frontier

Kay Tarble de Scaramelli

Between the fifteenth and eighteenth centuries, several European nations vied for a foothold in the Antilles and the Eastern Coast of South America, resorting to various forms of colonialism that differed in goals and strategies. The eventual conquest of the Guayana region resulted in dramatic processes of population decline and vast sociocultural transformations, even while native actions and responses posed significant challenges to the colonial intentions of the European powers. Pervasive and profound transformations were wrought in political, ritual, and social institutions in indigenous communities and beyond that affected both the construction of gender and sexuality. Unfortunately, many studies of the Spanish imperial project merely serve to reproduce the stereotypical vision of the penetrating conquest of the submissive female Indian (dark, untamed, virgin territory) by the White, European male (Stoler 1989; Voss 2008b). This "conquering discourse" that permeates much of the literature on colonial Latin America downplays the creative role that indigenous women played in both resistance, negotiation, and in the *mestizaje* process, a role that cannot be merely tagged as "traitor/whore" or "raped/victim" (Powers 2002). Although an ideology of patriarchy and male privilege prevailed throughout the empire, circumstances varied considerably in different colonial contexts, giving room for agency even within the program of domination and enculturation envisioned by the Crown and its agents (Lightfoot 2004, 2005).

Using an example from the Middle Orinoco, I present documentary and archaeological evidence for the long-term consequences of transformations in gender and sexuality. I argue that under the colonial regime some indigenous women were empowered by their productive capacities both in the biological and agricultural

I am most grateful to Barb Voss and El Casella for their invitation to participate in this venture. I am especially indebted to Barb Voss, who encouraged me to rethink the archaeological evidence from the Orinoco in terms of intimate encounters. Sandra Angeleri, of the Universidad Central de Venezuela, Diana Loren, and other participants at the Intimate Encounters workshop, as well as the anonymous reviewers, made valuable comments on earlier drafts of this chapter. Part of this research was financed by the Consejo de Desarrollo Científica y Humanística, Universidad Central de Venezuela, PI 05-00-6753-2007 and PI 05-16-4941-02.

realms and sought to negotiate social mobility through conversion to Catholicism, commodity production for personal economic gain, and, in some circumstances, sexual favors, concubinage, or marriage outside of their birth community. The intention here is neither to blame nor to exalt these women who were caught up in the colonial situation but to foreground the arenas of female agency that have been ignored in most historical accounts.

Archaeology provides a privileged window to the transformations in gendered relations on the Orinoco frontier, especially following the expulsion of the missionaries in the nineteenth century. Although Jesuits and Franciscans in the eighteenth and early nineteenth centuries left numerous and detailed accounts of their endeavors, the documental record for the ensuing Republican period is scanty and was produced mainly by explorers who describe only brief encounters with the local population. Therefore, the archaeological remains collected at settlements corresponding to this period of "documentary vacuum" are a valuable source for the comprehension of the readjustment of the Indians subsequent to the War of Independence (1810–1823). The collections obtained at ancient Mapoyo[1] residential sites offer a revealing glimpse of the lives of this indigenous people as they struggled to overcome the drastic population reduction that occurred during the Jesuit occupation in the eighteenth century (see Hull, Chapter 8, this volume, for a discussion of demographic decline in the Yosemite Valley). I discuss several lines of material evidence that give insight into the transformations in gendered relations that point to the active negotiation of female status and sexuality: ceramic remains, rock art, and settlement pattern. First I offer some historical background.

THE COLONIAL FRONTIER ON THE ORINOCO

The Orinoco region of Venezuela was on the edge of the Spanish Empire, both geographically and politically (Figure 9.1). Early conquest efforts centered on the quest for gold, and numerous expeditions attempted to locate the fabled riches, but to no avail. By the seventeenth century, once the allure of El Dorado had dissipated, the Spanish reassessed the potential value of the Orinoco as a strategic waterway that could facilitate communication between the eastern and western administrative centers of northern South America. However, the highly effective indigenous resistance led by the Carib and their Dutch allies had to be overcome before this goal could be achieved (Whitehead 1988). Following an unsuccessful attempt to settle along the Middle Orinoco in the 1680s, the Jesuits returned with military support to found a series of missions at strategic points, designed to permit control of the river (Rey Fajardo 1971; Useche Losada 1987; Whitehead 1988).

The missionaries offered protection from slave raids, exploitation by unscrupulous settlers, and, in some cases, sexual violence. The missionaries had a somewhat ambiguous sexual role because of their vows of celibacy, and several accounts describe their intervention on the behalf of women facing sexual exploitation (Bueno 1965; Gumilla 1944). Luring the prospective neophytes with coveted trade goods, the Jesuits relocated Indians to the missions, often at great distances, where they were expected to provide for themselves as well as for the relatively small contingency of missionaries and soldiers stationed there. The settlements were plagued by countless difficulties, including irregular and insufficient supplies, armed attacks, rebellions, and desertion by the neophytes. Epidemics of smallpox, measles, and other Old World diseases caused many fatalities in the missions, and most settlements were abandoned after only a short occupation (Gilij 1987, Vol. 1: 69–70; Morey 1979).

Under these precarious circumstances, indoctrination centered on the children, with a daily routine of schoolwork and catechism; the adults were dedicated to productive activities during most of the week in outlying settlements. The Jesuits were somewhat tolerant of local customs, in the form of dances and social gatherings, because they feared the neophytes would desert the missions if they felt that discipline was too strict (Gilij 1987, Vol. 3: 72–77). In the economic sphere, the missions served as centers for the exchange of manufactured goods in return for local products. They introduced cattle and other domesticated animals and attempted to instruct the neophytes in trades; nonetheless, these incipient efforts were brought to an end with the expulsion of the Order in 1767. Although neither the missionaries nor the Crown considered the missionary endeavor in the area to have been a success (Alvarado 1966; Rey Fajardo 1966, 1971), this initial colonizing effort set in motion a process that had profound effects on the cultural makeup of the region. The presence of the missionaries and their support group of soldiers, servants, and slaves promoted a restructuring of social and productive relations that lay the groundwork for future configurations of race, gender, and class.

The Late Colonial period (1768–1830) witnessed a shift in colonial strategy toward the foundation of secular settlements, where Indians were recruited as free labor for agricultural ventures (Lucena Giraldo 1991, 1998). Missionary activity in this period was reduced dramatically in the Middle Orinoco, and many of the earlier mission sites were abandoned. In the Llanos (plains) to the north and west of the Orinoco, feral cattle attracted poor, landless Whites from the capital, escaped slaves, and Indians fleeing from the missions. In the Llanos, these "marginal" individuals poached cattle and lived a nomadic life beyond the reach of the colonial authorities and laws.

Following the War of Independence (1811–1830), cattle ranching continued as the major economic activity in the Orinoco Llanos, and large tracts of land were privatized. Strict laws prohibiting free movement resulted in the incorporation of a small number of stable cattle hands on the ranches, and many others were reduced to vagrancy, contraband, and armed rebellion (Duncan Baretta and Markoff 2007). The new laws, combined with the construction of fences throughout the Llanos, forced groups such as the Pumé and Guahibo/Hiwi into the most marginal lands, where they have struggled to survive in the face of radically reduced territories (Metzger and Morey 1983; Mitrani 1988). Other indigenous groups retreated to areas marginal for ranching, such as the upland forests and the savannahs of Bolívar State, where they complemented subsistence activities with commerce in gathered products such as Tonka beans, rubber, and the sale of manioc in the form of *casabe* or *farinha*. In these areas, groups such as the Mapoyo, Piaroa, and Eñepá were able to maintain more traditional lifestyles and a degree of territorial control, as well as their indigenous identity, as they gradually recovered demographically. This contrasts markedly with the situation on the Upper Orinoco, where the rubber

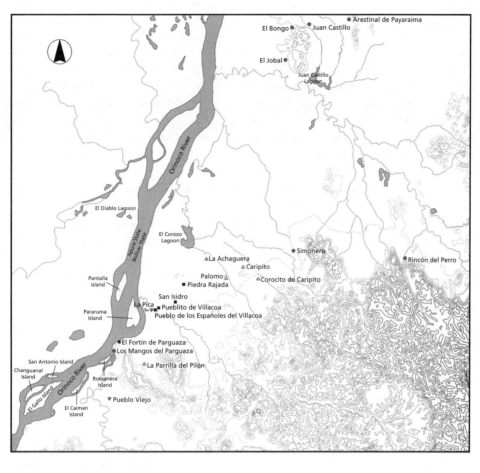

FIGURE 9.1. The Middle Orinoco region of Venezuela.

boom of the early twentieth century resulted in extreme violence and exploitation of the indigenous peoples of the area (Hill 1998).

SEXUAL POLITICS OF COLONIALISM

The sexual politics of colonialism on the Venezuelan Orinoco frontier entailed a complex field with multiple players. The relationships drawn on racial, ethnic, class, and gendered lines shifted through time, depending on the makeup of the colonial agents, the native population, and the economic and political milieu. Men of European descent arrived on the scene first as members of conquest expeditions and later as missionaries, soldiers, tradesmen, farmers, and cattle ranchers. Black slaves of African heritage accompanied these settlers, and runaway slaves sought refuge in remote forests. As noted earlier, the Llanos attracted numerous "marginal" men of diverse origin. Throughout the colonial period and well into the twentieth century, Indians by far outnumbered the colonists, even as they lost political control of their territories. During the conquest and Early Colonial period, it was difficult to attract European women to the distant frontier, and indigenous women were sought as sexual partners, whether consensual or not.

Jesuit accounts claim that indigenous women were often instrumental in bargaining for the terms of incorporation into the missions, and numerous documents stress the active influence of women in persuading their relatives to relocate to the settlements. Once in the missions, women played an important part in providing a viable subsistence base and, in some cases, in promoting the conversion to Catholicism. It was the women who did most of the cultivation and food processing; the men concerned themselves mainly with fishing, hunting, crafts, and trade. As Rivière has noted, the newly acquired iron tools and weapons alleviated several of the men's activities, such as tree felling, canoe making, and house construction, whereas women's tasks were not significantly altered by the introduction of these tools (Rivière 1987). This meant that women shouldered a major part of the more time-consuming activities in the fields and in the home, which led to discontent and complaints among the women (discussed subsequently).

Closely linked to the traditional division of labor was the political organization of the indigenous societies. Before European conquest, the groups of the Middle Orinoco were, for the most part, "egalitarian" in their social organization and political structure (Poeck 1974: 170, 174–175); men gained status and political clout through the demonstration of acumen in discourse, commerce, warfare, and the ability to accrue surplus for display (Gilij 1987, Vol. 2: 170–172; Gumilla 1944, Vol. 1: 131, Vol. 2: 103–110, 255). In most Orinocan groups, this surplus depended on a man's ability to attract several wives and, through time, children and in-laws, who contributed to the productive potential of the extended household (Gilij 1987, Vol. 2: 213–215; Rivière 1983–1984). Ritual knowledge and curative powers provided another route to status and power and often were combined in the person of the local headman or shaman. In either case, under traditional conditions, adult males had a definite advantage over other members of the society in the quest for political power, based, to a large extent, on the productive capacity of their wives and daughters.

To counteract this native power structure, the Jesuits set out to undermine the traditional sociopolitical organization and division of labor. They banned polygyny (Gumilla 1944, Vol. 2: 258–259) and appealed to the women to rebel against what they interpreted as lowly status and mistreatment in the hands of the native men (Gilij 1987, Vol. 2: 215–216; Gumilla 1944, Vol. 2: 76–79). They declared the ritual specialists to be their worst enemies and banned what they believed to be pagan or diabolical practices. Through these mechanisms, the missionaries attempted to subvert traditional courses to political and economic status and strove instead to insert the mission Indians into a patriarchal structure patterned on European forms of organization: monogamous, nuclear families, institutionalized political hierarchies with offices and chain of command, tributary obligations to the Crown, and conversion to Catholicism.

At the same time, the priests were shrewd in discovering certain tensions in native social relations and used them to their advantage. For example, they observed the bickering and jealousy among the co-wives in polygamous marriages and played on these emotions to promote monogamous unions. Gilij, the Jesuit priest who presided at the mission at La Encaramada, reported that the co-wives constantly fought for the favor of the husband and accused one another of being "ugly, lazy, or clumsy" (Gilij 1987, Vol. 2: 214). Nevertheless, after some time in the mission, he claims to have received a petition for baptism from a group of Tamanaco women who were all joined in polygamous unions. Gilij replied that he could only baptize monogamous adults, whereupon he reports that the women begged him to abolish the polygamous marriages and give each man only one wife. Following this incident, Gilij, seeing that he "had the women on his side," proceeded with greater force to abolish the polygyny in his Reduction.

In a similar vein, the Jesuits noted the complaints of the women in several of the Orinocan societies, such as the Betoy, who were said to have preferred to abort or kill their newborn daughters rather than allow them to suffer the hardships of a woman's life, and the women complained bitterly of the abuses they suffered in the hands of their husbands (Gumilla 1944, Vol. 2: 77–78). Although we need to question whether these incidents actually occurred, if they were the norm, or whether the Jesuit chroniclers were merely trying to justify their intervention and strategy to promote monogamous unions, it is interesting to note that similar incidents are cited in various texts. I argue that by gaining the confidence of the women and children, the Jesuits attempted to overcome some of the resistance to the mission regime and, at the same time, undermine the traditional forms of status and political power. It appears that some of the women used these circumstances to their benefit, in a strategy to gain social mobility in the mission context. For example, they took advantage of the opportunities to sell pottery and other craft items and surplus from their gardens to buy beads, cloth, and other sundries (Alvarado 1966: 311). The popularity of glass beads in Colonial period archeological contexts points to the impact of the missionaries on the ideals of modesty and sexual attraction, in which new modes of dress and adornment were adopted along with the monogamous unions (see Loren, Chapter 7, this volume).

Another arena for the transformation of gendered relations was the ceremonial sphere. The mission context may have contributed to what Brown has referred to as "gender revolutions," in which rapid shifts in belief and practice occur, often in the context of Christian conversion (Brown 2001: 207). In the Orinocan missions, there are documented occasions for the modification of traditional gender roles in ritual practice and the emergence of new ceremonial forms that explicitly rejected the secrecy and prohibitions against female participation that had prevailed prior to contact. Gilij describes a fascinating episode in which the Tamanaco and other groups under his supervision agreed to reveal to the women the sacred flutes that had been heretofore prohibited and to include the women as participants in the dances (Gilij 1987, Vol. 2: 241). I suggest that this incident reveals a change in attitude toward the sexuality of women, who were considered to be a source of pollution and danger in many traditional Lowland cultures. This kind of compliance to missionary control was not necessarily the norm in the missions, however, and in other cases the desacralization of ritual instruments and knowledge was sufficient excuse for the Indians to abandon the mission. In other instances, the rites continued to be carried out in secret, out of sight of the missionaries (Bueno 1965 94–95, 131; Gilij 1987, Vol. 2: 98).

The bestowal of sexual favors, concubinage, and marriage with nonindigenous men was common practice in the Colonial period, even as it is today. Following the Bourbon Reform in the late eighteenth century, contradictory policies concerning *mestizaje* arose in the Guayana region. Some administrators continued to condemn the practice, and others encouraged mixed marriages or unions (Lucena Giraldo 1991, 1998). Missionaries and other colonial agents noted that the offspring of Indian women and European, mestizo, or black men were healthier, perhaps because of increased immunity to the Old World diseases (Gumilla 1944, Vol. 2: 289–290; Useche Losada 1987), whereas unions with Indian men were often barren (Mansutti-Rodríguez 2003). Recent research indicates that the offspring of mixed marriages were regarded differently on the frontier compared with the urban centers to the north. Lucena Giraldo (1998) has found several documents that describe the population of Ciudad Real, a secular town founded in 1759. These residents were described in one text as "Españoles" (Spaniards), whereas in another document, these same residents were broken down in the following ethnic terms: *Blancos* (White), *Mulatos, Morenos* (Dark), *Indios* (Indians), and *De color quebrado* (of dark color or mixed blood). This is an excellent example of the process through which cultural ascription overrides "racial" or ethnic categories (for a similar example, see Voss 2008c). In this case, the need for colonial agents (Españoles) on an unattractive frontier led to a relaxation of the sharp distinctions upheld in the urban areas to the north, and unions of indigenous women to nonindigenous men can be construed to be a strategy to achieve social mobility.

It is likely that a similar blurring of boundaries occurred in indigenous communities where children of mixed marriage who were raised in the fold of an Indian community may have assumed that identity. An assimilation of this kind could even apply to the spouse. Gilij (1955 [1785] vol. 4, part 2, chapter 2; http://www.lablaa.org/blaavirtual/historia/enhia/enhia14b.htm) reports the case of a black slave who escaped to a Carib community, whereupon he abandoned his clothes, painted himself with achiote, and took a young woman as a wife or concubine (see Sheptak, Blaisdell-Sloan, and Joyce, Chapter 10, this volume, for examples in colonial Honduras).

ARCHAEOLOGICAL EVIDENCE FOR THE REDEFINITION OF GENDER AND SEXUALITY

The archaeological record offers an alternative and complementary source to texts, especially concerning subaltern sectors of the population who are often underrepresented or misrepresented in the written sources. Household archaeology, with its emphasis on living quarters and workspaces, provides a glimpse into the quotidian life of the actors as they operated within the colonial community and underlies many interpretations concerning acculturation and *mestizaje,* understood as the racial and cultural mixing. An alternative to this useful, but limited, view of past relations (cf. Voss 2008a) focuses on the long-term "effects of empire" (Coronil 2007) as they played out through time. Through the comparison of similar contexts from different time periods, the consequences of colonial intervention, both intended and unintended, come to light. Following this strategy, I analyze evidence for transformations in gendered relations and sexuality following the establishment of mission settlements in the Orinoco and their continued effects in the Late Colonial and Republican periods. Ceramic decoration, rock art, and settlement pattern provide contrasting material sources for tracing the transformations in ritual, social, and productive relations that took place through time.

Ceramic Production

Women were in charge of pottery production in most Middle Orinocan societies. Before European colonization, various ceramic traditions produced in the area are easily distinguished by differences in color, temper, form, and decorative style (Scaramelli 2006). Pottery was an essential item for the female domains of food preparation and service, transport, and storage, and it is ubiquitous in precolonial sites. Following colonization, locally made pottery continues to make up the major proportion (73 percent) of material goods found at the archaeological sites (15,829 ceramic fragments out of a total of 21,628 items including ceramic, stone, glass, and metal artifacts), although changes occur in paste, vessel form, and decorative modes. What can this tell us about the role of indigenous women and their negotiations with the colonial regime?

On one hand, the continuation of pottery production in the context of mission sites argues for the essential role of women as both makers, users, and breakers of pots in the colonial period. Very few iron or copper pots have been found at colonial sites, pointing to the dependence on local wares by both Indians and colonizers. The presence of the large ceramic griddle (*budare*) testifies to the production of *casabe,* a storable "bread" made from manioc (*manihot esculenta*), and *arepas,* corn cakes that served to sustain the mission settlements. Throughout the postcontact period, *budares* increase in proportion to other vessel forms, suggesting that *casabe* production, in the hands of women, gained importance, perhaps as a commodity to be traded beyond the community (Figure 9.2). At the same time, the large pots used to ferment *chicha,* prevalent in precolonial times, and so essential to the festivities surrounding the route to prestige and status of adult men, show a marked decline in the Early Colonial and Republican periods (Figure 9.2). This indicates a radical shift in the traditional gendered division of labor, forms of leadership, and status that prevailed even after the expulsion of the missions.

A notable decline in decorated pottery followed colonial intervention (from nearly 9 percent in precolonial sites to less than 2 percent in the Republican period). It is likely that the missionaries prohibited certain types of objects, such as figurines, body stamps, zoomorphic or anthropomorphic lugs, and incised and painted designs that they associated with pagan beliefs or rituals. It is also possible that as the neophytes were converted to Christianity, they abandoned certain rituals that involved

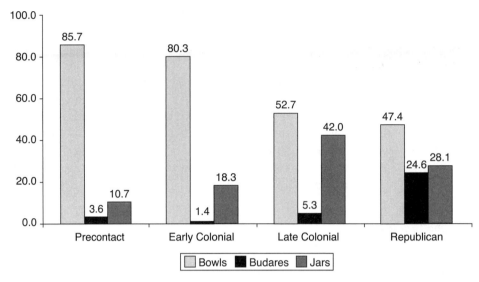

FIGURE 9.2. Distribution of grouped vessel forms according to period.

the more highly decorated wares. At the same time, population decline may have contributed to the simplification of ceramic designs and the loss of decorative techniques. The missions were fraught with epidemics of smallpox, measles, and other Old World diseases, with dire consequences for the neophytes. Under these circumstances, certain forms of knowledge may have been lost, resulting in inferior or simplified products, and the forced relocation to the multiethnic mission sites may have interfered with traditional training in craft production. The separation of parents and children during the week may have prevented the enculturation of young girls in the arts of potting and other crafts, resulting in the eventual simplification or loss of decorative techniques.

An increased volume of production for the market (Gilij 1987, Vol. 2: 257–258; Gumilla 1944, Vol. 1: 167) may have resulted in a reduction of time-consuming decorative techniques (Rice 1984). This commodification of ceramic production has been documented for the Republican period, and *Criollo* settlers (nonindigenous Venezuelan nationals) sought local wares for their own domestic consumption. The women potters may have abandoned the decorative modes that identified the pots as "indigenous" products in an expression of a new mestizo identity, especially in the case of marriage outside of the indigenous community.

A final factor contributing to the loss of decoration on the local pottery may be found in the replacement of decorated local tableware by imported dishes. The greatest decrease in decorated pottery occurs in the transition between Early and Late Colonial periods, with a notorious loss of incised flanges on bowls and small jars. It is precisely during this period that inexpensive, industrialized tablewares decorated with a variety of techniques and in a wide range of colors were introduced and adopted widely. By the Republican period, open plates and flanged bowls were no longer being produced in the local pottery, and pearlware and whiteware dishes became widespread, even in settlements identified as indigenous.

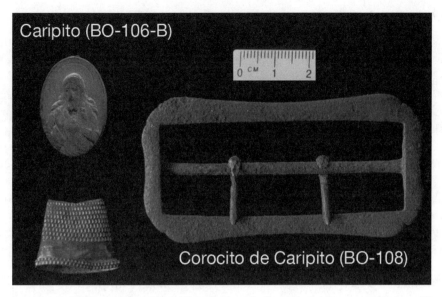

FIGURE 9.3. Catholic medallion, thimble, and buckle from Republican period sites. (Photo by Franz Scaramelli.)

Likewise, other items that may indicate a desire to emulate Western styles of dress and habits also gained popularity during this period. Glass beads, popular in colonial times, and incorporated into native aprons and armbands, give way to Catholic medallions, thimbles, and buckles (Figure 9.3) that suggest the increasing use of sewn clothing; medicine and perfume bottles and hair tonic indicate transformations in the realm of the body (Scaramelli and Tarble de Scaramelli 2005). Even following the expulsion of the missionaries, a modified sense of propriety and modesty can be inferred from the frequency of these items. Canned goods and beverage bottles also increase in frequency at the Mapoyo sites, signaling modifications of diet and drinking practice (Scaramelli and Tarble 2003; Scaramelli and Tarble de Scaramelli 2005). The fragile, but showy, cups and saucers that accompany coffee drinking are omnipresent in these Republican period sites. The incorporation of this exotic beverage, and the etiquette involved in its service, formed a "package" that served as a rank signifier, particularly in the feminine sphere of visitation and display. Its message was clearly one of distinction, in which only the persons with access to cash could obtain the exotic commodities (Tarble 2008). Further confirmation of the importance of these items can be found in their placement as funerary offerings associated with young women (Galarraga et al. 2003). I propose that these Western goods are being employed as status markers that serve to distinguish the women of certain indigenous communities from their more traditional neighbors and, at the same time, signify an aperture to contact with the growing *Criollo* population in the area. It is also interesting to note that serving dishes in the Republican period are much smaller in size, indicating the abandonment of communal meals and a trend toward organization in nuclear families. This, in association with the scattered settlement pattern to be described later in this chapter, seems to point to a modification in the modes of commensality that may have accompanied the transition to monogamous households.

Rock Art in the Orinoco

Orinocan rock art has been interpreted to be a graphic expression related to the masculine sphere during precolonial times (Tarble 1991; Tarble and Scaramelli 1999), although overt sexual depictions are rare. Most anthropomorphic figures are depicted as stick figures or as figures with rectangular bodies with few explicit sexual differentiations. Nonetheless, the objects and activities that prevail in the art in the region can be related to several spheres of traditional masculine dominance – hunting, basketry, and ritual – whereas motifs depicting activities in the female sphere of production (plants, foodstuffs) are not recognizable in the motifs. No scenes of copulation, birth, or pregnancy are evident. Zoomorphic motifs, important both as hunted species and as representations of mythical protagonists, are common. Artifacts portrayed in the rock art such as maracas (gourd rattles), baskets, and woven mats are made and used primarily by men (Guss 1989). Other ritual objects that have been identified in rock art, such as flutes, masks, and feather headdresses, are often described as being made and used by men only, and in some cases, women are forbidden to see the instruments and the ceremonies in which they are used, pending death (see, for example, Mansutti Rodríguez 2006). Although Overing (1986) is careful to point out that women play essential parts in the ceremonies in which these instruments are used in traditional contexts, both as "audience" and as hidden participants, there is a clear gender division in the conduction of the ritual sphere, and women and men must carefully observe proscriptions regarding food consumption, body fluids, and couvades to promote successful reproduction of the society. It can be argued, then, that the rock art minimizes the representation of the female contribution to production and reproduction, just as much of myth and ritual practice tends to embellish the male's role.

Following contact, there is a virtual cessation of the production of rock art in the Middle Orinoco, and outright iconoclasm involving the destruction or repainting with Christian symbols is found at several sites (Figure 9.4). To what extent the abandonment of rock painting is related to the adoption of Christian religion by indigenous neophytes or to the overzealous desire on the part of missionaries to destroy "diabolic" manifestations is difficult to assess. The changes noted may be due to the same factors discussed earlier regarding the decline in ceramic decoration. Nonetheless, as noted in reference to indigenous ceremonies and dances, there may have been some circumstances under which traditional ritual and sacred spaces were desecrated and abandoned as a part of the emergence of new cults in which gendered relations were profoundly transformed and the proscriptions on female participation were no longer enforced.

Settlement Pattern

Further insight into transformations in traditional relations between men and women can be found in the radical modification of settlement pattern and house style following colonial intervention. Before European contact, settlements were characterized by fairly dense accumulations of cultural remains, suggesting the construction of large, communal residences on sites that provided access to varied resources. The size of these settlements depended on the capacity of the headman

FIGURE 9.4. Motif of Christian cross, superimposed over earlier paintings at the Cueva Pintada site, located on Mapoyo lands in Bolívar State. (Photo by Franz Scaramelli.)

to attract and retain a viable, productive community. Mission strategy promoted the relocation of indigenous communities to mission sites, where different ethnicities built separate neighborhoods distributed on the edges of a central plaza where the church, fort, and missionary's residence were located (Gilij 1987, Vol. 3: 62–63).[2] Following the War of Independence, in the nineteenth century, a new settlement pattern ensued in which indigenous communities either receded to the upper reaches of the tributaries of the Orinoco or adopted a disperse pattern in the savannas inland from the main stream of the river. In the case of the Mapoyo, nuclear families began to build individual, rectangular houses, either isolated or in small groups in the savanna (Hernández Pérez 2008). These are visible in the archaeological record as shallow scatters of refuse, characterized by local and imported ceramic wares, glass bottles, manioc graters made from kerosene cans, gun-powder flasks, sardine cans, and other sundries obtained through trade. This pattern can be interpreted as a consequence of the earlier mission influence, in which monogamous unions gained precedence and communal dwellings were abandoned. These communities are located in secluded areas of the inland plains, set back from the main stream of the Orinoco. In contrast, the *Criollos* maintained the control of the major rivers where they established small towns dedicated to fishing, *vega* (riverbank) agriculture, and commerce. It is during this period that cattle ranches came to dominate the landscape of the lower Llanos, pushing the indigenous groups into the marginal lands of the area.

THE PAST MEETS PRESENT

Although the written record for the Republican period in the Middle Orinoco is scanty, archaeological remains provide insights into processes that were unfolding in the area as a consequence of the earlier colonial occupation. Despite the fact that the missions in the area were short-lived, their "effects" were vast and far-reaching in the local population, as evident in the Mapoyo community today and its forms of interaction with the national state. Exogenous domestics, such as cattle, pigs, chickens, plantains, mangoes, sugar cane, and rice, form a part of the local productive modes, just as an ever-increasing dependence on manufactured goods and foods amplifies the dependence on commerce with the *Criollos*. To meet these ever-increasing needs, traditional crops and "collectibles" have been converted into commodities. Mapoyo women continue to provide *casabe* and other products for the market (Figure 9.5) and, in some cases, have crossed ethnic boundaries to marry, often returning later to their birthplace with children and, on occasion, spouse.[3] Catholicism predominates in its various creative manifestations, Spanish is the dominant language, and shorts and T-shirts have replaced more traditional garb. The Mapoyo offer an example of resilience and strength in the face of colonial and neo-colonial situations. This is a community that opted to interact with the dominant sector of the Venezuelan nation, through support for the Republican army in the War of Independence, commerce, and intermarriage (Henley 1983; Scaramelli and Tarble 2000). Despite many transformations in their productive modes, division of labor, and religious practices, the Mapoyo have maintained an indigenous identity and a degree of territorial control, and they are avidly striving to keep astride of the political, social, and economic transformations that they face as a consequence of the impact of industrial bauxite development in the region. This situation contrasts with that of many of the other indigenous groups who entered into the mission system, such as the Tamanaco, Otomaco, Guamo, and Pareca, and who, following the War of Independence, were unable to maintain viable communities and were absorbed by other indigenous communities or into the *Criollo* sphere. The Mapoyo are a multiethnic community, that, as in the Northern California case cited by Lightfoot (Lightfoot 2005), has an "indigenous" identity, even while not conforming to essentialized notions of a "tribe."

FIGURE 9.5. Mapoyo woman baking manioc cakes (*casabe*) for sale on the market September 2010. (Photo by Franz Scaramelli.)

Within this long-term project of domination and control, it is often difficult to perceive the agency of the various subordinated sectors. How did the individual indigenous men and women frame their own "projects" (Ortner 2006) within the constraints of the colonial order and its asymmetrical relationships of power? What were the original intentions of these projects, and what were the unintended consequences? As indigenous women gained space, negotiating access to desired goods, participating in commerce, and marrying out, what did they find? Did it mean the loss of ties to their home and community? How much choice was involved, and how much was due to the violent appropriation of their bodies by nonindigenous men who considered themselves to be their racial superior, and, hence, in their "right"? To what extent did the choice to appropriate Western styles underlie strategies for the attainment of a perceived gain in status or economic well-being? These and other questions lie at the heart of sexual and racial attitudes as they play out in contemporary Venezuela and must be acknowledged, rather than hidden under the veil of equality or *mestizaje* that has dominated official ideology until recently.

On a broader, regional and national scale, the persistence of indigenous peoples in postcolonial Venezuela has connotations of a different order. Despite an ideology of *mestizaje*, laid out by the Liberator Simón Bolívar, in his vision for a unified country forged out of the blood of Indians, Africans, and Europeans, this "equalizing" national project was engendered by profound social hierarchies. As Coronil and Skurski have so cogently argued, "[t]he glorification of the postcolonial state has been cast in masculine terms of military strength and rational enlightenment, granting the state the mission to uplift and control a backward people, ambiguously gendered as both docile and dangerous" (Coronil and Skurski 2005: 24). In the popular national imagination, a gradient from barbarian to civilized is constructed using the more remote and less "acculturated" peoples, such as the Yanomami, as one end of the spectrum, through the "clothed" and bilingual indigenous groups, such as the Wayuú or Mapoyo, to the rural mestizo, but still barbarian, *Llanero*, the "virile" coastal Afro-descendents, to the "White," urban, middle and upper classes. At the same time, this gradient is construed in sexual terms, from the ambiguously "feminized" Indian to the dominant, "masculine," White.

More recently, under the aegis of the Bolivarian revolution, this ideology has come under scrutiny, and different sectors of the nation are seeking to deconstruct the connotations of *mestizaje* and to revive ethnic (indigenous and Afro-descendant), gendered, and class consciousness in a new vision designed to celebrate diversity in a multicultural, pluri-ethnic nation. It is paradoxical that this "revolutionary process" is reproducing and reinforcing several of the stereotypes that it purportedly set out to rectify. This is particularly the case regarding the role of the "Original Peoples" (*Pueblos Originarios*) in the construction of the national community in which official discourse glorifies the male indigenous warrior as a valiant example of resistance but gives minimal recognition to indigenous sectors that steered alternative courses in the face of colonial rule. This can be construed as a subtle reincarnation of "ethnic shame" that has characterized the enduring, ambiguous attitude toward the Indian in Venezuela as somehow inferior to the "high cultures" of Mesoamerica and the Andes. For many Venezuelans, the Indian is not a source of "ancient pride" except as a model of rebellion and resistance to the European colonizer (as in the case of the male *guerrero*). Indigenous women, portrayed as passive recipients of white blood in the *mestizaje* process or displayed as the occasional *guerrera* (female warrior), have been doubly silenced in official renderings of the colonial process (see Rubertone, Chapter 14, this volume), even as they contributed enormously to the creation of the national culture through both productive and spiritual knowledge and through their reproductive force.

NOTES

1. The Mapoyo are an indigenous people whose territory lies between the Suapure and Parguaza Rivers in the Middle Orinoco. The Mapoyo language forms part of the Carib family.
2. I have found no evidence for the construction of neophyte barracks at the Jesuit missions. The housing is described as multifamilial or as individual huts, depending on the different

ethnic group involved. Separate housing for children can be inferred from the fact that the adults spent most of the week at outlying sites, tending to the plantations.

3. For decades, Mapoyo women and men had to look outside their community to marry because of a shortage of available partners (Henley 1983). Men often took neighboring indigenous wives, and women were more likely to marry a *Criollo*. Many of these marriages terminated because of abuse or abandonment, and the women returned with their children. More recently, *Criollo* men have married into the community, where they maintain farms and livestock with the permission of the Captain. The offspring of these marriages are counted as Mapoyo if they remain in the community. Territorial conflicts in recent years have heightened ethnic consciousness, but there is not space here to discuss this topic adequately.

REFERENCES

Alvarado, E. d. 1966. "Informe reservado..." in J. d. Rey Fajardo S.J. (ed.), *Documentos Jesuíticos Relativos a la Historia de la Compañía de Jesús en Venezuela*. Caracas: Biblioteca de la Academia Nacional de la Historia, pp. 215–333.

Brown, M. F. 2001. "Worlds Overturned: Gender-Inflected Religious Movements in Melanesia and the Amazon," in Gregor, T. A., and D. Tuzin Berkeley (eds.), *Gender in Amazonia and Melanesia: An Exploration of the Comparative Method*. Los Angeles and London: University of California Press, pp. 207–220.

Bueno, O. F. M., R. 1965. *Tratado Histórico*. Caracas: Biblioteca de la Academia Nacional de Historia.

Coronil, F. 2007. "After Empire: Reflections on Imperialism from the Americas," in Stoler, A. L., C. McGranahan, and P. C. Perdue (eds.), *Imperial Formations*. Santa Fe, NM: School for Advanced Research Press, pp. 241–271.

———, and J. Skurski. 2005. *States of Violence*. Ann Arbor, MI: University of Michigan Press.

Duncan Baretta, S. R., and J. Markoff. 2007. "Civilization and Barbarism: Cattle Frontiers in Latin America," in Coronil, F., and J. Skurski (eds.), *States of Violence*. The University of Michigan Press, pp. 33–74.

Galarraga, A., M. Garaicoechea, M. G. Montoto, F. Scaramelli, and K. Tarble. 2003. "Contextos Culturales y Funerarios en la Cueva del Caño Ore, Edo. Bolívar, Venezuela." *Boletín de la Sociedad Venezolana de Espeleologia* 37 (diciembre):2–11.

Gilij, Felipe Salvador. 1955 [1784]. *Ensayo de Historia Americana: Estado Presente de la Tierra Firme*, Vol. 4, Bogotá, Editorial Sucre. Parte 2, capítulo 2. Available at http://www.lablaa .org/blaavirtual/historia/enhia/enhia14b.htm.

———. 1987. *Ensayo de Historia Americana*. Caracas: Biblioteca de la Academia Nacional de la Historia.

Gumilla, J. 1944. *El Orinoco Ilustrado*. Bogotá: Editorial ABC.

Guss, D. M. 1989. *To Weave and to Sing: Art, Symbol, and Narrative in the South American Rain Forest*. Berkeley: University of California Press.

Henley, P. 1983. "Los Wánai (Mapoyo)," in Coppens, W. (ed.), *Los Aborígenes de Venezuela*. Caracas: Fundacion La Salle de Ciencias Naturales, Instituto Caribe de Antropología y Sociología, pp. 216–241.

Hernández Pérez, A. L. 2008. "Etnoarqueología del espacio doméstico y comunitario del grupo Mapoyo de la comunidad de El Palomo, Municipio Cedeño, estado Bolívar-Venezuela." *Boletín Antropológico* 25(71):389–405.

Hill, J. 1998. "Violent Encounters: Ethnogenesis and Ethnocide in Long-term Contact Situations," in Cusick, J. (ed.), *Studies in Culture Contact: Interaction, Culture Change, and Archaeology*. Carbondale: Southern Illinois University at Carbondale, pp. 146–167.

Lightfoot, K. 2004. "Native Negotiations of Missionary Practices in Alta California." *Missionalia* 32(3):380–393.

———. 2005. *Indians, Missionaries, and Merchants: The Legacy of Colonial Encounters on the California Frontiers*. Berkeley and Los Angeles: University of California Press.

Lucena Giraldo, M. 1991. *Laboratorio Tropical: La Expedición de Límites al Orinoco, 1750–1767.* Caracas: Monte Avila Latinoamericana y Consejo Superior de Investigaciones Científicas.

———. 1998. "Gentes de infame condición." Sociedad y familia en Ciudad Real del Orinoco (1759–1772). *Revista Complutense de Historia de América* 24:171–191.

Mansutti-Rodríguez, A. 2006. *Warime: La Fiesta. Flautas, trompas y poder en el noroeste amazónico.* Ciudad Guayana, Venezuela: Fondo Editorial UNEG.

———. 2003. "Enfermedades y despoblamiento: El Orinoco Medio entre los siglos XVI y XVII," in Alès, C., and J. Chiappino Mérida (eds.), *Caminos Cruzados: Ensayos en Antropología Social, Etnoecología y Etnoeducación.* Venezuela: IRD Édictions, ULA GRIAL, pp. 69–100.

Metzger, D., and R. Morey 1983. "Los Hiwi (Guahibo)," in R. Lizarralde and H. Seijas (eds.), *Los Aborígenes de Venezuela, Volumen II: Etnologia Contemporánea I.* Caracas: Fundación La Salle de Ciencias Naturales, Instituto de Caribe de Antropología y Sociología, pp. 125–216.

Mitrani, P. 1988. "Los Pumé (Yaruro)," in J. Lizot (ed.), *Los Aborígenes de Venezuela. Volumen III: Etnologia Contemporánea II.* Caracas: Fundación La Salle de Ciencias Naturales, Instituto Caribe de Antropología y Sociología y Monte Avila Editores, C.A., 147–214.

Morey, R. V. 1979. "A Joyful Harvest of Souls: Disease and the Destruction of the Llanos Indians." *Antropologica* 52:77–108.

Ortner, S. B. 2006. *Anthropology and Social Theory: Culture, Power and the Acting Subject.* Durham, NC, and London: Duke University Press.

Overing, J. 1986. "Men Control the Women? The Catch 22 in the Analysis of Gender." *International Journal of Moral and Social Studies* 1(2):135–156.

Poeck, G. 1974. "Misión del río Orinoco en el Nuevo Reyno 1684," in J. Rey Fajardo (ed.), *Documentos Jesuíticos relativos a la Historia de la Compañía de Jesús en Venezuela.* Caracas: Biblioteca de la Academia Nacional de la Historia.

Powers, K. V. 2002. "Conquering Discourses of 'Sexual Conquest': Of Women, Language and Mestizaje." *Colonial Latin American Review* 11(1):7–32.

Rey Fajardo, J. d. (ed.). 1966. *Documentos Jesuíticos Relativos a la Historia de la Compañía de Jesús en Venezuela.* Caracas: Biblioteca de la Academia Nacional de la Historia.

———. 1971. *Aportes Jesuíticos a la Filologia Colonial Venezolana.* Caracas: Ministerio de Publicaciones, Departamento de Publicaciones.

Rice, P. 1984. *Pottery Analysis: A Sourcebook.* Chicago: University of Chicago Press.

Rivière, P. 1983–1984. "Aspects of Carib Political Economy." *Antropológica* 59–62:349–358.

———. 1987. "Of Women, Men and Manioc," in Skar, H. O., and F. Salomon (eds.), *Natives and Neighbors in South America: Anthropological Essays.* Göteborg: Göteborys Etnografiska Museum, pp. 178–201.

Scaramelli, F., and K. Tarble de Scaramelli. 2005. "The Roles of Material Culture in the Colonization of the Orinoco, Venezuela." *Journal of Social Archaeology* 5:135–168.

———, and K. Tarble de Scaramelli. 2000. "Cultural Change and Identity in Mapoyo Burial in the Middle Orinoco, Venezuela." *Ethnohistory* 47(3–4):705–729.

———, and K. Tarble. 2003. "Caña: The Role of Aguardiente in the Colonization of the Orinoco," in Whitehead, N. L. (ed.), *History and Historicities in Amazonia.* Lincoln: University of Nebraska Press, 163–78.

Scaramelli, K. L. 2006. *Picking up the Pieces: Ceramic Production and Consumption on the Middle Orinoco Colonial Frontier.* Chicago: Department of Anthropology, University of Chicago.

Stoler, A. L. 1989. "Making Empire Respectable: The Politics of Race and Sexual Morality in 20th-Century Colonial Cultures." *American Ethnologist* 16(4):634–660.

Tarble, K. 1991. "Piedras y Potencia, Pintura y Poder: Estilos Sagrados en el Orinoco Medio." *Antropológica* 75–76:141–164.

———. 2008. "Coffee, Tea, or Chicha? Commensality and Culinary Practice in the Middle Orinoco Following Colonial Contact." *Cuadernos de Arqueología Mediterránea* 17:53–71.

Tarble, K., and F. Scaramelli. 1999. "Style, Function, and Context in the Rock Art of the Middle Orinoco Area." *Boletín de la Sociedad Venezolana de Espeleología* 33(diciembre):17–33.

Useche Losada, M. 1987. *El Proceso Colonial en el Alto Orinoco-Río Negro (Siglos XVI a XVIII).* Bogotá: Fundación de Investigaciones Arqueológicas Nacionales, Banco de la República.

Voss, B. 2008a. "Domesticating Imperialism: Sexual Politics and the Archaeology of Empire." *American Anthropologist* 110(2):191–203.

———. 2008b. "Las Políticas Sexuales de Imperio en las Américas Españolas: Perspectivas Arqueológicas del San Francisco Colonial." *Cuadernos de Arqueologia Mediterránea* 17:31–52.

———. 2008c. *The Archaeology of Ethnogenesis: Race and Sexuality in Colonial San Francisco.* Berkeley and Los Angeles: University of California Press.

Whitehead, N. L. 1988. *Lords of the Tiger Spirit: A History of the Caribs in Colonial Venezuela and Guyana, 1498–1820.* Dordrecht, the Netherlands: Foris Publications.

TEN

IN-BETWEEN PEOPLE IN COLONIAL HONDURAS

Reworking Sexualities at Ticamaya

Russell N. Sheptak, Kira Blaisdell-Sloan, and Rosemary A. Joyce

Archaeological excavations on the north coast of Honduras at CR-337, an archaeological site we identify as the pre-Hispanic and colonial town Ticamaya (Figure 10.1), produced a stratigraphic record with radiocarbon dates as early as 1300–1400 CE and artifacts dating as late as the nineteenth century (Blaisdell-Sloan 2006; Wonderley 1984a, 1984b). According to sixteenth-century Spanish documents, Ticamaya was a critical settlement in Spanish and native military campaigns and political strategies in the early sixteenth century (Sheptak 2004, 2006, 2008).

The two parallel bodies of data produced by excavations and archival research are each material traces from the past, and each, we argue, is equally relevant *archaeological* data. Tacking back and forth between documents and other materials, we demonstrate that sexuality is a highly visible structuring principle in colonial Honduras, albeit more directly legible in documentary materials. That, we would suggest, is partly because the regulation of sexuality and the products of sexual liaisons was jurally relevant, requiring overt commentary (Brooks 2002; Twinam 1999).

The material dimensions of everyday life through which sexuality was mediated were largely, although not entirely, tacit. Yet if we turn to the archaeological excavations with the complexity of sexual relations immanent in documentary records in mind, we can transform the way we understand even such perennial standbys as chipped stone tools. Integrating experiential, practice, and performative theoretical perspectives, we change the way we see social relations at Ticamaya, showing that the supposedly immaterial domain of sexuality is material both in the substantive and the theoretical sense.

POINTS AND PALISADES: MATERIALIZING MASCULINITIES

The physical traces of sixteenth-century Ticamaya are invisible at first glance. The site extends across several fields formed as levees at the confluence of two rivers.

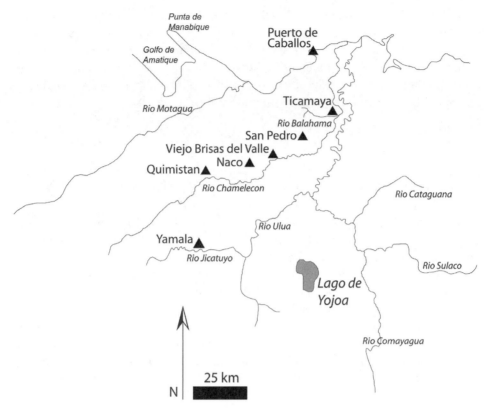

FIGURE 10.1. Map showing locations of early colonial places mentioned in text. Drawing by Rosemary A. Joyce.

Today the channel of the larger of these rivers, the Chamelecon, is mostly dry, as modern canals have diverted water to the parallel Ulúa River. The old course of the tributary river, called the Río Balahama in sixteenth-century documents, is visible on air photos as a channel that formerly drained what today is Lake Ticamaya (Pope 1985). The upper drainage of what once was the Río Balahama now joins a distinct channel to the Chamelecon and is known today as the Río Choloma (Figure 10.1).

Historical texts tell us that Ticamaya was located on the river, surrounded by a palisade and ditches (Sheptak 2004, 2006), suggesting a well-defined settlement. A program of systematic augur testing confirmed that buried site components extended continuously across a well-defined area of 140 by 215 meters. Artifact densities were highest near the riverbanks, suggesting a concentration of settlement in this area. Cesium magnetometer survey of a subarea of 1,900 square meters identified five clear magnetic anomalies, all evidence of denser occupation features. In every case, the nearest augur hole to a magnetic anomaly produced construction materials from typical perishable buildings. At the same time, there were many significant concentrations of artifacts located by auguring for which there is no corresponding magnetic anomaly.

Guided by these complementary methods, Blaisdell-Sloan (2006) intensively excavated five household areas within the site boundaries during two field seasons in 2001 and 2003. Her excavations defined features dating to the sixteenth century in three areas, which are the focus of our discussion here. These are the material remains of a town that was the site of negotiation of sexuality between indigenous and Spanish actors during the first generation of colonization.

Structure 3A

Excavations in Operation 3A, 3B, and 3D documented traces of a sixteenth-century house (Blaisdell-Sloan 2006: 134–136, 249, 254–255). The house was represented in the excavated area by a single posthole and hearth. Inside the hearth were the remains of a single broken vessel (Figure 10.2). A burned clay wasp's nest was probably attached to the building here when it was burned. Outside of the house, and six meters away, large pieces of utilitarian pottery were recovered in Operation 3C on an extension of the same surface, indications of an exterior working space. The hearth, the broken pot in it, and the range of associated artifacts securely indicate that this was a residential area.

The surface around the features that are the traces of the building yielded a wide variety and large number of artifacts and faunal remains. Artifacts included obsidian blade fragments, six projectile points unifacially chipped on blades, broken pieces of pottery, fragments of deer antler, and a small piece of sheet copper. Deer antler was widely used in pre-Hispanic Honduras for tools including awls and punches and those used today in removing corn kernels from the cob. Among the pottery represented are fragments of the types Algo Red, Carbano Brushed, and Cebadia Incised, which are utilitarian or domestic unslipped and red slipped bowls and jars used for food preparation and serving. Also present were fragments of the type Nolasco Bichrome, interpreted as imported from the indigenous town of Naco to the west (Figure 10.1) where it is preferentially used in wealthy, high-status households, primarily occurring in the form of dishes used in food serving (Urban 1993; Wonderley 1981, 1986).

As would be expected in a residential area, there were a significant variety of remains that probably relate to foods prepared and consumed in the area. Animal bone came from turtles, rodents, and white-tailed deer, and there were also remains from crustaceans and *jutes* marking the importance of marine resources at this riverside town. Plant remains were fairly rare overall at Ticamaya because of poor preservation, but tubers, probably manioc, and *Helianthus* and *Artemisia* seeds were recovered from inside the structure itself, near the hearth (Blaisdell-Sloan 2006: 254–255).

The entire area was covered with a thin level of soil before another sixteenth-century surface formed. These overlying sediments were mixed with large amounts of carbon, as if the building had been burned, an event also suggested by the finding of a burned wasp's nest. Blaisdell-Sloan (2006: 152) obtained a radiocarbon date from this building (Sample AA61409: 347 ± 37 BP, cal 1480–1520 CE or 1560–1630 at one sigma), which supports the artifact data that suggests its destruction happened in the first half of the sixteenth century.

FIGURE 10.2. Vessel broken in place on floor inside Structure 3A. Photograph courtesy of Kira Blaisdell-Sloan.

Structure 1A

Excavations in Operation 1A and 1D documented a second sixteenth-century structure which differed from Structure 3A in significant ways and may not have been purely residential in nature (Blaisdell-Sloan 2006: 122–124, 228, 248). One edge of the structure was defined by two 30-centimeter-diameter post holes located 4 meters apart on an east–west line. These postholes were each lined with plaster, covering the sides and the bottom of the hole, making it likely that the post, not just the hole, had originally been plaster covered (Figure 10.3). Remains of three previous structures in the same location were also documented. Structure 1B, the version immediately preceding Structure 1A, had features suggesting it was used pre-Hispanically for ritual (Blaisdell-Sloan 2006: 125). These included deposits located in the each of

FIGURE 10.3. Post hole lined with plaster inside Structure 1A. Photograph courtesy of Kira Blaisdell-Sloan.

the corners of the building, containing a total of five ceramic censers (Figure 10.4), tobacco seeds, and ocelot and coyote teeth. The continuity of occupation in this area and the relatively sparse artifact inventory from Structure 1A lead us to suggest the possibility that this later sixteenth-century structure was also a special-purpose building, possibly a church.

Ceramics were few and include fragments of Algo Red and unslipped bowls and jars. Obsidian blades were recovered, but there were no obsidian projectile points located in or around this structure. Animal bone recovered could be assigned to the Artiodactyla family, which includes deer, sheep, goats. Given the approximate dating of this structure, the bone is considered more likely to be from deer than from the introduced European domesticates.

The Fogón *(Oven)*

Excavations in Operation 2C and 2D uncovered a sixteenth-century firebox, possibly used as a pit oven, or as a ceramic kiln (Blaisdell-Sloan 2006: 131–132, 152, 169, 228–229, 249, 254). This structure was a 1-meter-diameter pit dug 50 centimeters deep, lined with burned clay. Within this was another clay structure about 50 centimeters in diameter that was built either for cooking or supporting pots during firing.

After it was no longer in use, this oven was filled with garbage including carbon, obsidian projectile points, turtle, peccary, white-tailed deer, and other animal bone fragments, as well as riverine snail and bivalve shells. Palaeoethnobotanical analysis

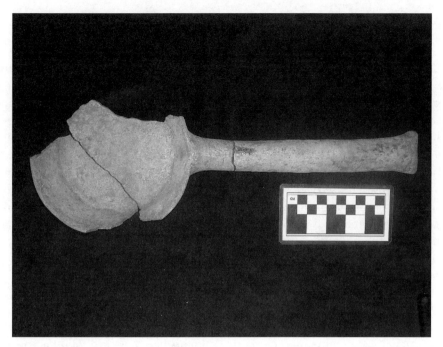

FIGURE 10.4. One of five censers found under the floor of Structure 1B. Photograph courtesy of Kira Blaisdell-Sloan.

identified carbonized maize seeds and tuber fragments. Ceramic types represented included Algo Red, Cebadia Incised, and an unnamed unslipped burnished ware, all consistent with domestic use ceramics for food preparation and serving. Blaisdell-Sloan (2006: 152, 309) obtained a radiocarbon date for a sample of carbon from the fill in this oven (AA61407 cal 1440–1520 CE, or 1590–1620 CE at one sigma).

Other Exterior Surfaces

Excavation in Operation 2A and 2B documented two successive surfaces assigned to the sixteenth century. The most recent of these was marked by small pits, and dispersed bits of *bajareque*, burned daub from local wattle-and-daub buildings (Blaisdell-Sloan 2006: 130, 254). Also detected in this area were varied plant remains including coyol palm seeds, *Carex* sp., *Paspalum* sp., *Mamillaria* sp., and lumps of tubers consistent with manioc or sweet potato. *Carex* and *Paspalum* are plants used for bedding or matting and come from wetland areas. Coyol palm fruits are consumed both as a food and fermented as an alcoholic beverage. These remains suggest this open area was most likely a workspace associated with nearby residences.

A second, more deeply buried surface can be assigned to the sixteenth century as well. This, too, is marked by small pits and dispersed bits of bajareque (Blaisdell-Sloan 2006:130, 182). No faunal or floral remains were detected from this surface or the pits dug into it. Nonetheless, it seems likely that the same kinds of activities took place in this area as on the slightly later surface.

Discussion

How do we move from the description of sixteenth-century deposits like these to thinking about sexuality and its negotiation? Our phenomenological perspective asks how the everyday experience of people at Ticamaya was shaped by the things they made and used (Blaisdell-Sloan 2006). Especially at a time of structural transformation, we might expect changes in the way that people at Ticamaya engaged with their material world, whether by intensifying existing practices or reshaping them.

Two material practices at sixteenth-century Ticamaya draw our particular attention: an intensified use of obsidian dart or arrow points, and the innovative construction of substantial fortifications. The first is evident from excavation results, the second, from textual analysis. Together, these practices provide a material basis for us to propose that the initial phase of colonization was accompanied by the emergence of a strongly marked masculinity based on participation in war, not evident materially in the earlier history of the region.

The excavated lithic assemblage included thirty-four projectile points, twenty-one (61 percent) recovered from early colonial contexts (Blaisdell-Sloan 2006: 236, 238). These are small obsidian dart points, base- or side-notched, chipped unifacially on prismatic blade segments (Figure 10.5). Points like these are found across the contemporary lowlands of Mexico, Guatemala, and Honduras (Pendergast, Jones, and Graham 1993: 67). They are understood as arrow or dart points used by warriors in battle against human opponents, an inference originally based on artistic depictions but also supported by edge-wear analysis and depositional contexts created in the violent conquest of ninth-century Aguateca, Guatemala (Aoyama 2005: 204).

At Ticamaya, contexts that produced a wealth of these armaments (Sub-Operations 3A, 3B, and 3D) also provide evidence of burning of residential features dated to the sixteenth century (Blaisdell-Sloan 2006: 134; 154). The abundant carbon around the oven in Operations 2C/2D indicates that burning happened here as well. The group of six obsidian projectile points discarded near the oven reinforces the inference that this exterior living area witnessed the performance of the warrior masculinity that either was developed or intensified during the long resistance against Spanish invasion.

Radiocarbon dates for the burned Structure 3A (AA61409: 347 ± 37 BP, cal 1480–1520 or 1560–1630 CE) and the *fogón* in Operation 2C/2D (AA61407 cal 1440–1520 or 1590–1620 CE) allow dating of these burned features to either the early sixteenth century or the decades of transition to the seventeenth century. The presence in residential Structure 3A of Nolasco Bichrome sherds, which are not made after the late pre-Hispanic period (Urban 1993), coupled with the complete burning of Structure 3A, suggest that it may be a house burned during the Spanish attack on the town in 1536 which was the decisive battle of Spanish colonization.

Unlike the unmistakably residential Structure 3A, Structure 1A showed no signs of burning. Yet it was clearly occupied during the early colonial period, built as a continuation of a pattern of remodeling buildings in this location. The lack of any sign of burning, plus the absence of obsidian projectile points from this area,

FIGURE 10.5. Projectile points made from obsidian blades. Photograph courtesy of Russell N. Sheptak.

suggests that during the period of resistance to Spanish incursions, not all parts of the town were equally affected by changes in practices or even by the events of the final battle at Ticamaya. If our suggestion that warfare facilitated the crystallization of a new masculinity is taken into account, Structure 1A would need to be characterized as a space where that masculinity was not being performed or was not highly visible.

Bajareque fragments, found on both sixteenth-century surfaces in Operation 2, are a product of burning, but there was no carbon or dark discoloration to indicate that intense burning occurred in this area of the site. In addition, no obsidian projectile points were recovered in this area, only segments of obsidian blades used in domestic tasks. When we juxtapose the material record from this exterior space with that noted near the *fogón*, it is again evident that there was not a uniform presence of the kinds of activities through which the newly emphasized warrior masculinity might have been performed.

An intensified demand for men, particularly young men, to play the part of warrior during more than a decade of active military resistance to Spanish incursion shaped the performance of masculinity by a generation of youths at Ticamaya in the 1520s and 1530s. Warrior masculinity was long established among the contemporary Maya of Yucatan, cultivated by the segregation of a cadre of young men who learned the art of war together and took part in other physical activities such as ball games and dances that displayed their strength and agility to audiences composed primarily of other men (Joyce 2000). Yet the kinds of evidence for warrior masculinity among the Yucatec Maya, including specialized young men's houses, artwork that glorified the young male body in motion, and overtly sexualized images of genitalia, are absent or less evident in pre-Hispanic northern Honduras. The military posture that developed in response to Spanish incursions into Honduran territories, leading to higher frequencies of small arrow or dart points in archaeological excavations at Ticamaya, changed the nature of everyday life and the kinds of masculine identity performed by those participating in warfare. It created an all-male sphere of activity that was at once violent and physical.

The second practice with material dimensions that we can associate with intensified warfare is the building of fortifications. Here, our primary evidence comes from sixteenth-century Spanish letters to the Crown describing in detail the nature of the fortifications around the towns resisting Spanish colonization (Sheptak 2004, 2006). These documents describe the fortifications at Ticamaya as a palisade composed of seven or eight rows of rough, heavy wood, with openings from which to shoot, and towers. Around the palisade were concealed holes forming additional obstacles for anyone intent on attacking. Access inside the palisade was possible by canoe from the river as well as from land.

Like all the features of the sixteenth-century town of Ticamaya, any traces of these fortifications are now buried, and Blaisdell-Sloan did not encounter anything interpreted as evidence for them. However, there is no reason to doubt the testimony of multiple descriptions recorded by the Spanish, who were frustrated in their attempts to defeat the defense of the town until they devised a plan to attack from the river with artillery mounted on a canoe. We thus need to think about Ticamaya as a spatially enclosed community in which everyday life took place under the literal shadow of possible aggression.

There is reason to think that fortifications were innovations in sixteenth-century northern Honduras, contributing to the shaping of warrior masculinity as something new. Although the burial of Ticamaya obscures the spatial layout of the town today, there are two well-studied contemporary late pre-Hispanic sites located upstream that have not been buried and have been thoroughly mapped (Figure 10.1). Naco, located on a small tributary of the Chamelecon River, covered an area of 90 hectares with a core of larger buildings in "a compact group near the river" and other structures distributed in clusters more widely spaced as the distance from this central group increased (Henderson et al. 1979: 172). A second documented site, Viejo Brisas del Valle, located along the Chamelecon between Ticamaya and Naco, similarly has no sign of fortifications or even a close spacing of buildings that might suggest there had once been perishable defensive walls (Neff et al. 1990). Nor do historical documents describe the sixteenth-century towns of the Naco valley as fortified.

Naco and other settlements near it were among the earliest in the region to receive Spanish visitors, toward whom they adopted a policy of hospitality and openness, shifting, once the hostile intentions of their visitors became clear, to avoidance by moving away from former town sites to live dispersed in the hills. People in the Ulúa River province had the opportunity to witness the interactions between the people of Naco and the Spanish and to prepare accordingly, receiving the first Spanish attempts at settlement with deadly force.

Fortifications, not unknown in the larger world to which these Honduran towns were connected, would have been one way to prepare for the visit of hostile outsiders. A study of fortifications in Yucatan and Guatemala describes walled precincts protecting the residences of the wealthy nobility in the northern Yucatan lowlands (Cortes Rincon 2007: 179–180), an area connected to the Ulúa River province by trade and visitation. With thick walls capable of supporting palisades, but lacking additional features (towers, ditches, or slit windows for shooting) described for Ticamaya, fortifications in northern Yucatec sites were usually added to a site originally founded with an open plan, in response to military threats. Some are described as having been built "hastily."

This leads us to consider the effects of living within enclosing fortifications on the experience of Ticamaya's inhabitants. The spatial layout of the settlement, as indicated by Blaisdell-Sloan's (2006) subsurface testing, was relatively compact. Clusters of artifacts and other cultural material tended to cover areas of 10 to 20 meters in diameter. This is within the range documented for groups of buildings and associated exterior spaces that were the normal residential architecture in pre-Hispanic sites in the Ulúa Valley, where house compounds averaged 12 to 15 meters in width. Using the upper range of artifact clustering documented by Blaisdell-Sloan as a proxy for residential group size, the mapped area of Ticamaya would have accommodated approximately seventy-five residential compounds. This compares favorably to the Spanish statement that in 1536 there were eighty men at Ticamaya (implicitly, in context, tribute-paying men, heads of households).

For the people of Ticamaya, everyday life would have taken place in relatively close proximity to other households. The encircling fortifications segregated the population inside from the broader world outside. As Spanish military incursions into the valley made venturing out risky, with the possible costs ranging from death or injury to kidnapping and forcible servitude, the everyday experience of warriors who were obliged to go out to campaign against the enemy would have been increasingly distinct from that of the people of the town as a whole. Although not the kind of segregation fostered by the institutionalization of young men's houses in Yucatan, the spatialization of differential experience could have had many of the same effects, reinforcing the separation from the general population of those developing a distinctive violent male masculinity shaped by the newly important activity of hunting other people using obsidian pointed projectiles.

PEOPLE IN PLACE: "A CHRISTIAN SPANISH WOMAN . . . FROM SEVILLA"

Historical documents provide us with additional insight into the effects of warrior masculinity on sexual relations across the initial divide between Spanish and indigenous people. On August 31, 1535, the governor of the Spanish colony in Honduras wrote to the king of Spain to report an incursion into his territory by a troop from Guatemala that intruded violently on the indigenous town of Yamala (Figure 10.1). In this document, Andres de Cereceda gives his side of a negotiation he entered into with the intruding troop, in which he effectively offered them the opportunity to obtain their own territory by undertaking the conquest of the as-yet-unpacified land immediately east, in the much larger valley of the Ulúa River. Here, acting from the site of Ticamaya, the indigenous leader Çocamba had led a successful campaign to limit Spanish incursion for a decade (Sheptak 2004, 2006, 2008).

Cereceda wrote that after a successful meeting with the leader of the intruding Spanish troop, Cristobal de la Cueva,

> concertamos que otro dia se partiese por su gente . . . para que habiendo reposado dos o tres dias, el Don Cristobal fuese con ochenta hombres a conquistar y castigar el Río de Ulúa, que mataron los Cristianos de Puerto de Caballos y a rozer el albarrada de Cacamba, . . . como por sacar de poder de aquel Cacique Cacamba una mujer Cristiana Española . . . he sabido que es de Sevilla, de los que mataron a Puerto de Caballos, decimos que era casada con uno de los muertos y por información de indios he sabido que el Cacique Cacamba la tiene por mujer

> [We agreed that the next day he would leave to rejoin his people . . . so that having rested two or three days, Don Cristobal would go with eighty men to conquer and punish the Río de Ulúa, that killed the Christians of Puerto de Caballos; and to raze the fortress of Çocamba . . . as well as to take from the power of the same *cacique* Çocamba a Christian Spanish woman . . . I have learned that she is from Sevilla, of those that were killed at Puerto de Caballos, they say that she was married to one of the dead, and according to information from the *indios* I have learned that the *cacique* Çocamba has her as a wife.] (AGI Guatemala 39 R.2 N.4)

The theme of the "captive woman" is a familiar one throughout the parts of the Spanish colonies where conflicts with indigenous people continued for multiple generations. As James Brooks (2002) argues in his study of similar histories in the southwestern United States, such exchanges, which went in both directions, were necessary parts of the processes of colonization that engaged ideas of kinship, shame, and honor. They were strategic, if violent, means through which new societies were forged.

The woman from Sevilla is an extraordinary presence in the early documentary history of the region. Cereceda's references to her are careful to clarify her status: she is not only from Seville, but specified as Spanish, as opposed to any other national origin. She is Christian – meaning no doubt could be shed on her family's origins in recently reconquered Andalusia, formerly a Moorish realm with tolerance for religious plurality, including an active Jewish population forced to convert or leave Spain. She was, Cereceda writes, married to one of the men killed in a raid on the coastal town of Puerto Caballos (Figure 10.1) established in 1524. The use of the term *casada* is significant, because it reinforces the legitimacy of her social position under Spanish law – she was, this passage implies, present in the Americas in a socially respectable role.

This description contrasts markedly with the status to which, from the perspective of Cereceda, she had been reduced by capture: the indigenous leader (*cacique*) has her as a *mujer*, literally "woman"; by definition, he could not be "married" to her because that would require a Christian ceremony, and Çocamba was not yet converted. Cereceda tells us he has long had the desire to remove the "woman from Sevilla" from the captivity he imagines she is suffering, based on information he has gained from questioning Indian informants.

Brooks (2002:17–18) suggests that "the capture of 'enemy' women and children was . . . one extreme expression along a continuum of exchange . . . they could serve as agents and objects of the full range of exchanges, from the peaceful to the violent." The reason that Cereceda gives for his interest in recovering the woman from Sevilla is specifically because "she is held as much among the Indians that arrive there in friendship; from whom he [Çocamba] has learned that there are Christians in the territory, saying that he cannot for his strength resist; even though he has killed Christians he could be pardoned." For Cereceda the woman from Sevilla was serving as a kind of ambassador in the heart of domestic life of his fiercest enemy.

Brooks (2002: 19–26) reviews the significance such cross-cultural, cross-religion sexual liaisons already had in Iberian society during the centuries of the *reconquista*, the slow war to recover control of the peninsula that reached its end in the 1490s. The participants in the initial colonization of Honduras were at most one generation removed from a society in which such marriages were sometimes tactical, sometimes outcomes of battle, and not yet the uneasy objects they would rapidly become as Spanish society in the sixteenth century focused on a process of purification of bloodlines in the peninsular homeland as much as in the new distant colonies.

ALTERNATIVE EXCHANGES: GONZALO GUERRERO AND JERONIMO DE AGUILAR

The focus in discussions of cross-cultural capture in processes of colonization has primarily been European women. However, the Spanish–indigenous conflict in northern Honduras also involved the alternative exchange of a shipwrecked male captive who married into indigenous society.

Cereceda failed in his attempt to convince de la Cueva to undertake a military campaign against Çocamba in 1535. However, the urgency of his colony's situation led him to send the treasurer of the colony to Guatemala to seek the assistance of the governor of that province, Pedro de Alvarado. Alvarado promptly undertook a march that brought him to Honduras at a point when the colonists were threatening to leave en masse.

Cereceda succeeded in convincing Alvarado that there was enough wealth to share if he simply defeated the indigenous leaders of the Río de Ulúa. Cereceda reported to the king on the successful outcome of this campaign in a letter of August 1536, after the establishment by Alvarado of the cities of San Pedro and Gracias a Dios and the reformation of Puerto Caballos in late June. In his report, Cereceda describes the surrender of Çocamba and reports that he

declaro que durante el combate que había tenido lugar dentro de la albarrada, un cristiano español llamado Gonzalo Aroca había sido muerto de un escopetazo. Es el que vivía entre los indios de la provincia de Yucatán, y además, es el que dicen que arruinó al adelantado Montejo . . . ese Español muerto en el combate, estaba desnudo, con tatuajes en el cuerpo y usaba los adornos que emplean los indios.

[declared that during the combat that had taken place inside the walled enclosure, a Spanish Christian named Gonzalo Aroca had been killed by gunfire. He is the one that lived among the Indians of the province of Yucatan, and as well, he is the one that they say ruined the Adelantado Montejo [governor of Yucatan] . . . this Spaniard died in combat, was nude, with tattoos on his body and used the ornaments that the Indians employ.] (AGI Guatemala R.2 N.6)

passage echoes a well-known description by Bernal Diaz del Castillo of the
ter Hernan Cortes had with surviving Spanish victims of an early shipwreck
the coast of Yucatan. One, Jeronimo de Aguilar, who had taken some form of
vows and was celibate, was recovered by Cortes and served as one of his two principal
interpreters in his campaign against the Mexica state.

A second, named by Bernal Diaz "Gonzalo el marinero" – "the sailor, Gonzalo" –
was later identified as Gonzalo Guerrero – Gonzalo, the warrior. When Gonzalo
came to meet with Cortes along the eastern coast of Yucatan in 1519, he declined
to be repatriated to the Spanish forces. Bernal Diaz reports a speech (written many
decades later, and thus to be taken as the sentiments expected rather than the
literal words of Gonzalo) in which he said he needed to stay because he was married
(*casado*) and had children and because his body was ornamented in the manner of
the people of the land.

Gonzalo reportedly had originally been a prisoner of the lord of one of the major
Maya states of eastern Yucatan and eventually rose to the position of warrior and was
married to a daughter of the *cacique*. His participation in the defense of the Ulúa
Valley was at least the second time he had come to aid Çocamba, bringing dozens
of canoes of warriors with him.

Like the woman from Sevilla, Guerrero can be seen as a captive spouse. In his
case, we have the reported speech in which he cites his parentage of children as the
reason he no longer can return to the Spanish cause. Spanish authorities emphasize
his identity as a Christian in accounts that express frustration with his participation
in battles against them.

We see two codes of identity at work here: one of cross-cultural marriage, which
Brooks (2002) notes was already important in Spain and which paired with adoption worked to create social bonds across otherwise hostile boundaries in Spanish
America; the other, the expectation that religion would prevail as a form of identity
outweighing kinship. As the counterpart to Gonzalo, Jeronimo de Aguilar had made
no ties of marriage or kinship, and through his religious devotion, remained loyal
to a Spanish identity that Gonzalo never explicitly denied but that, implicitly, his
altered body negated.

That religious identity could outweigh other forms of identity is implicit in the
treatment of Gonzalo's ally in the Ulúa campaign, Çocamba. The Spanish crown
acknowledged Cereceda's report in a letter dated June 30, 1537. In a marginal
note, the passage is titled "el gran señor se llamaba soamba, el que se redujo a
christiano" [the great lord that they called Soamba, he that was made a Christian].
The Spanish monarch cites Cereceda's report that Alvarado undertook a successful
campaign against

un Gran Señor que diz que hay en esa tierra que se llama Soamba que es el que a
hecho a los christianos todos los daños que les an venido en ella, al qual cerco y
lo tomo preso con todos los principales de esa tierra y se tornaron christianos por
su voluntad y se concertaron de seguir de paz, lo qual habia sido causa que todo el
resto de esa provincia diese la obediencia

[a Great Lord that they say they have in that land that is called Soamba who is the one
that has done all the damage to the Christians that have occurred to them in that

land, who he [Alvarado] came near and took prisoner with all the principal people of the land and they converted to Christian by their own will and they undertook to continue in peace, which has been the cause that all the rest of this province has given obedience.] (AGCA A1.23 Legajo 4575 Expediente 39528 Folio 39)

The language of the passage describing Çocamba borrows from that used by Cereceda to describe Gonzalo. The Spanish king does not comment on the troubling report of the renegade Spanish Christian who did not live to be subdued and convert.

Nor do we hear explicitly in this or any other source we have reviewed to date about the disposition of the woman from Sevilla. Her Christianity was apparently never in doubt, as Cereceda attributes to her explicit attempts to persuade Çocamba that he could be pardoned even his killing of other Christians, as indeed was the outcome. The children of Gonzalo, who remained in Yucatan, and any children who were the product of the decade-long relationship between Çocamba and the woman from Sevilla, are equally unmentioned in these sources, although they clearly were first-generation, in-between people.

Blaisdell-Sloan (2006: 281) argued that the increase in frequency of obsidian dart points in sixteenth-century contexts was closely linked to the militarization of the town during its defense, an intensification of masculinities of warfare that allowed Gonzalo and Çocamba to become prominent leaders. It may seem that the people mentioned are unusual figures and that their impact on processes of colonization may have been minor. However, we suggest that they represent only the most obvious examples of people engaged in sexual relations across boundaries of national citizenship and religion in areas where Spanish colonial campaigns were contested. Spanish colonial documents hint at other such liaisons, with men of the Spanish forces and women from indigenous villages engaging in relationships that fall at the other end of the spectrum of sex and violence that Brooks (2002) has sketched out in his study of the U.S. Southwest.

SHADOWY FIGURES: "THEY TAKE PLEASURE . . . IN AN ESTANCIA OUTSIDE THE TOWN"

In his letter of August 1536, Cereceda gave a detailed account of the insubordination from which he was suffering when Alvarado arrived. Among the crimes he accuses the principal Spanish mutineers of committing occurs a curious phrase: they were, he notes, inclined to "tomar placer" in "una estancia fuera del pueblo" – they took pleasure in an establishment (a dwelling or ranch) outside the Spanish town of Buena Esperanza, established near the indigenous town of Quimistan (Figure 10.1).

Cereceda was even clearer in a letter of December 1535: he needed to report a scandal to the king, that there were men marrying outside the Spanish population: "they go to their women and houses," again using the term *mujeres*, "women," to mark the difference from formalized Christian marriages that would be expected of these men. Cereceda links this fraternizing to the fact that few of the men of his colony were legally married. So he sought a contingent of married men for the new colony, presumably to be accompanied by their wives.

It is clear that sexual behavior of the Spanish forces in the young colony was only loosely controlled (see also Loren, Chapter 7, this volume). In 1544, Cristobal de Pedraza, the first resident bishop of Honduras, assigned the role of "Protector of the Indians," reported as one of his pastoral problems the continued practice of unmarried sexual liaisons between Spanish men and indigenous women. In the absence of other modes of formalized social relations, sex served as a means for individuals to create connections across divides of language, culture, and social norms.

This two-decade-long history of cohabitation, undertaken by men and women even less clearly identified than the nameless "woman of Sevilla," was critical to the initial survival of the colony (see also Croucher, Chapter 5, this volume). Cereceda's letters provide a plaintive account of the inability of the Spanish to feed themselves, for lack of knowledge of the local climate (planting their first crops at the wrong time of year) and because they were incapable of warding off the raids of unpacified groups who took cattle and horses from the pastures. Cohabitation with indigenous women in the rural hamlets where the indigenous population was initially welcoming to the Spanish ensured that a greater number of the Spanish population survived, even as it threatened the integrity of the newly founded Villa de Santa Maria de Buena Esperanza, of which no material trace has been identified.

Even after the founding of San Pedro, and the refounding of Puerto Caballos, sexual relations across the populations likely were critical to the survival of the colonial population (see also Hull, Chapter 8, this volume). The fifty Spanish *vecinos* (citizens) of the initial population of San Pedro dwindled to eight by 1591. These were completely untenable population numbers for the city to survive, yet it clearly did. Unacknowledged residents without the rights of *vecindad* (citizenship), which required legitimacy, pure Spanish descent, and unquestioned Christian background (Twinam 1999), must have been the majority of the population of the district of San Pedro. Although Gonzalo, Çocamba, and the woman from Sevilla provide marked examples singled out for roles in leading resistance and accommodation, they stand for countless other in-between people who forged the new colonial order, from the household out.

CONCLUSION

Evidence available for Ticamaya allows us to see the renegotiation of sexuality and intersecting identities at an intimate scale (see also Voss, Chapter 11, this volume). A combination of documents and excavated archaeological materials forms the basis for understanding the positions of men and women in the early sixteenth century.

At the beginning of colonization, both forms of evidence suggest that intensification of militarization reconfigured expressions of masculinity grounded in the role of the warrior. At the same time, opportunities for sexual liaisons across categories of national origin and civil status provided for new expressions of both masculinity and femininity.

The realization of such opportunities is represented on one hand by the figure of Guerrero – a "renegade" Spaniard whose new identification with indigeneity resulted directly from his status as the father of mixed-race children. Equally a product of these new possibilities is the "captured bride," the "woman of Sevilla" who served as the intermediary in Çocamba's understanding of Spanish adventurers in his territory.

The primary way that early-sixteenth-century colonization in Central America took place was through independent campaigns by troops of men who lived together, traveled together, voted on new projects, and split the spoils from successful campaigns among themselves. Cristobal de la Cueva's insurgent troop was one of these, and like other such troops, it terrorized the local population as it entered Honduras from Guatemala with extreme violence.

The performance of an indigenous warrior masculinity, an innovative part of the experience of residents of towns such as Ticamaya in the early sixteenth century, created structurally similar all-male groups bound by achievement in violent confrontations. Like the Spanish troops with whom they fought, the warriors of the Ulúa province traversed the landscape in all-male groups, living apart from women, children, and men not engaged in warfare who occupied the houses inside the fortified towns.

As in the colonial situations in the southwestern United States that Brooks (2002) discusses, sexual liaisons were the major means through which Spanish and indigenous populations forged points of connection that officially were not possible in sixteenth-century Honduras. These alliances created a new social landscape in which sexuality mediated race, class, and social status, whether the object of new sexual relations was a captured Spanish sailor, an indigenous woman in a rural household accepting a foreign soldier in her bed, or a woman from Sevilla who survived the destruction of a military encampment to become the guide to Spanish culture for the indigenous man who found his calling in violent resistance to colonization.

REFERENCES

Aoyama, Kazuo. 2005. "Classic Maya Warfare and Weapons: Spear, Dart, and Arrow Points of Aguateca and Copan." *Ancient Mesoamerica* 16:291–304.

Blaisdell-Sloan, Kira. 2006. *An Archaeology of Place and Self: The Pueblo de Indios of Ticamaya, Honduras (1300–1800 AD).* Ph.D. dissertation, Department of Anthropology, University of California – Berkeley.

Brooks, James F. 2002. *Captives and Cousins: Slavery, Kinship, and Community in the Southwest Borderlands.* Chapel Hill: University of North Carolina Press.

Cortes Rincon, Marisol. 2007. *A Comparative Study of Fortification Developments Throughout the Maya Region and Implications of Warfare.* Ph.D. dissertation, Department of Anthropology, University of Texas – Austin.

Henderson, John S., Ilene Sterns, Anthony Wonderley, and Patricia Urban. 1979. "Archaeological investigations in the Valle de Naco, Northwestern Honduras: A preliminary report." *Journal of Field Archaeology* 6:169–192.

Joyce, Rosemary A. 2000. "A Precolumbian Gaze: Male Sexuality among the Ancient Maya," in Schmidt, Robert A., and Barbara L. Voss (eds.), *Archaeologies of Sexuality.* London: Routledge Press, pp. 263–283.

Neff, Theodore, Patricia A. Urban, and Edward M. Schortman. 1990. "Late Prehistoric Developments in Northwestern Honduras: Preliminary Report on the 1990 Investigations at Viejo Brisas del Valle." Tegucigalpa, Honduras: Instituto Hondureño de Antropología e Historia, Report in the archives of the Institute.

Pendergast, David, Grant Jones, and Elizabeth Graham. 1993. "Locating Maya Lowlands Spanish Colonial Towns: A Case Study of Belize." *Latin American Antiquity* 4:59–73.

Pope, Kevin 1985. *Paleoecology of the Ulúa Valley, Honduras: An Archaeological Perspective*. Ph.D. dissertation, Department of Anthropology, Stanford University, Stanford, California.

Sheptak, Russell N. 2004. *Noticias de un cacique indígena de la época colonial: Una contribución a la historia colonial de Honduras*. Tegucigalpa, Honduras: VII Congreso Centroamericano de Historia. Available at http://hcentroamerica.fcs.ucr.ac.cr/Contenidos/hca/cong/mesas/cong7/docs/1_6.doc.

Sheptak, Russell N. 2006. "Rereading Çicumba's Documentary Record." Paper presented at the 71st annual meeting of the Society for American Archaeology, San Juan, Puerto Rico.

Sheptak, Russell N. 2008. "Çoçumba Contested: Documentary and Material Traces of Early Colonial Indigenous Practice." Paper presented at the 73rd annual meeting of the Society for American Archaeology, Vancouver, Canada.

Twinam, Ann. 1999. *Public Lives, Private Secrets: Gender, Honor, Sexuality and Illegitimacy in Colonial Spanish America*. Stanford, CA: Stanford University Press.

Urban, Patricia. 1993. "Naco Valley," in Henderson, John S., and Marilyn Beaudry-Corbett (eds.), *Pottery of Prehistoric Honduras*. Institute of Archaeology Monograph 35. Los Angeles: University of California, pp. 30–63.

Wonderley, Anthony. 1981. *Late Postclassic Excavations at Naco, Honduras*. Latin American Studies Program, Dissertation Series, No. 86. Ithaca, NY: Cornell University Archaeology Program-Latin American Studies Program.

———. 1984a. "Rancho Ires Phase (Colonial) Test Excavations," in Henderson, John (ed.), *Archaeology in Northwestern Honduras: Interim Reports of the Proyecto Arquologico Sula, Volume 1*. Ithaca, NY: Cornell University Archaeology Program-Latin American Studies Program, pp. 4–26.

———. 1984b. "Test excavations of the Naco (Late Postclassic) Phase," in Henderson, John (ed.), *Archaeology in Northwestern Honduras: Interim Reports of the Proyecto Arqueologico Sula, Volume 1*. Ithaca, New York: Cornell University Archaeology Program-Latin American Studies Program, pp. 27–66.

———. 1986. "Material symbolics in Pre-Columbian Households: The Painted Pottery of Naco, Honduras." *Journal of Anthropological Research* 42:497–534.

ELEVEN

THE SCALE OF THE INTIMATE

Imperial Policies and Sexual Practices in San Francisco

Barbara L. Voss

Sexuality and intimacy are often conflated with the micro-scale realms of social life: the marriage bed, domesticity, the household, the family. Archaeologists studying sexuality and colonization have consequently focused directly on household deposits and personal identities. This study, like many others in this volume, rejects this simplistic equation between sexuality and the micro-scale. Rather, I understand sexuality and intimacy to be *points of articulation* among personal, familial, institutional, economic, religious, and governmental fields of social practice. In this, I take inspiration from Foucault's observation that sexuality is "an especially dense transfer point for relations of power . . . useful for the greatest number of maneuvers and capable of serving as a point of support, as a linchpin, for the most varied strategies" (Foucault 1978: 103).

In this chapter, I explore multiple scales of intimacy and sexual politics by juxtaposing two historical contexts that have rarely been considered related. One context is the Spanish "discovery" and subsequent settlement of the San Francisco Bay in California in the late eighteenth and early nineteenth centuries – events that were, without question, colonial. The other is the influx of Chinese immigrants to the same region in the mid- to late nineteenth century, following the U.S. annexation of California. Although immigration policies during this period are rarely interpreted as "colonial," attention to macro- and micro-scale sexual politics exposes the "imperial effects" (Coronil 2007) of sexual regulations aimed at Chinese immigrants to the United States during this period.

Research at the Presidio of San Francisco National Historic Landmark is conducted in partnership with the Presidio Trust and the National Park Service. This chapter presents my views as an independent researcher and does not represent the policies of either agency. The Market Street Chinatown Archaeology Project is funded in part by Stanford University, History San José, and the City of San José Redevelopment Agency in cooperation with Chinese Historical and Cultural Project and Past Forward, Inc. Deb Cohler, El Casella, Bryn Williams, two anonymous reviewers, and other contributing authors to this volume generously provided comments on earlier drafts of this chapter.

This unlikely comparison reveals surprising consistencies in the deployment of sexuality across two quite different historical periods. In both instances, the intersection of racial segregation with sexual regulation resulted in profound disruptions of familial relations among subjugated populations. Simultaneously, same-sex labor regimes generated new homosocial contexts in which affective relationships among men became increasingly central to daily life.

SPANISH-COLONIAL SAN FRANCISCO

The San Francisco Bay (Figure 11.1) offers one of the most protected natural harbors along the Pacific Coast of North America. Anthropologists have conventionally described Native Californian societies before colonization as "complex hunter-gatherers" (e.g., Blackburn and Anderson 1993) who lived in villages ranging from 150 to 300 people, with groups of villages comprising a district that shared a common dialect and political and religious leadership (Milliken 1995).

The San Francisco Bay region was largely unaffected by European empire-building until the late eighteenth century, when Alta California came under Spanish rule during that empire's final territorial expansion into North America. In 1776, Juan Bautista de Anza led a caravan of 193 settlers – 2 priests, 37 male soldiers, 11 male civilians, 35 adult women (mostly wives of the male soldiers and civilians), and 110 dependent children – on a nine-month journey from Tubac, Arizona, to the San Francisco Bay (Langellier and Rosen 1996). The colonists established three settlements: a military presidio (San Francisco) at the mouth of the bay; a religious mission (also named San Francisco but more popularly called Dolores) about 4 miles inland from the Presidio; and a civilian pueblo (San José) at the south end of the bay. Colonial settlement of the San Francisco Bay region eventually expanded to include six missions and three civilian pueblos, along with two additional military fortifications along the mouth of the bay.

Following the Spanish imperial policy of *reducción*, colonists directed Native Californians living in the San Francisco region to live in missions, where they were converted to Christianity and instructed in agriculture and colonial trades. Although some Native Californians came to the missions voluntarily, most relocations occurred under duress (Milliken 1995). Other Native Californians were recruited or impressed as laborers at the Presidio of San Francisco (Voss 2008a) and at *ranchos* granted to colonists (Silliman 2004).

Marriage in Colonial San Francisco

From the beginning, imperial policies shaped the sexual and gendered composition of San Francisco's colonial settlements and the relationships that formed between colonizers and Native Californians. Marriage was a particularly contested institution, not only in eighteenth- and nineteenth-century San Francisco but throughout the history of Spain's empire in the Americas. Debates centered on two interrelated themes: the validity, and advisability, of cross-racial marriage and the relative authority of parents, the Church, and the state in granting and sanctioning marriages. In

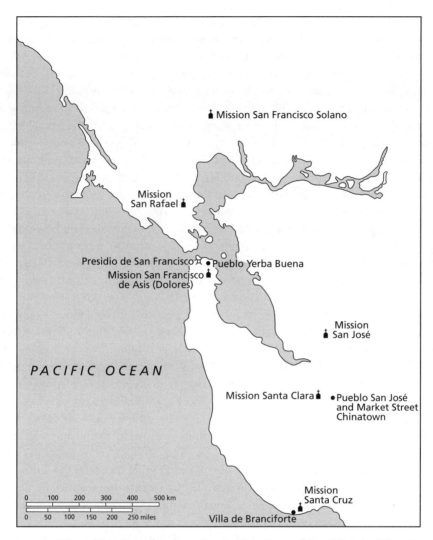

FIGURE 11.1. Map of San Francisco Bay, showing locations of Spanish-colonial settlements and the site of the Market Street Chinatown.

some contexts, intermarriage was promoted to foster alliances between prominent colonial and indigenous families. Simultaneously, from the early 1500s onward, military policy and colonial laws such as the 1629 Policy of Domestic Unity and the 1776 Royal Pragmatic on Marriage established barriers to interracial marriages in the colonies (Mörner 1967: 26–27; Castañeda 1993).

Archaeological scholarship on interethnic households in the Spanish Americas has demonstrated that negotiations of Spanish-colonial regulations of marriage varied considerably across location and period (Voss 2008d). For example, although racial intermarriage was commonly practiced in some colonial settlements (e.g., Deagan 1983), in others, many male colonists elected to remain legally single rather than marry indigenous women (see Voss 2008d: 869). Colonial regulation of intermarriage concerned the legitimation of colonial households and the classification of their offspring and did not suppress interracial sexual relations. The pervasive archaeological evidence for indigenous women's influence in the material culture of colonial homes in many regions of the Spanish-colonial Americas has led Rothschild (2003) to note that intermarriage was only one of several ways that colonists acquired Native American women's labor and services, including sexual services.

The politics and practices related to marriage in Spanish-colonial San Francisco illustrate the complex interactions between imperial regulation of sexuality and colonial sexual practices. Juan Bautista de Anza enrolled San Francisco's colonial settlers during a special campaign that recruited not individual soldiers but married couples with proven reproductive capabilities. He planned that each soldier–wife pair would bring six children with them to the new colonial settlement; in the end, the actual average was closer to three children per couple (Chapman 1916).

State involvement in the colonists' sexual relationships continued far beyond their initial recruitment. As the settlement matured, the colonists were almost entirely endogamous. This was not simply a matter of personal choice: under frontier military regulations, marriages had to be approved by the Presidio's commanding officer, who was charged with enforcing the Royal Pragmatic on Marriage. Similarly, Native Californians living at missions, classified as *neofitos* (neophytes), found that mission priests had complete authority in sanctifying preexisting indigenous marriages (including dissolution of polygamous marriages) and in permitting new marriages (Milliken 1995; Newell 2009). Both Presidio commanders and mission priests discouraged colonial-indigenous intermarriage in San Francisco. During 1776–1834, only six marriages between colonists and Native Californians were recorded in San Francisco. Most of these were among older widows and widowers whose first marriages had been within their community of origin (Milliken et al. 2005: 128–129).

The archaeological record of the Presidio of San Francisco provides a window into the material outcomes of colonial endogamy. In La Florida, the Caribbean, and the U.S. Southeast and Southwest, where interracial marriage and concubinage were common, colonial household deposits usually contain high frequencies of Native American material culture and foodstuffs (e.g., Deagan 1983; Deagan and Cruxent 1993; Loren 1999; Rothschild 2003). In contrast, excavation at the Presidio of San Francisco indicates that colonists there maintained firm material boundaries between themselves and local Native Californian populations. Only 10 of approximately 465,000 artifacts – approximately 0.002% – recovered during excavation of the Presidio of San Francisco's main quadrangle during 1993–2000 are objects that are associated with Native Californian material culture traditions (Voss 2008a: 160). For example, colonial households used vesicular basalt grinding stones imported from present-day Mexico rather than adopting ubiquitous groundstone tools used by Native Californians. The content of the colonial diet consisted overwhelmingly of cultivated cereals and legumes and domesticated stock. Although this staple diet was supplemented by a small quantity of wild game, those foods most closely associated with Native Californians – shellfish and acorns – are conspicuously absent from colonial residential deposits, even though they are abundant in the environment surrounding the Presidio. Similarly, none of the ornamentation typical of Native Californian dress – beads, earrings, pendants, and hair ornaments carved from shell, bone, and antler – is present in the deposits associated with colonial house-holds (Voss 2008a).

This paucity of Native Californian artifacts in the Presidio's main quadrangle is especially puzzling because historical records indicate that many Native Californi-ans labored in the quadrangle, as servants, construction workers, crafts workers, prisoners of war, and Indian Auxiliary militias. Despite constant physical proximity between colonists and Native Californians, Native Californian material culture was not incorporated into colonial residential life. It is only in areas well outside the quadrangle itself that archaeologists have encountered colonial-era deposits that contain substantial quantities of Native Californian material culture and foodstuffs. It was not a lack of contact between colonists and Native Californians but rather the imperial regulation of intimate relationships that fostered a material divide between the Spanish-colonial settlers and the Native Californians among whom they lived.

Military Conflict and Labor Regimes

At the same time that colonial marriages were highly regulated, military conflict during San Francisco's Spanish-colonial era was highly gendered and sexualized. Only men could enlist in the colonial military. Consequently, combat zones – located well beyond the colonial settlement – were highly masculinized regions of social life. Soldiers from the Presidio of San Francisco routinely attacked Native Californian villages in the coastal mountain ranges and the Central Valley to the east, south, and north of the Presidio. This created a region of colonial encounters in which colonial women were largely absent.

Not coincidentally, rape was sometimes deployed as an unofficial military tactic, generating "a disturbing pattern of wholesale sexual assault" against Native Californi-ans (Castillo 1994: 283). Ethnohistoric and archaeological evidence has shown that some Native Californian communities reconfigured their villages to resist sexualized military violence, relocating areas for food processing, basket making, hide prepa-ration, and other tasks from the villages' periphery to the center of tightly packed houses. In some cases, ditches were excavated around housing clusters to deter colo-nial troops from entering on horseback (Voss 2008c: 197–198). At the very least, these spatial transformation moved Native Californian women's daily routines to the interior of indigenous villages; perhaps Native Californian women's movement across the broader landscape was also circumscribed by the threat of colonial sexual violence.

Sexualized warfare produced gendered labor regimes. After a battle victory, colo-nial soldiers separated prisoners of war by age and gender, sending women and children to the nearest mission to be converted to Christianity. Captured Native Californian men were usually escorted to the Presidio of San Francisco, where they were sentenced to convict labor – primarily construction and agricultural work – for several months to a few years (Figure 11.2). As military conflict increased through-out the colonial occupation, so, too, did the number of adult Native Californian men laboring at the Presidio of San Francisco, from five to twenty workers in the 1780s to as many as a hundred during the 1800s–1810s (Voss 2008a: 77–83).

The settlement's increased reliance on Native Californian laborers transformed the gendered relations of local production. For example, the soldiers and their families were initially responsible for constructing their own houses. Archaeological research has revealed that over time, architectural production shifted from a small-scale endeavor shared by colonial men, women, and children to a centrally organized undertaking carried out by work gangs of Native Californian men under the direction of colonial soldiers (Voss 2008a: 173–202). Analysis of locally produced ceramics indicates a similar shift from household-based production to centralized production in workshops run by master crafts workers and colonial soldiers who supervised Native Californian laborers (Voss 2008a: 203–232).

The homosocial environments created by sexualized military combat and colonial labor regimes linked the violence of colonization outside the Presidio settlement to the mundane routines of production within the settlement itself. Whereas the outcomes of combat were uncertain and posed significant risk to the colonial soldiers, construction projects and craft production were venues in which small numbers of colonial men could more securely control the labor and bodies of male Native Californians. Perhaps the most significant product of these male homosocial labor regimes was not the buildings and craft goods themselves but the routine interactions that consolidated hierarchical relationships between colonial officers and rank-and-file soldiers, and between colonial men and indigenous men. The sexual politics of empire forged tight interconnections among colonial policies, military strategies, and the daily routines of colonial domestic life.

FROM FRONTIER OUTPOST TO SETTLER STATE

Typical of many regions of the world, the colonization of the San Francisco Bay region occurred in multiple waves. Spanish rule was supplanted in 1821 by California's incorporation into the newly independent nation of Mexico, a period in which subjugation of Native Californian populations shifted from mission and military institutions to privately held agricultural *ranchos* (Silliman 2004). The Mexican *rancho* economy ended abruptly when the United States annexed California as part of the spoils of the 1846–1848 Mexican–American War. With liberal relocation and immigration policies bolstered by sensationalist accounts of gold discovery at Sutter's Mill, the newly formed State of California was rapidly occupied by both U.S.-born and foreign-born settlers. In 1845, the nonnative population of California numbered 5,600 people. By 1850, it had surged to 93,000; by 1860, to 380,000; and it reached nearly 2.5 million by 1900 (Hornbeck and Fuller 1983: 51, 68).

Because California's statehood is often framed in U.S. history as the "liberation" of California from Mexican rule, the historical events that followed are rarely interpreted as imperial projects. However, Coronil's (2007: 243) model of "imperial effects" (see also Voss, Chapter 2, this volume) draws attention to the *intensification* of colonial projects during early California statehood. For example, Native Californians were targeted by military extermination campaigns and forced removal to reservations (Hurtado 1988). California's former Spanish-colonial/Mexican population was largely politically disenfranchised and dispossessed of their landholdings

FIGURE 11.2. Native laborers being escorted by a Presidio soldier. Detail from *View of the Presidio of San Francisco*, by Louis Choris, 1816, color engraving. Courtesy of the Bancroft Library, University of California, Berkeley.

(Haas 1995; Sánchez 1995). Immigrant workers, recruited as laborers in the rapidly expanding resource extraction, transportation, and manufacture industries, were differentially treated and at times segregated on the basis of country of origin. In sum, California quickly came to resemble other breakaway settler colonies through rapid geographic expansion into previously uncolonized inland regions, the formation of "internal colonies" through Indian reservations, and the racial segregation of worker populations.

CHINESE IMMIGRATION AND POST-STATEHOOD IMPERIAL EFFECTS

The case of Chinese immigration provides a poignant example of neo-colonial sexual politics in the early decades of California's statehood. Chinese immigrants, most from the southern province of Guangdong, comprised a significant portion of new settlers in California, numbering 35,000 in 1860 and 120,000 in 1900. In San Francisco Bay area counties, Chinese residents consistently accounted for 7 to 15 percent of the total population during 1860–1890 (Yu 2001).

Even as California's politicians and business owners promoted Chinese immigration as a reliable source of cheap labor, state and federal laws aimed to ensure that Chinese residents remained "perpetual foreigners" (Lowe 1996), ineligible for citizenship, unable to testify in court, and prohibited from owning land (Baxter 2008; Voss and Allen 2008). Because the U.S. Constitution grants citizenship to all persons born within the country's borders, preventing Chinese citizenship required intensive regulation of Chinese immigrants' sexuality and reproduction. All the immigration laws aimed at Chinese immigrants specifically targeted their sexual and reproductive relationships. The 1875 Page Law prohibited the immigration of Chinese and Japanese "prostitutes," a category that was indiscriminately applied to nearly all single Asian women attempting to immigrate. This was followed in 1882 by the Chinese Exclusion Act (renewed in 1892, 1902, and 1904), which prohibited Chinese laborers from sponsoring the immigration of their wives and children. Concurrently, in 1880, California's anti-miscegenation laws were expanded to prohibit marriage between whites and "Mongolians," the legal term used at that time for people of Asian descent (Gyory 1998; Hsu 2000; Takaki 1998).

Thus, as with the settlement of the Presidio of San Francisco nearly a century earlier, the gendered and sexual composition of the Chinese population of the San Francisco Bay area was profoundly shaped by state regulation. By the late nineteenth century, the ratio of Chinese men to Chinese women in the United States had increased to 21 to 1 (Yu 2001: 5). The combination of anti-miscegenation laws, the Page Law, and the Chinese Exclusion Act generated profound structural constraints on the sexual and reproductive lives of Chinese immigrants.

Sexual Politics and the Archaeology of the Market Street Chinatown

My own research on Chinese immigration has centered on the Market Street Chinatown in San Jose, California. Located at the southern tip of the San Francisco Bay, San Jose was one of three core population centers for Chinese immigration from the 1860s onward (the other two being San Francisco and Los Angeles). The Market Street Chinatown encompassed a two-block area of downtown San Jose that had formerly been the site of the Spanish-colonial pueblo. Artifacts from the site were recovered in the 1980s through a salvage excavation during urban development. Local Chinese Americans were instrumental in advocating for archaeological excavation at the site before its destruction. Their involvement continues through the current Market Street Chinatown Archaeology Project, which is a collaborative partnership between Chinese Historical and Cultural Project, History San José, Past Forward, Inc., and Stanford University.

Founded in the early 1860s, the Market Street Chinatown housed more than 1,000 Chinese, predominantly adult men alongside a smaller number of merchant and professional families (Figure 11.3). It was also the cultural and economic headquarters for more than 2,000 additional Chinese, also predominantly adult men, who worked in agriculture, industry, mining, and domestic service in the surrounding area. The community was a thriving center of Chinese American culture and a fragile refuge from anti-Chinese racism and violence. In May 1887, during a period of heightened hostility against San Jose's Chinese residents, the Market Street Chinatown was destroyed by an arson fire. Despite open pressure to leave the region, within a few days, its former residents established two new communities on the outskirts of the growing city (Yu 2001).

The spatial organization and material culture of Chinese American archaeological sites such as the Market Street Chinatown cannot be understood without taking into account the effects of ethnosexual discriminatory legislation. Prohibited from owning land, Chinese immigrants formed business consortiums that rented urban lots from white landowners and developed these leaseholds into mixed residential/commercial Chinese neighborhoods. Residential and commercial buildings faced inward toward a shared internal network of alleyways, outdoor cooking facilities, and other public spaces in the center of the block. By and large, people in the Market Street Chinatown lived in two kinds of residences. Tenements provided short- and long-term housing for adult men, who slept in shared rooms and used common cooking areas and other facilities. Merchants, who could sponsor their wives and children for immigration, operated stores that provided housing not only

FIGURE 11.3. Market Street Chinatown, San Jose, California, in 1877. Courtesy of History San Jose.

for the merchant and his family but also for business partners, clerks, employees, boarders, and visitors (Yu 2001).

State regulation of Chinese immigrants' sexuality is reflected in the very structure of the archaeological record. In city blocks adjacent to the Market Street Chinatown, non-Chinese archaeological deposits dating to the same period consist largely of informal trash pits and household privies located in the rear yards of discrete house lots. In contrast, the Market Street Chinatown archaeological record consists primarily of formally constructed wood-lined trash pits that were located along the edges of buildings, public outdoor areas, and alleys (Voss 2008b). Such deposits cannot be attributed to individual households or families. Instead, they indicate community-level organization of refuse disposal along with the collective organization of residential life and spatial integration of commercial and domestic activity.

Split Households

The scarcity of conventional "households" in historic Chinatowns has led many scholars to mistakenly characterize these communities as bachelor societies. Yet for many Chinese immigrants and Chinese Americans, a flexible understanding of the relationship between family and place enabled the endurance and reproduction of Chinese families despite forced separation. About two-fifths of Chinese men residing in the United States in the late nineteenth and early twentieth centuries were married to women who lived in China, forming bi-continental "split households" (Hsu 2000). Some married before immigrating to the United States, whereas others returned to their home villages to wed after arranging the marriage through correspondence with family members and the fiancé. In split households, the timing of sexual affection between spouses, and the couple's management of sexual reproduction, required careful planning and considerable expenditure.

Although physical contact was infrequent, the marriages and extended kin networks formed through split households were characterized by strong emotional and economic bonds, maintained through correspondence and remittances. For male kin, reunification was possible through immigration, and fathers and uncles living abroad encouraged their Chinese-born sons and nephews to join them as laborers in the United States. This practice led to multigenerational chains of immigration within families. By the mid-twentieth century, some Chinese families had lived and worked in the San Francisco Bay area for three or more generations, but all of the family members were Chinese-born.

Because most Chinese immigrants maintained familial and social lives that spanned two continents, the materiality of their daily lives was geographically dispersed. For example, members of Chinese Historical and Cultural Project have cautioned that archaeologists should not expect to be able to evaluate economic status from the household objects recovered from the Market Street Chinatown (Voss 2005).

Tableware ceramics, which are commonly used by historical archaeologists as an index of economic status, provide one example of this. The majority of tableware ceramics recovered from the Market Street Chinatown are inexpensive bowls and plates (Table 11.1). Bowls are overwhelmingly Asian porcelains. Nearly half (48.9 percent) of the bowls are decorated in a single pattern, Bamboo. Typically costing only two to five cents per piece (Sando and Felton 1993), Bamboo pattern porcelain bowls were the cheapest ceramic available at this time. Most plates recovered from the Market Street Chinatown are British-produced white earthenwares. Here again the most abundant category is the least expensive within its class – plain undecorated vessels (Miller 1980, 1991).[1]

A conventional interpretation of this tableware assemblage would likely stress the impoverishment and low purchasing power indicated by the high frequency of cheap ceramics.[2] However, this archaeological index of impoverishment is contradicted by what might be termed the monumental landscape of the Market Street Chinatown and of the residents' home villages in Guangdong. Within the Market Street Chinatown, merchants and district associations raised funds to construct a temple, which occupied a prominent central place in the community. Its wooden walls were festooned with papers publically displaying the names of those who donated cash and goods for its construction and upkeep. The open lower floor of the temple served as a multipurpose community room, and the upper floor contained the altar, constructed of ornate lacquer woodwork, gilt statues, incense burners and candlesticks, and a brass gong, all imported from China. Several elements of the temple survive today and are now curated in the Chinese American Museum in San Jose (Yu 2001).

Table 11.1. Bowls and plates cataloged from the Market Street Chinatown collection[*]

	Bowls		Plates	
	No. MNV[**]	% MNV	No. MNV	% MNV
Asian porcelains	**328**	**91.6%**	**48**	**23.4%**
Bamboo	175	48.9%	NA[2]	NA[†]
Four Flowers	81	22.6%	35	17.1%
Celadon	51	14.2%	0	0.0%
Other Asian porcelain	21	5.9%	13	6.3%
Euro-American improved earthenwares	**30**	**8.4%**	**153**	**74.6%**
Plain white earthware	18	5.0%	85	41.5%
Shell-edged	0	0.0%	12	5.9%
Transfer printed	5	1.4%	29	14.1%
Other British-American improved earthenwares	7	2.0%	27	13.2%
Other ceramics	**0**	**0.0%**	**4**	**2.0%**
Total	358	100%	205	100%

[*] Approximately 40 percent of the tableware ceramic assemblage have been cataloged as of this analysis. This analysis includes all cataloged sherds that represent vessels that were conventionally used for single servings (ca. 10–25cm diameter). Smaller saucers and condiment dishes, and larger serving vessels, are excluded from this analysis.

[**] Minimum Number of Vessels

[†] The bamboo pattern was only used on single-serving bowls and was not available in plate form.

Similarly, nineteenth-century remittances sent by San Jose's Chinese to their home villages in Guangdong not only increased the personal wealth of the immigrants' families but also underwrote substantial building projects. "New Villages" were established throughout the region, composed of clusters of so-called foreign houses, built with brick and concrete and decorated with stained glass, Greek-style columns, domed roofs, and front porches. Remittances were also used to build schools, orphanages, hospitals, railroads, bridges, paved roads, electric grids, and public lighting that transformed the region's infrastructure (Dehua 1999: 28–29; Hsu 2000: 40–54). Patronage of public works and community facilities were highly prioritized by split households.

The contrast between daily life in the Market Street Chinatown, in which most residents slept in crowded tenements and ate simple meals off cheap ceramic bowls and plates, and the opulent architecture and high standard of living that was enabled by remittances to Guangdong, speaks to a materially divided life. Without doubt, most residents of the Market Street Chinatown worked in low-paid professions such as domestic service and agricultural labor. Archaeological evidence such as the ceramic assemblage would conventionally be interpreted as evidence of impoverishment. However, we must also ask whether the consumer purchasing patterns evident in the ceramic assemblage indicate economic *constraint* or deliberate *restraint*. Residents of the Market Street Chinatown appear to have responded to discriminatory regulations and separation from their families by developing a shared commitment to community-oriented spending.

Archaeological Traces of Homosociality

The geographic separation of adult men from their children and their female kin meant that the Market Street Chinatown was strongly characterized by homosociality. With a highly skewed gender ratio, many residents' daily interactions and immediate affective ties revolved around friendships, business relationships, and associations that formed among men.

Archaeologists studying Chinese immigrant workers in agricultural, mining, logging, and railroad camps have described collective bunkhouses formed by four to twelve Chinese men, who pooled resources to purchase food and other necessities and to hire cooks and housekeepers (usually other Chinese men who could not pursue wage labor because of injuries or poor health; e.g., Gardner 2004; Hardesty 1988; Van Bueren 2008). In urban communities such as the Market Street Chinatown, most immigrant men lived in tenements. Perhaps tenement residents also organized themselves into domestic units, as Chinese men living in more rural areas are known to have done. Historical accounts also indicate that stores were central to the lives of San Jose's Chinese men. Far beyond serving a mercantile function, stores served as headquarters for district associations and labor recruiters, offered inexpensive ready-made meals, and provided a sense of community perhaps comparable to present-day neighborhood bars or coffeehouses (Yu 2001).

Research conducted on the Market Street Chinatown collection by Michaels (2005) and Williams (2004, 2008) provides archaeological perspectives on homosociality in this urban Chinese community. Michaels' research centered on sixteen peck-marked ceramic vessels recovered from the Market Street Chinatown (Figure 11.4). Peck marks are Chinese characters chipped by hand onto mass-produced vessels; in many regions of China today, it is a common practice to peck-mark plates and bowls with symbols of good luck. It is likely that nineteenth-century immigrants carried this tradition to the Market Street Chinatown. Michaels' analysis, however, found interesting variations in both the meaning and the context of the peck marks. Of the twelve marks that could be translated, only five are wishes or blessings. These were recovered from features associated with stores that, as noted earlier, often sold ready-made meals. In contrast, seven peck marks represent individual names, family names, or nicknames, a practice that Michaels' sources indicate was not common in China itself. Interestingly, Michaels found these name-marked vessels were primarily recovered from features associated with tenements and were absent from the features associated with stores (Michaels 2005: 132). Michaels interprets this modification of traditional peck marking as a "hybridized art form" related to the stresses of daily life in the crowded living quarters in tenement houses (Michaels 2005:132).

Michaels' research on peck-marked ceramics is complemented by Williams's studies of opium pipes and alcohol cups at the Market Street Chinatown (Williams 2004, 2008). Although stereotypically associated with Chinese immigrants, opium consumption was widespread throughout the U.S. population during the mid- and late nineteenth century. In fact, the commercially available opiate-rich pills, tinctures, and patent medicines commonly used by Euro-Americans were far more potent and addictive than the opium paste that was smoked by Chinese immigrants

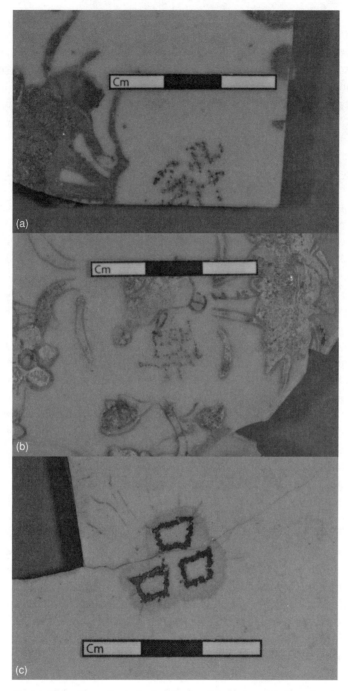

FIGURE 11.4. Examples of peck-marked vessels from the Market Street Chinatown. (a) "Mahn," a family name, and (b) "Drunk," possibly a personal nickname, are on Chinese export porcelain plates decorated with the Four Flowers pattern that were recovered near tenement housing. (c) "Sir," possibly referring to a military rank, is on a plain British whiteware plate recovered from a feature near stores and a restaurant. Translations by Scott Wilson and Young Xie as published in Michaels 2005:129. Photos courtesy of the Market Street Chinatown Archaeology Project.

(Courtwright 2001). Williams's analysis of ninety-five ceramic opium pipe bowls from the Market Street Chinatown collection provides a very different picture of the consumption of this social drug than historical accounts would suggest. First, although Euro-American observers described opium smoking as carried on in secretive gathering places ("opium dens"), Williams found that pipe bowl sherds were primarily found in association with domestic refuse and were distributed evenly throughout residential and commercial areas, indicating that opium was smoked in a wide variety of spatial and social contexts. Second, Williams found that the pipe bowls themselves showed "a remarkable degree of formal diversity both within and between features. . . . There are no two pipes that are exactly alike" (Williams 2004: 223), pointing to individuality within a widely shared social practice.

Williams has also studied alcohol-related artifacts from Feature 20, a trash pit located near a store, the temple, and several tenement buildings. Feature 20 included six glass Euro-American alcohol bottles, one small glass tumbler, and three tiny porcelain cups, decorated in Four Flowers pattern (Clevenger 2004). The tiny cups are particularly notable because they were traditionally used at festivals and other social gatherings to drink potent Chinese distilled liquors such as *ng ga pei* (Wegars 2001). In this case, the social context of alcohol consumption is ambiguous: the alcohol in the bottles, likely whiskey or gin, could have been served to customers at the nearby store, distributed at a temple festival, or passed among roommates in one of the tenements. In any case, Williams notes that the apparent use of the tiny porcelain cups to drink Euro-American spirits may indicate a novel articulation of Chinese *wu* masculine ideologies in this immigrant setting. *Wu* masculinity, hegemonically associated with the working class and with warriors, emphasizes the joining of strength with restraint and wisdom. Drinking potent alcohol in specialized tiny cups allowed men to display fortitude and self-discipline simultaneously (Williams 2008: 59–61).

Notably, both Michaels and Williams focused on commensality as routine yet significant material practices through which social relations among men were forged and negotiated. Interestingly, the objects related to these practices reveal a strong tension between collective allegiance and individual identity. Roommates might draw their meal from a common pot, but some men ate from personal rice bowls they had carefully marked with their nickname or family name. At the end of a long day, men relaxing together in their tenement housing might sit and smoke together, but each man's pipe bowl was uniquely decorated. Convivial drinking strengthened men's relationships with each other and also served as a venue for displaying individual fortitude and control of the self. Eating, smoking, and drinking were moments in the day when men living at Market Street consolidated their relationships with each other while simultaneously expressing their individuality.

It would be a mistake to celebrate the new social worlds forged by Chinese immigrants in the face of ethnosexual discrimination without also acknowledging the personal losses that resulted from U.S. immigration policy. Poems and letters written by Chinese immigrants frequently spoke of their loneliness. Merchants' children who grew up in San Jose's Chinatowns recalled being doted on by dozens of "uncles" who longed for their own families (Yu 2001). For most, family reunification was a deferred dream "that stretched into decades until death made reunification impossible" (Hsu 2000: 91). Not unlike the Native Californian men laboring at the Presidio of San Francisco a century earlier, for Chinese immigrants in San Jose, one "imperial effect" was the profound disruption of family life.

DISCUSSION

Throughout this chapter, I have interwoven three core arguments: methodological, historical, and social. Methodologically, I have argued against the assumption that sexuality is only associated with the micro-scale and demonstrated that it is a point of articulation between macro- and micro-scale aspects of colonialism. An archaeology of the intimate thus requires us to investigate every scale available to our discipline. We are no more be able to "find" the intimate only within the close confines of a dwelling place than we can investigate a world system solely through a map on the wall. It is only through tracing the material links that bind together colonial policy with so-called private life that we will be able to understand the links between imperial formations and intimate relations.

The second argument, historical in nature, uses Coronil's model of "imperial effects" to question the "post"-colonial status of California statehood. Comparing the sexual politics of eighteenth- and nineteenth-century California reveals some surprising congruencies: gender segregation, combined with the regulation of interracial sexuality, disrupted heterosexual kinship relations, and generated male homosocial environments among some subaltern populations. In both cases, the separation of adult men from their children and their female kin – by force or by design – was closely linked to labor regimes.

The ruptures between California's Spanish-colonial period and its early statehood are substantial enough to resist interpreting these congruencies as continuity. Rather, the similarities between the two cases could be symptoms of what anthropologist James C. Scott terms a "structural family resemblance" (Scott 1990: 21) between these contexts of domination. Tracing the sexual consequences of statist policies in mid- and late-nineteenth-century California exposes a practical politics of imperialism that was cloaked with rhetorics of nation-building and economic development.

The third argument concerns the intimate lives of subaltern populations. I have demonstrated that eighteenth-century Native Californians and nineteenth-century Chinese immigrants in the San Francisco Bay area came under increased sexual scrutiny and regulation. The options available to these subaltern men to form cross-sex romantic, sexual, and family relationships were starkly diminished. Indeed, the disruption and distanciation of subaltern personal relationships is echoed in many other studies presented here (e.g., Croucher; Casella; Dawdy; Hull; and Tarble de Scaramelli, this volume).

In both Spanish-colonial and early American San Francisco, sex-segregated labor regimes produced new homosocial contexts in which affective relationships among men became increasingly central to daily life. While developing this chapter, I was often pointedly asked why I "avoided" discussing same-sex *sexuality* in the foregoing discussions of same-sex *sociality*. Before addressing this persistent question, I want to draw attention to the politics of the question itself. Present-day folk models of sexuality, especially male sexuality, often posit that men living in single-sex environments "need" to turn to each other for sexual release. Such folk models resonate strongly with medico-psychological classifications that differentiated between "situational" and "congenital" homosexuality from the late nineteenth century onward (Bland and Doan 1998). They also evoke "hydraulic" models of sexuality, for example, those prevalent in Freudian psychology, that assume a universal sexual drive that requires management and release (Freud 1975 [1910]).

Cross-cultural studies have not only documented the ubiquity of same-sex sexual practices across cultures but also demonstrated that the cultural meaning of sexual practices, both cross-sex and same-sex, differs profoundly according to context. It is a reasonable assumption that in any social context – heterosocial or homosocial – there were likely a fair number of people who engaged in same-sex sexual practices. The question that seems anthropologically and archaeologically relevant is not *whether* some men in homosocial environments were having sex with each other, but rather what cultural forms and institutions gave cultural meaning to these sexual practices.

In the case of Native Californian men who were captured or recruited to work at Spanish-colonial presidios and Mexican-era *ranchos*, it is well-documented that laborers actively resisted Spanish-colonial/Mexican labor demands (e.g., Castillo 1989; Hurtado 1988). Group-level tactics of resistance, including negotiations, refusal, flight, armed resistance, and establishment of inland fugitive communities, most likely relied on strong affective relationships among the laborers who were willing to risk their individual safety for their fellows. Whether these affective relationships included sexual relationships is a matter of speculation (see also Funari and Carvalho's discussion, Chapter 15 in this volume, of the historiographic challenges in reconstructing sexuality in Brazilian maroon communities).

For the immigrant men who shared tenement housing at the Market Street Chinatown several decades later, there is much stronger documentary and archaeological evidence of the social organization of formal and informal homosocial relationships. To the extent that same-sex sexuality was or was not part of Chinese immigrant men's affective relationships with each other, same-sex sexuality does not seem to have contributed to specific categories of identities or relationships, nor is there any indication that same-sex sexuality was particularly stigmatized or persecuted. Instead, what is well documented are social institutions that tied individual men to larger communities. The men's financial support of the temple and their patronage of Chinatown stores linked them with institutions that provided ritual and domestic services and fostered community sociality. District associations and intergenerational male kinship (especially father–son and uncle–nephew) forged strong bonds between immigrant men by reinforcing their shared connection with their home villages. These affective ties have left an indelible mark on the archaeological record: a shared commitment to faraway relatives fostered economic restraint in personal expenditures. Convivial eating, smoking, and drinking in these contexts were occasions when men used material culture to express their own, and witness each other's, individuality.

Conclusion

This chapter, in dialogue with other case studies presented in this book, reveals strong structural similarities in the sexual politics of colonial projects. Through the intersections of racialization, labor regimes, and sexual regulation, the weight of imperial institutions bore down hard on the affective relationships of those subject to colonial rule. In such contexts, kinship, marriage, parenting, and sexuality were sites of struggle as well as locations of refuge.

Although there may have been structural similarities in colonial institutions, the case studies in this book show a great degree of variation in how subaltern communities responded to these oppressive conditions. From mine marriages in South Africa (Weiss, Chapter 4) to split households linking San Jose and Guangdong, from prison motherhood in Australia (Casella, Chapter 3) to rogue colonialism in Louisiana (Dawdy, Chapter 16), and from gladiators' memorials in the Roman empire (Garraffoni, Chapter 13) to stone monuments to Native American leaders in New England (Rubertone, Chapter 14), those subject to colonial rule fought to preserve affective and kinship relationships with incredible creativity and innovation.

Notes

1. The less expensive Bamboo porcelain pattern was not produced in vessel forms other than single-serving bowls, so Bamboo would not have been an option for plate purchases.
2. Plain white earthenwares were preferred by some nineteenth-century consumers because of their aesthetic qualities. At the Market Street Chinatown, the consistency in the selection of lowest-cost bowls, which happen to be decorated, and lowest-cost plates, which were plain, suggests that price sensitivity was likely a stronger factor than aesthetics in consumer decisions about ceramic purchases.

References

Baxter, R. Scott. 2008. "The Response of California's Chinese Populations to the Anti-Chinese Movement." *Historical Archaeology* 42(3):29–36.

Blackburn, Thomas C., and Kat Anderson, eds. 1993. *Before the Wilderness: Environmental Management by Native Californians.* Menlo Park, CA: Ballena Press.

Bland, L., and L. Doan, eds. 1998. *Sexology in Culture: Labeling Bodies and Desires.* Chicago: University of Chicago Press.

Castañeda, Antonia I. 1993. "Marriage: The Spanish Borderlands," in Cook, J. E. (ed.), *Encyclopedia of the North American Colonies*, Vol. II. New York: Maxwell Macmillan International, pp. 727–738.

Castillo, Edward D. 1989. "The Native Response to the Colonization of Alta California," in Thomas, D. H. (ed.), *Columbian Consequences: Archaeological and Historical Perspectives on the Spanish-colonial Borderlands West.* Washington, DC: Smithsonian Institution, pp. 377–393.

———. 1994. "Gender Status Decline, Resistance, and Accommodation among Female Neophytes in the Missions of California: A San Gabriel Case Study." *American Indian Culture and Research Journal* 18(1):67–93.

Chapman, Charles Edward. 1916. *The Founding of Spanish California: The Northwest Expansion of New Spain, 1687–1783.* New York: Macmillan Company.

Clevenger, Elizabeth Noelani. 2004. *Reconstructing Context and Assessing Research Potential: Feature 20 from the San José Market Street Chinatown*. Master's thesis, Stanford University, Stanford, CA.

Coronil, Fernando. 2007. "After Empire: Reflections on Imperialism from the Américas," in Stoler, A. L., C. McGranahan, and P. C. Perdue (eds.), *Imperial Formations*. Santa Fe, NM: School for Advanced Research Press, pp. 241–271.

Costanso, Miguel. 1992 [1769]. *Diario del viege de tierra hecho al norte de la California*. Lafayette, CA: Great West Books.

Courtwright, David T. 2001. *Dark Paradise: A History of Opium Addiction in America*. Cambridge, MA: Harvard University Press.

Deagan, Kathleen. 1983. "The Mestizo Minority: Archaeological Patterns of Intermarriage," Deagan, K. (ed.), in *Spanish St. Augustine: The Archaeology of a Colonial Creole Community*. New York: Academic Press, pp. 99–124.

———, and José María Cruxent. 1993. "From Contact to *Criollos*: The Archaeology of Spanish Colonization in Hispaniola." *Proceedings of the British Academy* 81:67–104.

Dehua, Zheng. 1999. "Guangdong *Qiiaoxiang* Architecture," in Pan, L. (ed.), *The Encyclopedia of the Chinese Overseas*. Cambridge, MA: Harvard University Press, pp. 28–29.

Foucault, Michel. 1978. *The History of Sexuality, Volume I: An Introduction*. New York: Random House.

Freud, S. 1975 [1910]. *Three Essays on the Theory of Sexuality*. New York: Basic Books.

Gardner, A. Dudley. 2004. "The Chinese in Wyoming: Life in the Core and Peripheral Communities," in Zhu, L., and R. Estep (eds.), *Ethnic Oasis: The Chinese in the Black Hills: South Dakota History*. Pierre: South Dakota Historical Society Press.

Gyory, Andrew. 1998. *Closing the Gate: Race, Politics, and the Chinese Exclusion Act*. Chapel Hill: University of North Carolina Press.

Haas, Lisbeth. 1995. *Conquest and Historical Identities in California 1769–1936*. Berkeley: University of California Press.

Hardesty, Donald L. 1988. *The Archaeology of Mining and Miners: A View from the Silver State*. Ann Arbor, MI: Society for Historical Archaeology.

Hornbeck, David, and David L. Fuller. 1983. *California Patterns: A Geographical and Historical Atlas*. Palo Alto, CA: Mayfield Publishing Company.

Hsu, Madeline. 2000. *Dreaming of Gold, Dreaming of Home: Transnationalism and Migration between the United States and South China, 1882–1943*. Stanford CA: Stanford University Press.

Hurtado, Albert L. 1988. *Indian Survival on the California Frontier*. New Haven, CT: Yale University Press.

Langellier, John Phillip, and Daniel B. Rosen. 1996. *El Presidio de San Francisco: A History under Spain and Mexico, 1776–1846*. Spokane, WA: The Arthur H. Clark Company.

Loren, Diana DiPaolo. 1999. *Creating Social Distinction: Articulating Colonial Policies and Practices along the 18th Century Louisiana/Texas Frontier*. Ph.D. dissertation, Binghamton State University of New York.

Lowe, Lisa. 1996. *Immigrants Acts: On Asian American Cultural Politics*. Durham, NC: Duke University Press.

McKeown, Adam. 2004. "Global Migration, 1846–1940." *Journal of World History* 15(2):155–189.

Michaels, Gina. 2005. "Peck-Marked Vessels from the San José Market Street Chinatown, A Study of Distribution and Significance." *International Journal of Historical Archaeology* 9(2):123–134.

Miller, George L. 1980. "Classification and Economic Scaling of 19th Century Ceramics." *Historical Archaeology* 14:1–40.

——— 1991. "A Revised Set of CC Index Values for Classification and Economic Scaling of English Ceramics from 1787–1880." *Historical Archaeology* 25(2):3–14.

Milliken, Randall. 1995. *A Time of Little Choice*. Menlo Park, CA: Ballena Press.

_____, Lawrence E. Shoup, and Beverly Ortiz. 2005. *The Historic Indian People of California's San Francisco Peninsula*. Draft Report prepared for the National Park Service, Golden Gate National Recreation Area, San Francisco, California, by Archaeological Consulting Services, Oakland, CA.

Mörner, Magnus. 1967. *Race Mixture in the History of Latin America*. Boston: Little, Brown, and Company.

Newell, Quincy D. 2009. *Constructing Lives at Mission San Francisco: Native Californians and Hispanic Colonists, 1776–1821*. Albuquerque, NM: University of New Mexico Press.

Pan, Lynn. 1999. "Emigration from China," in L. Pan (ed.), *The Encyclopedia of the Chinese Overseas*. Cambridge, MA: Harvard University Press, pp. 48–49.

Rothschild, Nan A. 2003. *Colonial Encounters in a Native American Landscape: The Spanish and Dutch in North America*. Washington, DC: Smithsonian Books.

Sánchez, Rosaura. 1995. *Telling Identities: The California Testimonios*. Minneapolis: University of Minnesota Press.

Sando, Ruth Ann, and David L. Felton. 1993. "Inventory Records of Ceramics and Opium from a Nineteenth Century Chinese Store in California," in Wegars, P. (ed.), in *Hidden Heritage: Historical Archaeology of the Overseas Chinese*. Amityville, NY: Baywood Publishing Company, pp. 151–176.

Scott, James C. 1990. *Domination and the Arts of Resistance: Hidden Transcripts*. New Haven, CT: Yale University Press.

Seed, Patricia. 1988. *To Love, Honor, and Obey in Colonial Mexico: Conflicts over Marriage Choice, 1574–1824*. Stanford, CA: Stanford University Press.

Silliman, Stephen W. 2004. *Lost Laborers in Colonial California: Native Americans and the Archaeology of Rancho Petaluma*. Tucson: University of Arizona Press.

Stoler, Ann Laura. 2001. "Tense and Tender Ties: The Politics of Comparison in North American History and (Post) Colonial Studies." *Journal of American History* 88(3):829–865.

Takaki, Ronald. 1998. *Strangers from a Different Shore: A History of Asian Americans* (updated and revised edition). New York: Back Bay Books/Little, Brown, and Company.

Van Bueren, Thad M. 2008. "Late Nineteenth-Century Chinese Farm Workers in the California Mother Lode." *Historical Archaeology* 42(3):80–96.

Voss, Barbara L. 2005. The Archaeology of Overseas Chinese Communities. *World Archaeology* 37(3):424–439.

_____. 2008a. *The Archaeology of Ethnogenesis: Race and Sexuality in Colonial San Francisco*. Berkeley: University of California Press.

_____. 2008b. "Between the Household and the World-System: Social Collectivity and Community Agency in Overseas Chinese Archaeology." *Historical Archaeology* 42(3):37–52.

_____. 2008c. "Domesticating Imperialism: Sexual Politics and the Archaeology of Empire." *American Anthropologist* 110(2):191–203.

_____. 2008d. "Gender, Race, and Labor in the Archaeology of the Spanish Colonial Americas." *Current Anthropology* 49(5):861–897.

_____. 2008e. "Poor People in Silk Shirts: Dress and Ethnogenesis in Spanish-colonial San Francisco." *Journal of Social Archaeology* 8(3):404–432.

_____, and Rebecca Allen. 2008. "Overseas Chinese Archaeology: Historical Foundations, Current Reflections, and New Directions." *Historical Archaeology* 42(3):5–28.

Wegars, Prescilla. 2001. *Chinese Artifact Illustrations, Terminology, and Selected Bibliography*. Moscow: Asian American Comparative Collection, Laboratory of Anthropology, University of Idaho, p. 11.

Williams, Bryn. 2004. "Opium Pipe Tops at the Market Street Chinese Community in San Jose." *Proceedings of the Society for California Archaeology* 17:219–227.

———. 2008. "Chinese Masculinities and Material Culture." *Historical Archaeology* 42(3):53–67.

Yang, Philip Q. 1999. "Sojourners or Settlers: Post-1965 Chinese Immigrants." *Journal of Asian American Studies* 2(1):61–91.

Yu, Connie. 2001. *Chinatown, San Jose, USA*. San Jose, CA: History San José and Chinese Historical and Cultural Project.

SECTION III

COMMEMORATIONS

TWELVE

LIFE AND DEATH IN ANCIENT COLONIES

Domesticity, Material Culture, and Sexual Politics in the Western Phoenician World, Eighth to Sixth Centuries BCE

Ana Delgado and Meritxell Ferrer

INTRODUCTION

Sexuality in the ancient Mediterranean colonial world is a *tropos* that appears in the work of Foucault. In *Le gouvernement de soi et des autres* (Foucault 2008), a set of lectures focused on the correlation between morality and power, Foucault relates the story of Plato's visit to the Greek colony of Syracuse and the horror Plato felt upon seeing that the Greek colonists lived in an *Italic way*, going from feast to feast, eating until they were full, and never sleeping a night without company (Plato, *Letters* VII, 326b). Plato's negative reaction to the intimate relations and the sense of pleasure of the Syracuse people of the fourth century BCE proves that in the ancient Greek colonies, sexuality was not a matter of the simple transposition of the intimate relations prevailing in the founding metropolis.

Foucault's work has had a clear influence on the study of sexuality in antiquity, particularly in the field of Greek and Roman studies (Halpering et al. 1990; Larmour et al. 1998). The continuous references to intimate relations in antiquity in the writings of this French thinker have caused an explosion of studies on this topic. Most of these studies are proposals that endorse Foucault's constructivist perception and his vision of the relationship between sexuality and power.

However, more current studies about intimate relations in ancient colonial settings have not been given proper attention. In these colonial studies, a uniform view still prevails that erases the differences between colonial settings and their motherlands, grouping them under a supposed homogeneity that is always metropolitan. The persistence of this monolithic image derives mainly from the lack of impact, until recently, that postcolonial approaches have had on the study of ancient diasporas, colonies, and empires (cf. van Dommelen 1998, 2006).

Consequently, the exploration of the construction of sexuality in colonial settings has been one of the fundamental contributions postcolonial approaches have made in the past few decades to the academic fields of geography, history, anthropology, and historical archaeology. Postcolonial approaches have highlighted the links between colonial and imperial projects and the sexual politics imposed in these settings, uncovering an enormous variety of histories that speak to metropolitan continuities as well as colonial discontinuities (Casella and Voss, Voss, Chapters 1 and 2, this volume).

Postcolonial studies point out that colonies, borderlands, and other contact zones are productive arenas for the metamorphosis and construction of new sexualities. This dynamic is fundamentally related to the enormous social and cultural heterogeneity that usually characterizes such spaces, where displacement and hybridization break preestablished identities and power relations. Colonies are spaces where people of different social and cultural origins cohabit, provoking an encounter of diverse ways to understand and to construct social, gender, power, and sexual relations and identities. Such an encounter entails a conflict between different world understandings, and therefore between diverse sexual attractions, senses of pleasure, intimate relationships, and sexual identities. These understandings are transformed and renegotiated in colonial settings, leading to new sexualities that do not correspond to those we find in either the founding metropolis or in local indigenous groups.

Colonial metamorphoses happen in a framework in which power relations are changing and dynamic. From this perspective, and following Foucault's thesis, several postcolonial critics have highlighted the dynamics of the relationship existing between the colony and the founding empire and the divergence of the sexual politics prevailing in each of these scenarios. In fact, they have argued that sexuality is an essential part of the domination project imposed, developed, and contested in colonial contexts (McClintock 1995; Phillips 2006; Stolcke 1974; Stoler 1989, 2002).

These critical works suggest that discourses about sexuality and intimate relations are a fundamental resource in creating cultural and social differences between settlers and local peoples and therefore are central to the construction of the hierarchies of colonial communities. We particularly note the earlier studies of Stolcke (1974) and Stoler (1989) regarding the importance of colonial sexual regulation for the construction of categories such as class and race. These authors emphasized the importance of practices and discourse regarding sexuality and, in Stoler's case, the relevance of domesticity. Previously, these two criteria – sexuality and domesticity – had been considered unconnected to both the public sphere and the male-dominated realm of politics. However, as Stoler points out, "assessment of civility and the cultural distinctions on which racial membership relied were measured less by what people did in public than by how they conducted their privates lives – with whom they cohabited, where they lived, what they ate, how they raised their children, what language they chose to speak to servants and family at home" (Stoler 2002: 6).

Sexual politics and domestic representations used to define the inclusion in or exclusion from colonial communities and to differentiate social hierarchies, have varied dramatically according to time and locale. Authors such as Stoler (1989, 2002) and Voss (2008b: 868–870) have drawn attention to the remarkable diversity of sexual regulations and cohabitation politics existing among peoples of different cultural origins in modern colonial worlds, noting that such politics and regulations are related to either global colonial dynamics or particular colonial projects. In ancient colonial and imperial worlds, and more specifically among the Phoenician and Punic diaspora communities, we observe the same diversity (see also López-Bertran, Chapter 6, this volume).

In this chapter, we examine the complexities of two Phoenician colonial settings – the southern Iberian Peninsula and western Sicily – between the eighth and sixth centuries BCE. Material culture from domestic and funerary contexts of these two colonial settings reveal an everyday life marked by the intimate cohabitation of people of different origins. Houses, graves, food, and objects used in daily life and funerary rituals reveal important differences between these two Phoenician contexts in relation to their hegemonic gender identities and relations, domestic representations, and sexual politics.

PHOENICIAN DIASPORA IN THE MEDITERRANEAN

Between the ninth and sixth centuries BCE, Phoenician groups founded several colonies along the Mediterranean. These colonists came from the eastern Mediterranean coast, in particular from the narrow coastal strip that extends from the current coast of Syria to Mount Carmel (see Figure 12.1). In this area, Phoenicians lived in diverse city-states such as Arwad, Byblos, Beirut, Sidon, or Tyre, all important harbors and artisanal centers with a long tradition of interregional trade.

In the ninth century BCE, Phoenician merchants expanded their commercial networks into the western Mediterranean. From the middle to the close of the eight century, numerous groups of Phoenician people moved to the west. In some cases, they were drawn by trade, in others, by the new social and economic opportunities these territories offered away from the tribulations, sieges, and deportations then taking place in the Levantine Phoenician cities that, as in other Near East regions, were threatened by the war machine of the Assyrian Empire.

Colonists coming from Levantine Phoenician cities settled in many lands along the Mediterranean coast (see Figure 12.1). These immigrants formed small neighborhoods in indigenous centers and founded new colonies on lands not previously permanently occupied by local populations. They maintained important social, cultural, and economic bonds with their motherlands and preserved and re-created the memory of their land of origin, including their language, scripture, habits, rites, cosmologies, and material culture. However, these were quickly altered through contact with new lands and new peoples (Delgado 2008a). The re-creation of that memory in the lands that hosted this diaspora favored the construction of a collective identity, a Phoenician identity, shared by the different people scattered along the Mediterranean.

This shared identity favored the creation of social networks that bound together Phoenician peoples settled across diverse Atlantic and Mediterranean areas and conferred on them an important advantage in commercial and economic relations. The cultural and economic dynamics that characterize the migration and establishment of Phoenicians in the west have been defined as one of the main examples of commercial diaspora in antiquity (Aubet 2001; Delgado 2008a: 377–380).

Historical Dynamics, Domesticity, and Heterogeneity in Western Phoenician Colonies

Phoenician colonies were inhabited by a socially, culturally, and ethnically heterogeneous population, as is documented by the literary and archaeological information. Narratives that relate the founding of some of these colonies allow us a glimpse of the various social groups and the diverse geographic origins of the people who participated in this process. The foundation myth of Carthage is a good example. This account tells of the exile of several members of the royal family of Tyre, who fled this Phoenician metropolis with the intent of founding a new city in the western Mediterranean. During their journey, they stopped in Kition, a Phoenician enclave in Cyprus, where eighty Cypriot maidens joined the expedition.

Material culture from Carthage, especially from its earlier levels, suggests that, together with Phoenician and Cypriot colonists (Kourou 2002), other populations from different Mediterranean areas, and even Atlantic territories, took part in the creation of new settlements in the West. These other groups appear to have also participated in the construction of a commercial network that, in a few decades, came to be controlled by Phoenician sailors (Delgado 2008a: 368–369). The importance of such western groups in the establishment of these centers is also suggested by the archaeological evidence from other Phoenician settlements, where most of the wares recovered from the older layers are made using technologies and shapes typical of native western Mediterranean populations.

The prevalence of daily life cultural remains from western native populations in Phoenician settlements disappears after some decades, between the second half of the eighth century and the beginning of seventh century BCE. From this moment, there is a change in the dominant material culture of western Phoenician settlements. In the colonies, we now see that landscapes, spaces, bodies, and practices that refer to the eastern Phoenician metropolis are preferentially re-created and re-elaborated. This markedly oriental material culture suggests that colonial peoples, in their lifeways, were deliberately seeking to differentiate themselves from the native groups with whom they coexisted and, at the same time, points to a clear Phoenician hegemony in the dominant power relations of these colonial centers.

However, archaeological evidence in some workplaces, and particularly from domestic and funerary areas, indicates that Western Phoenician colonies always hosted ethnically diverse populations. Funerary evidence and archaeological records obtained in many excavated domestic contexts of several western Phoenician centers demonstrate that cohabitation between persons of diverse cultural origins was a common practice in the colonies, at least among some social groups.

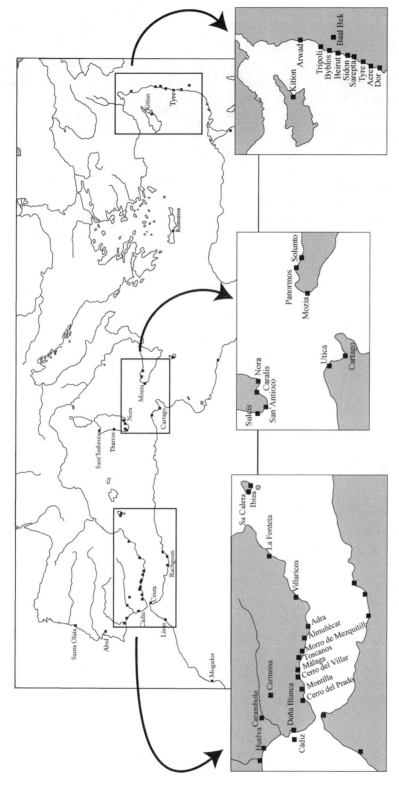

FIGURE 12.1. Mediterranean and Atlantic Phoenician cities, enclaves, and colonies.

199

The studies we have carried out in Cerro del Villar, a Phoenician colony close to modern-day Malaga in southern Spain, provide an example (Delgado 2005, 2008b; Delgado and Ferrer 2007). The material culture found in the excavated houses of this settlement strongly suggests the presence of mixed domestic groups. In some of the houses, handmade pots adapted for cooking boiled cereal foods are associated with spherical bowls adapted for the consumption of these liquid or semiliquid foods. These handmade pots and bowls are closely related to cuisines, diets, and foodways typical of the local populations. In the same colony, in other domestic structures, plates, manners of consumption, and cooking devices typical from Levantine cuisine prevail. Notable among these cooking devices are the ovens used mainly for baking bread, the daily food for most of the households in ancient Near Eastern communities (Meyers 2002; Spanò 2005). In other Phoenician settlements of southern Iberia, dwellings have been found with mixed or mestizo kitchens and manners of consumption. In these spaces, culinary techniques of diverse origins and plates associated with foods belonging to diverse traditions are found together (Delgado 2008b; Martín Córdoba et al. 2005; see Figure 12.2).

The inhabitants' diet in these excavated colonial houses also shows differences that suggest cohabitation in the colony – and in the majority of its households – of people of diverse ethnic and social origins. From the botanical data of southern Iberian Phoenician settlements, we know that barley was the basis of the diet, setting them apart from the food preferences of eastern Phoenician cities. In Levantine urban centers, wheat was the most consumed cereal, at least among those social groups not of low rank. However, the diet of colonial populations is closer to the dietary preferences of southern Iberian native peoples, or to low-ranking groups of eastern Phoenicia, for whom barley was the dominant food. The consumption of some meats demonstrates this conclusion even more clearly. An especially relevant example is pig, the consumption of which in the Canaanite area was limited to clearly defined social and ethnic groups and which excluded the vast majority of the inhabitants of the eastern Phoenician cities (Hesse 2000). However, in the faunal remains in Phoenician colonies of southern Iberia and the central Mediterranean, pig is relatively frequent.

Because of the lack of any systematic work in this direction, we have little information on social patterns and sexual attributions related to food preparation among the native western communities. However, we have some interesting evidence on this subject from the Canaanite area during the first and second millennia BCE. Archaeological, iconographic, and literary evidence suggests that in this area, household milling, cereals preparation, and baking activities – the basis of most households' daily diet – were carried out mainly by women (see especially Meyers 2002; Spanò 2005). Although there is some textual evidence that explicitly mentions male participation in bread preparation (Amadasi Guzzo 1993: 115), these references are mostly related to a kind of specialized production carried on outside of the domestic sphere.

From these data, we infer that in domestic spaces of eastern Phoenician cities and towns, food preparation, in particular that of cereals and cooking, was a task principally carried out by women. Probably the same pattern, although altered because of the encounter and conflict with other gender systems, was reproduced

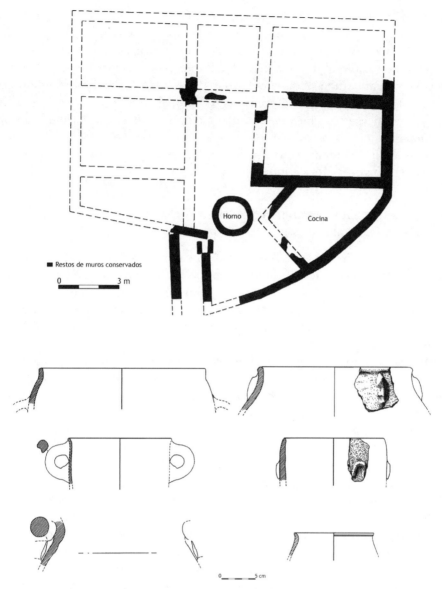

FIGURE 12.2. House from Chorreras with bread oven and diverse cooking traditions cookware registered in its surrounding areas. Adapted from Martín Córdoba et al., 2005: figures 4, 11, n. 10, 18, n. 3, 19, n. 1 y 2, 20, n. 3, and 21, n. 3).

in the west by Phoenicians settlers. We argue, therefore, that the heterogeneity of culinary techniques and daily diet present in Phoenician colonies demonstrates the presence of women of diverse social and ethnic origins. In these peninsular Phoenician enclaves, women of oriental, native, or mestiza origin coexisted, and most would have had an essential role in the feeding and the care of the households to which they belonged.

The central role of women in the daily preparation and distribution of food to household members, at least in those groups not part of the social elite (that is, the majority of groups), gave them a decisive role in their kinship groups, regardless of their origin, and thus in these diaspora communities. Just as in Syrian–Palestinian settlements or western native centers, these women carried a decisive weight in the colonies because of the role they played in crucial activities for the social and economic welfare of their household groups, and therefore of their communities. Women of oriental origin or descent, native women, and mestizas worked in the productive processes in which their household groups were involved and probably, as is documented in Canaan, also participated and controlled critical aspects of religious life and domestic ritual, such as the ancestors' cult and the care of the dead (Delgado 2008b; Dever 2005; Meyers 2005b).

THE COLONIAL CEMETERIES IN SOUTHERN IBERIA: TOMBS AND GENEALOGIES

During the second half of the eighth century BCE, some decades after the settlement of the first Phoenician colonists in southern Iberia, the first cemeteries were set up. The appearance of these first tombs corresponds with a period of consolidation of colonial adventure in the region. Almost all of these tombs or groups of burials are situated some distance from their associated settlements, which suggests that by the end of the eighth century BCE, most colonies had appropriated a small territory. Through the memory of their dead, the colonists constructed and marked out their own sense of place. Tombs, cemeteries, and funerary rituals materialized the ties between the settlers, their ancestors, and their new land, creating areas where a colonial identity was built and negotiated – a collective identity that defined the colonists in relation to their place of origin and to the local communities now around them.

In Mediterranean Andalusia, funerary areas consisted mainly of isolated tombs, funerary chambers, or small groups of no more than twenty graves. Each Phoenician colonial settlement had several cemeteries, but these contain only a small number of tombs. This low number of graves suggests that not all the residents of the colonies had the right to be buried in the settlements' cemeteries, implying that burial in these areas was limited by restrictive principles (Delgado 2008a: 454–455; López Castro 2006: 76–77). These restrictions were probably based on (1) age, a conclusion suggested by the absence of children in Phoenician necropolis; (2) status, implied by the use of symbols associated in the Near East with power and monarchy, such as the alabaster urns (see Figure 12.3); and (3) genealogy, indicated by the grouping of tombs and the construction of some funerary chambers to reproduce the shape of a house. In these colonial settlements, the social identity of the deceased and of their relatives was displayed through the use of a particular funerary space, which expressed their inclusion in, or exclusion from, a family or domestic group. Genealogy seems to have constituted one of the main ways of delineating the new social hierarchies created in these Phoenician colonies.

The importance of genealogy in establishing social hierarchies in the colonies is clearly demonstrated in the necropolis of Trayamar. This is a small cemetery set up at a late stage, in the second half of the seventh century BCE, built of ashlar walls and made up of only five chamber tombs. Several individuals were buried in

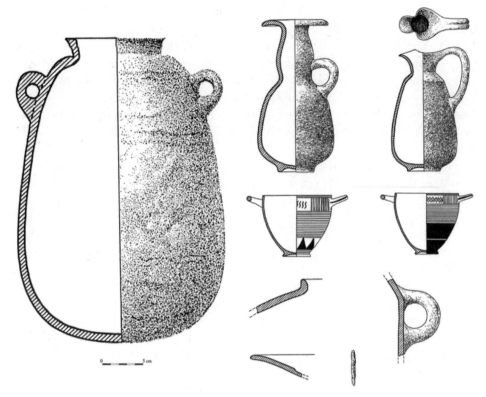

FIGURE 12.3. Urn and grave goods from Laurita necropolis Tomb 19 (Pellicer 1962: fig. 32).

each of these chambers, suggesting that they acted as repositories for a family group (Schubart and Niemeyer 1976). This monumental necropolis stands on a hill on the bank of the Algarrobo River, above Morro de Mezquitilla, one of the earliest Phoenician settlements established in this area. The proximity to the colony and the uniqueness and monumental construction of the funerary space suggest that the cemetery was established in memory of the ancestral founders of the community (Delgado 2008a: 455–456). The funerary chambers of Trayamar may have been reserved for families who belonged to the colonial elite and claimed descent from the first settlers to arrive in the area.

Food and Funerary Rituals

In the necropolis of Trayamar, and in other Phoenician cemeteries along the coast of Malaga, funerals were a re-elaboration of Levantine funerary rituals, in which food and purification rites play a central role. The funerary practices for which we find evidence in the tombs of these Phoenician colonies reveal that the colonial elite built and displayed their status, gender, and colonial identity by looking to the East.

The dead are accompanied by a set of ritual objects that reproduce eastern Phoenician funerary ceremonies. These include oil lamps, amphorae, trilobular jugs, mushroom jugs, vessels for food (commonly red slip plates), and drinking cups. Deposition of these types of grave goods reflects funerary rituals involving a number of practices. The making of offerings and pouring of libations of some kind of liquid, possibly wine or mead, is indicated by the presence of trilobular jugs and drinking vessels. The purification and anointment of the deceased or the space in which they will rest is demonstrated by containers for oils – mushroom jugs, oil lamps, and vessels in which aromatic oils were burnt. Finally, amphorae and plates reveal the offering of foodstuffs. Moreover, in these funerary contexts, food, drinks, or libation oils can be represented by the vessels themselves, without any actual contents, with the presence of the empty vessel thereby signifying these substances.

Some of the practices materialized by grave goods found in the tombs involve actions, or the expression of relationships, largely attributable to women. This attribution, although problematic, is based on the assumption that in funerary contexts, colonial elites constructed gender roles in the same manner as they displayed status – by emulating Near Eastern practices. These female tasks probably included those materialized by vessels for ointment and oils and vessels used for serving and consuming food.

In the Near East, and specifically in the Canaan area, we know from literary and documentary evidence about the primary role women played in the purification and preparation of the dead for burial or before and after cremation and in the continuing care of the dead (Dever 2005: 239–241). The Bible talks about the role women had in caring for and preparing the deceased, as well as in mourning them. For example, Lazarus' corpse was kept and looked after by his sisters (John 11), and Jesus' corpse was cared for and anointed by Mary and Mary Magdalene (Matthew 27:61; 28:1; Marc 16:1; Luke 24:1; John 20:1). We can assume a similar link between women and the ritual use of food, which is evidenced by the presence of vessels used for the preparation and consumption of food found in tombs.

To understand how grave goods participate in the construction of gender identities and relations, it is important to take into account that these goods can materialize a relationship between the people who used them in life, whether it be with the deceased or with other people participating directly or indirectly in the funerary rites (Brück 2006). The objects that we find in tombs can act as an extension of a person, representing that person. Unlike our Cartesian thought, in other worlds, like Phoenician world, objects are inalienable from those who used or touched them (Strathern 1988). From this point of view, the inclusion in the funerary deposit of objects related to food and care of the body materializes the bonds that existed between the deceased and the women who fed and cared for them during their lives, prolonging those bonds in the afterlife. The presence of these objects among grave goods reveals the centrality of caregiving and those women acting as caregiver in the funerary discourse of this colonial sphere.

Funerary Meals and Social Hierarchies

In these funerary contexts, food constitutes one of the principal means of constructing identity and demonstrating social solidarity. It marks the inclusion or exclusion of a group, acts as a marker of status and age, and is highly involved in the definition and negotiation of gender roles (see, for example, Goody 1982; Twiss 2007).

In the Phoenician colonies of southern Iberia, the involvement of food in this negotiation of social relations is most visible in the celebration of funerary feasts. The clearest evidence of what these feasts involved comes from Trayamar's necropolis. Dozens of pottery sherds have accumulated around the funerary chambers from vessels used in feasts celebrated both at the time of burial and also periodically after the tomb was closed. These periodic feasts honored the bond between the hosts and their buried ancestors. Through these celebrations, which the material evidence suggests were well attended, members of the colonial elite emphasized their position within the community, legitimizing their high status through their genealogies and their links with colonial founders (see Hamilakis 1998; Hastorf 2003). In these places and through these acts, elites built up a social memory that was fixed and materialized by the deposition of the goods used during the feasts on the same spot where their ancestors were buried.

The vessels used to serve food in these ceremonies were mainly red-slip plates (Schubart and Niemeyer 1976: 142–143, figures 20–23). In fact, we do not find other types of vessels, such as handmade or greyware bowls, among the scattered fragments. The latter two bowl types reflect the traditional foods and consumption patterns of the local communities in southern Iberia. It is notable that although these bowls are found in several household contexts within the Phoenician colonies of coastal Andalusia, as we see in Cerro del Villar or in Morro de Mezquitilla, the settlement associated with the necropolis of Trayamar, they are not found in remains of the funerary feasts (Schubart and Niemeyer 1976).

Another significant exclusion from the material remains of these feasts is that of objects connected to cooking. Strikingly, cooking pots are absent from around the tombs, nor are they found among grave goods inside the tombs. However, cooking pots, including handmade cooking pots, are used in these settlements in other ritual practices. For example, cooking or storage pots are common in domestic rituals carried out for the foundation of a new house, and for the beginning of a new life cycle within the domestic context. Ritual practices of this kind are known from Morro de Mezquitilla itself, as well as from Cerro del Villar.

In all Phoenician necropolis along the coast of Andalusia, grave goods that reflect indigenous methods of preparing or consuming foods are notably absent. Handmade pottery, greyware, or hybrid productions that reproduce local shapes, forms, or technologies are not deposited in the tombs. However, these objects are commonly found in the houses of the associated colonial settlements and were clearly used on a daily basis by the inhabitants. One of the few exceptions to this phenomenon is the presence of some fragments of a cooking pot and two greyware bowls found in a tomb in the necropolis of Laurita, in Almuñecar (Pellicer 1962: figures 3 and 4).

Funerary rituals and feasts reflect a discourse of power, a discourse that we should not confuse with the realities of daily life unfolding in the colonies. The discourse of power expressed in these funerary contexts excluded many of the women and indigenous people and their descendants who lived in the colonies. This discourse of power only affected elite groups, who legitimized their hegemony through it. Elites constructed their status and reinforced their social distinction by emphasizing their distance and separation from the local world through an emulation of Near Eastern models. The exclusion of indigenous material culture from these funerary deposits suggests that in these southern Iberian colonies, the elites favored social and sexual restrictions against relationships of mixed-ethnicity to legitimate their hegemonic status and power within the group. These discourses and practices must be related to Foucault's concept of the bond between power and sexuality. Several postcolonial thinkers, such as Stoler (1989, 2002), have expanded on this idea to show the relationship between sexual regulations prevailing in colonies and domination projects of their elites. Likewise, these contextual and historical under- standings of power and sexuality have entailed studies that favor non-monolithical and nonessentialist perceptions but stress the diversity of sexual regulations and politics in colonial settings. This diversity can be glimpsed in Phoenician colonial world where materialities used in the funerary discourse regarding power, gender, ethnicity and sexuality show clear differences among colonies, as we can see through the Phoenician cemeteries in western Sicily.

MOTYA, A PHOENICIAN SETTLEMENT IN WESTERN SICILY

The prevailing sexual politics related to the construction of colonial hierarchy and identity in Mediterranean Phoenician contexts presents notable differences. In other Mediterranean areas, material culture linked to domesticity and, partic- ularly, to the ties between living family groups and their dead are clearly diverse from those we have seen in southern Iberia. This variance suggests the existence of a difference in the politics that regulated intimate relationships among peo- ple of diverse ethnic and social origins. To demonstrate this variance, we analyze Motya, another Phoenician enclave located in the central Mediterranean. This set- tlement was a Phoenician colony situated in western Sicily, where food, cooking, and serving vessels were used differently in funerary rituals, and thus in the con- struction of colonial identities and hierarchies, than we have seen in southern Iberia.

Motya, founded during the second half of the eighth century BCE, was the first Phoenician colony established in Sicily. In this case, the Phoenicians situated them- selves on an unoccupied island close to the coast. Currently, we know little about daily life in this colony, particularly in its first years of existence. The excavations carried out on Motya since the beginning of the twentieth century have focused only on the monumental spaces or places significant from the perspective of institutional power – the walls, the harbor, the Cappidazzu sanctuary, the necropolis, and the tophet.

Phoenician Funerary Rituals in Western Sicily: The Necropolis of Motya

Fortunately, the detailed excavation of the funerary areas of this colony gives us the opportunity not only to explore the daily life and life cycle of the inhabitants but also to visualize some of their caregiving practices for the world of the dead.

Between the end of the eighth century and the first half of the sixth century BCE, Motya's colonists set aside two burial areas, the tophet and the necropolis. The former appears to have been a ritual area reserved for the burial of certain fetuses, newborns, and children less than one year old (Bernardini 2005). The latter is the area principally designated for the burial of some adult members of the colony. Both funerary spaces are located in Motya's northwestern area, which during the first years of the colony seems to have been the area allocated for communal functions.

One hundred sixty-one burials have been excavated from the necropolis, out of which 157 are adult cremations, and the remaining 4 are children. The juvenile burials, tombs 148, 152, 154, and 159, use a distinct method of burial, the *enchytrismoi*, or pot burial (Ciasca et al. 1978). The quantity of burials we find is notably few if we assume that Motya was inhabited from the end of the eighth century to the beginning of the sixth century BCE. This implies the existence of a highly restrictive burial system, as in coastal Andalusia. However, in contrast to what we have seen in southern Iberia, the restriction in this case is not based on genealogy, as far as the material evidence reveals. In Motya's necropolis, we do not observe any grouping that could suggest the presence of family units. On the contrary, the restriction seems to be based on age, as demonstrated by the existence of a funerary space exclusively for child deposits, the *tophet*, and the fact that the four child burials in the main necropolis reveal a totally different method of burial, inhumation as *enchytrismoi*.

Recognition as a member of the colony is also an important factor in these burial rituals and practices. The early establishment by the colonists of a funerary space on the same island not only demonstrated a strong initial intent to stay and to belong but also created a space of constant mnemonic reference, visible to all who lived in or visited the colony. Furthermore, the funerary restrictions identifiable in the necropolis – that is, the right to be buried or to bury one's dead there – suggests that this space acted as a means of legitimizing the social hierarchies that existed within the community. However, at Motya these hierarchies were not materialized through grave goods left in the tombs, which are relatively homogeneous, but would have been demonstrated in other stages of the funerary ritual, in the right even to be buried there, and certainly in the actions of the living.

Food, Cookery, and Funerary Rituals

The funerary rituals visible through the burials of Motya's necropolis are characterized by a high homogeneity, both in the treatment of the dead and in the type and quantity of the objects deposited in the tombs. The dead are accompanied by a highly standardized set of ritual objects that demonstrate the adoption of the same Near Eastern funerary practices seen in other Phoenician colonies. This set of objects is made up of a trefoil jug, a mushroom jug, a vessel for food, and, occasionally, a fineware vessel for drinking, or, in other words, vessels representing liquids, ointments, and foods. However, funerary rituals and grave goods retain their own unique characteristics, which reflect the colony's distance from the mother city and from other colonies within the Phoenician network. In the cemetery on Motya, these distinctions are observed in two main examples. First, instead of the typical funerary urns used for the dead, amphorae, cists, stone boxes, or simple fosse are found. A second distinction is in the type of vessel holding the food offerings deposited with the dead. In this case, the widespread presence of a cooking pot, either handmade or wheelmade, rather than the traditional red-slip plate, emphasizes vessels used in

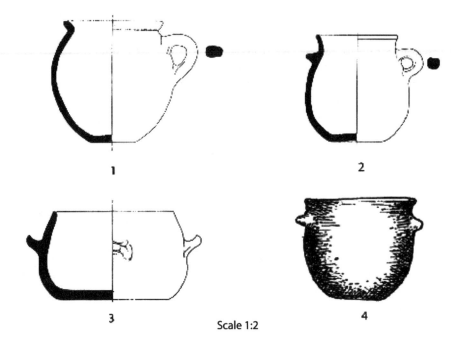

1

2

3

Scale 1:2

4

Figure 12.4. Different kinds of cooking pots present in Motya's necropolis (after Spanò 2000: figures 42, 44, and 45).

the preparation of food, rather than only for serving, in marked contrast to colonies in southern Iberia.

From the 161 excavated burials in Motya's necropolis, 111, or 69 percent of the total, contain one or more cooking pots. Moreover, is interesting to note that the presence of a serving plate does not exclude the presence of a cooking pot. Among the seven deposits that contain a plate as a part of the grave goods, four deposits, from tombs 80, 82, 95, and 145, also include a cooking pot (Ciasca et al. 1978).

The cooking pots found in Motya's necropolis point toward different methods of cooking than those predominant in the Canaan area or in Phoenician colonies of the western Mediterranean. The most common type of cooking pot is one-handled, either handmade or wheelmade, with a globular body, flat bottom, and single circular handle. This type is found throughout Phoenician colonies, at particular in central Mediterranean sites (Bartoloni 1983: figures 8 d and 8e, 9f, and 10k; Vegas 1998: 148, 157, and figure 4). However, found together with this type of pot are other vessels used for cooking that point to a variety of cooking practices as diverse as the indigenous populations of the central Mediterranean (Botto and Salvadei 2005; Delgado and Ferrer 2007). Among these vessels the presence of the *pignatta*, a cooking pot typical of indigenous Sicilian communities, stands out (see Figure 12.4).

The heterogeneity demonstrated by the cooking pots found in this necropolis, which indicates the diversity of cooking practices, and, more generally, different ways of doing things, points again to the variation between Motya and the Phoenician colonies in southern Iberia. When compared with southern Iberia, the visibility of indigenous elements among the grave goods at Motya suggests, on one hand,

Stelae 833   Stelae 792   Monte Polizzo

FIGURE 12.5. Stela 800 and 792 from Mozia's *tophet*, and Monte Polizzo's bowl with anthropomorphic handle (after Moscati and Uberti 1981; Mühlenbock 2008: figure 51).

different gender constructions, and on the other hand, the prevalence of different sexual politics. In particular, this indicates a difference with regard to the social and sexual intermixing of ethnicities and the social recognition of women of non-Phoenician origin as well as their descendants within elite groups or community recognized memberships.

The presence in the necropolis of noneastern cooking pots suggests that buried within the funerary space of Motya are the relatives of people – primarily women – with diverse Mediterranean origins. Because they are buried in the necropolis, they were fully accepted members of this heterogeneous colonial community. The power discourse in this case, illuminated by the grave goods and funerary rituals, does not marginalize women and people of local origin but rather integrates them, forming a discourse of hybridity.

This discourse of hybridity is also reflected in the representations of the female body engraved on the funerary stelae of the *tophet* at Motya that represent social practices related to mourning. Some stelae present women playing musical instruments such as flutes and, especially, tambourines, a practice related to funerary songs and to frighten away demons. Other stelae represent women who show or touch their breasts. Taking into account the mortuary context, these gestures should not be interpreted as a sexual offering or practice (especially because these women are dressed) but as a corporal expression of pain typical of Canaanite mourning practices, which also include putting the hands on the head. These corporal expressions are common in Phoenician funerary iconography and literary narratives (Olyan 2004: 31).

Most of the engraved feminine bodies in these stelae represent stereotyped female bodies that reproduce eastern conventions about feminine corporality. However, one of the stelae, number 792 (Moscati and Uberti 1981), does not look back to eastern models but looks instead to modes of corporality typical of the indigenous Sicilian world (see Figure 12.5). The representation of indigenous corporalities – also in stereotyped ways – correspond with the evidence from pottery: that women of non-Phoenician origins participated actively in mourning their relatives who were buried in Mozia's cemeteries. This also informs us about the social recognition of these women by the colonial community.

Likewise, the differences between these corporal representations suggest possible sexual agreements and disagreements produced in these heterogeneous worlds (see Loren, Chapter 7, this volume). These representations, although they are not explicitly sexual, suggest interesting disagreements between prevailing forms of sexual attraction and their representation. Eastern literary narratives are explicit in references to the vulva and the hair as focal elements in masculine heterosexual desire. In fact, "eastern" feminine figures represented in these stelae fit with this masculine literary taste by showing women whose hair is shoulder length and worn loose. Sexual attraction exerted by hair in eastern Phoenician world contrasts, however, with Sicilian-styled representations of women in which hair is absent and all attraction is focused around the eyes.

Pots, Women, and Colonial Identities

The high visibility of cooking vessels in Motya's funerary rituals suggests that a different way of constructing colonial identity existed here than that observed in southern Iberia, in which some women played a more central role as they acted to reinforce family and community bonds.

The substitution of red-slip plates for cooking pots in a small number of the funerary deposits at Motya indicates differences in the type of food offered, its significance, and the relationship between the person making the offering and the deceased. Red-slip plates signify the acts of serving and consuming, whereas pots reflect the cooking process, the transformation of produce into food, and collective nourishment rather than a single serving. Moreover, cooking pots are closely linked to the household and, in particular, to those who prepare the daily meals (in the Phoenician world, preferentially women). At this point, it is interesting to note that many of the cooking pots found in the tombs of Motya seem to have been used before deposition (Spanò 2000).

In the necropolis on Motya, the cooking pot represented an extension of the household and a continuation of the relationship between the deceased and the woman or women who cared for them during their life. The pot deposited in these burials symbolized the house – understood in a social sense – and the bonds among its members, constructed social and emotionally through the daily practices of eating. These pots materialized on the one hand the emotional and nurturing bonds between some women and those whom they cared for and prolonged these bonds after death. On the other hand, it signified the role of these caregiving women as the pillar or nexus of the family, and perhaps the community as a whole. This practice is also observed in other geographic areas and historical contexts. For example, Gilchrist (2005), in her study of medieval cemeteries from southeastern England, identified several burials that contained ashes from domestic hearths. According to Gilchrist, the presence of these ashes represented the extension of a woman's role as the person charged with maintaining the fire in the hearth and caring for the household. It was, therefore, a woman's duty that, as the burials on Motya also suggest, extended beyond the grave.

In sum, the evidence from Motya demonstrates that the role of some women as caregivers, independent of their place of birth or descent, constituted a central part of the discourse of colonial identity in this Phoenician settlement, illuminating in this regard a profound difference from other Phoenician contexts in the Western Mediterranean.

CONCLUSIONS

Through this comparative analysis of the funerary discourse of two Phoenician colonial contexts, we can see that colonial identity – understood as a collective sense of belonging which differentiates the members of the community from their mother city and from the other Phoenician colonies or local settlements around them – is constructed and defined in a radically different way in each context. This disparity is principally due to differences in the social, sexual, and ethnic composition of each colonial group; the manner and extent of relations with local peoples; and the definition and negotiation of gender identity and relations. It also indicates differences in the sexual politics prevailing in each colony. In both settings, the study of funerary spaces offers us the possibility of observing how gender is constructed and displayed differently and also how the colonial elites maintained diverse sexual discourses and politics related to interethnic intercourses to define colonial hierarchies and community membership.

REFERENCES

Amadasi Guzzo, M. G. 1993. "Sacrifici e banchetti: Bibbia ebraica e iscrizioni puniche." In Grotanelli and Parise (eds.), *Sacrificio e Società nel Mondo Antico.* Roma: Laterza, pp. 97–122.

Aubet, M. E. 2001. *The Phoenicians and the West. Politics, Colonies and Trade.* Cambridge: Cambridge University Press.

Bartoloni, P. 1983. *Studi sulla cerámica fenicia e punica di Sardegna.* Collezione di Studi Fenici. Rome: CNR.

Bernardini, P. 2005. "Per una rilettura del santuario tofet: il caso di Motya." *Sardinia, Corsica et Baleares Antiquae* 3:55–70.

Botto, M., and Salvadei, L. 2005. "Infagini alla necropolis arcaica di Monte Sirai. Relazione preliminare sulla campagna di scavi del 2002." *Rivista di Studi Fenici* 33:81–168.

Brück, J. 2006. "Death, Exchange and Reproduction in the British Bronze Age." *Journal of European Archaeology* 9(1):73–101.

Ciasca, A., Tusa, V., and Uberti, M. L. 1978. *Motya IX.* Roma: C.N.R.

Delgado, A. 2005. "Multiculturalidad y género en las colonias fenicias de la Andalucía mediterránea". In Spanò, A. (ed.) *Atti V Congresso Internazionale di Studi Fenici e Punici,* vol. II. Palermo: Università degli Studi di Palermo, pp. 1249–1260.

_____. 2008a. "Fenicios en Iberia," in Gracia, F. (ed.), *De Hispania a Iberia.* Barcelona: Arielpp, pp. 347–474.

_____. 2008b. "Alimentos, poder e identidad en las comunidades fenicias occidentales." *Cuadernos de Prehistoria de la Universidad de Granada* 18:163–188.

_____, and Ferrer, M. 2007. "Cultural Contacts in Colonial Settings: The Construction of New Identities in Phoenician Settlements of the Western Mediterranean." *Stanford Journal of Archaeology* 5:18–42.

Dever, W. G. 2005. *Did God Have a Wife? Archaeology and Folk Religion in Ancient Israel*. Cambridge: Eerdmans.

Foucault, M. 2008. *Le gouvernement de soi et des autres: cours au collège de France (1982–1983)*. Paris: Gallimard.

Gilchrist, R. 2005. "Cuidando a los muertos: las mujeres medievales en las pompas fúnebres familiares." *Treballs d'Arqueologia* 11:51–72.

Goody, J. 1982. *Cooking, Cuisine and Class*. Cambridge: Cambridge University Press.

Halperin, D., Winkler, J., and Zeitlin, F., eds. 1990. *Before Sexuality: The Construction of Erotic Experience in the Ancient Greek World*. Princeton, NJ: Princeton University Press.

Hamilakis, Y. 1998. "Eating the Dead: Mortuary Feasting and the Politics of Memory in the Aegean Bronze Age Societies." In Branigan, K. (ed.), *Cemetery and Society in the Aegean Bronze Age*. Sheffield, England: Sheffield University Press, pp. 115–132.

Hastorf, C. 2003. "Andean Luxury Food: Special Food for the Ancestors, Deities and the Elite." *Antiquity* 77:545–554.

Hesse, B. 2000. "Animal husbandry and human diet in the Ancient Near East." In Sasson, J. M. (ed.), *Civilizations of the Ancient Near East*. Peabody: Hendrickson, pp. 203–222.

Kourou, N. 2002. "Phéniciens, Chypriotes, Eubéens et la fondation de Carthage." *Cahier du Centre d'Études Chypriotes* 32:89–111.

Larmour, D., Miller, P., and Platter, C. eds. 1998. *Rethinking Sexuality: Foucault and Classical Antiquity*. Princeton, NJ: Princeton University Press.

López Castro, J. L. 2006. "Colonials, Merchants and Alabaster Vases: The Western Phoenician Aristocracy." *Antiquity* 80:74–88.

Martín Córdoba, E., Ramírez Sánchez, J. D., and Recio Ruiz, A. 2005. "Nuevo sector urbano fenicio en el yacimiento de Las Chorreras (Vélez-Málaga, Málaga)." *Ballix* 2:1–33.

McClintock, A. 1995. *Imperial Leather: Race, Gender and Sexuality in the Colonial Context*. New York: Routledge.

Meyers, C. 2002. "Having Their Space and Eating There Too: Bread Production and Female Power in Ancient Israelite Households." *Nashim* 5:14–44.

——— 2005. *Households and Holiness: The Religious Culture of Israelite Women*. Minneapolis, MN: Fortress.

Moscati, S., and Uberti, M. L. 1981. *Scavi a Motya, le stele*. Rome: CNR.

Mühlenbock, C. 2008. *Fragments from a Mountain Society*. Gothenburg, Germany: University of Gothenburg.

Olyan, S. M. 2004. *Biblical Mourning: Ritual and Social Dimensions*. Oxford: Oxford University Press.

Pellicer, M. 1962. *Excavaciones en la necrópolis púnica "Laurita" del Cerro de San Cristóbal (Almuñécar, Granada)*. Excavaciones Arqueológicas en España, 17. Madrid: MEC.

Phillips, R. 2006. *Sex, Politics and Empire: A Postcolonial Geography*. Manchester, England: Manchester University Press.

Plato. 1997. *Complete Works* (John M. Cooper, ed.). Indianapolis, IN: Hackett.

Schubart, H., and Niemeyer, H. G. 1976. *Trayamar: los hipogeos fenicios y el asentamiento en la desembocadura del río Algarrobo*. Excavaciones Arqueológicas en España, 90. Madrid: MEC.

Spanò, A. 2000. "La ceramica fenicia della Sicilia." In Bartoloni and Campanella (eds.), *La ceramica fenicia di Sardegna. Dati, problematiche, confronti*. Rome: CNR, pp. 303–331.

——— 2004. "I luoghi della morte: impianti funerari nella Sicilia fenicia e punica." In González-Prats (ed.), pp. 205–252.

——— 2005. "Pappe, vino e pesce salato. Apunti per uno studio della cultura alimentare fenicia e punica." *Kokalos* XLVI(I): 417–464.

Stolcke, V. 1974. *Marriage, Class and Colour in Nineteenth-century Cuba: A Study of Racial Attitudes and Sexual Values in a Slave Society*. London: Cambridge University Press.

Stoler, A. L. 1989. "Rethinking Colonial Categories: European Communities and the Boundaries of Rule." *Comparative Studies in Society and History* 31:134–161.

——— 2002. *Carnal Knowledge and Imperial Power: Race and the Intimate in Colonial Rule*. Berkeley: University of California Press.

Strathern, M. 1988. *The Gender of the Gift: Problems with Women and Problems with Society in Melanesia.* Berkeley: University of California Press.

Tilley, C., Keane, W., Kuechler, S., Rowlands M., and Spyer, P., eds. 2006. *Handbook of Material Culture.* London: Sage.

Twiss, K. 2007. *The Archaeology of Food and Identity.* Carbondale: Southern Illinois University Press.

van Dommelen, P. 1998. *On Colonial Grounds.* Leiden, the Netherlands: Archaeological Studies Leiden University.

———. 2006. "Colonial Matters. Material Culture and Postcolonial Theory in Colonial Situations," in Tilley, C., Keane, W., Kuechler, S., Rowlands M., and Spyer, P., (eds.). *Handbook of Material Culture.* London: Sage, pp. 267–308.

Vegas, M. 1998. *Cartago fenicio-púnica: las excavaciones alemanas en Cartago 1975–1997.* Cuadernos de Arqueología Mediterránea 4. Barcelona: Bellaterra.

Voss, B. 2008a. *The Archaeology of Ethnogenesis: Race, Sexuality, and Identity in Colonial San Francisco.* Berkeley: University of California Press.

———. 2008b. "Gender, Race, and Labor in the Archaeology of the Spanish Colonial Americas." *Current Anthropology* 49:861–893.

THIRTEEN

READING GLADIATORS' EPITAPHS AND RETHINKING VIOLENCE AND MASCULINITY IN THE ROMAN EMPIRE

Renata S. Garraffoni

INTRODUCTION

Classical sources have been used to provide broad parallels and contrasts with the present. Although many types of archaeological and historical information are available about the Roman Empire, Hingley (2005) states that a core issue in modern scholarship is how to approach the relationship between power and identity. Since the sixteenth century, the Romans sometimes have been understood to be part of a shared European identity; conversely, at times the Romans were categorized as "others." Roman violence and power have both attracted and repulsed scholars throughout the past two centuries, resulting in different interpretations of the Roman past. For example, the consequences of Roman imperialism have been understood at times as beneficial to native societies because of supposed material improvement and cultural "progress" experienced by native societies. The Roman system of domination, therefore, became an example of what a modern empire should be and consequently inspired colonialist policy during the end of nineteenth century into the beginning of twentieth, with the violence of the process seldom acknowledged (Hingley 1996, 2000, 2001, 2005, Shepherd, Chapter 17, this volume).

In the 1970s, however, this perception of the Roman Empire began to be challenged. The so-called nativist approach, developed mainly by British scholars,

A preliminary version of this chapter was first read at World Archaeology Congress 2008 for the session "Intimate Encounters, Post-colonial Engagements: Archaeologies of Empire and Sexuality." I thank my colleagues for their comments on that occasion and also for comments offered during the workshop held at Stanford University in April 2009. During December 2008 and March 2009, I was based at University of Birmingham, United Kingdom, as a British Academy Fellow, allowing me the time to complete up-to-date reading and to finish this chapter. I thank Mary Harlow, Anthea Harris, and Ray Laurence for their support and the Museo Arqueológico y Etnológico de Córdoba (Spain) for the permission to publish the photos of the tombstones. The ideas expressed here are my own, and I am solely responsible for them.

pointed out the importance of material culture in the study of local communities. This new scholarship balanced the record of the elite with an awareness of cultural negotiation in different areas of the empire (Delgado and Ferrer, Chapter 12, this volume). This approach emphasizes that native people were not only "assimilated" into the Roman order but also participated in the creation of new orders.

Hingley (2005) has pointed out that in both approaches, the idea of Romanization, or becoming Roman, was constructed from a male elite point of view, because the focus of classical studies has been on elite male writings and material culture. Hingley himself did not develop a gender-focused approach to understanding the effect of the Roman Empire on native people, because his main focus was to reconceptualize Romanization as a modern colonialist concept. However, his scholarship enables us to seek alternative models with which to construct a more critical and balanced interpretation of the Roman Empire and its people. This paves the way toward a more reflexive approach to Roman material culture or, as Shepherd points out in this volume, to confront the presence of the past and its absences.

Inspired by Hingley's critical approach and motivated by a desire to bring underrepresented Roman people into archaeological discourse, I believe that a focus on the tombstones and epitaphs of gladiators can aid in understanding native people's daily lives. This chapter focuses on gladiators' tombstones found in Rome and Hispania (Roman Spain), especially those paid for by women. My goal is to understand the emotional lives of men and women who, during the Roman Empire, were defined as outsiders through violence, sexuality, or death but who developed relationships to sustain and comfort each other. Although these tombstones are seldom studied, I believe that, as archaeological data, they create gendered places of memory. They also contribute to a better understanding of the dynamics of human relationships (Rubertone, Chapter 14, this volume).

As Voss and Schmidt (2000) have shown, material culture has an unique role to play in telling the history of people who are invisible or misrepresented in written sources. I believe these tombstones can help us to understand how common men and women were affected by Roman power, as well as their responses to "imperial effects" (Voss, Chapter 2). My intent here, then, is to examine the ways in which the archaeological record, particularly epigraphy, can suggest new perspectives on the gladiators' experience, allowing us to rethink our perceptions of the Roman Empire, violence, sexuality, and masculinity. Considering that these are ephemeral concepts for which meanings can change through time, their transitory nature requires that we develop new theoretical approaches to understand the postcontact cultural changes among Romans and native people. As the tombstones chronicle diverse experiences and are places of memory, I suggest they challenge us to construct alternative interpretative models to understand those whose desires and worldview were not always visible.

UNDERSTANDING THE ROMAN ARENA

Theatrical combat involving gladiators were held for more than five centuries. In this analysis, I focus on the first century CE period, a time when the Roman Empire was well established. During this period, there was a substantial increase in gladiatorial presentations and wild-beast hunts. Many masonry amphitheaters were built in various parts of the Roman Empire to support these shows (Edmondson 1996; Figure 13.1). In addition, there were gladiator schools supported by the Roman emperor, as well as a variety of formal professions linked to the Roman arena.

Since the nineteenth century, scholars have been trying to explain the gladiator phenomenon, which encompassed religiosity, blood, masculinity, and violence. The interpretation of the Roman arena remains a controversial subject to this day. For example, some scholars argue that arena spectators were an idle mob that lived for *panem et circenses* (bread and circuses). In theories of Romanization, the amphitheaters are understood as a symbol of Roman masculinity and power (Garraffoni 2005). These studies have focused on literary sources and have paid more attention to audiences than to the gladiators themselves. Although it is difficult to find gladiator voices in the literature, as such sources describe the gladiators from the viewpoint of the elite, archaeology can provide unique evidence of those voices through inscriptions, which potentially become an important source for capturing aspects of a gladiator's day-to-day life (Garraffoni 2008; Garraffoni and Funari 2009). Because archaeology connects materiality to social relations and breaks the silences of the written record, it provides a different approach to gladiator combats. However, it is important to emphasize that to bring archaeological evidence to the center of this analysis also means to use a unique data set for producing alternative models through which to rethink the Roman past. In this context, it is also necessary to rethink theoretical underpinnings, and I suggest here that postcolonial thought seems to be the most appropriate tool with which to recognize the particularity of marginalized lives in the Roman Empire. Peter Ucko (1995) has already noted that postcolonial thought can help us rethink normative models based on similarity and underline the specificity of each social stratum. Recent historical archaeological literature criticizes the assumption of a one-to-one correspondence between text and material culture and proposes to study documents and archaeology in their respective contexts (e.g., Courtney 2007; Funari, Jones, and Hall 1999; Funari and Zarankin 2001; Laurence 2005).

Although in the 1990s Cullen (1996) observed that classical archaeologists had shown little inclination to examine theoretical approaches to the ancient past, in the past decade this situation has been changing. The development of postmodern theory led to a skepticism of meta-narratives and helped classicists refine the sensitivity to differences and "otherness." Recent approaches view the Roman Empire as an intricate pattern of inequalities (e.g., Hingley 2005).

Using a postcolonial epistemological approach, I focus on material culture – the gladiators' tombstones – to discuss memory, neglected lives, and the role of women in shaping the identity of the deceased gladiator and in memory-keeping. First I discuss the main approaches to the gladiators' lives. Then I focus on the role of archaeological research to confront silences and contribute alternative perspectives to understand excluded pasts.

THE GLADIATORS' DAILY LIVES

As the gladiators fought in the arena, the focus on the experience of the warrior in battle, their virtues in the face of death, and the masculinity involved in public fights

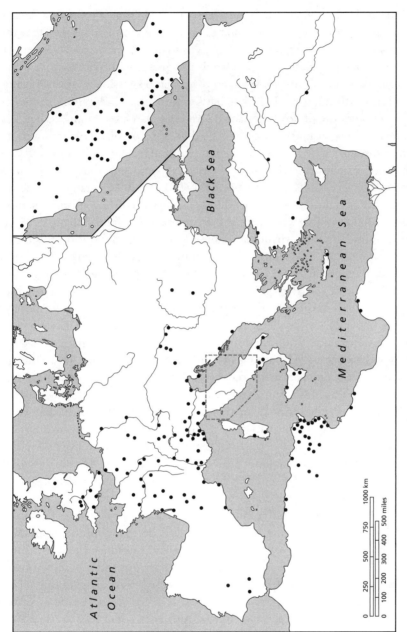

FIGURE 13.1. The most important Roman arenas (Weeber 1994: 20).

217

was prioritized. Such scholarship neglected social and family networks, sexualities, and desires, thus preserving an understanding of common people's lives that relied on an exclusively normative model of what it was to be a Roman male. It is important to emphasize that the gladiators practiced a stigmatized profession, so that the images of masculinity that are constructed from that profession are not the same as the masculinity attributed to elite men. This complexity can be found in Seneca's writings.[1] Although the philosopher considered the gladiators infamous because of their profession, he constantly evoked the gladiator as a powerful metaphor to teach the virtue of disdain for death, a virtue he felt essential for the formation of the ethos of a warrior or a political leader. Seneca constantly moves between the notions of virtue and infamy in establishing the moral values that should be taught to members of the elite. Such values articulate in different ways according to rank, status, or occupation: what would be worthy for the formation of the ethos of a man of virtue would be different from the virtues available to a man of infamous profession.

Commenting on Seneca, some scholars contend that he admitted the importance of the gladiatorial performance as a pedagogical element to prepare the Roman soldier for death (Barton 1993; Cagniart 2000; Wistrand 1992). However, this approach relates the gladiators' infamous condition to their status as social pariahs: men without identity or memory seeking to be recognized by Roman society. Following this approach Edwards, for instance, contends that gladiators, as with prostitutes and actors, were infamous because they sold their own flesh; they lived to provide sex and violence for the pleasure of the public (Edwards 1997: 67, 77, 85). Barton (1993), Gunderson (1996), and Wiedemann (1995), like Edwards, conclude that legal disabilities stripped the gladiators of the social and cultural characteristics that gave identity to most men in Roman society. According to this perspective, these legal restrictions condemned the gladiators to live as a homogenous mob, a collective social pariah; they became, as Edwards has suggested, "the gladiator," a naked figure, defined only by his weapon (Edwards 1997:78).

Approaches based mainly on literary sources create hermetic categories of masculinity and of the identity of the common people. Such a narrow idea of masculinity links the gladiators' lives to elite ideas of morality and masculinity (although they may have also helped to shape the warrior ethos and disdain for death). The limited sense of "identity" for the common people condemns them to an anonymous journey, seeking social acceptance. These models lead us to imagine that all those who fought in Roman arenas were men without personal history or identity. We see them only as men who lived to serve special purposes, some as victims of Roman cruelty and violence, others condemned to an obscure social life or reduced to bodies for public display and entertainment. Thus, important details of their lives are concealed. One such detail, for example, would be that during the early principate, the gladiators comprised not only slaves or bandits condemned to fight but also free persons who decided to live and work as gladiators (Ville 1981). Another point obscured by such hermetic concepts is the fact that at the end of the first century CE, there was an increase in the presence of women in the gladiatorial troops (Briceño Jáuregui 1986; Vesley 1998; McCullough 2008).

The presence of women and freemen choosing to fight in the arenas reveals a heterogeneity among the gladiatorial troops. Their presence, and the records of institutional proceedings such as gladiatorial contracts, allow us to contend that these men and women made choices and could not be described as belonging to a homogenous mob. Although the conscious choice to become a gladiator may seem odd to modern sensibilities, when we examine their commemorative tombstones, erected by wives or friends, we encounter surprising evidence. This evidence exposes the complexity of human relations in the Roman past, a complexity seldom found in the older interpretive models mentioned earlier. In this context, I believe that a gender archaeology approach to the tombstones can shed light on the evidence and help us to rethink aspects of the gladiators' daily lives and intimacy.

WHY A GENDER APPROACH TO THE GLADIATORIAL COMBAT?

As noted earlier, the few studies done on gladiators' daily lives have constructed a negative image of them: they were condemned to the status of social pariah, infamous people who provided violence and sex for the delight of elite audiences. The studies from the 1990s served an important historical role in having reinserted the figure of the gladiator into the scholarly discourse and in proposing new interpretations for the combats. However, these studies were constructed on an idea of universal male aggression. The gladiators are described by their armor categories, their weapons, their violence, and their bloodthirstiness; their essential nature becomes "warriorhood." Because the Roman arena was a highly masculinized region of social life, I suggest it is important to rethink this approach. Same-sex social environments can be complex and challenge us to look for points of articulation, searching beyond the "aggressiveness," for example, to consider the inhabitants of these environments in a more contextual analysis. As Casella and Voss (Chapter 1) have pointed out, it is important to rethink masculinized environments, sexuality, and intimacy, articulating them within the context of personal, familial, institutional, economic, and religious practices. Or, in other words, it is necessary to consider the gladiators as lovers, husbands, fathers, and men who could express their worldview and share it with friends, both male and female.

Gilchrist (1999) has already pointed out that masculinist theories can challenge monolithic and essentialist views of "male." Such theories also provide tools to reexamine masculinity and to consider it as a multidimensional and socially acquired quality. Gender archaeology thus helps us to rethink naturalized approaches to masculinity and femininity, reminding us that those categories are neither absolute nor static because they are constituted within specific societies. The concern with gender gives impetus to new types of data analysis and inspires innovative ways of approaching past social relations (Sorensen 2007). Using this epistemological context, it is possible not only to rethink some aspects of the gladiators' daily experiences but also to highlight the contributions of women in shaping their memories.

APPROACHING THE ROMAN TOMBSTONES

Alföldy (2003) comments that during the Augustan period, there was an increase in the use of inscriptions. On the basis of MacMullen's classic study on epigraphy (MacMullen 1982), Alföldy argues that the Romans developed an epigraphic habit and turned inscriptions of the most varied types into an efficient communication medium. Inscriptions spread symbolic values and reached public opinion in distinct spheres, becoming vital to a broader knowledge of Roman society and economy. Among the extensive diversity of inscriptions from Rome and the Roman provinces, tombstones thus became important evidence for the study of moral, legal, and hereditary relationships between the deceased and a commemorator.

Saller and Shaw (1984) indicate that tombstones furnish more than three-quarters of the entire corpus of Latin inscriptions.[2] Many tombstones give us no more than names, but thousands of others offer additional details, such as age at death or the name of the commemorator, allowing us to study relationships between commemorator and deceased. Most analyses of this type of evidence are usually focused on the epitaphs of elites, not only because they are so plentiful but also because there has been greater interest among historians in mapping the kin and local status of Roman politicians. In this context, tombstones constitute an important data set for classicists, especially those interested in family relationship analysis, to define the political web in the Roman provinces.

It should also be noted that although tombstones and epitaphs were common in Roman culture, historians and epigraphists have paid more attention to the inscriptions themselves than to the surfaces on which they were embossed or the places in which they were found. Funari (1994) has defined this as a crossroad of epigraphic studies. According to Funari, the main difficulty produced by this omission is that some experts publish translations of inscriptions but do not comment on the material context in which they were found, creating a void between material culture and epigraphy. As a result, epigraphists end up ignoring archaeologists' work, and vice versa, impeding a dialogue that could be useful for both specializations.

Studying the tombstones and epitaphs as material culture can help construct a better understanding of daily life in the Roman provinces. Inscribed tombstones were central to Roman culture because they were a media for place-making or memory-keeping. They were used to bring the past into the present and to remind people of the finitude of life. Tombstones usually were located on roadsides outside of the city walls and were intended to reveal to passersby not only who was lying there but also some aspect of his or her life. Not everyone could afford them, but the *Collegia* (guilds or associations) helped common people pay for tombstones and provide an appropriate burial (Alföldy 1984). Unfortunately for archaeological purposes, the majority of Roman tombstones have not been found in situ because they were used to construct new buildings during the medieval period. Therefore, it can sometimes be difficult to date some tombstones or to reconstruct their original context. Even with these problems, those that have survived can help us reconstruct fragments of anonymous lives otherwise lost in a landscape of elite-dominated references.

GLADIATOR TOMBSTONES FROM ROME AND ROMAN SPAIN

The tombstones I selected comprise a particular type of data because they commemorate deceased gladiators. Although some scholars, such as Sabbatini Tumolesi or Hope, have pointed out that gladiator tombstones are not numerous, are in a poor state of preservation, or are too fragmentary, they nevertheless help us to understand gladiator games from a different perspective, allowing us to glimpse aspects of the worldviews and family relationships of individual gladiators (Hope 1998, 2000a,

2000b; Sabbatini Tumolesi 1971, 1974, 1980, 1984, 1988). Despite Hope's assertion that only professional gladiators would have received formal burial rites, with the majority buried in mass graves (Hope 2000a: 97), memorials to individual gladiators reveal the everyday life of the gladiators, especially the gendered relationships that tombstones express between the deceased and their commemorators.

Tombstones were erected by friends or relatives and help us to understand how memories and social roles were constructed. Sabbatini Tumolesi reminds us that epitaphs and tombstones commemorated the dead gladiator as an individual; instead of indicating, as in inscriptions announcing a spectacle, the number of men scheduled to fight, the epitaphs give us a few words about an individual's life and history (Sabbatini Tumolesi 1980: 150). Most gladiator epitaphs were written in irregularly shaped and positioned letters, indicating the humble origin of those commemorating the dead gladiator. However, additional inscriptions with more regular letters indicate that some gladiators could afford professionally made tombstones. In either case, the few words written on a tombstone inform us about aspects of the gladiator's skills and allow us glimpses of a private life, including the presence of friends, fellow fighters, and relatives.

For this analysis, I selected epitaphs from both Rome and Roman Spain. My goal has been to compare epitaphs and tombstones from two parts of the empire, the main city (Rome) and the provincial area of Córdoba (Roman Spain). It is also important to remember that the territory of Hispania was one of the first to be dominated by the Romans after they left the Italic peninsula and that the Roman presence in Hispania lasted several centuries. During the first century CE, many masonry amphitheaters had already been built in Roman Spain (Figure 13.1), which has allowed retrieval of a great diversity of the material culture of the gladiators, including the tombstones. Although the tombstones I selected are all of the first century CE, were professionally made, and refer to an urban funeral context, there are some differences I would like to stress. First, the tombstones from Rome discussed later in the chapter were collected in a series of books titled *Epigrafia anfiteatrale dell'occidente romano* edited by Sabbatini Tumolesi (1984). As noted earlier, none of the tombstones and epitaphs from Rome were found in their original context. Most are fragmentary, and most are now housed in various Italian museums. Although provenance is unknown, the tombstones can be dated by the material they are made of and the lettering style of the inscription. The examples from Roman Spain, however, are of a known archaeological context. They were unearthed between 1948 and 1954 during excavations on a necropolis in Córdoba (Figure 13.2) and were published by Garcia y Bellido (1960). Since excavation, these tombstones have been housed in Córdoba's Archaeological Museum. They comprise a corpus of eleven inscriptions. Garcia y Bellido (1960) notes they are well preserved and are all inscribed in the same format. Most have marble surfaces (for example, see Figures 13.3 and 13.4).

I selected eleven tombstones – seven from Rome and four from Córdoba. I believe this sample is representative of the ways in which gladiators were represented in the funerary context and of the role of women in shaping their memories. As Hope has stressed (2000a: 94), the tombstones provided a forum open to manipulation. Thus, they construct ideal memory rather than reflect reality.

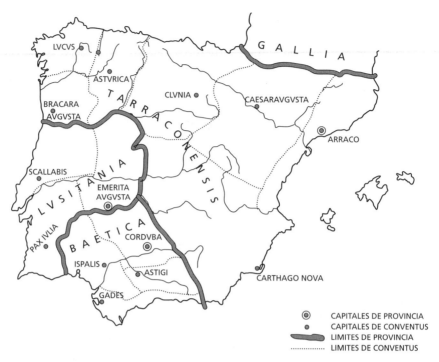

FIGURE 13.2. Roman Spain and Cordoba, Baetica (Gozalbes Gravioto 2000: 262).

FIGURE 13.3. Satur's tombstone, marble (Museo Arqueólogico y Etnológico de Cordoba, Spain; number CE012342).

FIGURE 13.4. Actius' tombstone, marble (Museo Arqueólogico y Etnológico de Cordoba, Spain; number CE010681).

ROME

Tombstone 1:

A(ulus) POSTUMIUS
ACOEMETUS
DOCTOR
MYRMILLON(um)[3]
[Aulus Postumius Acoemetus, Murmillos trainer]

Tombstone 2:

GRATUS
DOCTOR MURM(illonum)
V(ixit) A(nnis) XXVII[4]
[Gratus, Murmillos trainer, he was 27 when he died]

Tombstone 3:

D(is) M(anibus) S(acrum)
APOLLONIO
THRAECI, SC(aeua)
LIB(ero), VI[5]
[To the Manibus gods, Apollonius, Thracian, left-handed, freedman, fought 6 times]

Tombstone 4:

Amanus, Sam(nes), Ner(onianus),
v(ictoriarum) III, (coronarum) II[6]
[Amanus, Samnites, neronian, 3 victories, 2 crowns]

Tombstone 5:

> L(ucius) Lucretius, tr(aex), vict(oriarum) XIIX[7]
> *[Lucius Lucrecius, Thracian, 18 victories]*

Tombstone 6:

> C(aius) IVLIVS
> IVCVNDVS
> ESSEDARIVS
> V(ixit) A(nnis) XXV
> FILIA PATRI[8]
> *[Caius Iulius Iucundus, Essedari, he was 25 when he died. From his daughter]*

Tombstone 7:

> C(aius) Futius Hyacintus doct(or) opl(omachorum).
> Futia C(ai) l(iberta) Philura fecit[9]
> *[Caius Futius Hyacintus, Oplomachus' trainer.*
> *Futia Philura, freedwoman has done it.]*

The preceding tombstones from Rome all have regular letters, harmoniously distributed on the surface of the tombstone. Tombstones 1 and 2 belong to two *doctores*, the Latin word for a trainer of gladiators. Aulus Postumius Acoemetus and Gratus were both trainers of a specific type of gladiator, the Murmillo. This indicates that each man fought for a period as a Murmillo gladiator and later became a trainer. Both thus survived combat and spent the remainder of their lives training young gladiators. Aulus was a free citizen and Gratus a slave. According to Sabbatini Tumolesi, Aulus was of Greek origin.

Sabbatini Tumolesi also comments on the origin of Amanus, the gladiator commemorated by tombstone 4. Amanus came from a Syrian family, according to his name. Although Amanus was a slave, and Aulus a freeman who died as a trainer, the tombstones of both men tell us their armor categories and indicate aspects of their careers. Amanus, who fought in Samnite armor, trained in the *ludus neronianus*, a gladiator training school in southern Italy in operation during Nero's reign. Thus, Amanus was born to a Syrian family, lived and trained in southern Italy, and passed away in Rome. This career, which includes three victories and two prizes, indicates the gladiator's geographic mobility.

Tombstone 3 belongs to Apollonius, a freedman who fought as Thracian. He fought six times before dying and was left-handed, a skill that was always commemorated because it was more difficult to fight against somebody who carried the sword in his left hand.

Lucius Lucretius, tombstone 5, is another Thracian who fought and won eighteen bouts. Even if we presume that this number of victories is inflated, it is interesting to note that Lucius fought in multiple presentations and survived for some years afterward. This tombstone particularly, but also each of the others already noted, reminds us that in Rome, as in other parts of the empire, gladiator presentations were not necessarily simple slaughters. Many professional gladiators survived multiple contests, and some could go on to become trainers and die outside of the arena.

Others established affective relationships, such as Caius Iulius Iucundus (tombstone 6) and Caius Futius Hyacintus (tombstone 7). The former belonged to the Essedari armor category and was commemorated by his daughter. Even if we assume that someone else paid for the tombstone, because the girl would have likely been too young to actually provide for this, it is important to emphasize that her mention indicates that some gladiators may have had children. Because this tombstone emphasizes the daughter's presence, it represents persuasive evidence that women played an important role in commemorating a gladiator's death. The second tombstone noted earlier, of Caius Fuitius Hyacintus, is more explicit in this aspect. His tombstone, very well preserved, indicates that Futia Philura was responsible for having it made. She was a freedwoman, probably Caius' concubine, and was responsible for guaranteeing his memory by paying for the tombstone and having it engraved.

The epitaphs are short, and their simplicity leads some scholars to point out the features they share with Roman military epitaphs. Like gladiator tombstones, the military variety also presented the soldier's biographical information, such as province of origin, rank, unit, and age (Gregori 2001; Hope 2000a: 111–112). Military tombstones were erected in faraway lands, after a battle, by comrades commemorating the skills of a deceased colleague. Roman gladiator tombstones are thus as valuable as the tombstones of Roman soldiers for the information they provide. They support a clearer understanding of the diverse ethnic origins of the gladiators. They provide information about individual gladiatorial careers. And they provide insight into the dynamics behind the games themselves, given that we find many gladiators continued to work in a capacity related to the games, as trainers, even past their combat years. Although the gladiatorial matches can be understood as a highly masculinized environment, epitaphs from tombstones 6 and 7 highlight the role of women, figures seldom otherwise mentioned in connection with the gladiatorial presentations. We find that an important figure to guarantee the memory of a gladiator could be female.

ROMAN SPAIN

Although the essential characteristic of a tombstone is to be concise, tombstones from Roman Spain are more complex and provide more background on the role of women in commemorating the gladiators. These tombstones from Hispania also allow us to consider the presence of interethnic households.

Tombstone 8:

> Mur(millo). Cerinthus. Ner(onianus). II. Nat(ione) graecus.
> An(norum) XXV. Rome Coniunx bene merenti de suo posit. T(e) R(ogo)
> P(raeteriens) D(icas) S(it) T(ibi) T(erra) L(euis)[10]
> *[Murmillo Cerinthus, neronian, fought two times. He was Greek.*
> *He was twenty-five when he died. Rome, his wife, has paid for this tombstone.*
> *I ask you, passerby, say "Let the earth be light upon you."]*

Tombstone 9:

> Actius, mur(millo), uic(it) VI,
> Anno XXI, H(ic) s(itus) e(st) s(it) t(erra) l(euis).

Uxor uiro de suo quot quisquis uestrum mortuo.

Optarit mihi it ili di faciant. Semper uiuo et mortuo.[11]

[Actius, Murmillo, won six times. He was twenty-one years old when he died. Here he lies. His wife has paid for this tombstone with her money. Whatever you wish on me and on him the gods will do to you, dead or alive.]

Tombstone 10:

SATVR MVR(millo) IVL(ianus) XIII

BASSUS. L(iberatus). MVR(millo) I. I

H(ic) S(iti) S(unt). S(it) V(obis). T(erra). L(evis)

CORNELIA SEVERA

VXOR D(e) S(uo). D(edit)[12]

[Satur, Murmillo, iulianus, he fought 13 times.

Bassus, freedman, Murmillo, won one palm and one crown. They lie here. Let the earth be light upon them. Cornelia Severa, wife, has paid for this tombstone with her money.]

Tombstone 11:

MUR(illo) FAVSTVS NER(onianus)

XII VER(na) ALEX(andriae) AN(orum) XXXV

H(ic) S(itus) E(st) APPOLONIA VXOR ET HERMES TR(ax)

DE SVO POSVERVNT[13]

[Murmillo Faustus, neronian, he fought 12 times. He was born as a slave at Alexandria and was 35 when he died. Here he lies. Apollonia, his wife, and Hermes, a Thracian gladiator, paid for the tombstone with their money.]

Like the tombstones found in Rome, all the tombstones from Córdoba in Hispania were produced in the first century CE. Although additional tombstones from this area are irregularly lettered, made by friends or paid for by the troops, I have chosen to comment on those described here because they document the presence of women, illuminating the active role of women in choosing the words to describe their partners or friends. Such tombstones also allow us to reflect on the intimate encounters and interethnic cross-sex relationships that were made possible only through the increase in gladiator troops and their movement throughout the Roman Empire.

Like tombstones 6 and 7 from the city of Rome, tombstones from Hispania were also made by professionals, but with notable differences. The tombstones from Roman Spain have longer epitaphs and allow us insight into the gladiators and their social context. According to tombstone 8, Cerinthus, a Murmillo gladiator who trained at neronian's school, was of Greek origin. As with Amanus, mentioned in tombstone 4, Cerinthus also traveled with his troop: he trained in Italy, but died in Roman Spain. He was twenty-five years old when he died. He left a wife, Rome, also a slave, who paid for his tombstone.

García y Bellido (1960) has commented on an interesting detail in this inscription: the word *coniunx* (wife) in the epitaph was not usually used among slaves. Another remarkable detail is that the woman, Rome, chose to underscore that she paid for the tombstone with her own money: *bene merenti de suo posit.*

On tombstones 9, 10, and 11 we find a similar situation. Tombstone 9 was dedicated to Actius, tombstone 10 to Satur and Bassus (freedmen), and tombstone 11 to Faustus. On each of these tombstones we find the word *uxor*, which refers to a "wife." As with *coniunx*, this word was not usually used to refer to a slave's concubine, but rather to freewomen married to Roman citizens. Although no female name appears on tombstone 9, on the other two, we find the term applied to both the freedwoman Cornelia Severa and the slave Appolonia. It is a plausible assumption that, because they paid for the tombstones, these women also selected the messages to be engraved there. Again, each commemorative tombstone not only commemorates the gladiator's life but also suggests that his partner had an active role in shaping the memory of that life through an engraving to intervene against forgetfulness. Because these tombstones were excavated from the necropolis, it conceivable that the women chose epitaphs as a way to construct a dialogue with passersby, not only commemorating the deceased but also asserting their own place in this provincial society.

All the tombstones also give us details of the gladiators' lives. We read that Actius was a slave who fought as a Murmillo and won six times. He was twenty-one when he died, and his wife left a warding-off message to protect them both from any uncharitable thoughts a passerby might have.

Tombstone 10 is unusual in being dedicated to two gladiators, Satur and Bassus. Satur trained at the *ludus* of Julius Caesar in Capua (southern Italy), fought thirteen times, and died in Roman Spain. His friend Bassus won two prizes, a crown and a palm. It is not clear which of these men was Cornelia Severa's partner, but García y Bellido (1960) suggests she was married to Bassus. This tombstone allows us to consider that fellow gladiators could be buried together and the women who were close to them outside of the arena.

Tombstone 11 also showcases friendship and family links. Fautus, commemorated by this tombstone, was born a slave in Alexandria, trained in Capua (southern Italy), and died in Roman Spain. His wife, Apollonia, and his friend, Hermes, a gladiator of another armor category, paid for his tombstone. This tombstone, as with tombstone 10, indicates that women, as well as friends from the gladiatorial troops, were present in the gladiators' lives and that such relationships were important in preserving the memory of the deceased gladiator.

This question of women companions is seldom explored in studies of the lives of gladiators. As Vesley (1998) has pointed out, we do not have many sources through which to study female gladiators, but I believe this type of evidence enables us to imagine women and their role outside of the arena. Even if we take into account that some tombstones are not signed, as in tombstones numbers 1 through 5, or that some were made by comrades from the gladiatorial troops, the tombstones paid for by women provide alternative possibilities and approaches to explore. They help us understand gladiators in a social context, commemorated as friends, partners, or fathers. They also emphasize a woman's role in constructing the memory of a companion and in choosing the words to celebrate his life. Some, like number 11, are more precise in stating the birthplace of the gladiator, and others underscore the possibility of expressing feelings and protection for the deceased lover. I suggest, then, that although the arena is a highly masculinized environment, women nevertheless sometimes had active roles in that arena through commemorating the deceased gladiators' lives and experience.

The tombstones allow us to see these men in a complex social net that involved interethnic households and cross-class relationships, including even intimate relationships between free and enslaved persons. Through the commemorative words these women chose, we learn of gladiators born in different areas of the empire, who trained in specific schools, married, and died far away from their birthplaces. Furthermore, we see that because these women's lives took on a public dimension through the inscriptions, they themselves became visible, challenging an environment dominated by male references.

The tombstones I selected for this case study provide an idea of the diversity of the epitaphs and of their importance as an alternative source of biographical details and the social lives of otherwise obscured individuals. Even in their variety, the tombstones help us understand these people from a more humanistic approach. Reading the epitaphs one learns of the gladiators' mobility throughout the Roman Empire, their legal status (slave, freedman, or free), their friendships and family, their skills and abilities, and the ways in which their memory was constructed by friends and lovers. In addition, the armor category of some gladiators, important enough to include on a tombstone, does not seem to be a symbol of shame, as some scholars have suggested, but, I believe, a positive expression of professional pride, or, as Hope has suggested (2000a), a claim to membership in a community.

This evidence comprises a compelling corpus, encouraging us to think about these men not just as a narrowly defined group but as people who shared life, feelings, and intimacy. The tombstone is an epigraphic source that can help us understand the gladiators not only as representatives of aggressive masculinity but as individuals playing different roles: winner or loser in the arena, professional, father, lover, friend, slave, or freedman. The tombstones also require us to recognize that many gladiators are still remembered because of their concubines' wishes. They could afford the tombstones, and it is possible to imagine that in commemorating the deceased gladiator, they also claimed their position in local society. Saller and Shaw (1984: 127) have noted that it was not only the wealthy who wished to perpetuate their own histories but that people of humble origins also sought to avoid the anonymity of the mass grave. The gladiators would have been no different. In light of that awareness, I suggest that the deceased gladiator and his concubine became visible through the tombstone. They could be seen by passersby and acted to construct a particular discourse of memory that enables us to think not only about ephemeral affairs but also about different forms of long-term social bonds, such as nuclear families and interethnic households. Tombstones, then, can be understood as a special type of material culture, dedicated to memory-making and memory-keeping. They provide clues to the intimate encounters between people who were born under and affected by the Roman Empire but who seldom appear in scholarly discourse. As I have suggested in a previous study, I believe these tombstones represent valuable alternative archaeological sources that allow us to think in terms of a more complex social context, understanding the gladiators' lives not as enclosed in an isolated male world but as lives constructed among the women and men with whom they shared their lives, intimacy, and desires (Garraffoni 2005, 2008).

CONCLUSION

The tombstones I have commented on here are a singular corpus because they allow us to reach gladiators' lives. They provide a different type of discourse, one informed not by the elite point of view found in written sources but by the perceptions of friends and relatives who helped construct the memories of the gladiators. Although most of these inscriptions are concise, through case studies of thoughtfully selected samples, it is possible to recover voices otherwise seldom heard by scholars. In this context, the tombstones still direct our attention to a specific type of discourse, one encompassing socially constructed and reinterpreted memories. Through the tombstones, it is possible to celebrate individual lives, not only reconstructing the gladiators' experiences in the arena but also establishing them in their social networks. One may consider the tombstones to be fragmentary, but they nonetheless remind us of men who trained, rested, had friends, and sometimes even married and had children. In sum, they lived, and as they lived, they were not alone but shared their values and experiences with confidantes.

Finally, I believe these epigraphic sources are important evidence for not only capturing aspects of the gladiators' experience but also documenting the presence of women in keeping the memory of the gladiators alive. In this context, the tombstones challenge us to deconstruct analytical categories based on the idea of the gladiator as a symbol of aggressive masculinity, allowing us to envision them in a complex social context of interaction with men and women of different social backgrounds and ethnic origins. This new perspective should remind us that the purpose of archaeology is to study the historical nature of specific social, cultural, and gender relationships, observing, in this case, the details and complexities of the Roman past, and avoiding universal assumptions. Instead of a uniform or global interpretation of who the gladiators were or of the armor category they belonged to, this epigraphic evidence focuses on local variety in a specific context, allowing us to avoid analytical approaches based on Western notions of what a warrior should be.

NOTES

1. See, for instance, Seneca's text *On the Brevity of Life*, especially chapter 13.
2. Saller and Shaw indicate that there were approximately 250,000 known inscriptions at the time of publication (1984).
3. Catalogue number 55 (Sabbatini Tumolesi, 1988).
4. Catalogue number 56 (Sabbatini Tumolesi, 1988).
5. Catalogue number 95 (Sabbatini Tumolesi, 1988).
6. Sabbatini Tumolesi, 1988: 77–78.
7. Sabbatini Tumolesi, 1998: 81–82.
8. Catalogue number 67 (Sabbatini Tumolesi, 1988).
9. Sabbatini Tumolesi, 1988: 61–62.
10. García y Bellido, 1960: 127–128.
11. García y Bellido, 1960: 134–135.

12. García y Bellido, tombstone 01
13. García y Bellido, tombstone 04.

REFERENCES

Alföldy, G. 1984. *Römische Sozialgeschichte.* Stuttgart, Germany: Franz Steiner.

Alföldy, G. 2003. "La cultura epigráfica de los romanos: la diffusion de un medio de comunicación y su papel en la integración cultural," in Remesal, J. et al. (eds.), *Vivir en tierra extraña: emigración e integración cultural en el mundo antiguo.* Barcelona: Universitat Barcelona, pp. 137–149.

Barton, C. A. 1993. *The sorrows of the Ancient Roman.* Princeton, NJ: Princeton University Press.

Briceño Jáuregui, M. 1986. *Los gladiadores de Roma: estudio histórico legal y social.* Bogotá, Colombia: Instituto Caro y Cuervo.

Cagniart, P. 2000. "The Philosopher and the Gladiator." *Classical World* 93(6):607–618.

_____. 2007. "Historians and Archaeologists: An English perspective." *Historical Archaeology* 41(2):34–45.

Cullen, T. 1996. "Contributions to Feminism in Archaeology." *American Journal of Archaeology* 100:409–414.

Edmondson, J. C. 1996. "Dynamic Arenas: Gladiatorial Presentations in the City of Rome and the Construction of Roman Society during the Early Empire," in Slater, W. J. (ed.), *Roman Theater and Society.* Ann Arbor: University of Michigan Press, 69–112.

Edwards, C. 1997. "Unspeakable Professions: Public Performance and Prostitution in Ancient Rome," in Hallet, J. P., & M. B. Skinner (eds.), *Roman Sexualities.* Princeton, NJ: Princeton University Press, pp. 66–95.

Funari, P. P. A. 1994. "Bretanha romana – Estudos recentes sobre a Arqueologia da Bretanha romana." *Revista de História da arte e Arqueologia* 1:249–252.

_____, Jones, S., and M. Hall. 1999. *Historical Archaeology – Back from the Edge.* London: Routledge.

_____, and Zarankin, A. 2001. "Abordajes arqueológicos de la vivienda doméstica en Pompeya: algunas consideraciones." *Gerión* 19:493–512.

García y Bellido, A. 1960. "Lapidas funerarias de gladiadores de Hispania." *Archivio Español de Arqueologia* 33:123–144.

Garraffoni, R. S. 2005. *Gladiadores na Roma Antiga: dos combates às paixões cotidianas,* São Paulo: Editora Annablume/FAPESP.

Garraffoni, R. S. 2008. "Funerary Commemoration and Roman Graffiti: How Epigraphy Can Contribute to Rethink Gladiators," in Hainsmann, M., and Wedenig, R. (eds.), *Instrumenta Inscripta Latina II.* Klagenfurt: Verlag des Geschichtsvereines für Kärten, pp. 119–132.

_____ and Funari, P. P. A. 2009. "Reading Pompeii's Walls: A Social Archaeological Approach to Gladiatorial Graffiti," in Wilmott, T. (ed.), *Roman Amphitheatres and Spectacula: A 21st Century Perspective.* Oxford: Archeopress, pp. 185–193.

Gilchrist, R. 1999. *Gender and Archaeology – Contesting the Past.* London: Routledge

Gozalbes Gravioto, E. 2000. *Caput celtiberiae.* Cuenca, Spain: Ediciones de la Universidad de Castilla-La Mancha.

Gregori, G. L. 2001. "Aspetti sociali della gladiatura romana," in Regina, A. (ed.), *Sangue e arena.* Rome: Electa, pp. 15–27.

Gunderson, E. 1996. "'The Ideology of the Arena," *Classical Antiquity* 15(1):113–151.

Hingley, R. 1996. "The 'legacy' of Rome: The Rise, Decline and Fall of the Theory of Romanization," in Webster, J., and N. Cooper (eds.), *Roman Imperialism: Post-Colonial Perspectives.* Leicester: University of Leicester Press, pp. 35–48.

_____. 2000. *Roman Officers and English Gentlemen – the Imperial Origins of Roman Archaeology.* London: Routledge.

_____, ed. 2001. *Images of Rome: Perceptions of Ancient Rome in Europe and the United States in the Modern Age. Journal of Roman Archaeology Supplementary Series 44,* Ann Arbor: Cushing-Malloy.

_____. 2005. *Globalizing Roman Culture.* London: Routledge.

Hope, V. M. 1998. "Negotiating Identity and Status: The Gladiators of Roman Nîmes," in Berry, J., and R. Laurence (eds.), *Cultural Identity in the Roman Empire*. London: Routledge, pp. 179–195.

_____. 2000a. "Contempt and Respect – The Treatment of Corpse in Ancient Rome," in Hope, V., and E. Marshall (eds.), *Death and Disease in the Ancient City*. London: Routledge, pp. 104–127.

_____. 2000b. "Fighting for Identity: The Funerary Commemoration of Italian Gladiators," in Cooley, A. (ed.), *The Epigraphic Landscape of Roman Italy*. London: University College of London, pp. 93–113.

Laurence, R. 2005. "The Uneasy Dialogue between Ancient History and Archaeology," in *The Cities of Vesuvius: Pompeii & Herculaneum*. Sidney: MacGuare University, pp. 99–111.

MacMullen, R. 1982. "The Epigraphic Habit in the Roman Empire."*American Journal of Philology* 103:233–246.

McCullough, A. 2008. "Female Gladiators in Imperial Rome: Literary Context and Historical Facts." *Classical World* 101(02):197–209.

Sabbatini Tumolesi, P. L. 1971. "Gladiatoria I." *Rediconti dei Lincei* XXVI:735–746.

_____. 1974. "A proposito di alcune iscrizioni gladiatorie veronesi." *Atti dell'Istituto Veneto di scienze, lettere ed arti* CXXXIII:435–448.

_____. 1980. *Gladiatorum paria: annunci di spettacoli gladiatorii a Pompei*. Rome: Edizioni di Storia e Letteratura.

_____. 1984. "A proposito do *CIL*, VI, 31917 da Praeneste (?)," in *Bullettino della Comissione Archeologica Comulale di Roma* LXXXIX 1:29–34.

_____. 1988. *Epigrafia anfiteatrali dell'Occidente Romano I – Roma*. Rome: Edizioni Quasar.

Saller, R. P., and Shaw, B. 1984. "Tombstones and Roman Family Relations in the Principate: Civilians, Soldiers and Slaves." *Journal of Roman Studies* LXXIV:124–156.

Seneca. 1932. *De Brevitate Vitae*. Moral Essays II, Loeb Classical Library Series. Cambridge, MA: Harvard University Press.

Sorensen, M. L. 2007. "On Gender Negotiation and Its Materiality," in Hamilton, S., et al. (eds.), *Archaeology and Women – Ancient and Modern Issues*. London: University College London, pp. 41–51.

Tilley, C. 1998. "Archaeology as Social-Political Action in the Present," in Whitley, D. S. (ed.), *Reader in Archaeological Theory – Post Processual and Cognitive Approaches*. London: Routledge, pp. 305–330.

Ucko, P. 1995. "Archaeological Interpretation in a World Context," in *Theory in Archaeology – A World Perspective*. London: Routledge, pp. 1–27.

Vesley, M. 1998. "Gladiatorial Training for Girls in the Collegia Iuvenum of the Roman Empire." *Echos du Monde Classique/Classical Views* XLII(17):85–93.

Ville, G. 1981. *La gladiature en Occident des origines la mort de Domitien*. Paris: De Boccard.

Voss, B. L., and Schmidt, R. A. 2000. "Archaeologies of Sexuality: An Introduction," in Voss, B. L., and Schmidt, R. A. (eds.), *Archaeologies of Sexuality*. London: Routledge, pp. 1–32.

Weeber, K.-W. 1994. *Panem et circenses: Massenunterhaltung als Politik im antiken Rom*. Mainz am Rhein, Germany: Philipp von Zabern.

Wiedemann, T. 1995. *Emperors and Gladiators*. London: Routledge.

Wistrand, M. 1992. *Entertainment and Violence in Ancient Rome – The Attitudes of Roman Writers of the First Century AD*. Göteburg, Sweden: Acta Universitatis Gothoburgensis.

FOURTEEN

MONUMENTS AND SEXUAL POLITICS IN NEW ENGLAND INDIAN COUNTRY

Patricia E. Rubertone

INTRODUCTION

On September 21, 1883, the Rhode Island Historical Society dedicated a boulder monument to Canonicus, a seventeenth-century sachem (or "chief") of the Narragansett, in the city of Providence's oldest public cemetery (Figure 14.1). In a ceremony filled with European Americans' speeches, poems, and patriotic songs, a Narragansett man had the dubious honor of unveiling the monument, and a little Narragansett girl presented a bouquet of flowers to the Indian Commissioner. Neither is reported to have said a word.

For members of the Society with antiquarian tastes and romanticized views about the Native American past, the dedication fulfilled a plan to commemorate "the friendly deeds of the sons of the forest by erecting to each a simple and inexpensive monument" that had lingered almost for forty years (Rhode Island Historical Society 1875: 68). The idea was proposed when opinions linking Native American decline and assimilation and the nation's historic destiny were gaining popularity across the United States. With predictions about vanishing Native Americans disappearing into the melting pot seeming increasingly undeniable, European Americans were assured that the time for implementing the plan for commemorating the "sons of the forest" had come. Not surprisingly, the monument envisioned for Canonicus, the most illustrious "son of the forest" considered worthy of commemoration, appeared on the landscape only after Rhode Island declared the Narragansett people "extinct"

I thank Barbara Voss and Eleanor Casella for inviting me to write this chapter and to participate in sessions at the Sixth World Archaeology Congress and at Stanford, where it was presented as a work-in-progress. I am indebted to Paula Dove Jennings and Loren Spears, and also Kate April, at the Tomaquag Indian Memorial Museum for their time and knowledge, and for giving me access to Red Wing's Collection. Numerous individuals at the Little Compton Historical Society, Pettaquamscutt Historical Society, Providence Public Library, Rhode Island Historical Society Library, and the Haffenreffer Museum of Anthropology, all provided valuable assistance with the research. William Simmons and John Norder offered suggestions that helped sharpen my ideas and broaden my perspective. Ella Sekatau has given me insights about Indian Rocks and more for which I am forever grateful.

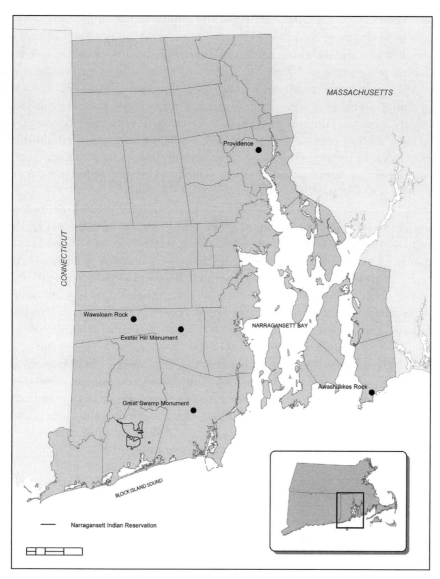

FIGURE 14.1. Map of Rhode Island showing locations of the Awashunkes, Wawaloam, Exeter Hill, and Great Swamp Monuments and the present-day boundaries of the Narragansett Indian Reservation (produced by Colin Porter).

and terminated its formal relations with the tribe. Nearly two hundred years after devastating losses in a bitter conflict between Indians and colonists called King Philip's War (1675–1676) and the insults of sustained colonialism, the Narragansett had become in the eyes of many European Americans so dwindled in number, divorced from place, and diluted by blood that they ceased to exist as a tribe.

Although detribalization, the common term for Rhode Island's dissolution of the Narragansett's tribal status, and commemoration implied finality, these processes were instead merely footnotes to an ongoing and more contentious saga of colonialist erasure (Rubertone 2008b). Rhode Island's "Indian problem" and Native people did not disappear after detribalization nor did monument-building cease. The sale of the tribe's remaining land base except for a few acres did not end disputes over property boundaries and resource use, and citizenship did not resolve persistent tensions about perceptions of Narragansett identity. As these nagging problems wore on, and the Narragansett, much like other New England Indians, strove to keep their cultural practices, nurture communal ties, and survive in American society, European Americans continued to memorialize them. The monuments raised consigned the Narragansett to a commemorative landscape where particular historical interpretations of them as friends or adversaries were concretized. Consequently, who was remembered and how they were recalled represented only a mere fraction of Native people and their experiences with the colonizers.

Short of making a case for building counter-monuments to redress these silences, I examine the sexual politics of monuments and the tensions surrounding them, arguing that the underrepresentation and misrepresentation of Native women on commemorative landscape was one of the many ways that colonialism attempted to reshape their lives. Such monumental oversights that marginalized and misconstrued the influential roles of Native women as community leaders and cultural nurturers was a form of symbolic violence perpetrated on their memory that underrated their value in ways that resonate even today. Arguably, spatial expressions of masculinity, and often enough sexuality, that discouraged women's use of public, commemorative spaces created cartographies that underwrote dispossession by imposing real or imaginary limitations on Native women's mobility. In exploring how Native women in New England negotiated the sexual politics of commemorative spaces, I show how they used monuments as theaters of action where, through public performances, they critiqued colonialism, affirmed cultural knowledge, and challenged their invisibility and that of their communities.

REMEMBERED AS HONORARY MEN

Only two Native women were commemorated with free-standing boulders in Rhode Island. One, inscribed "In memory of Awashonks Queen of Sogkonate & friend of the white man" (Figure 14.2), is located in Little Compton, a town historically associated with the Saconet. During the seventeenth century, they lived in an ancestral homeland encompassing settlements and camps stretching from the coast inland, as did other Native peoples around Narragansett Bay to whom they were linked by kinship, exchange, and politics. After King Philip's War, they were given a piece of land three-quarters of a mile square that oral history says surrounded one of their villages and that written accounts place in the vicinity of where Isaac Champlin Wilbour created a parklike, nature preserve enhanced with bridges, roads and paths, poetic verses, and commemorative boulders to local Indians, including the much-storied Awashunkes, in the latter nineteenth century (Brownell 1970: 287–288; VHB/Vanasse Hangen Brustlin 2003).

Known as a squaw sachem, a loose iteration of the term *saunks* translated as "the Queen, or Sachim's wife" (Williams 1936 [1643]: 141), Awashunkes was a leader in her own right (e.g., Grumet 1980; Richmond and Den Ouden 2003). She appears in the official records of Plymouth Colony, which had jurisdiction of her homeland, and

FIGURE 14.2. Awashunkes Boulder in Wilbour Woods from the Little Compton scrapbook. Ink on Paper, n.d., RHi X17 473 (courtesy of the Rhode Island Historical Society).

Rhode Island between 1671 and 1683. At a time of increasing tensions and hostilities in southern New England, she emerges as an independent-minded leader whose name shows up in connection with matters related to land sales and intercultural politics (Plane 1996). She is featured prominently in Benjamin Church's diary of King Philip's War in which the military leader of Plymouth described her leading a dance "in a foaming sweat" at a large gathering of Saconet and other Indians during the early days of the conflict. He reported that upon his arrival, she broke away from the dance – a ritual southern New England Indians referred to as a *nickòmmo* that they held in times of general crisis and at other important turning points in their lives – sat down, called her nobles around her, and ordered him into her presence to discuss the impending war (Church 1975: 69–70). She was characterized by her skill and intelligence as a negotiator but also by the detailed physical description of her body. In Church's estimation, she was "savage but honorable" (Plane 1996: 147), an opinion that was repeated across the centuries – from 1716 when his account appeared in print, to the moment the monument was raised in her memory in the nineteenth century.

However, her "savage but honorable" image did not offer immunity from an accusation of infanticide brought against her in an English court of law in 1683 for aiding and abetting the murder of her daughter's newborn child (Plane 1996). Considering that infanticide was rarely prosecuted in seventeenth-century (and early-eighteenth-century) New England, the case points to "a literal *embodiment* of colonization" (Plane 1996: 154) in which Native women's bodies and sexual behavior became the sites of struggle and increased scrutiny and regulation by colonists (Voss, Chapter 2, this volume). Although neither she nor her daughter were found guilty – the daughter was punished for fornication (sexual intercourse outside of marriage) and Awashunkes chastised for having the woman who accused her and her family of the murder whipped – gender and sexuality served as a "formidable ally of colonization" (Brown 1993) that provided additional cause for colonial intervention aimed at undermining her authority. Awashunkes was an especially vulnerable target of the colonists' efforts at eroding the political autonomy of Native authorities because her public role as a leader defied the colonial society's gender expectations. She was atypical for a woman but only from the perspective of the colonizers.

The other boulder monument is engraved: "To the memory of Wawaloam, wife of Miantonomi, 1661." It sits in what has been identified as a small historical cemetery in Exeter, Rhode Island, although the stone neither marks her grave nor gives her date of death. When and where Wawaloam died is unknown, as is the year and place of her birth. Although these facts of her life are undocumented and her lineage difficult to sort out precisely from colonial records, one aspect of her life that is fairly certain is that she was married to Miantonomi, an articulate and charismatic Narragansett sachem. She was probably the wife who traveled with him to Connecticut in 1638 along with their children and a large entourage to attend a meeting aimed at negotiating a treaty that would ease intertribal and intercultural tensions (LaFantasie 1988: 182–183). She is mentioned in a letter written by Roger Williams in 1639 that says she gave a basket to Mrs. Winthrop, the wife of the governor of the Massachusetts Bay Colony, which her husband brought to Boston along with gifts of wampum (LaFantasie 1988:196). Four years later, Miantonomi was dead, assassinated by his enemy, Uncas, the leader of the Mohegans. The oldest of her three sons (no daughters are mentioned in written sources) died young. The other two survived childhood and grew into adults.

Wawaloam comes into view again in 1661, when she gives testimony about land given by her late husband and his deceased uncle, the chief sachem Canonicus, to an Indian named Sosoa (Potter 1835: 248). In the affidavit, also signed by her second son, she affirms that she was Miantonomi's wife. The date inscribed on her monument (1661) underwrites her ties to him by marriage. However, her testimony also underscores her knowledge of and active role in matters regarding colonial land transactions so important to her community (e.g., Richmond and Den Ouden 2003). Although Wawaloam's life is overshadowed by her husband's in colonial records, she appears as knowledgeable and competent, as well as sensible and kind.

She may not have harbored any pretension to assume leadership as a sachem, but she appears at crucial moments in which her presence, actions, and opinions were valued. In the colonizing society where women were not meant to be visible, her public role marked her as anomalous.

The paucity of monuments to Native American women in Rhode Island (and North America in general) makes a telling statement about how they have been mostly rendered anonymous in the colonial gaze. The two Native women visibly remembered with boulder monuments were commemorated because they are relatively prominent figures in the chronicles of Indian-European relations in seventeenth-century New England. More precisely, Awashunkes and Wawaloam were commemorated because they exhibited attributes of leadership admired *in* and *by* men in the colonizing society, but considered unusual for women, and not because they demonstrated abilities in other dimensions of their lives respected in Native communities. That these Native women were recognized with boulder memorials, the same kind of monuments European Americans raised to male sachems, made them by extension "honorary men" (see Norkunas 2002).

However, discussions of Native American women and public monuments in New England cannot be only about whether they were visibly remembered and if so, how their lives were evaluated by monument builders or what types of tangible memorials were considered suitable for them (see also Garraffoni, Chapter 13, this volume). To confine inquiries to these questions would confirm the colonialist inscription of public space as male space. In light of ideas about place as memory and experience, and feminist and postcolonial approaches in geography that question the extent to which people are compelled by dominant structures of identity reproduced on the landscape (e.g., Duncan 1996; Kern 2005; Mackintosh 2005; McDowell 2008), I focus attention on performances and contests in public commemorative spaces. Looking beyond the way that gendered identities were constituted by monuments to how they were negotiated in contradictory ways is crucial to destabilizing European American conceptions of power inscribed in the public sphere and illuminating experiences and memories silenced by notions of space that are dichotomized by invariable categories of gender, race, class, and sexuality. Additionally, the recognition that the experiences of Native American women, and more broadly, women of color, in public, commemorative spaces may not conform to the spatial prescriptions of exclusion, intimidation, and movement is critical to decolonizing archaeological studies of monuments and what they can ideally accomplish (Rubertone 2008a).

INDIAN ROCKS AND ROCK WOMEN

Bridging these experiences and memories, and indeed archaeologies, begins with the acknowledgment that memorial boulders erected by European Americans were not the only "Indian Rocks." For Narragansett and other New England Native peoples, rocks were also media of place-making and memory-keeping. Natural features such as rock outcrops and glacial erratics, as well as purposeful constructions such as stone heaps or rows, often identified special places of remembrance, the meanings of which were inextricably connected to their specific location on the landscape rather than defined by a carved inscription (e.g., Fawcett 2000; Mavor and Dix 1989; Simmons 1986). Whether referencing distant ancestors, named individuals, or other attachments, "Indian Rocks" were about an indigenous sensibility of place. Their stories learned in childhood and over a lifetime guided generation after generation of those who would listen, providing them with moral guideposts, lessons about struggle and survival, and warnings about danger and outsiders. Native women and men knew the importance of these rocks and the sacred spaces beneath and around them within their ancestral homelands as places to be revered, remembered, and revisited. They were places where the ancestors' voices resonated loud and firm and where the identities of Native men and women were assured even when threatened by colonialism and accelerated exposure to European American ways (see Basso 1996).

Although Native men and women knew the meanings and power of rocks in their ancestral homelands to their histories and identities, they were also acutely aware that European Americans' boulder monuments were disempowering in that these tangible memorials materialized claims about their disappearance and other misconceptions about their lives. The gendered and sensual qualities European Americans perceived in rocks they used as monuments and the masculine labels they attached to them – "rugged," "kingly boulders," "as tall as an average man," and not in the least, fitting memorials "to the manly qualities of the possessors of the soil" (Commission on the Affairs of the Narragansett Indians 1884: 19, 23, 31; Providence Sunday Journal 1912) – hardly describe how Native women and their communities interpreted these rocks.

Knowing the power of rocks to tell stories and that European Americans' boulder monuments were no exceptions, some Native people represented their tribes at non-Indian dedication ceremonies (Fawcett 2000). On such occasions, they often stood silent or were pushed to the sidelines, maybe shook hands with a president of the United States or gave flowers to a local official, or participated in the theatrics of an unveiling or uttered a few words. Some would also represent their tribes at pageants, anniversaries, and other celebrations held at monument sites that attracted mostly non-Natives for whom the messages inscribed in stone created first impressions and reinforced existing ones about New England Indians (see Trouillot 1995). The presence of living Indians at these events said Indians were still around despite the monuments' pronouncements. Nevertheless, their participation posed the risk of incurring the cynicism of non-Natives, who might perceive them as token survivors or doubt their genuineness, or inviting criticism from Indians in their own communities who might question the value of playing any part in these celebrations.

Starting in the 1920s, some New England Indians from different descent groups and tribal affiliations, especially many living in the region's cities and towns, joined fraternal organizations that actively promoted the revitalization of Native culture. One of these organizations, the Indian Council of New England, encouraged public performances and ceremonies as a means to increase local Native peoples' visibility and raise public awareness of their shared histories of survival. To accomplish these goals, the council launched an ambitious plan to erect and dedicate at least forty or fifty or even as many as a hundred monuments across southern New England to commemorate important sachems and great events in the Narragansett's past (Indian Council of New England n.d.; McMullen 1994). The proposal was opposed by Gladys Tantaquidgeon, a young Mohegan woman, who had been approached

FIGURE 14.3. Dedication of the Exeter Hill Monuments (October 28, 1923) from the Haffenreffer Museum's Bicknell Archive (courtesy of the Haffenreffer Museum of Anthropology, Brown University).

about becoming involved in the project. In a letter forwarded to Thomas Bicknell, a non-Native member of the council, who had devised the plan, she questioned the wisdom of raising even forty memorials by intimating that educational and other projects could serve as a living memorial more beneficial to Native people. Her polite rebuke registered impatience with romanticized ideas about New England Indians' past at the expense of their present lives, but it also hinted at tensions that came from her experiences as a representative of her tribe at public events where indigenous histories of place were ignored (see Fawcett 2000).

Despite Tantaquidgeon's objections, the council went ahead with its plan to raise and dedicate monuments, although far fewer than proposed. Ironically, the first monument unveiled was another boulder memorial to Wawaloam, also in Exeter. It was situated within a group of three boulders that commemorated her along with her husband and the place where they lived. Her monument is inscribed "Wawaloam, Sunck-Squaw." The writing on Miantonomi's rock reads only "Miantonomi" and that on the boulder commemorating the settlement, "Aspanansuck Village – 1620." Compared to Miantonomi, Wawaloam's identity was marked on the monument to make her known, as it was on the other rock remembering her that also identified her as the wife of a sachem. By furnishing the name and date of her "village" in a public space, the Exeter Hill monument connects her to place and community in ways the other monument does not. It begs the possibility of filling in details of her life and ties to an ancestral homeland, rather than merely valorizing her through her husband or simply recognizing her as an "honorary man."

A photograph of the dedication ceremony shows a large and mixed gathering of Indian men, women, and children standing around the monuments with the tall, bearded Bicknell and another non-Native man in the foreground (Figure 14.3). A local newspaper reported that the "roadside was lined two to three cars deep" and that there were so many townspeople and Indians that the event had the semblance of an old home day (Providence Journal 1923). The occasion was an old home day in ways more profound than supposed by this reference to popular homecoming festivals for native-born sons and daughters of New England towns; it offered a venue where Narragansetts no longer living close to the former reservation could reunite with family and friends and rediscover places they knew only vaguely or might have forgotten. Not in the least, the event also ushered in an era of increasing pride and activism during which New England Native peoples would become intimately involved in planning dedications and ceremonies at monuments, rather than just being invited guests.

To Remember, Instead of Being Remembered

Following the dedication of the Exeter Hill monuments, the activities of the New England Indian Council continued to focus largely on events such as dedications, but also powwows and reenactments, as would those of other intertribal organizations (McMullen 1994). These celebrations and performances were not exclusively cultural and social; they also were increasingly mobilized as political actions aimed at challenging contested Native identity. Performances became more elaborate and stylized, with some Native participants taking on "Indian" dress, names, and rhetoric. Men in particular began to wear clothing widely recognized in White society as "Indian," such as Plains-style feather bonnets, shirts, leggings, breechclouts, moccasins, and jewelry that became standard regalia intended to alter perceptions about their cultural identity as Indians.

However, Native women, at least most of them during the 1920s and 1930s, wore street clothes typical of European American attire at these public events that they often accessorized with long, multiple bead necklaces reaching below their waists (McMullen 1996). The necklaces were personal history made with beads the women had accumulated during their lives as gifts they received when they were named, came of age, and married, and others they exchanged among themselves when they spent time together weaving and doing beadwork (Rubertone 2001; Turgeon 2004). That they did not initially mark their bodies as "Indian" in their dress as they moved through these event venues, or did so in subtle ways not readily recognizable to non-Natives who probably did not grasp the meaning of beads in their life histories (cf. Loren, Chapter 7, this volume), contrasts with how European Americans inscribed Native women's identities on monuments. On commemorative boulders, they were the marked case, a *squaw sachem*, and not simply a sachem because in the thinking of European Americans, a male sachem was considered the norm and was therefore unmarked (Plane 1996: 151). Comfortable in their own social skins and cultural knowledge despite the powerful effects of colonialism on their lives, Native women did not see an immediate need to call additional attention to themselves as "Indian" by their attire at public events.

Their manner of dress, both clothing and hairstyles, had changed since the seventeenth century, accommodations to the colonizers' efforts to "civilize" them and economic forces that altered the material conditions of their mundane cultural practices. However, clothing and hairstyles were also tactics that Native women (and men) sometimes employed to disguise or camouflage their appearance in interactions with the dominant culture because of persistent prejudices and the added stigma of mixed blood in the later colonial period (e.g., Clifford 1988; Doughton 1997). Although photographs (e.g., Figure 14.3) show the clothes that Native women wore and the ways they styled their hair, a more intriguing question, as Devon Miheusah (2003:4) proposes, may be about the personal thoughts, community memories, and experiences behind these women's gazes, rather than what their appearance might imply about becoming colonial or being Indian.

Although many Native women felt it was unnecessary to use clothing to connect their inside and outside selves at public events, some did opt to dress in ways that met the expectations of the colonialized society to broadcast their Indianness. Whether they donned regalia or not, some women became actively involved with public monuments as doers who took history into their hands, rather than continue to be silenced (Tarble de Scaramelli, Chapter 9, this volume; Trouillot 1995). These women could be labeled activists or preservationists, but they had been called so many names under colonialism and suffered the indignities of so many stereotypes that romanticized them, eroticized them as symbols of "savage" sexuality, represented them as drudges or vagrants, misidentified their ancestry or tribal affiliation, or for that matter, recognized them as honorary men not to want any more (Heffernan and Medlicot 2002; Kammen 1991; Richmond and Den Ouden 2003; Mihesuah 2003; O'Brien 1997). Their actions and increasingly visible and vocal roles in public spaces were not motivated by a desire to have their contributions recognized with monuments or to rectify the exclusion of generations of Native American women on the commemorative landscape by insisting that monuments be raised to them. Instead, they acted in the role of rememberers who came to play enormously influential roles by using some monuments as stages for orchestrating public events at which they recounted counterfactual histories of their communities. The Great Swamp Monument serves as a case in point.

GENDER AND SEXUAL POLITICS OF DANGEROUS PLACES

The Great Swamp Fight Monument was raised in 1906 by the Societies of Colonial Wars, a male, lineage-based, patriotic organization, to commemorate the Narragansett's defeat by colonists in an assault that occurred on December 19, 1675. In the fight, a surprise attack on a Narragansett settlement sheltered deep in Great Swamp (near the present-day South Kingstown) early in King Philip's War, wigwams were burned and a large number of Narragansett women, children, and men were killed, along with refugees from neighboring Wampanoag homelands. For the Narragansett and other New England Native people, the day would go down in infamy as a brutal massacre, but it would also be a defining moment for the colonists claiming victory who would write about Narragansett history as a downward spiral of defeat, decline, and disappearance (Rubertone 2001: xiv). With the war still raging, New England men and women, English colonists and Indians alike, began to memorialize the events of war and fight for control of its history (Drake 1999; Lepore 1998).

FIGURE 14.4. The Great Swamp Monument (photograph by Patricia Rubertone).

The monument consists of a tall, granite shaft rising erect above a low, grass-covered artificial mound (Figure 14.4). Encircling the shaft at the base of the mound are four large, block-shaped boulders representing the colonies of Massachusetts, Plymouth, Connecticut, and Rhode Island. The rugged shaft resembles an obelisk, which has been called "the quintessential male memorial form, an overtly phallic symbol of male power" (Norkunas 2002: 95). The obelisk has a long history as a monument used to valorize males, having its origins as a symbol used to proclaim military prowess and rulers' victories in ancient Egypt and taking on the more specific connotation of a military memorial under the Romans (Borg 1991). As a material form of memory, it embodies masculine ideals of conquest and domination that are typically considered to be prominent features of monuments representing war in a heroic light. Although not all war memorials are obelisks, that particular shape not only signals the importance of a particular military engagement but may also serve to emphasize its role as a formative event in the history of a nation (Foote 1997).

In addition to having a crude obelisk as a centerpiece, the Great Swamp Fight Monument is a public space where men's experiences and narratives filled with masculine and sexualized references have dominated the discourse. Written accounts tell of the European American men who commissioned the monument; and the Narragansett men who hauled the obelisk-like stone through the swamp with their team of oxen when the efforts of twelve horses failed. The written accounts also report of the European American men, who traveled into the swamp, accessible only by a rough cart path, on the day of the dedication and withstood pounding, torrential rains long enough to carry out a twig and turf ceremony, an old English rite of land conveyance used to establish colonial possession, as a symbolic declaration of their intent to hold onto the monument site (Seed 1992; Society of Colonial Wars 1906).

FIGURE 14.5. Women visiting the Great Swamp Monument, c. early 1900s (courtesy of the Pettaquamscutt Historical Society).

After the bounds of the site were "beaten out," three Narragansett men unveiled the monument.

We also learn of other European American men who overcame the logistical challenges of traveling over rough terrain and through the soggy and seemingly impenetrable swamp to visit the monument after the dedication. Some came to install memorial tablets, and once to consume "a hot and delicious" and ample catered lunch on banquet tables in a tent pitched just a short distance from the monument (Rhode Island Historical Society 1917). In the 1930s, young men in the Civilian Conservation Corps, a federal work-relief program, had their youthful energies disciplined at Great Swamp by building a new road, parking area, and footpath to the monument (Hyde 1938). Without belaboring the point any further, narratives and experiences of men, and masculine and sexualized metaphors of landscape penetration and conquest – key elements of colonialism – have permeated European Americans' written accounts of the monument. These gendered and sexualized interpretations by *and* about men have propagated understandings of this commemorative space and expectations about how it should be experienced that have sent a strong message that the Great Swamp Fight Monument was no place for women (cf. Dawdy, Chapter 16, this volume).

Attention to these subjectivities would have constrained the parameters and nature of women's engagement with the monument. An undated photograph, probably taken in the early 1900s (perhaps slightly before or after the dedication judging from the unkempt landscape), shows some women, seemingly European American and otherwise anonymous, in this sea of male references (Figure 14.5). The purpose of their visit is undocumented, but one can suppose that the outing was chaperoned by men to protect them in a place that as a swamp was long considered "hideous and dangerous" by colonizers (Lepore 1998: 84) and, as a public space at the turn of the nineteenth century, was thought to be particularly threatening to women by the larger society and not meant for them (Mackintosh 2005; Valentine 1989).

There are no written or visual records of Native American women at the monument until the 1930s. Although their grandmothers of generations ago, other blood relatives, and kin had been massacred at Great Swamp, at a location not far from the monument, the voices, let alone the faces, of these seventeenth-century women were not recorded. Nevertheless, their cries could be heard and their spirits seen by their descendants, who would have been told about Great Swamp's importance as children. Like others in their communities, Native women would have visited Great Swamp and expressed their grief by conducting their own private ceremonies of remembrance despite the intrusiveness of the commemorative obelisk and boulders.

Under the direction of some Native women, notably a Narragansett-Wampanoag woman known as Princess Red Wing, who knew well that rocks could be used to send messages different from those inscribed in written history (or as she imputed "history"), the Great Swamp Fight Monument became the stage for the "Great Swamp Massacre Ceremony" (Figure 14.6; Red Wing 1972). As originally conceived and performed, the ceremony was a public celebration of New England Native peoples' mutual accounts of survival and their "shared colonial history" with Whites (Lilley 2006; Murray 2004). Red Wing's personal papers and the published accounts in the collections of the Tomaquag Indian Memorial Museum in Exeter provide a rich archive suggesting that elements of the public remembrance rite have stayed in place more or less intact as it developed into an annual event and pilgrimage that continues through today.

Among these practices is the lighting of fires to the past, present, and future that have long provided the framework for the ceremony. Songs, dances, poems, roll calls of the war dead from old and modern conflicts, pipe ceremonies, speeches (some by non-Natives), and other innovations have been incorporated at different times since the ceremony's inception in the 1930s. Both men and women wore full regalia that became more reminiscent of the older clothing styles of the Northeast Woodlands than the western Plains, although the regionally-appropriate style was more popular among younger people and some women (Boissevain 1975; McMullen 1994, 1996). Performed mostly by Narragansett, Wampanoag, and other local Indians, the Great Swamp Massacre Ceremony has publicly recounted counterfactual histories of the seventeenth-century melee to challenge interpretations reproduced by the monument.

In contrast to the ceremonies conducted at other public monuments, and even those enacted at the 1906 dedication of the Great Swamp Fight Monument, local Native women were not merely spectators or absent at the Great Swamp Massacre Ceremony. They performed dances, lit fires, recited prayers, sang songs, and wailed rueful laments that made them visible and their voices heard. Although they did not act alone, their parts in the public ceremony, whether in the lead as mistress of

FIGURE 14.6. Narragansett and other Indians at the Great Swamp Massacre Ceremony, 1962 (courtesy of *The Providence Journal*).

ceremonies or in supporting roles, were crucial to asserting contested tribal identities, resistances, and survival. Some of the early pageantry, poetics, and conciliatory gestures of brotherhood toward Whites were later criticized by various local Indians, although others recognized that the speech and mannerisms were necessary components of their public performances at a certain historical moment. There have also been times, notably in the 1970s, when the Great Swamp Massacre Ceremony served as a platform for making bolder and broader assertions about injustices suffered by the region's Native people. Some Indians say they seriously contemplated destroying the monument but decided to let it stand as a symbol of racism that they could point to in teaching their children important lessons about Native peoples' struggles to survive.

In 1978, the annual pilgrimage to Great Swamp for the public ceremony, although still rekindling somber memories, was more celebratory (Providence Journal 1978). Because of the efforts of Ella Sekatau, a remarkable Narragansett woman and powerful cultural and political presence in her community and across Indian New England, land lost by the terms of detribalization (plus additional acreage) was reinstated to her tribe in an out-of-court settlement of a suit filed against Rhode Island and certain non-Indian landowners. The return of 1,800 acres, considerably less than claimed, was nevertheless a major victory. The decision supported the Narragansett's contention that Rhode Island had acted illegally in buying their reserved land because the action violated the U.S. Indian Trade and Intercourse Act of 1790 that requires the federal government to supervise or approve the disposing of tribal land (Herndon and Sekatau 1997). With that victory in hand, the Narragansett submitted their petition to the Department of Interior for federal recognition backed by copious documentation that Sekatau was instrumental in preparing.

However, before that task was completed (and five years before federal acknowledgment would be received), the Great Swamp Massacre Ceremony offered a venue from which to announce the successful outcome of the land case, a triumph that made the inscription on a memorial tablet describing the Narragansett's defeat especially inappropriate. Interestingly, highly contentious words such as "crushed by" had already been gouged out and overwritten with the letters "GENICID." In an eclectic array of graffiti that includes initials, names, dates, symbols of peace and romantic love, and undecipherable scribbling as artifacts of experiences and agencies falling outside what was culturally sanctioned by this public space, the term resonates comfortably in the language of native resistance (e.g., Macdonald 1998; Ouzeman 2003; Phillips 1999). Although the identities of the person (or persons) responsible are unknown, the purposeful erasure and overwriting provide a compelling visual statement of engagement with the monument that inscribes an alternative memory of the significance of December 19, 1675, than the official message carved by European Americans.

As important as the Great Swamp Fight Monument is as a vivid reminder of colonialism and the ways it implicated gender, sexuality, and race, and as a site from which Native women (and men) countered with their own versions of the seventeenth-century event it commemorated and commented on their experiences as survivors, the locale has other meanings to Narragansett people. Rather than a site of penetration and conquest represented in the tropes of the colonists, Great Swamp was – and is – a place of encounter and persistence. Within ancestral homelands across New England and northeastern North America, swamps are special sites of memory-making and memory-keeping, not danger, where Native people connect with each other and their ancestors (Hamell 1987). Accordingly, Great Swamp would have been a place of refuge where they sought protection from enemies as they did in King Philip's War; it would also have been a place of renewal where they reconnected spiritually with ancestors dwelling in this landscape by performing rites at times when they were not facing the threat of attack or the likelihood of public attention.

That they chose the monument as the site where they would publicly reclaim their history comments on the power of the locale despite – but also because of – the imposed monument. Native women who crafted and took charge of the Great Swamp Massacre Ceremony were not motivated by a sense of their own victimhood or by a desire to reverse the dominant society's thinking about gender, sexuality, and space by identifying the commemorative public space as specifically female. They had never been out of place at Great Swamp, except by the rules of behavior dictated by European American society that defined public spaces as male domains and pressured women to act submissively or negotiate these spaces only in the company of male protectors (Norkunas 2002: 101). Great Swamp was never only about Native women or for that matter, just about men, but about community and its survival.

CONCLUSIONS

Monuments to Native Americans in New England were gendered in ways that reflected colonialist, and overwhelmingly masculine, political imaginings and processes of place-making in European American society in the late nineteenth and early twentieth centuries. Consequently, these monuments may be viewed as an aspect of colonialism that has exerted powerful forces on perceptions of Native women and, more generally, about the nature of the colonial experience. Native women who were actively involved in public events at these commemorative spaces, whether as representatives of their tribes or as activists who orchestrated and participated in counterfactual remembrances, challenged assumptions about their invisibility and about the exclusionary politics of the public domain. Their activities were pathways to gaining respect and understanding of Native New England people's culture and history that cannot be underestimated.

Without diminishing their accomplishments, the ways Native American women remembered and were remembered on the commemorative landscape indicate the importance of considering gender and sexuality in archaeological studies of place in colonial settings. More specifically, the observations offered about the sexual politics of monuments highlight the value of examining critically how gender, sex, and sexuality intersect with ethnicity, race, and class to shape experiences and memories (e.g., Conkey 2005). In addition, this research also underscores the need for more work that focuses specifically on (and includes dialogues with) Native women and women of color, whose presence in, memories of, and engagement with monuments are typically blurred by commemorative processes, and sometimes by the totalizing claims of postcolonial and feminist theories.

Although revisionists bemoan the scarcity of monuments to Native American women and lobby for additional public memorials that value Native women vastly underrated in historical chronicles, historians and anthropologists have exposed the sexual politics of empire and colonization underwriting these absences that give insights to why this exclusion has taken place. However, archaeologists offer the possibility of bridging the sexual politics of monuments and Native peoples' memories and experiences by bringing fine-grained attention to the small-scale processes of daily practices in the material record that add texture, depth, and different meanings to these sites. Not in the least, archaeology informed by the cultural wisdom of indigenous knowledge can point to other experiences and attachments, ostensibly encompassing places of intimate spiritual, social, and sensual encounters within and beyond the geographies of monuments unseen through the lens of the colonized landscape.

As a space of colonial encounters where ongoing historical, political, and moral understandings and relationships were and are being continuously worked out (Clifford 1997: 192; Pratt 1992: 6–7), monuments are ideal sites for studying colonialism and its intersections with gender, sexuality, ethnicity, race, class, and other categories through which identities are constituted, produced, reproduced, and controlled. In New England and elsewhere in the colonized world, they are places where Native women and members of their communities encounter and negotiate colonialist, and specifically gendered and sexualized, representations of their ancestors and "the colonial project" that reverberate in their own everyday lives. Historical archaeology as a hybrid practice can productively show how the architects of commemoration made these versions of the colonial past visible on the cultural landscape, illuminate "lived experiences" they rendered invisible, and uncover processes intended to reverse colonialist assertions they would not have predicted. An emphasis on interlocking conflicting understandings and practices within the asymmetries of colonial social relations can ultimately contribute to decolonizing how we think about the colonial experience, the effects of empire and colonization on gender and sexuality, and monumental archaeology as a source of national identities rooted in colonial struggles.

REFERENCES

Basso, Keith. 1996. *Wisdom Sits in Places: Landscape and Language among the Western Apache*. Albuquerque: University of New Mexico Press.
Boissevain, Ethel. 1975. *The Narragansett People*. Phoenix, AZ: Indian Tribal Series.
Borg, Alan. 1991. *War Memorials: From Antiquity to the Present*. London: Cooper.
Brown, Kathleen. 1993. "Brave New Worlds: Women's and Gender History." *William and Mary Quarterly* 50(2):311–328.
Brownell, Carlton C., ed. 1970. *Notes on Little Compton*. Little Compton, RI: Little Compton Historical Society.
Church, Benjamin. 1975. *Diary of King Philip's War, 1675–1676*, with an Introduction by Alan and Mary Simpson. Chester, CT: Pequot Press.
Clifford, James. 1988. "Identity in Mashpee," in *The Predicament of Culture: Twentieth Century Ethnography, Literature, and Art*. Cambridge, MA: Harvard University Press, pp. 277–346.
———. 1997. *Routes: Travel and Translation in the Late Twentieth Century*. Cambridge, MA: Harvard University Press.
Commission on the Affairs of the Narragansett Indians. 1884. *Fourth Annual Report of the Commission on the Affairs of the Narragansett Indians, Made to the General Assembly at its January Session, 1884*. Providence, RI: E. L. Freeman and Company.
Conkey, Margaret W. 2005. "Dwelling at the Margins, Action at the Intersection? Feminist and Indigenous Archaeologies," *Archaeologies* 1(1):9–59.
Doughton, Thomas L. 1997. "Unseen Neighbors: Native Americans of Central Massachusetts, A People Who Had 'Vanished'," in Calloway, Colin G. (ed.), *After King Philip's War: Presence and Persistence in Indian New England*. Hanover, NH: University Press of New England, pp. 207–230.

Drake, James D. 1999. *King Philip's War: Civil War in New England, 1675–1676.* Amherst: University of Massachusetts Press.

Duncan, Nancy. 1996. *Bodyspace: Destabilitizing Geographies of Gender and Sexuality.* London: Routledge.

Fawcett, Melissa Jayne. 2000. *Medicine Trail: The Life and Lessons of Gladys Tantaquidgeon.* Tucson: The University of Arizona Press.

Foote, Kenneth E. 1997. *Shadowed Ground: America's Landscapes of Violence and Tragedy.* Austin: University of Texas Press.

Grumet, Robert S. 1980. "Sunksquaws, Shamans, and Tradeswomen: Middle Atlantic Coastal Algonkian Women during the 17th and 18th Centuries," in Etienne, Mona, and Eleanor Burke Leacock (eds.), *Women and Colonization: Anthropological Perspectives.* New York: Praeger Scientific, pp. 43–62.

Hamell, George R. 1987. "Mythical Realities and European Contact in the Northeast during the Sixteenth and Seventeenth Centuries." *Man in the Northeast* 33:63–87.

Heffernan, Michael, and Carol Medlicot. 2002. "A Feminine Atlas? Sacagewea, the Suffragettes, and the Commemorative Landscape in the American West, 1004–1910." *Gender, Place and History* 9(2):109–131.

Herndon, Ruth Wallis, and Ella Wilcox Sekatau. 1997. "The Right to a Name: The Narragansett People and Rhode Island Officials in the Revolutionary Era," in Calloway, Colin G. (ed.), *After King Philip's War: Presence and Persistence in Indian New England.* Hanover, NH: University Press of New England, pp. 114–143.

Hyde, Gerald H. 1938. "Historic Great Swamp Opened at Last." *The Regional Review* 1(6).

Indian Council of New England. n.d. Scrapbook of Thomas W. Bicknell of the Indian Council of New England (1923–1925). Bristol, RI: Haffenreffer Museum of Anthropology, Brown University.

Kammen, Michael. 1991. *Mystic Chords of Memory: The Transformation of Tradition in American Culture.* New York: Vintage Books.

Kern, Leslie. 2005. "In Place and at Home in the City: Connecting Privilege, Safety and Belonging for Women in Toronto." *Gender, Place and Culture* 12(3):357–377.

LaFantasie, Glenn W., ed. 1988. *The Correspondence of Roger Williams,* Vol. 1. Hanover, NH: Brown University Press and University Press of New England.

Lepore, Jill. 1998. *The Name of War: King Philip's War and the Origins of American Identity.* New York: Alfred A. Knopf.

Lilley, Ian. 2006. "Archaeology, Diaspora and Decolonization." *Journal of Social Archaeology* 6(1):28–47.

Macdonald, Bradley J. 1998. "Border Signs: Graffiti, Contested Identities, and Everyday Resistance in Los Angeles," in Spener, David, and Kathleen Staudt (eds.), *The U.S.–Mexico Border: Transcending Divisions, Contesting Identities.* Boulder, CO: Lynne Rienner Publishers, pp. 169–184.

Mackintosh, Phillip Gordon. 2005. "Scrutiny in the Modern City: The Domestic Public and the Toronto Local Council of Women at the Turn of the Twentieth Century." *Gender, Place and Culture* 12(1):29–48.

Mavor, James W., Jr., and Byron E. Dix. 1989. *Manitou: The Sacred Landscape of New England's Native Civilization.* Rochester, VT: Inner Traditions International.

McDowell, Sara. 2008. "Commemorating Dead 'Men': Gendering the Past and Present in Post-Conflict Northern Ireland." *Gender, Place and Culture* 15(4):335–354.

McMullen, Ann 1994. "What's Wrong with this Picture? Context, Conversion, Survival, and Development of Regional Native Culture and Pan-Indianism in Southeastern New England," in Weinstein, Laurie (ed.), *Enduring Traditions: The Native People of New England.* Westport, CT: Bergin and Garvey, pp. 113–150.

———. 1996. "Soapbox Discourse: Tribal Historiography, Indian-White Relations, and Southeastern New England Powwows." *The Public Historian* 18(4):53–74.

Mihesuah, Devon Abbott. 2003. *Indigenous American Women: Decolonization, Empowerment, Activism.* Lincoln: University of Nebraska Press.

Murray, Tim. 2004. "In the Footsteps of George Dutton: Developing Contact Archaeology of Temperate Aboriginal Australia," in Murray, Tim (ed.), *The Archaeology of Contact in Settler Societies*. Cambridge: Cambridge University Press, pp. 200–225.

Norkunas, Martha. 2002. *Monuments and Memory: History and Representation in Lowell, Massachusetts*. Washington, DC: Smithsonian Institution Press.

O'Brien, Jean M. 1997. "'Divorced' from the Land: Resistance and Survival of Indian Women in Eighteenth-Century New England," in Calloway, Colin G. (ed.), *After King Philip's War: Presence and Persistence in Indian New England*. Hanover, NH: University Press of New England, pp. 144–161.

Ouzman, Sven. 2003. *News from the Edge: Graffiti, Archaeology and Identity in Post-Apartheid Southern Africa*. Paper Prepared for the Stanford-Berkeley Joint Center for African Studies Popular Culture in Africa Conference, Stanford University, Palo Alto, California.

Phillips, Susan A. 1999. *Wallgagin': Graffiti and Gangs in L.A.* Chicago: University of Chicago Press.

Plane, Ann Marie. 1996. "Putting a Face on Colonization: Factionalism and Gender Politics in the Life History of Awaskunkes, the 'Squaw Sachem' of Saconet," in Grumet, Robert S. (ed.), *Northeastern Indian Lives, 1632–1816*. Amherst: University of Massachusetts Press, pp. 140–165.

Potter, Elisha R. 1835. *The Early History of Narragansett. Collections of the Rhode Island Historical Society 3*. Providence, RI, Rhode Island Historical Society.

Pratt, Mary Louise. 1992. *Imperial Eyes: Travel Writing and Transculturation*. London: Routledge.

Providence Journal. 1923. "Exeter Unveils Memorial," *Providence Journal*, October 29:5.

———. 1978. "Pilgrimage Marks 1675 Massacre of Tribe," *Providence Journal* (September 25), p. A3.

Providence Sunday Journal. 1912. "North Burial Ground's Public Memorials," *Providence Sunday Journal* (May 26), Section 5, p. 10.

Red Wing. 1972. "Indian Communications," *College Composition and Communication* 23(5):350–356.

Rhode Island Historical Society. 1875. *Proceedings of the Rhode Island Historical Society 1874–1875*. Providence, RI: Printed for the Society.

———. 1917 *Proceedings at the Dedication of a Tablet to the Memory of Major Samuel Appleton, November 3, 1916*. Providence: Rhode Island Historical Society.

Richmond, Trudie Lamb, and Amy E. Den Ouden. 2003. "Recovering Gendered Political Histories: Local Struggles and Native Women's Resistance in Colonial Southern New England," in Calloway, Colin G., and Neal Salisbury (eds.), *Reinterpreting New England Indians and the Colonial Experience*. Boston: The Colonial Society of Massachusetts, pp. 174–231.

Rubertone, Patricia E. 2001. *Grave Undertakings: An Archaeology of Roger Williams and the Narragansett Indians*. Washington, DC: Smithsonian Institution Press.

———. 2008a. "Engaging Monuments, Memories, and Archaeology," in Rubertone, Patricia E. (ed.), *Archaeologies of Placemaking: Monuments, Memories, and Engagement in Native North America*. One World Archaeology Series 59. Walnut Creek, CA: Left Coast Press, pp.13–33.

———. 2008b. "Memorializing the Narragansett: Placemaking and Memory Keeping in the Aftermath of Detribalization," in Rubertone, Patricia E. (ed.), *Archaeologies of Placemaking: Monuments, Memories, and Engagement in Native North America*. One World Archaeology Series 59. Walnut Creek, CA: Left Coast Press, pp.195–216.

Seed, Patricia. 1992. "Taking Possession and Reading Texts: Establishing the Authority of Overseas Empires." *William and Mary Quarterly* 49(2):183–209.

Simmons, William S. 1986. *Spirit of New England Tribes: Indian History and Folklore*. Hanover, NH: University Press of New England.

Society of Colonial Wars. 1906. *A Record of the Ceremony and Oration on the Occasion of the Unveiling of the Monument Commemorating the Great Swamp Fight, December 19, 1675, in the Narragansett Country, Rhode Island; Erected by the Societies of Colonial Wars of Rhode Island and Massachusetts, October 20, 1906*. Boston: Merrymount Press.

Trouillot, Michel-Rolph. 1995. *Silencing the Past: Power and the Production of History.* Boston: Beacon Press.

Turgeon, Laurier. 2004. "Beads, Bodies, and Regimes of Value: From France to North America, c. 1500–1650," in Murray, Tim (ed.), *The Archaeology of Contact in Settler Societies.* Cambridge: Cambridge University Press, pp. 19–47.

Williams, Roger. 1936 [1643]. *A Key into the Language of America*, 5th ed. Providence: Rhode Island and Providence Plantations Tercentenary Committee.

Valentine, Gill. 1989. "The Geography of Women's Fear." *Area* 21(4):385–390.

VHB/Vanasse Hangen Brustlin. 2003. *Determination of Eligibility for the National Register of Historic Places (Wilbour Woods).* Report prepared for the Rhode Island Department of Transportation. On file at the Little Compton Historical Society.

FIFTEEN

GENDER RELATIONS IN A MAROON COMMUNITY, PALMARES, BRAZIL

Pedro Paulo A. Funari and Aline Vieira de Carvalho

INTRODUCTION

Archaeology has long studied materiality for new insight into the cultural aspects of colonial settings. Narratives about empire include such interpretive models as creolization, ethnogenesis, hybridity, syncretism, and transculturation (Casella and Voss, Chapter 1, this volume). These subjects are also linked to the body and to gender relations. In this chapter, we focus on applying some of these questions to the context of Palmares, a seventeenth-century *maroon* settlement in South America.

BRAZILIAN SETTING

The practice of African and native enslavement between the sixteenth and nineteenth centuries is not exclusive to Brazil or Latin America. This phenomenon was the result of the European colonization project, beginning in the fifteenth century, which imposed diaspora communities and relationships on new territories throughout the globe. The European colonial adventure in the Americas (S. Hall 2006: 395) shaped common experiences among various ethnic groups representing multiple identities, including experiences of conflict, violence, negotiation, and peace. Among various aspects of the fight against slavery in Brazil, we address the concepts of *maroon*, *cimarón* (cimaroon), and *quilombos*.

These three terms describe the same movement but each has a unique historical meaning. The noun *maroon* comes from the Spanish word *cimarón*, which was originally used for domesticated cattle that escaped to the woods. When used in describing runaway slaves, the meaning of *maroon* changed, coming to mean a reaction against slavery. Thus, the underlying implication of the word *maroon* was that slaves were not capable of making choices or mobilizing politically. In the slave owners' universe, slaves were thought of and referred to as mere domesticated animals.

In contrast, the term *quilombo* (kilombo), the origin of which can be traced to languages of African coastal regions of the Congo and Angola, was used to describe the movement of insurgent warriors (Slenes 2005: 20) particularly renowned for their structured military organization. As slaves, the *quilombolas*[1] were still considered mere property but were now seen as something more than a kind of "cattle." They were understood as possible fighters. As such, they were considered an imminent threat to order in colonial society.

In Brazil, with its history of Portuguese colonization, the term *quilombo* has been broadly used from colonial days to the present. The meanings imprinted on the term, however, change according to the contexts in which the *maroons* are studied, and more importantly, according to the research interests of the scholars studying them. It is this element of varied scholarly interests that determines the character of research carried out on Brazilian *maroons*.

Throughout the twentieth century, into the beginning of the twenty-first, researchers have sought to understand the phenomena of the *maroons* as a cultural and political form of the struggle for freedom. These researchers have examined the multiple cultures and identities present within the *maroons*, as well as how *maroons* negotiated this pluralism and the types of internal and external conflicts the *maroons* experienced. Thus, in the modern country of Brazil, marked by authoritarian governments, and even more by social inequality, the *maroons* have become a constantly reconstructed mirror for contemporary society's understanding of itself. The *maroons* have often thus become one more arena in the search for our identity.

Identities are a recent issue in social theory in general, and in archaeology in particular. Identity has long been at the core of anthropological research, but identities in the plural, as fluid, ever-changing, and unstable, have been discussed in postmodern times in new and creative light, fostering diversity rather than homogeneous, stable, and univocal identity definitions of early anthropological theory (Jones 1997; Garraffoni, Chapter 13, this volume). As Barbara L. Voss notes (2008a: 13), identity is a contested field, fraught with epistemological and political implications. Identity has long been understood as a normative concept, rooted in the etymology of the word itself: *idem* in Latin means "the same." However, there is no word in Latin for identity; the concept is a modern invention. The word is attested in English from 1570 and was used in the seventeenth century to refer to individuality or personality. Not until the nineteenth century was the term used to describe the condition of being identified in feeling and interest as, for example, in Victorian British Prime Minister William Gladstone's description of Homer: "he is in visible identity with the age" (Little et al. 1955: 951). Identity as a bounded and fixed set of features is thus linked to the emergence of nation-states and nationalism, as the ideology of homogeneity. The nation is conceived as formed around shared, self-designating beliefs, a social relation with both temporal depth and bounded territory (Grosby 2005: 14–15). The concept of modern nation states as bounded, coherent entities composed of similar-minded people is also related to colonialism, and to the opposition between different and homogeneous identities (Gosden 2004). The invention of races as homogeneous human groups is kin to the new nation-state. The idea of nation has played a crucial role in the origins and development of racial thinking (Shepherd, Chapter 17, this volume). The idea of nation enabled a new boundary between "them" and "us," based on race (Rattansi 2007: 36–37). Even when differences are accepted, they are framed as two bounded national identities, as put so clearly by Ernest Renan in 1848: "Every nation is a unity, with its temples, gods, poetry, heroic traditions, fantastic beliefs, laws and institutions. It has a particular way of understanding life, plays a special role in mankind and has a unique function in the human spirit" (p. 868).[2]

Shared values are a political program, a matter of shared desires, *une affaire de volonté* (Todorov 1989: 308). Early social theorists such as Emile Durkheim emphasized that each society is a bounded entity, like an organism, even if plagued by disease, which must be extirpated for the sake of the common good. Norms were shared, and when people did not respect those norms, they were considered detrimental to the collective. The way to enforce norms was to indoctrinate people in discovering what they really were (or should be): *deviens ce que tu es* (Bourdieu 2001: 181). Latter-day conservatives continue to define identity as a process of discovery of oneself as part of a bounded, homogeneous entity: "The concept of identity implies similarity to oneself, as a condition for psychic and social life. Accordingly, it is much closer to re-cognition than to knowledge" (Meneses 1987: 182).

Those normative models have been criticized in recent decades for their oppressive aspects and implications. Fluidity, diversity, plurality, conflicts, and contradictions are some of the recurrent subjects in postmodern epistemology (Rago and Funari 2008). This move from normative models to less rigid and oppressive discourses has also been important in archaeology in general, and in historical archaeology in particular. In the volume *Historical Archaeology: Back from the Edge*, the editors stressed the importance of issues of identity, nationalism, and ethnicity (Funari et al. 1999), reflecting discussions resulting from a 1989 World Archaeological Congress (WAC) conference (WAC 2) in Venezuela. Those discussions led to a session in India at WAC 3, and then to the publication of the volume, subsequently presented at WAC 4 in South Africa. Identity issues also feature largely in two recently published volumes, *Historical Archaeology* and *The Cambridge Companion to Historical Archaeology* (Hall and Silliman 2006; Hicks and Beaudry 2006).

In dialogue with the discussions about identities, researchers are attempting to break with an intellectual tradition that connects human sexual manifestations with biological determinism. Since 1960, with the feminist movement, science has suggested leaving aside simplistic categories such as "man" or "woman," with their respective appropriate – or inappropriate – behaviors. Instead of biologically determined sex, questions related to gender and sexuality itself are now seen as aspects of identity. The current intent is to understand how sexual differences previously attributed to the biological sexes are culturally organized (gender) and how a broad spectrum of sexual relations (sexuality) is constituted (Schmidt and Voss 2000). Within this theoretical context, human sexual expressions are understood as historically constituted, not as natural, unquestionable behaviors (Foucault 1980).

In archaeology in particular, there has been a recent drive to develop theories and methods that will allow us to connect material remains to questions of gender and sexuality. The book *Archaeologies of Sexuality* (2000), edited by Robert A. Schmidt and Barbara Voss, is an example of this pioneering work, which is not only theoretical and methodological, but also political. This publication, presenting a spectrum of archaeological scholarship that investigates gender and sexuality in various historical moments and geographic locations, breaks a great silence in archaeology.

Gender and sexuality studies are an innovative trend in Brazilian history and archaeology. In the Brazilian context, we aim at understanding how gender relations were normalized as part of the European colonial endeavor during the shaping of the modern world (Lawrence and Shepherd 2006: 69). Material culture studies, combined with historical documents, enable us to understand the dialogues resulting from subjective and plural identities. In this way, Palmares provides an opening for the discussion of gender identities in colonial and native settings.

Within this context, we examine a variety of issues relating to identity in the making as we interpret this fugitive settlement forged by escaped slaves and indigenous South Americans. Palmares represents a community that offered an alternative to the oppression of seventeenth-century colonial society in Brazil (Hall and Silliman 2006: 13). In several prior scholarly works, the authors have studied a variety of issues relating to Palmares, this odd rebel polity (Funari and Carvalho 2005, with references). In this chapter, we discuss the ways in which identity perceptions shape our understanding of the polity and, particularly, how gender images have been perceived. As we argue, female-positive approaches, grounded in heterarchical epistemologies, can prove useful for understanding different, liberating readings of the past.

THE CONTEXT

To understand the constitution of the Palmares Quilombo, it is necessary to return to the fifteenth-century Marine Expansion pursued by Portugal in search of new routes to the Indies. In 1415, the Portuguese overtook the island of Ceuta and initiated an expansion process through Africa. In the following decades, they crossed the southern Atlantic and arrived at the territory that constitutes modern-day Brazil. During the second half of the sixteenth century into the early seventeenth, when commerce with the Indies proved to be unprofitable for Europeans, the Portuguese implemented a new type of production in the newly discovered lands: the processing of sugar cane.

Many sugar mills that used the slave labor of Africans and local Indians, known as Negroes of the land, were set up on the coast of Bahia and Pernambuco. Sugar-cane processing returned a profit not only for Portugal but also for Holland, which was responsible for refinement of the product. As the Portuguese dedicated themselves to the implementation of the sugar mills, they also began to face the escape of Black and Indian slaves. Together, these slaves founded the Palmares Maroon (Figure 15.1).

During the period of the Iberian Union (1508–1640), when Portugal was incorporated into the Spanish Crown under the power of Philip II, Palmares, located about 60 kilometers inland from the Brazilian coast, received new inhabitants. According to the historiography about the *maroon*, which is addressed later in the chapter, it was not only Indians and blacks lived in the *maroon*, but also Jews, witches, and Muslims. By 1612, the Portuguese had begun to acknowledge the settlement as a powerful and dangerous refuge for the slaves.

The religious disputes existing in Europe in the seventeenth century also had repercussions for daily life in the Brazilian colony, and thus for the Palmares Maroon. Philip II, king of Catholic Spain, forbade Holland to do commerce with Brazil (which belonged to Spain through the Iberian Union). This proclamation was motivated by the loss of Spanish territories in the Netherlands. The Dutch, mostly Protestants, invaded Brazil in 1630 to search for sugar, but also in response to the actions of Philip II. The Dutch authorities then dominating the region of Pernambuco also recognized the danger of the Palmares settlement, but despite all military efforts, they were unable to destroy it.

With the end of the Iberian Union in 1640 and the 1654 expulsion of the Dutch from Brazil, colonial authorities and mill owners combined military forces in a drive to destroy the Palmares Maroon. In response, the Palmarinos began to attack farms along the coast to obtain weapons, free slaves, and exact revenge on the mill owners and overseers. In one of the many conflicts, infantry captain Fernão Carrilho imprisoned about two hundred members of the *maroon*. In response to these developments, Ganga-Zumba, military chief of the Palmares Maroon, sought to resolve the situation through negotiations. He proposed to the governor of Pernambuco, Aires de Souza e Castro, that the inhabitants of Palmares would disarm if, in exchange, they were granted ownership rights over the lands of Palmares and personal freedom for all those born in the *maroon*.

As a result of Ganga-Zumba's proposition, discord arose inside the *maroon*. Another military leader, Zumbi, led the opposition against Ganga-Zumba, organizing Palmares' continued resistance to the colonial forces. In 1687, the governor of Pernambuco placed Domingos Jorge Velho, a *Bandeirante*, in command of the campaign against Palmares. After seven years of attempts Velho, leading an army of colonists, Indians, and *mamelucos* (mix of Indian and white ancestry), finally destroyed the settlement. Zumbi was not captured until November 20, 1695.

THE IDENTITIES CONSTRUCTED BY HISTORICAL NARRATIVES: FROM RACE TO GENDER

Since the end of the seventeenth century, descriptions of the Palmares Maroon have been based on what is considered official written documentation. Understandings of Palmares have therefore been drawn from political, military, and religious documents. The interpretation of this documentation, done by chroniclers, archivists, historians, sociologists, anthropologists, lawyers, and playwrights, resulted in the elaboration of two images of Palmares. The first image gives us the poignant example, "worthy of pity," of an overmatched slave revolt opposed by powerful colonial authorities; the second image exalts the *maroon* as an example of the heroic resistance of a defiant black people.

The valuation of cultures believed to be pure and static, allowing a romanticized analysis of the *maroon* as a place of escape from the slave plantations, was in vogue in the social sciences in the 1930s and 1940s. Roger Bastide, a French sociologist responsible for important studies on African American religion, was one important thinker in this historiographic current. With the end of the Second World War, and the discovery of the Nazi concentration camps, social science scholars began to rethink the concept of "culture" in light of new understandings about the political repercussions of this concept.

In the specific case of the studies of Brazilian *maroons*, particularly those focused on Palmares, historians of the 1960s fought extensively against the studies of

FIGURE 15.1. The Palmares Maroon (1597–1694) occupied an area straddling the modern Brazilian states of Alagoas (AL) and Pernambuco (PE), highlighted in the map.

Palmares that circulated in the 1930s and 1940s. The central goal of the new line of historiography moved from examining the cultural manifestations (especially religious manifestations) to understanding the settlement as representative of a social struggle against slavery. The slave – captive, runaway, or free – was understood as a political agent who could corrupt the basis of the slavocratic system extant in the Portuguese colony. Clóvis Moura (1959) and Décio Freitas (1978) represent important scholars working within this new context.

Moura and Freitas understood slave rebellion and the existence of the Palmares Maroon through the lens of Marxist theories. Within an analytical context of class struggle, these scholars argued that Palmares was inherent to slavery – in other words, that it existed only because of class exploitation. At the same time, the appearance of *maroons* is ambivalently perceived as responsible for making the slave system more unstable and especially for wearing it out. The various types of slave revolts, among them the formation of *maroon* settlements, are now considered to be ways through which black people recovered the human dignity they had been deprived of in the condition of slavery. Moura and Freitas, journalists as well as scholars, engaged the public at large with descriptions of the punishments suffered by the slaves, the difficulties faced by the *quilombolas* in their escapes, and the type of free life that existed inside the *maroons*. In Zumbi, the warrior, they constructed a hero worthy of admiration.

This new analysis of the Palmares Maroon is fundamentally based on economic theory, and this economic approach is also applied to explain the daily life of the *quilombolas*, including descriptions of gender relations. In the book *Palmares: A Guerra dos Escravos* (1978), Freitas addresses the presence of women in the *maroon*: "the first Palmarians were too few to constitute a really viable economic and social community. To begin with, there weren't enough women. This forced them to go down to the plantations periodically in order to kidnap females, not only black but also Indian, mulatto and white women. The need for kidnapping women from other races was due to the scarce number of black women in the plantations and sugar mills since slave-owners preferred to acquire men" (pp. 37–38).

The scarceness of women in colonial society, and the purported need for the *quilombolas* to reproduce to maintain a sustainable community that would meet Freitas's criteria for economic and social viability seems to justify, for him, the kidnappings. Freitas notes that it was not only black women who were forcefully taken to the *maroon*, but that kidnappings also included women who fit his definition of "other races," such as Indian, mulatto, and white women. For Freitas, the argument for economic viability justifies even the racial variety among the kidnapped women. This theory is undermined, however, by other accounts, cited by Freitas himself, asserting that many "free women of humble condition ran away out of their own free will with the black *palmarinos*." If this is the case, then numbers and scarceness explain nothing.

To explain the voluntary escape of these women, Freitas is forced to turn to the argument that this was a common practice not only in Brazil but also in the United States. He states: "The fact should not cause much admiration. Even in the United States in the eighteenth century it was fairly common to see the escape of white women – Irish, Scot and English – reduced to 'indentured servants' – in the company of black and mulatto men" (1978: 37–38).

However, arguing that such practice is common does not explain its motivations. Because Freitas's goal was to analyze the Palmares Maroon as a struggle for freedom against slavery, he is not concerned with gender relations within the settlement. He notes as an aside that at Palmares women had more than one husband, which he characterizes as polyandry (from the Greek: *poly-* many, and *andro-* man). However, again, his understanding of this polyandry focuses only on the numbers. His argument is that because there were few women in either colonial society or the *maroon*, these women would have had many male partners as a simple matter of the continuing survival of the settlement.

Working within his specific research context, Freitas is not concerned with questions regarding desire, or definitions of feminine and masculine, among other areas of research more typical of the field of gender and sexual relations. Ultimately, his search is for a Palmares representative of the political struggle for freedom, that is, as an answer to the slavocratic system, not one that can give him insight into sexual issues.

In this same period, Abdias do Nascimento (1980) glorified Palmares as a heroic example of the power of black people in the New World. A self-designated African-Brazilian intellectual, Nascimento preached an immediate Pan-Africanism (the union of all the "People of Africa" – descendants of Africans born on other continents), whose inspiring model would be the Palmares Maroon.

The scholars just cited longed to recover, "through exhaustive and empirical research," the Palmares Maroon as it "really" was, according to historian Célia Marinho Azevedo (2000). However, they present a *maroon* full of the expectations, doubts, and answers that are characteristic of the period lived by each researcher. The colonial *maroon* no longer represents a historical event alone but has come to symbolize the struggles of the present. Previously a symbol of "black weakness and inferiority," it has now moved to representing a concrete example "of African richness and power."

Social movements, particularly the varied currents of the black nationalist movement, also interpreted Palmares as an inspiring example of African resistance in Brazil. Since the nineteenth century, there have arisen a series of Brazilian organizations with the goal of rebuilding the dignity of black people in the country. The Palmares Maroon was incorporated into the history taught by these movements, and Zumbi became more than a black hero, he became a national hero. A Brazilian rapper called Rappin Hood, born in a poor area of the city of São Paulo, and who specifically refers to himself as black, describes Zumbi and Palmares: "My grandfather told me about the 400 years of slavery of the black people in Brazil and about Zumbi's fight. Today hip hop gave me the knowledge to notice that the main leader of the biggest of *maroons*, Palmares, is more current than ever: he fought for social equality, for the rights of black people as citizens, and for a humanitarian distribution of income" (2002).

As a national hero, Zumbi, along with the Palmares Maroon, have also been adopted by other political movements. In 1995, Luiz Mott, professor of Anthropology at Federal University of Bahia, and president of the Gay Group of Bahia (GGB), declared that Zumbi, among other historic personalities of Brazil, had been gay. This claim was based on civil suits, letters, books, quotations, and other documents. In an interview with *Istoé Online Magazine* Mott said: "Zumbi's nickname was sueca (Swedish woman), he never had a wife, he came from the Angolan ethnicity of "quibanda," where homosexuality was institutionalized, he was raised by a priest in Alagoas who called him 'my little nigger' and, when he was assassinated in 1695, his penis was cut off and shoved into his mouth" (interview given to the journalist Flávio Sampaio – *Istoé Magazine* online, no date).[3]

The responses to Mott's statements were violent. The lecturer had his car windows broken and his house walls painted with graffiti. Aside from the question of Zumbi's sexuality, an issue not yet debated in academia, the Luiz Mott case brought to the surface the controversial nature, in current Brazilian society, of discussions about gender and sexual relations. For now, it seems there is no room for homosexual heroes.

ARCHAEOLOGICAL NARRATIVES: IDENTITY AS AN AXIS

In 1992 and 1993, Charles Orser Jr. (1996), Michel Rowlands (1999), and Pedro Paulo Funari (1999) opened archaeological excavations at the settlement of Palmares, seeking data to complement the many previous approaches to the Palmares Maroon. Interpretation of the artifacts – the objects produced or modified by human actions – from the daily life of the *quilombolas*, together with the analysis of the written sources, suggest alternative visions of the *maroon*.

Through this new approach, fresh areas of inquiry took on greater importance. These included the existence of other outcast groups inside the settlement such as witches, Muslims, and Jews (already mentioned in the written documentation), the commercial role played by Palmares, and the connections between the *maroon* and the colonial authorities.

The archaeological work done in an area of Serra da Barriga in the modern state of Alagoas, financed by national and international institutions, is illustrative of the researchers' findings (Figure 15.2). During field work in Serra da Barriga, fourteen *archaeological* sites were identified, only one of which, site 11, dated from after the Palmares Maroon. Dating was determined through the presence of majolica or glazed ceramics. In total, 2,448 artifacts, over 90 percent of which are ceramic, were collected (Funari 1996).

Although the three archaeologists discussed subsequently analyzed the same artifacts, each of them produced a very distinct Palmares Maroon.

The American archaeologist Charles Orser, Jr. works from a perspective of global historical archaeology. Orser states that the Palmares Maroon did not form an isolated unit fighting for a pure culture because it was integrated into a complex web of direct and indirect relations with both the lower-class inhabitants of the colony, and the Europeans. The colonists would have had ongoing dealings with Palmares not only through commercial transactions but also in the private spheres of daily life, because the ordinary citizens of the colonies shared an identity much closer to that of the inhabitants of Palmares than to the farm owners and other local elites of the colonies.

In this interpretation, the Palmarian settlement was part of a web of relations that allowed connection with several parts of the world. The Palmares Maroon, just as for slave plantations in the southern United States and in rural farming areas in Ireland, is understood as the result of capitalist forces, modernity, Eurocentrism, and colonialism. In Orser's work, we see the creation of a broad model that attempts to explain and interconnect all humanity after the year 1415.

Grounded in archaeology of ethnicity perspectives, Brazilian archaeologist Pedro Paulo Abreu Funari emphasizes the relationship between people. Funari's primary focus is that the *maroon* was a place where people of various ethnic and cultural backgrounds would have lived together. This ethnic pluralism originated in the historical and strategic situation of the *maroon*. The Palmarinos established themselves in a region populated by natives, colonial villagers, farmers, the Dutch, and other groups deemed outcast. Therefore, the *quilombos* were not isolated communities; they lived not only in conflict with these colonial groups but also, and necessarily, in interaction with them. Such ongoing contact transformed Palmares not into a

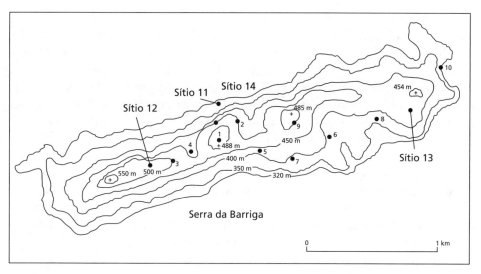

FIGURE 15.2. Serra da Barriga, showing the fourteen sites investigated during field work done in 1992 and 1993. The location of the sites seems accidental, with the exception of the nineteenth-century site 11. The remaining sites are located on the mountaintop or on the southern side of the range, with a possible alignment of observation sites on the southeast flanks. Sites 10, 13, 8, 6, 9, 7, and 5 form an east–west line on the southern side of the mountains facing onto the Mundau River. Although still early to hypothesize about the functionality of the sites, the occupation density of which has not yet been determined, future field work should determine the relationship of the general layout to individual *quilombola* settlements. (*Source:* Funari 1996: 38.)

faithful copy, nor even a modified reconstruction of previous experiences (exclusively African); on the contrary, these contacts consolidated the *maroon* as a unique experience.

In an archaeology of ethnicity, the settlement is understood as a space of debate, where identities, fluid as they are, can only be defined for the purpose of analysis, or better, with a didactic goal. The settlement is seen as an example of interactions between different social elements. Thus, it is understood as an example for our current society of the possibility of a peaceful, tolerant existence among people with fluid and diverse identities. The goal of an archaeology of ethnicity is not to build an explanatory model applicable to *quilombola* settlements throughout the Americas but rather to value the historical context in which the Palmares Maroon appeared. In this it resembles the archaeology of domination and resistance.

British archaeologist Michael Rowlands interprets the Palmares Maroon through a perspective of domination and resistance research, noting that Palmares society was a plural structure in which, for example, slavery was an accepted practice. In this view, the *maroon* is understood as a society very similar to colonial society. Similar to the colonies, distinctions existed in Palmares between the elite and the other inhabitants of the *maroon*. For Rowlands, these repeated distinctions of class, as well as differences based on gender and ethnicity, explain the existence of slavery in the Palmares Maroon.

Within the archaeology of domination and resistance, Palmares is perceived as the result of a combination of contexts. These shaping contexts include the experience of slavery, the existence of sugarcane plantations, the presence of European merchants and traders, and the presence and culture of the Indians and the Dutch. The Brazilian Portuguese colony, and later the Dutch colony, were characterized by very specific social structures that were reproduced, in part, in the Palmares Maroon. The settlement offers evidence that the concept of resistance may mean more than simply the escape of slaves or the defense of a pure cultural identity. Palmares, as an extension of colonial society, expands our understanding of "resistance" to include the ideas of negotiation and interaction.

Another group of researchers associated with North American archaeologist Scott Joseph Allen conducted new archaeological investigations in the Serra da Barriga in 1996. Working within the theoretical framework of ethnogenesis archaeology, Allen (2001) focused on very specific dynamics in Palmares. For him, the key fact is that the *quilombolas* created a new culture and identity in an alien natural and social environment. Their clothes, names, artifacts, and other cultural expressions (material or nonmaterial) were constructed by joining traditional elements, mostly African, with colonial elements. These articulations served to differentiate the Palmarinos from the various groups belonging to the slave society of the Dutch, Portuguese, and Brazilian colonists. Palmarian identity was consolidated through contact between many cultures, thereafter manifesting an identity of its own, specific to the *maroon*.

Within ethnogenesis archaeology, the Palmares Maroon is offered as proof that the *maroons* in the Americas were born out of a need to defend a sole, cohesive identity, formed through a mix of other identities such as Indian and African, against the cultural threats of colonial society. Ethnogenesis archaeology diverges from the archaeology of ethnicity and the archaeology of domination and resistance in its focus on cultural cohesion. Global historic archaeology follows a similar path, although it emphasizes a cohesion present among all human beings, not specific to only the Palmares Maroon.

The archaeological theories just described, informing varied analyses of the Palmares Maroon, emphasize different aspects of the settlement. For this reason, when analyzed together, they provide a multifaceted representation of the *maroon*. According to scholar Kathryn Woodward, the representation can be understood as a cultural process that "establishes individual and collective identities, and the symbolic systems in which they are based supply us with possible answers to the questions: who am I? what could I be? who do I want to be? Discourses and the systems of representations construct the places from where the individuals can position themselves and from which they can speak" (Woodward, 2000: 17).

The archaeological narratives about Palmares, reimagining the *maroon* through the filter of different theories, produce unique places where contemporary people can look for support to imagine and experience alternative identities for themselves and for others.

According to archaeologists Michael Shanks and Christopher Tilley, these places generated from within diverse archaeological theories can be conceived of as political choices. For Shanks and Tilley, archaeological studies, understood not only as fieldwork but also as the theoretical base of the researcher, are a political act. From this perspective, the texts produced by scholars of material culture should ideally create dissonance and invite students of the human past to constant reflection and debate (Shanks and Tilley, 1987).

Each archaeological interpretation of the Serra da Barriga sites created a unique Palmares Maroon, the images of which provoke certain reactions not only in the academic world, where they were conceived, but also in the world outside of the universities.

INTIMATE ENCOUNTERS AT PALMARES: GENDER, ARCHAEOLOGY, AND US

Archaeology provides a unique opportunity to address our understanding of colonialism and sexuality (Hall, Chapter 19, this volume). A fugitive polity such as Palmares is a case in point. Palmares is widely acknowledged and revered as an anticolonial, antislavery settlement. However, sexuality, intimacy, gender roles, and interpersonal relations are neglected subjects in the context of Palmares. Power relations at the micro-level, it seems, are still not accorded importance or relevance as subjects for serious scholarly inquiry. This is partly due to a lack of adequate attention to material evidence. Historical narrative built on written sources is prone to several biases. First and foremost, such written sources systematically disregard ordinary daily life, including the realm of intimacy. This is the result of the limitations of written documents, which are historically the product of an elite male outlook. The value of archaeology, however, is that it enables us to connect material remains with social relations, overcoming the biases of documentary narratives (Funari et al. 1999).

As sensual interactions mediated through bodies and artifacts, colonial encounters go beyond words. As in Roman and Greek society, examined in other chapters of this volume, the colonial world did not dissociate body, power, and materiality. As Pascal Quignard has stressed, "Greek and Roman societies did not dissociate biology and politics. The body, the city, the sea, the country, the war, the poetic work, all were the result of the same vitality; they were equally exposed to the same allures of fertility" (1994: 85).[4]

Sensuality was thus at the heart of colonial encounters at Palmares. Field work encounters with the archaeological record are also sensual and subjective, grounded in our own experiences and standpoints. The knowledge produced in such circumstances is thus at once empirical and theoretical – born from our own experience (*empeiria*) and from our own view points (*theoria*; Funari 1995). Knowledge is thus situational, rather than neutral, perceived through our bodies (Rago and Funari 2008) using our senses. The material evidence of Palmares provides us with the opportunity not only to feel the powerful impression of the landscape and its defensive character (Figure 15.3), but also to experience, for example, how runaways saw and touched glazed pottery (Figure 15.4).

POLYANDRY AND MATERIALITY

Polyandry, a sanctioned sexual relationship between one woman with more than one man, is a thorny subject. Biological perspectives focus primarily on the reproductive

FIGURE 15.3. Photos of Belly Hill (Serra da Barriga). (Photo: Pedro Paulo Funari.)

aspects of such relationships. As Jeanne and David Zeh propose (1996: 1711), "by mating with more than one male, females can potentially exploit post-copulatory mechanisms for minimizing the risk and/or cost of fertilization by genetically incompatible sperm." For a long time, polyandry has been considered by several scholars as extraordinary and counterintuitive. As David Schmitt has stressed "Overall, the extant evidence suggests that polyandry is not an evolved strategy in humans, but rather is a mating behavior that can emerge given harsh ecological circumstances, limited ability for men to accumulate resources, and peculiar inheritance rules" (2005: 264).

However, considering the cultural diversity of human societies, an approach based purely on "biological strategy" seems insufficient to understand properly the emergence and historical persistence of polyandry as a legal, socially supported contractual relationship in several cultural contexts. Even some patriarchal societies acknowledge the existence of polyandry as a de facto, if not de jure, practice, so much so that both Roman and Hebrew legal systems recognize only female descent, as the mother is the only sure parent (*mater certa, pater incertus*) (Cohen 1985). In a classic essay, Jack Goody linked polyandry to property, "Where women are propertied they are initially less free as far as marital arrangements go, though the unions into which they enter are more likely to be monogamous (or even polyandrous)" (2004: 116).

In archaeology, polyandry has been less frequently explored than polygamy and monogamy for many reasons, not least of which may be a male gender bias among historical researchers. In the case of fugitive settlements, polyandry may have played a variety of roles – not only to foster genetic success but possibly also as a way of empowering women and the community at large. This possibility takes on greater significance if we remember that the polity was fundamentally grounded in a resistance to the existing colonial power structures.

FIGURE 15.4. Photos of glazed potsherds from Palmares. (Photo: Pedro Paulo Funari.)

The materiality of polyandry is as yet an underexplored subject in archaeology. However, it is possible to examine the polyandry hypothesis through the main archaeological interpretive frameworks that have been used to understand material culture at Palmares.

The global network theory pioneered by Orser is not directly concerned with gender issues, but it might support the idea of polyandry as a local response to a global situation. The limited number of women on the plantations would inevitably lead to an imbalance in the male–female ratio in the settlement. Polyandry might result from this external situation. Archaeological evidence from Palmares could be reexamined to see whether polyandry materialized through an unusual relationship in the quantity and quality of male-associated artifacts to female-associated artifacts.

An anthropological approach that emphasizes inner contradictions in the settlement, such as that used by Michael Rowlands, addresses the topic of polyandry by focusing on differences in material evidence between groups located within the settlement itself. Polyandry, from this perspective, would be first and foremost interpreted as a response to the dynamics of the polity itself. By itself, a low population of women would not necessarily result in polyandry, particularly if men were controlling and centralizing social and material relations in the community. Although we cannot yet definitively assert that polyandry did develop at Palmares, if it did, a domination and resistance perspective would predict that there would be measurable variations in the proportion of male to female objects found in different areas of the settlement.

The ethnogenesis interpretive model, developed by Scott Allen, would examine polyandry as another cultural practice that contributed to the creation of a new homogeneous Palmarino identity. If polyandry was practiced at Palmares, it would have contributed to the differentiation of the runaway polity from colonial society. The Palmarinos' diverse sexual relationships would have existed in opposition to colonial laws and mores. Through this perspective, we would predict that the material evidence resulting from polyandry would be found in artifacts of local manufacture that express the distinctiveness of Palmares. Decorative motifs in pottery, for example, such as female genitalia, would shock colonial society and present the new Palmarino society as a bounded community with unique institutions such as polyandry.

Our own approach stems from a postmodern concern with fluidity and multiple identities. Polyandry in this context is not necessarily a stable, official institution but a practice among others. Sexuality and gender roles are understood as always in mutation. Third-gender roles, same-sex relationships, and a variety of male and female social relations were probably at work in this runaway settlement. If so, polyandry should be understood as one mode of relationship among a variety of possibilities.

The sexual politics of the past were as richly varied and complex as those of the present (Voss 2008b). The materiality of diverse sexual roles and relationships, including polyandry, should be sought in the full spectrum of material evidence, through an open-minded attention to the possible presence of diversity. A recognition of sexual variety in the archaeological record depends on a fresh approach to the archaeological record, rather than on new evidence alone. The outlook for those innovative archaeological approaches is encouraging. We hope this chapter contributes to such initiatives.

NOTES

1. *Quilombola* is the term used to described the people who lived in the *maroons*.
2. *Chaque nation, avec ses temples, ses dieux, sa poésie, ses traditions héroïques, ses croyances fantastiques, ses lois et ses institutions, représente une unité, une façon de prendre la vie, un ton dans l'humanité, une faculté dans la grande âme* (Renan 1848: 868).
3. Available at http://www.terra.com.br/istoegente/43/reportagens/rep_gays.htm.
4. "*les sociétés grecque et romaine ne dissociaient pas biologie et politique. Le corps, la cité, la mer, le champ, la guerre, l'oeuvre étaient confrontés à une seule vitalité, exposés au mêmes appels de fécondité.*"

References

Allen, S. J. 2001. *Zumbi Nunca Vai Morrer – History, race, politics, and the practice of Archaeology in Brazil.* Ph.D. dissertation, Department of Anthropology, Brown University, Providence, Rhode Island.

Azevedo, C. M. M. 2000. "A Nova História Intelectual de Dominick La Capra e a noção de raça," in Rago, M., and R.A.O. Gimenez (eds.), *Narrar o passado, repensar a história.* Campinas, Brazil: Editora IFCH, pp. 175–197.

Barléu, G. 2005. *O Brasil holandês sob o Conde João Maurício de Nassau: história dos feitos recentemente praticados durante oito anos no Brasil e noutras partes sob o governo do Ilustríssimo João Maurício Conde de Nassau (1584–1648).* Brasília: Senado Federal; Conselho Editorial.

Bourdieu, P. 2001. *Langage et Pouvoir Symbolique.* Paris: Éditions Fayard.

Carneiro, E. 1966. *O Quilombo dos Palmares.* Rio de Janeiro: Editora Civilização Brasileira.

Cohen, S. 1985. "The Origins of the Matrilineal Principle in Rabbinic Literature." *AJS Review* 10:19–35.

Freitas, D. 1978. *Palmares – A Guerra dos Escravos.* Rio de Janeiro: Graal.

Funari, P. P. A. 1995. "Mixed Features of Archaeological Theory in Brazil," in Ucko, P. (ed.), *Theory in Archaeology, A World Perspective.* London: Routledge, pp. 236–250.

———. 1996. "A Arqueologia de Palmares – Sua contribuição para o conhecimento da história da cultura afro-americana," in Reis, J. J., and F. S. Gomes (eds.), *Liberdade por um fio.* São Paulo: Contexto, pp. 26–51.

———. 1999. "A Arqueologia e a Cultura Africana nas Américas." *Estudos Ibero – Americanos,* Pontifíca Universidade Católica do Rio Grande do Sul (PUCRS), XVII(2):61–71.

———, and A. V. Carvalho. 2005. *Palmares, ontem e hoje.* Rio de Janeiro: Jorge Zahar.

———, and F. S. Noelli. 2002. *Pré-história do Brasil.* São Paulo: Contexto.

———, S. Jones, and M. Hall. 1999. "Introduction: Archaeology in History," in Funari, P. P. A., M. Hall, and S. Jones (eds.), *Historical Archaeology, Back from the edge.* London: Routledge, pp. 1–20.

Foucault, M. 1980. *The History of Sexuality, Volume 1.* New York: Vintage Books.

Gomes, Flávio dos Santos. 2005. *A Hidra e os pântamos.* São Paulo: Unesp/Polis.

Goody, J. 2004. "Inheritance, Property, and Marriage in Africa and Eurasia," in Parkin, R. and L. Stone (eds.), *Kinship and Family.* Oxford: Blackwell, pp. 110–118.

Gosden, C. 2004. *Archaeology and Colonialism: Cultural Contact from 5000 BC to the Present.* Cambridge: Cambridge University Press.

Grosby, S. 2005. *Nationalism.* Oxford: Oxford University Press.

Hall, M., and S. Silliman. 2006. *Historical Archaeology.* Oxford: Blackwell.

Hall, S. 2006. *Da Diáspora.* Belo Horizonte, Brazil: UFMG.

Hicks, D., and M. Beaudry. 2006. *The Cambridge Companion to Historical Archaeology.* Cambridge: Cambridge University Press.

Hood, R. 2002. "Zumbi e Palmares." *Revista MTV.* São Paulo: Setembro.

Jones, S. 1997. *The Archaeology of Ethnicity, Constructing Identities in the Past and Present.* London: Routledge.

Lawrence, S., and N. Shepherd. 2006. "Historical Archaeology and colonialism," in Hicks, D., and M. C. Beaudry (eds.), *The Cambridge Companion to Historical Archaeology.* Cambridge: Cambridge University Press, pp. 69–89.

Little, W., H. W. Fowler, and J. Coulson, eds. 1955. *The Oxford Universal Dictionary.* Oxford: Clarendon Press.

Meneses, U. B. 1987. "Identidade cultural e Arqueologia," in *Cultura Brasileira.* São Paulo: Ática, pp. 182–190.

Moura, C. 1981. *Os Quilombos e a rebelião negra.* São Paulo: Brasiliense.

———. 1959. *Rebeliões da Senzala – Quilombos, Insurreições, Guerrilhas.* São Paulo: Ed. Zumbi.

Nascimento, A. 1980. *O Quilombismo – documentos de uma militância pan-africanista.* Petrópolis: Editora Vozes.

Orser, Jr., C. 1996. *A Historical Archaeology of the Modern World.* New York: Plenum Press.

Quignard, P. 1994. *Le sexe et l'effroi*. Paris: Gallimard.

Rago, M., and P. P. A. Funari. 2008. *Subjetividades Antigas e Modernas*. São Paulo: Annablume.

Rattansi, A. 2007. *Racism*. Oxford: Oxford University Press.

Renan, E. 1848. *L'Avenir de la science*. Paris: Calmann Lévy.

Rowlands, M. 1999. "Black Identity and Sense of Past in Brazilian National Culture," in Funari, P. P. A., M. Hall, and S. Jones (eds.), *Historical Archaeology – Back from the Edge*. London: Routledge, pp. 328–344.

Sampaio, F. "Eram eles gays?" *Istoé Magazine online*. Available at http://www.terra.com.br/istoegente/43/reportagens/rep_gays.htm.

Shanks, M., and C. Tilley. 1987. *Social Theory and Archaeology*. London: Polity Press.

Schmidt, R. A., and B. L. Voss. 2000. *Archaeologies of Sexuality*. London: Routledge.

Schmitt, D. P. 2005. "Fundamentals of Human Mating Strategies," in Buss, D. M. (ed.), *The Handbook of Evolutionary Psychology*. Hoboken, NJ: Wiley, pp. 258–291.

Slenes, Robert W. 2005. "O escravismo por um fio?" in Gomes, Flávio dos Santos (ed.), *A Hidra e os pântamos*. São Paulo: Unesp/Polis, pp. 15–24.

Todorov, T. 1989. *Nous et les autres*. Paris: Éditons du Seuil.

Voss, B. L. 2008a. *The Archaeology of Ethnogenesis: Race and Sexuality in Colonial San Francisco*. Berkeley: University of California Press.

———— 2008b. "Sexuality Studies in Archaeology." *Annual Review of Anthropology* 37:317–336.

Woodward, Kathryn. 2000. "Identidade e Diferença: uma introdução teórica e conceitual," in da Silva, T. T. (ed.), *Identidade e Diferença*. Petrópolis, Brazil, Ed. Vozes, RJ, pp. 7–72.

Zeh, Jeanne, and Zeh, David. 1996. "The Evolution of Polyandry I: Intragenomic Conflict and Genetic Compatibility." *Proceedings of the Royal Society: Biological Sciences* 263:1711–1717.

Section IV

Showing and Telling

SIXTEEN

SEXUALIZING SPACE

The Colonial Leer and the Genealogy of Storyville

Shannon Lee Dawdy

INTRODUCTION

In 1879, Lafcadio Hearn described New Orleans (Figure 16.1) from the point of view of the Devil who had come to the southern city on a weekend break from a winter working in Chicago. The Devil was paying a visit to an old lover. He wrote, "the Devil could not suppress a sigh of regret as he gazed with far-reaching eyes along the old-fashioned streets of the city, whose gables were bronzed by the first yellow glow of sunrise. 'Ah!' he exclaimed, 'is this, indeed, the great City of Pleasure ... the fair capital which once seemed to slumber in enchanted sunlight, and to exhale a perfume of luxury even as the palaces of the old Caesars? Her streets are surely green with grass; her palaces are gray with mould; and her glory is departed from her. And perhaps her good old sins have also departed with her glory'" (Hearn and Starr 2001: 173–174).

Literary convention of a more fanciful era encouraged writers to personify cities, boats, buildings – and even whole nations – as women. However, the image of New Orleans as a feminine figure is remarkably vivid and persistent and of a particular character. New Orleans is not simply feminine; the city is imagined as a sexually experienced woman wise in the ways of commerce. Sometimes she is the welcoming, aged courtesan. Other times she is a tragic, fallen figure as in the popular interpretation of the song, "House of the Rising Sun."

How can something as large and potentially impersonal as a cityscape become not only gendered but sexualized in the imagination? Thinking archaeologically, what are the *material* bases for the sexualization of the New Orleans landscape? New Orleans shares with other port cities a reputation for sexual license, though probably few would dispute that it enjoys an exaggerated cachet as a port of call for pleasure. Most notoriously, the city is famous for the legalized red-light district known as Storyville, which operated from 1897 to 1917. Archaeological research on Storyville and sites such as the Rising Sun Hotel in the nearby French Quarter provoke questions regarding the social and historical context of this experiment in the segregation of sexual activity. Rather than chalking up Storyville to the paradoxes of late Victorian morality in what has become a Freudian or Foucauldian reflex, I argue instead that the roots of Storyville go back to the city's earliest days, when it became a destination for male adventure travel. Over time, three mutually reinforcing factors began to sexualize New Orleans within the American sphere and, later, spaces within it: the Atlantic economy's sexual division of labor, a modern masculinity reproduced through certain forms of consumption, and the orientalizing gaze of colonialism. At the broadest theoretical horizon, this paper explores how "space" itself can be sexualized.

Sexualizing Space

It is not easy to sexualize space. By this I mean two things. First, I mean that the processes through which a society may cordon off spaces or develop specialized architectures for certain sexual practices are likely to be the result of multiple political and economic factors, complex rationalities, or compromises meant to mediate contradictions in social categories. Thus, the few archaeological studies we have of "sex in space" chart landscapes full of tension and uncertainty, such as the cloisters of barely contained female celibacy (Gilchrist 1994, 2000), the ephemeral leatherman district of San Francisco (Rubin 2000), contested gay "pick-up" sites (Schofield and Anderton 2000), female prisons rife with sneaky behavior (Casella 2000, Chapter 3, this volume), plantation compounds accommodating concubinage (Croucher, Chapter 5, this volume), same-sex work camps (Weiss, Chapter 4, this volume), and colonial mission sites that attempted to regulate Native American sexuality and contacts with Spanish colonizers (Voss 2000).

The second way in which "sexualizing space" is not easy is that it is not easy for the archaeologist to map sexual practices that may have been spatially specific but artifactually understated. This paradox confronts us despite the fact that landscape analysis is central to an archaeological approach and even though sex is undoubtedly one of the most basic of human practices subject to social norms, if not regulation. The artifactual clues are few and far between – with the only consistent exception being sites of prostitution (e.g., McGinn 2002; Seifert and Balicki 2005; Yamin 2005) and perhaps bathhouses (Eger 2007). It is notable that even the recently expanded study of brothels tends to rely on the identification of documented red-light districts. The overdetermined legibility of these neighborhoods means that the sexual map is already drawn; we do not need archaeology to detect prostitution.

What is particularly difficult to map are the most frequent encounters – those informal, interpersonal sexual exchanges in homes, fields, boats, outbuildings, offices, and yards (see also Croucher, Chapter 5, this volume). Social perceptions about the acceptability of sexual exchanges in these locales (or even in the various rooms of a house – bedroom versus kitchen, etc.) may be available to us through texts in historic period contexts, but this helps only with proscription, not practice. An important exception occurs, however, when that proscribed space is large enough to encompass an entire community. When larger spaces are imagined to be sexualized, sexual practices are entailed (or at least are imagined to be entailed) in the other structures that shape social life – such as economics, politics, or religion. All sex is group sex. The anthropological task is to trace social processes that determine where, when, and how sexual exchanges take place, and what shared sexual meanings are read into other domains of life. From the viewpoint of outsiders, the commercial spaces of New Orleans came to be seen as illicit and titillating. Dialectically, this process of sexualizing the city entailed economic-legal conditions that encouraged female property holding and women's involvement in the hospitality trades in the colonial period interacting with a series of "misrecognitions" of the meanings of this independence by (largely Anglo) visitors and clientele. Tracing the genealogy of Storyville will help us understand this dialectic, which is as much the material story of a particular economy as it is an account of the emergence of a representation. Storyville was a place where sex transactions and other transactions flowed metonymically one into the other.[1]

Like any genealogy (or archaeology), I begin with the most recent generation and work backward. I begin by working from the archaeological sites that provoked this query and then put them into an interpretive context. I argue that it is impossible to understand Storyville without understanding New Orleans' colonial past. The leer that colonial adventurers cast on this port town and its residents fed certain social and economic formations. These formations have in turn reproduced the colonial leer, now known as the tourist gaze. These gendered economic transactions and the attendant colonial leer – a particular form of affective perception – transformed New Orleans from a gridded, flexible *space* (Tuan 2001) in the early French colonial period to a sensual creole *place* in the territorial period – or a destination and a landscape filled up with meaning.

Part of New Orleans' serpentine character is due to the twists and turns of its history. The French took possession of the vast Louisiana colony in 1699, and New Orleans was established as its new colonial capital and Mississippi River port in 1718. Vastly outnumbered by Native Americans, settlers and slaves concentrated in the Lower Mississippi Valley near New Orleans throughout the French period, which lasted until 1768. The following year, the colony was transferred to Spanish authorities. In the late eighteenth century, the population and wealth of the city grew. This was one reason the territory attracted Thomas Jefferson and other American interests. As a result of peace treaties in Europe, Louisiana was briefly returned to the French under Napoleon, only to be sold the following year, in 1803, to pay for war debts. After the Louisiana Purchase, Americans and multinational entrepreneurs flooded the city in the territorial period (ca. 1803–1815), both for its own rewards and as a gateway leading to Latin America, the Caribbean, and the Trans-Mississippi West. Thereafter, the population grew exponentially in the first half of the nineteenth century, from about 8,000 in 1803 to 120,000 in 1850. Although a large influx of refugees from Haiti and Napoleonic France helped keep French language and culture alive, local creoles were vastly outnumbered by Anglo, German, and Celtic immigrants and visitors by the 1830s. In the French period, the economy focused on subsistence agriculture, a small number of exports, and a lively smuggling trade; in the Spanish period, sugar plantations fed the city. Under the Americans, sugar and slavery expanded further, as did cotton and all manner of trade as the Mississippi River became an important thoroughfare for the agricultural heartland. Although the city's racial makeup fluctuated over the years, it tended toward equilibrium between whites and people of color under the two colonial regimes, with a relatively tolerant environment for free people of color and little

residential segregation. American rule and new immigration in the nineteenth century tipped the balance toward a white majority while imposing ever stricter racial
structures.

The Sites

Storyville

As one of the most famous red-light districts in American history, Storyville probably
needs little introduction. Its fame has been amplified by the photographs of Ernest
Bellocq, Louis Malle's film *Pretty Baby*, and many jazz biographies. This approximately four-by-four city block area nestled between the French Quarter, the Central
Business District, and Faubourg Tremé (Figure 16.2) was a fairly typical downtown
neighborhood throughout most of the nineteenth century, having a mixture of
townhouses and modest creole cottages. The area was bounded by Basin Street, an
important transportation artery, first for small canal boats and later for a city rail
line (established 1875). The city's oldest extant cemetery also bordered the neighborhood and bustling Canal Street – New Orleans' Main Street – lay just one block
away. The neighborhood was centrally located, adjacent to the heart of the city's
commercial heart and cultural life.

By 1887, a Sanborn Fire Insurance map lists a "female boarding house" on Basin
Street (Gray et al. n.d.). In New Orleans of this era, this designation was often a
euphemism for a brothel.[2] By 1895, the prevalence of brothels in this district war-
ranted publication of the first "Blue Book." Blue Books were Michelin-like guides
to the services and amenities of New Orleans' "underworld," paid for by advertising (Figure 16.3). The money brought to the area through prostitution paid for
renovations of some of the buildings, as well as the construction of several ornate
Edwardian and Victorian houses in the early 1900s. In fact, the advertisements in
the Blue Books stress the architecture and appointments of the better "houses" and
"sporting palaces" (other local euphemisms) such as that for Josie Anderson's establishment (Figure 16.4), whose house can be seen in the only known streetscape
photograph of the district (Figure 16.5). After studying legalized zones of prostitution in Holland and Germany, the City of New Orleans decided to designate
this area as a controlled prostitution district in 1897. Legalization spurred rapid
development. The push for legalization was led by Councilman Sidney Story, who
probably did not intend to be immortalized with "The District's" nickname. Storyville flourished until 1917, when the U.S. Department of the Navy demanded it be
shut down on the eve of U.S. entry into World War I (Long 2004). During its heyday,
Storyville was home to some of the most elegant brothels in the United States, as
well as backstreets full of dilapidated houses cut up for 50-cent cribs. It was a dense,
specialized development. On the 1909 Sanborn, sixty-five "female boarding houses"
were listed on just three of the city squares in the neighborhood (Gray et al. n.d.).
It is estimated that at its peak, Storyville housed 200 brothels and approximately
1,500 prostitutes. This was not simply a sexualized landscape; it was sexual zoning.

After the shuttering of Storyville, which in fact took a concerted effort by police
over the next two decades, the houses and taverns were razed to the ground to make

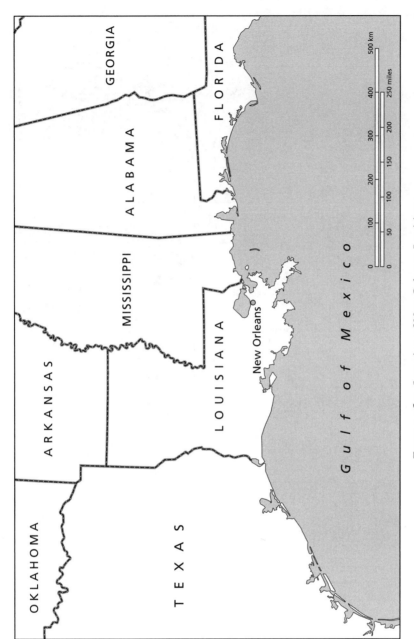

FIGURE 16.1. Location of New Orleans, Louisiana.

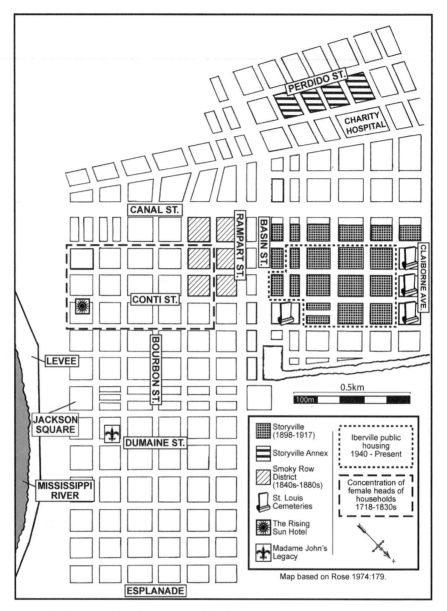

FIGURE 16.2. Sites and districts discussed in the text (created by Joe Bonni for S. Dawdy).

room for the Iberville Public Housing Project in the 1930s, which today still sits atop most of the former red light district. In 1999, Earth Search, Inc. was contracted to conduct archaeological monitoring during renovations at Iberville (Gray et al. n.d.). Although archaeologists were restricted to small areas where construction required monitoring, they did identify features and intact deposits that date to the Storyville era. Recovered artifacts include ironstone ceramics, hand-painted whitewares, an enameled tin wash basin, and a Hoyt's Nickel Cologne bottle.

More important, this first archaeological study of the area introduced a spatial approach to understanding Storyville, investigating the gaudy façade of Basin Street,

FIGURE 16.3. Cover of a Storyville Blue Book (courtesy of the Hogan Jazz Archive, Tulane University).

with its ornate mansions and loud music halls that greeted passengers deboarding the Spanish Fort Rail Line, as well as the backstreets filled with small cribs. Although segregated from the rest of the city as a legal district during the height of Jim Crow legislation, many of the "houses" boasted in their advertisements about the multiple skin tones from which to pick among the working girls. Although technically black men were banned from patronizing these establishments, they were commonly employed as musicians, bouncers, and bartenders; personal accounts indicate that the laws enforcing their sexual segregation were loosely enforced as well. New Orleans' reputation as a place with a lax sexual code was thoroughly entangled with its reputation for a lax racial code. The exoticism of New Orleans' fair-skinned, French-speaking women of color, and the social experience of a racially jumbled neighborhood jostling with intimate encounters, added an extra illicit thrill for male customers coming from whiter or more strictly segregated hometowns.

Rising Sun Hotel

The Rising Sun Hotel Site, located at 535 Conti Street in the French Quarter, is owned by the Historic New Orleans Collection, which sponsored field excavations between December 2004 and April 2005 (Dawdy et al. 2008). The Collection's planned construction of a new archival storage facility presented a unique opportunity for archaeological research. Excavations of ten 1 by 1 meter units preceded demolition of an early twentieth-century garage that had sealed the site since 1915. Deposits dating before 1840 are well preserved across the site and can be tied to documented occupations. The lot has a complex history, but the components relevant to this chapter date between 1796 and 1882, when the site was used by several proprietors of hospitality establishments.

Following a devastating citywide fire in 1788, the lot was redeveloped between 1791 and 1796. Between 1796 and 1809, a wood frame structure newly built on the site served as a residence and boarding house owned by Widow Margaret Clark Chabot. Her most notable guest was William Clark (no known relation), who resided in New Orleans for three months in 1798 before joining Meriwether Lewis for their overland expedition. When Mrs. Chabot died, the property passed through a handful of owners and operators but maintained its profile as a house of hospitality. It served first as a combination coffeehouse and hotel and then as a tavern and hotel. This last establishment opened in 1821 under the name "Rising Sun Hotel" but burned down a year later in an intense fire that took the lives of two men. It was replaced soon after with a more substantial brick hotel and billiards hall. The site continued to be used as a hotel through about 1882.

At the time of the excavations in 2005, media attention zoomed in on the Rising Sun Hotel component. "Rising Sun" was actually a fairly common motif in the eighteenth and nineteenth centuries used by Anglo taverns and coffeehouses. Nevertheless, the old American folksong "House of the Rising Sun," first recorded in the 1930s, has played a key role in imagining New Orleans. The lyrics are most often interpreted as the words of a fallen woman working in a brothel and gambling house, although other plausible interpretations have been offered (Anthony 2007).

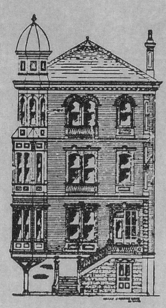

The Arlington

NOWHERE IN this country will you find a more complete and thorough sporting house than the ARLINGTON

Absolutely and unquestionably the most decorative and costly fitted out sporting palace ever placed before the American public.

The wonderful originality of everything that goes to fit out a mansion makes it the most attractive ever seen in this or the old country.

THE ARLINGTON

The Arlington, after suffering a loss of many thousand dollars through a fire, was refurnished and remodeled at an enormous expense, and the mansion is now a palace fit for a king.

Within the great walls of this mansion will be found the work of great artists from Europe and America. Many articles from various expositions will also be seen, and curios galore.

PHONE MAIN 1888

225 N. Basin

FIGURE 16.4. Advertisement from Storyville Blue Book (courtesy of the Louisiana Collection Tulane University).

The actual hotel called "Rising Sun" is quite well preserved in a fire-burned rubble level. Among the artifacts are an unusually high number of faience rouge pots – or French cosmetic jars (approximately five times the number found at residential sites of the same era). An 1821 advertisement for the hotel reads, "Gentlemen here may rely upon finding attentive Servants" and "the best entertainment." Although the twenty-first-century reader is inclined to interpret these lines as euphemisms for prostitution, the language is consistent with other hotel advertisements of the period. Archaeology offers no clear forensic evidence; there are no items associated with birth control or feminine hygiene like those found at other documented brothel sites. Even the rouge pots are an ambiguous form of evidence. As I address elsewhere (Dawdy and Weyhing 2008), if the pots did hold rouge, these beauty products could have been used in theatre performances or, equally plausibly, belonged to male dandies staying in the hotel and participating in the male fashion of the time, which made liberal use of face powder and rouge. The historical record likewise offers no smoking gun. No police records survive from the period nor is the site located within known antebellum red-light districts (Schafer 2009).

The Rising Sun Hotel was replaced soon after with a more substantial brick hotel and billiards hall known as the Richardson Hotel. Between 1828 and 1882, the hotel went through several renovations and name changes. Before the Civil War, it maintained its profile as a "gentleman's hotel" but was geared to serve a more upscale clientele than the Rising Sun. The new owners added more rooms and new amenities, and the hotel prospered during the steamboat era. As with the Rising Sun Hotel component, only male proprietors and resident employees are listed in the relevant censuses. After the war, the hotel followed the rest of the French Quarter, falling into disrepair during a period of economic decline, although it remained in operation probably up through 1882. The hotel housed a larger number of resident employees than in earlier periods, many of whom were Irish and included several women. Again, however, neither the archaeology nor the archival records strongly suggests prostitution.

Madam John's Legacy

This search to understand the roots of New Orleans' sexualized landscape has led me back to an excavation I conducted in 1997 at a historic house in the French Quarter known as Madame John's Legacy (Dawdy 1998). Located on Dumaine Street, this "French Indies"–style house is a rare representative of the architectural style that typified the town in the French colonial period. The site's first owner-operator provides another case study, but from the era just before Madame Chabot's boarding house. From the 1720s to the 1770s, the long-lived Elizabeth Real Pascal Marin operated an inn on the site. She outlived two husbands, both ship captains and smugglers. Notarial documents record that Elizabeth, although so illiterate she was uncomfortable signing even a mark for her name, had almost continuous power-of-attorney rights for her absent husbands' affairs. Although the men are listed in the early censuses as innkeepers, Elizabeth was the active proprietor. After her second husband died, Elizabeth was listed in a Spanish census of 1778 as an innkeeper in her own right. Like Madame Chabot's arrangement, Elizabeth's daughter lived with her and assisted in running the business (Dawdy 1998).

Archaeology at the site confirmed that walls of Elizabeth's house survived the disastrous fire of 1788 and were used in its reconstruction that same year. Excavations in the rear courtyard included a spectacularly well-preserved trash pit dating to the fire. Below and above this trash pit were deposits associated with the French colonial and early American occupations. The site has been particularly useful for establishing a baseline regarding diet, trade, and the Native American influence in eighteenth-century New Orleans. The components associated with Elizabeth's operation of the inn suggests that she attempted to provide French "comfort foods" to her traveling soldiers, sailors, and traders, as well as a clean, well-appointed European ambience, not unlike Madame Chabot's establishment. Like Madame Chabot, by the end of her life, Elizabeth was reasonably wealthy and politically well connected, although there was no man heading her household for the greater part of her business career.

CONTEXT AND INTERPRETATION

Divisions of Labor

These occupations and their artifact assemblages reflect differences of scale, class, and business type, as well as demographic and economic changes over time. However, gender was a consistent factor in the hospitality trade from the French founding of the city in 1718 through the antebellum era. Until the demographic surge of the territorial period (ca. 1803–1815), women owned and operated a large share of the boarding houses and inns, if not the majority. Their role in the food trade was even more significant. Travel writers in the early nineteenth century marveled at the women who milled the streets vending pies and other prepared foods. They operated many of the stalls in the "French Market," and the earliest recorded Creole recipes came from the kitchens of women of color who prepared most of the meals.

In colonial Louisiana, the distinctive civil code inherited from Paris meant that there were large numbers of land-holding women, regardless of their marital state as single, married, or widowed. Inheritance law gave daughters an equal share in their parents' estate, and marriage law encouraged the signing of prenuptial contracts in which propertied women could set aside their holdings and decide not to combine it with their future husband's as community property. Even women of relatively modest means often opted for these contracts to protect their children in the event that they predeceased their husband. Compared with British and American women, French colonial women had much greater access to property and much greater control over it (Baade 1978; Baker 1995). This state of domestic law continued under the Spanish regime and was so entrenched by the time the Americans took over that in Louisiana several types of inheritance law coexisted, and savvy women of Anglo descent opted for the French system. Notarial records from the colonial period also contain hundreds of documents related to the business affairs of *marchandes*, or businesswomen of all colors, who ran plantations, sawmills, merchandise stores, and bakeries (Dawdy n.d.). They sold eggs, milk, and oil. They ran taverns, made shoes, tailored clothes, and taught school.

Outside of legal marriage, New Orleans also fostered a large number of property owners and household heads among free women of color, in about equal numbers to women identified as white or European (Clark 2007; Thompson 2009). Many, although not all, of these women gained their property, independence, and, in some cases, freedom, through liaisons or common law marriages with free white men in a local custom known as *plaçage* (or "placement"). Although locally these relationships were accorded a modicum of discreet tolerance, to visiting eyes these households were likely viewed as sexually and racially licentious, adding to the overall impression of New Orleans' sexualized landscape. In the late antebellum era, Anglo writers fetishized unsegregated local balls where such liaisons may have been sparked, dubbing them "Quadroon Balls" (Clark 2007). Because the women involved in these arrangements often improved their material standing through informal marital support and inheritance – often including the acquisition of a "Creole cottage" (cf. Croucher, Chapter 5, this volume), the ambiguity of the transactional landscape was likely enhanced, especially for those exotifying it from the outside. Spatially, the residences of free women of color tended to be in the same Bourbon street area of the French Quarter near white female-operated hospitality establishments, as well as in the Tremé neighborhood that later surrounded the Storyville district.

Censuses provide three snapshots of the city in 1731 (French period), 1779 (Spanish period), and 1805 (Territorial period). Tabulating those households listed with a female head gives us a picture of the relative economic independence of women. Over time the total percentage of New Orleans' households listed with a woman in charge increased steadily from 22 percent in 1732 to an astounding 41 percent in 1815. Most of this gain reflects the demographic equalization of women-to-men overall in the population, but it also reflects the fact that by 1805, more than one-third (or 36 percent) of all free women in New Orleans were heads of their own households (compared with 28 percent in the French period and a brief dip in the Spanish period to 19 percent that corresponded to a demographic bulge of young unmarried women). Whichever year is selected, the numbers and ratios of women householders, and likely property owners, in New Orleans outpaced that of Anglo American port towns for which we have comparable statistics (Carr 2000). To put this in another perspective, in the census of 2000, only 12 percent of U.S. households are headed by single women, *less than at any time in early New Orleans*. In 1805, there were proportionately three times as many female-headed households in New Orleans as there are today in the general population.

In the territorial period (ca. 1803–1815), city directories began to be produced, providing a sample of the city's business establishments. This data suggests that the ratio of female householders reflected in the census are proportionate to their presence among business owners involved in the hospitality trades. An 1822 city directory for New Orleans boasted that the town was home to 350 "taverns, grocers, and billiards halls." Approximately one-fifth (20 percent) of the subscriber businesses were owned by women, although it is certain that the smaller boarding houses and food-vender businesses are not included, making the actual percentage likely higher.

Woman-owned hospitality businesses did not compete uniformly with male establishments. Women did not own any of the fancier luxury hotels noted by travelers, and their hospitality businesses tended to cluster in the same areas where female-headed households clustered – that is, in the upriver end of the French Quarter along Bourbon Street and short stretches of perpendicular streets branching off

FIGURE 16.5. Basin Street during Storyville's heyday (courtesy of the Hogan Jazz Archive, Tulane University).

of it, including Conti Street. Madame Chabot herself owned two other properties on Bourbon Street. Although Bourbon Street is today synonymous with libidinal tourism in New Orleans, in the eighteenth and early nineteenth centuries, the only feature that seems to have distinguished this area from the rest of the Vieux Carré was that it hosted a concentration of female-headed households and modest hospitality concerns operated by women. Although it would be surprising if prostitution was *not* present in a port town, the historical and archaeological evidence provides no indication thus far that this woman-dominated transactional landscape was known for prostitution. In fact, the archaeological evidence from Madame Chabot's boarding house and Elizabeth Real's inn suggests concerted efforts to define material and social respectability. The assemblages included fine gilded porcelain, silver candlesticks, and matching creamware and pearlware table settings. This attention to food presentation was in marked contrast to the assemblages from the male-operated Rising Sun Hotel component, which, although much larger in artifactual volume because of the fire that destroyed the building, contained a hodgepodge of outdated and well-worn soup bowls and serving vessels dominated by unmatching annular wares. Further, both of the woman-operated businesses had only moderate amounts of liquor-bottle glass and drinking vessels (fewer than ten each) compared with the Rising Sun, where liquor bottles and ornate, expensive wine and cordial glasses numbered at least forty-seven vessels across just four 1-meter excavation units. Even in this pretemperance era, female hostellers may have sought to avoid the impropriety too much drinking might have encouraged. Although the archaeological evidence from Storyville is too uncontrolled to measure, the artifact profile that emerges from other known prostitution sites shows a pronounced focus on liquors, and French champagne especially (Seifert et al. 2000). Despite this difference, however, both types of establishments emphasized a "feminine touch" to their hospitality in the form of fancy wares and decorative furnishings.

In the colonial and antebellum eras, a gendered economic zone of concentrated female householders and businesswomen lay immediately across Rampart Street from what would later become Storyville (Figure 16.2). The adjacent neighborhoods seem to share a connection. After the closing of the red-light district, madames migrated back to this part of the French Quarter so that, by the 1950s, Bourbon Street had acquired its seedy allure of door-by-door topless bars (Wiltz 2001). Thus, these small subdistricts of New Orleans – Bourbon Street and Storyville – were gendered before they were sexualized, but they were gendered by older, unmarried, and economically independent women. In the colonial and antebellum period, the women who controlled these spaces had a reputation for knowing how to handle money, if not men. However, this did not require sexual contact. For the most part, that seems to have come later. Between the 1840s and 1890s, legitimate woman-owned boarding houses catering to male boarders were gradually replaced by the euphemistic "female boarding houses," and the figure of New Orleans as the hospitable aging courtesan began to appear in romantic travel literature.

Masculine Consumption

As early as the 1720s, the New Orleans economy was strongly oriented toward the male traveler, from soldiers to *coureur de bois*, Irish smugglers, Kaintucks, Mexican sailors, Virginia slave traders, flat-boat pilots, cotton merchants, steamboat gamblers, and new immigrants stopping off before staking a claim in the west. A large percentage of New Orleans' year-round residents made their living hosting and feeding these men or tending to their ships and cargo. Even before the Louisiana Purchase of 1803, "gentlemen's establishments" in the form of boarding houses, hotels, coffeehouses, taverns, and canteens were cropping up all over New Orleans. The frontier boom economy of the 1810s and 1820s pushed this development into overdrive. In 1821, crowding was so bad, the city's Board of Health specified that boarding houses and taverns had to provide a minimum of "twelve cubic feet of air" per lodger, which works out to a coffin-like dimension of a 2 foot by 6 foot space.

In May 1806, Louisiana's territorial government (1805–1812) passed one of its first laws: "An Act to regulate Inns and Houses of Entertainment" (Louisiana Gazette 1806). The first section dictates the conditions innkeepers must meet to maintain their license, and other sections proscribe signage and the posting of rates, outlaw gambling, and restrict selling liquor to Indians, slaves, and soldiers. At the end of the act, however, Section 9 reads simply: "And be it further enacted, *That nothing in this act contained shall be construed as to extend to the city of New Orleans*" (emphasis added). The new American authorities actually *legislated* that New Orleans was to become an anything-goes port of pleasure for male travelers. This not only set it apart economically and morally from the rest of the massive territory of frontier Louisiana, it distinguished the city from other port towns in the United States where at least nominal regulation was attempted.

Mobile male consumers arrived in late colonial and early antebellum New Orleans looking for drink, food, and entertainment. They found that women had established themselves as providers of these goods and services early in the colonial period.

Because of a convergence of French legal code, demographics, and colonial conditions, they had a stronghold on the local economy. To visiting eyes, the landscape of early New Orleans, with its large number of female-headed households and businesswomen, must have looked like a strikingly woman-dominated space. With a port economy that had evolved to serve traders in the Atlantic economy, it was also a very hospitable place. Visitors developed an appetite for what they perceived as local exotic delicacies: French wine, Cuban cigars, and Creole food. Women provided many of these comforts.

Balls, music, and theater entertainments were also provided and expected. Billiards and gambling were all the rage in 1820s and 1830s New Orleans and were important activities of male sociability. Although forms of billiards have been played since the 1600s in both France and England, a new wave of popularity resulted in the rapid evolution of the game in the late 1700s and early 1800s. By 1820, the city boasted several public billiard halls, including the one at the Richardson Hotel.

The archaeological evidence from Madame Chabot's boarding house, Elizabeth Real's Inn, the Rising Sun Hotel, and the later Richardson Hotel speak to a hospitality industry offering familiar European or Anglo-American "comfort foods" such as Bordeaux wine, beef stew, and cheese but also to an economy of pleasure consumption that took place in the context of concentrated male sociality. Refined cordial glasses, imported brandies and wines, and tobacco seeds from cigar stock were found even at the rough and tumble "gentleman's" tavern at the Rising Sun Hotel. One implication of this context is that sharing the experience of going to a brothel may have been more important as a homosocial experience than a heterosexual one.

Pleasure Destination

These gendered dynamics to production and consumption in New Orleans trace back to the early colonial period. The city served the same needs that other port towns do – to restock, rest, and restore travelers and their vessels, and as an entrepôt. From the viewpoint of colonial actors New Orleans also represented a pleasure destination, a place to relieve the hardships of travel, military service, or backcountry land clearing. Elizabeth Real's inn and Madame Chabot's boarding house were among many establishments that catered to frontier men.

Travel narratives from the French period frequently describe the pleasures of a visit to New Orleans. One of the most remarkable accounts is that by Pierre Caillot, whose manuscript describes a stay-over in Louisiana in 1729–1730 and provides what may be the first description of a carnival, or Mardi Gras, celebration held in the city. Caillot devotes several pages to describing how he passed two or three nights of carnival celebrations in 1730 masking, singing, and reveling. He heralds the sensuous pleasures of the colony and the ways in which French drinks and delicacies were enjoyed on special occasions in New Orleans, recounting, "In effect, I began that evening to taste the first pleasures in the colonies." The height of the celebrations occurred at the home of Madame Rivard on Bayou St. Jean, where he fell in love with the young Mlle. Carrière. They ate, drank, and stayed up the entire night singing and dancing (Caillot 1730: 159).

Caillot's entire description is alive with sensual stimuli, of which food and drink comprise one part of an intense and pleasurable whole that centers unabashedly on sexual pleasures. While describing his trek through the woods to his hostess' party at the house she owns on the outskirts of town, he reports, "Assuredly, I thought that this day was made for love affairs." He and his fellows teased and flirted with the girls at the party. After three hours of music and dancing, the hostess invited Caillot's party to join them for a late-night meal that went on for hours with a table of forty-six guests where men far outnumbered women. After the meal, "our pleasure expanded infinitely because Baccus had quit his empire to go find Venus" and he did not leave until 5 o'clock in the morning (Caillot 1730: 160–163).

As Caillot's depictions of hospitality and entertainment in early New Orleans demonstrates, the town was enjoyed by travelers for the tastes of home and the opportunities for heterosexual encounters it offered. In the later Spanish period, this pattern continued, although the diversity of travelers was greater and the quotidian gender ratio had reached bizarre proportions. On the day he arrived in New Orleans, June 6, 1797, traveler Francis Baily wrote in his journal:

> I was then shown into a large saloon, where there were thirty or forty gentlemen at breakfast, with all the doors and windows wide open, for though it was so early it was very hot. Here I recollected a number of faces that I had seen before in my travels, and which to meet again in an unknown and foreign country was a double satisfaction to me. Having been informed that I could be accommodated with board and lodging here, I took my seat at the table, and joined them in their repast. . . . The house was kept by Madame Chabot, an Irish lady, but who had married a French man in this country, by whom she had an agreeable daughter about sixteen or seventeen years old. (Baily 1856: 298–299)

Baily goes on to describe Madame Chabot's daughter in barely disguised amorous terms. She was known to pick up her guitar and play for the men in the garden while they enjoyed afternoon tea, employing whichever language they preferred (French, Spanish, or English). This same savvy daughter later took over her mother's several properties and businesses, including the Rising Sun Hotel, the site of Baily's description and her teenage home.

These examples highlight two things that distinguished New Orleans from the plantations and smaller posts of the colony. The first was its market full of imports and its selection of cabarets, breweries, and inns. The second was the presence of hostesses. Free women resident in the colony concentrated in the city, as did free women of color in the Spanish and antebellum periods. In the woman-dominated spaces of the port town, men sought the pleasures of home. Enough women obliged – either out of business acumen, necessity, or personal reasons of their own – to establish the foundations of New Orleans' hospitality industry. Among the perceptions that shaped, and were shaped by, this demand economy was a sexual imagination – a colonial leer. When the traveling man descended on New Orleans, leaving the male-dominated environments of military forts, navy ships, and trading convoys, he entered a woman-dominated space. Over time, this woman-dominated *space* became a sexualized *place*.

Conclusion

Despite the shifting gender ratios and economic dynamics in a fast-changing city, two prevailing forces remained constant in New Orleans: a large influx of single or unattached male travelers of all classes and a stable and growing class of propertied free women ready to cater to them. The demand economy they created together was not atypical for port towns, but it was exaggerated in New Orleans because of the multiplicity of its routes and the peculiarities of the legal system. Traveling men in New Orleans expected to find a free port, meaning a port free of both moral and economic regulation, as legislated by the territorial government. The overtones of women offering pleasures and comforts to men in the form of food, bedding, music, and laughter were probably enough to extend the impression of the city's sexual availability to Anglo and European visitors unaccustomed to such a visible class of female proprietors. Commercial sex probably occurred, but there is no evidence to suggest that before the Civil War, it was any more prevalent in New Orleans than any other port town.

Geographer Lawrence Knopp urges us to apply "a conception of urban spaces as social products, in which material forces, the power of ideals and the human desire to ascribe meaning are inseparable" (1995: 158). This is what I have tried to do here in showing how certain forms of economic relations, like those between proprietors and patrons, can be ascribed with sexual fantasies, which in turn produce new material relations. My aim has been to show how New Orleans went from being a gendered *space* to a sexualized *place*. From the earliest French days, the city was gendered in a quite literal fashion – women possessed the land, the buildings, the goods. They owned the space. As men came through, they imagined themselves taking from the feminine city what they needed to create their masculine selves, creating a demand and circulation of exotic commodities and stages for entertainment. The business-women of New Orleans facilitated masculine consumption and the production of a homosocial landscape. Men experienced the city together, as men. They shared her. Ultimately it was the "desire to ascribe meaning" to this gendered economy that led to New Orleans becoming a sexualized place. That is the colonial leer.

Notes

1. I am focusing here deliberately on the heterosexual relations that take place outside marriage via short-term liaisons and/or through prostitution, an area that, in fact, could use greater attention (Voss 2008: 330).
2. To define terms, a *brothel* is a building regularly used for prostitution organized on the model of a hotel, boarding house, or tavern (and may mix these functions), often serving as a residence for prostitutes (synonymous with bawdy house or bordello). A *crib* is a single cell-like room or connected series of such rooms used exclusively for paid sex and not otherwise occupied or used.

References

Anthony, Ted. 2007. *Chasing the Rising Sun: The Journey of an American Song.* New York: Simon & Schuster.

Baade, Hans W. 1978. "Marriage Contracts in French and Spanish Louisiana: A Study in 'Notarial' Jurisprudence." *Tulane Law Review* 53:3–92.

Baily, Francis. 1856. *Journal of a Tour in Unsettled Parts of North American in 1796 and 1797 by the Francis Baily, President of the Royal Astronomical Society [posthumous]*. London: Baily Bros.

Baker, Vaughan B. 1995. "Cherchez les Femmes: Some Glimpses of Women in Early Eighteenth-Century Louisiana." In Conrad, Glenn R. (ed.), *The French Experience in Louisiana*. University of Southwestern Louisiana, pp. 470–493.

Caillot, Pierre. 1730. *Relation du Voyage de la Louisiane ou Nouv.lle France fait par le Sr. Caillot en l'année 1730*. Ms. 2005.11, The Historic New Orleans Collection.

Carr, Jacqueline B. 2000. "A Change 'As Remarkable as the Revolution Itself': Boston's Demographics, 1780–1800." *New England Quarterly* 73(4):583–602.

Casella, Eleanor C. 2000. "Doing Trade": A Sexual Economy of Nineteenth-Century Australian Female Convict Prisons. *World Archaeology* 32:209–221.

Clark, Emily. 2007. *Atlantic Alliances: Marriage among People of African Descent in New Orleans, 1759–1830*. Workshop, École des Hautes Études en Sciences Sociales.

———. n.d. "Marchandes Publiques: The Business of Women in French New Orleans."

Dawdy, Shannon Lee. 1998. "Madame John's Legacy (16OR51) Revisited: A Closer Look at the Archaeology of Colonial New Orleans." New Orleans, LA: University of New Orleans.

———. 2008. *Building the Devil's Empire: French Colonial New Orleans*. Chicago: University of Chicago Press.

Dawdy, Shannon Lee, D. Ryan Gray, and Jill-Karen Yakubik. 2008. *Archaeological Investigations at the Rising Sun Hotel Site (16OR225), Vol. I*. University of Chicago, submitted to Historic New Orleans Collection.

Dawdy, Shannon Lee, and Richard Weyhing. 2008. "Beneath the Rising Sun: 'Frenchness' and the Archaeology of Desire." *International Journal of Historical Archaeology* 11(3):370–387.

Eger, Asa A. 2007. "Age and Male Sexuality: 'Queer Space' in the Roman Bath-House. *Journal Roman Archaeology, Suppl. Ser.* 65:131–51.

Gilchrist, Roberta. 1994. *Gender and Material Culture: The Archaeology of Religious Women*. London: Routledge.

Gilchrist, Roberta. 2000. "Unsexing the Body: The Interior Sexuality of Medieval Religious Women," in Schmidt, Robert A., and Barbara L. Voss (eds.), *Archaeologies of Sexuality*. New York: Routledge, pp. 89–103.

Gray, D. Ryan, Howard Earnest, Benjamin Maygarden, and Jill-Karen Yakubik. n.d. *Archaeological Monitoring and Limited Test Excavations at the Iberville Public Housing Project*. On file, Earth Search, Inc., New Orleans, Louisiana.

Hearn, Lafcadio, and S. Frederick Starr. 2001. *Inventing New Orleans: Writings of Lafcadio Hearn*. Jackson: University Press of Mississippi.

Knopp, Lawrence. 1995. "Sexuality and Urban Space: A Framework for Analysis," in Bell, David and Gill Valentine (eds.), *Mapping Desire: Geographies of Sexualities*. New York: Routledge, pp. 136–149.

Long, Alecia. 2004. *The Great Southern Babylon*. Baton Rouge: Louisiana State University Press. Louisiana Gazette (June 10, 1806): c2 p. 3.

McGinn, Thomas A. 2002. "Pompeian brothels and social history." *Journal Roman Archaeology* 47:7–46.

Rubin, Gayle. 2000. "Sites, Settlements, and Urban Sex: Archaeology and the Study of Gay Leathermen in San Francisco, 1955–1995." in Schmidt, Robert A., and Barbara L. Voss (eds.), *Archaeologies of Sexuality*. New York: Routledge, pp. 62–88.

Schafer, Judith Kelleher. 2009. *Brothels, Depravity, and Abandoned Women: Illegal Sex in Antebellum New Orleans*. Baton Rouge: Louisiana State University Press.

Schofield, John, and Mike Anderton. 2000. "The Queer Archaeology of Green Gate: Interpreting Contested Space at Greenham Common Airbase." *World Archaeology* 32:236–251.

Seifert, Donna J., Elizabeth B. O'Brien, and Joseph Balicki. 2000. "Mary Ann Hall's First Class House: The Archaeology of a Capital Brothel," in Schmidt, Robert A., and Barbara L. Voss (eds.), *Archaeologies of Sexuality*. New York: Routledge, pp. 117–128.

Seifert, Donna J., and Joseph Balicki. 2005. "Mary Ann Hall's House." *Historical Archaeology* 39:59–73.

Shamos, Mike. *A Brief History of the Noble Game of Billiards.* Available at http://www.bca-pool.com/aboutus/history/start.shtml.

Thompson, Shirley E. 2009. *Exiles at Home: The Struggle to Become American in Creole New Orleans.* Cambridge, MA: Harvard University Press.

Tuan, Yi-Fu. 2001. *Space and Place: The Perspective of Experience.* Minneapolis: University of Minnesota Press.

Voss, Barbara L. 2000. "Colonial Sex: Archaeology, Structured Space, and Sexuality in Alta California's Spanish-Colonial Missions," in Schmidt, Robert A., and Barbara L. Voss (eds.), *Archaeologies of Sexuality.* New York: Routledge, pp. 35–61.

_____. 2008. "Sexuality Studies in Archaeology." *Annual Review of Anthropology* 37:317–336.

Wiltz, Christine. 2001. *The Last Madame: A Life in the New Orleans Underworld.* New York: Da Capo Press.

Yamin, Rebecca. 2005. "Wealthy, Free, and Female: Prostitution in Nineteenth-Century New York." *Historical Archaeology* 39:4–18.

SEVENTEEN

SHOWING, TELLING, LOOKING

Intimate Encounters in the Making of South African Archaeology

Nick Shepherd

INTIMATE ENCOUNTERS

The kind of intimacy that interests me here is not intimacy between persons in the past nor between people and objects (although both have their place in the story that follows), but rather the intimacy that arises in the relation between an archaeologist and her or his materials. That is, I am interested in intimacy in the act of knowledge construction. The conception that I have of the site and the moment of knowledge construction is that these are inherently intimate, also ambiguous, unstable, subject to risk and overdetermination. It becomes the job of the disciplinary discourse to normalize and contain this process, to draw off the element of risk and playfulness. It is the job of an analysis like this one to restage the drama and intimacy of these encounters, as a way of understanding better the nature of the discourse and the forms of knowledge that do and do not arise from it. Intimacy, overdetermination, disavowal: such is the tight knot of telling and not telling, showing and not showing, which exists at the heart of each archaeological encounter.

I focus on two historical encounters. Both involve the South African archaeologist John Goodwin (1900–1959) and indigenous people of the Cape (Figure 17.1). What these encounters have in common, besides their approximately coeval nature (both date to the decade of the 1930s) and the fact that they belong to the same general part of the world, is that both are made available to us through sets of photographs in the archive. They also both involve encounters between the person of the archaeologist and sets of bodies framed as objects – black bodies – one group living, the other dead. In the overdetermined contexts of colonialist archaeology, I use these encounters to frame an enquiry into the place of imagination and desire in the making of archaeological knowledge. In the second place, I am interested in forms of public exhibition and display, in the idea of an archaeological gaze, and in a local history of looking. In the third place, I am interested in exploring the resonances that arise among the archive, the photographic artefact, and the body in

FIGURE 17.1. The site of Oakhurst Cave is located about 15 kilometres east of the town of George (marked on map).

the grave. Centrally, I am interested in forms of archaeological and scientific practice and the limits of discourse and in the forms of subtle and overt violence that shadow them and that create their counterparts, the categories of the unspeakable, the unshowable, and the unthinkable.

The first of the two encounters that I describe involved the so-called Tweerivieren Bushmen. This was the same group of N/u-speaking San/ Bushmen that had been exhibited at the Empire Exhibition in Johannesburg in 1936, having been assembled by cultural entrepreneur and Bushman "specialist" Donald Bain at Tweerivieren in the Southern Kalahari. Goodwin encountered them when they were exhibited at the Rosebank Show Grounds, close to the University of Cape Town, in early 1937. The second encounter was with the dead hunter-gatherers of Oakhurst Cave, exhumed by Goodwin over a number of field seasons between 1932 and 1935. Intimate encounters with the newly exhumed dead, the resultant photographs evoke a proliferating set of responses. Intended as acts of impartial capture for science, both encounters became unexpectedly ambiguous and open-ended. There is the question of what Goodwin made of them. There is also the question of what we make of them in a postcolonial present.

A further note by way of orientation: John Goodwin, the South African–born, Cambridge-trained, archaeologist, played a formative role in the development of the discipline locally. The first person to hold a university position in archaeology in South Africa, in 1929 he published (together with Peter van Riet Lowe) a classification of the southern African Stone Ages that remains a standard work of reference (Goodwin and van Riet Lowe 1929). He went on to found the Archaeological Society of Southern Africa and to be the first editor of its journal, the *Southern African Archaeological Bulletin*. The archive relating to Goodwin's life and work is housed in the manuscripts and archives division of the University of Cape Town Library. Along with manuscripts and typescripts, lecture notes, field notebooks, an extensive personal and professional correspondence, short stories, and undergraduate poems, it also contains several thousand black-and-white photographic prints and negatives. Previous studies of mine have focused on Goodwin's unacknowledged black coworkers (styled as "boys"), on the localization of a disciplinary project in archaeology and its role in the development of a distinctive settler modernity, and on aspects of Goodwin's fiction writing (Shepherd 2002, 2003). Part of my own process in writing this study has been the decision not to reprint any of these images here. For those that are interested, they are in the University of Cape Town library and may be consulted. Ultimately, they are where Goodwin left them, in the layered depths of the archive, a kind of death in life. Far be it for me to grant them a second life through republication.

SCIENCE AND SPECTACLE IN THE SOUTHERN KALAHARI

The events of 1936–1937 leading up to the public display of a group of N/u-speaking San at the Rosebank Showgrounds fall into three parts. First, the main protagonist and prime mover of events, Donald Bain, great-grandson of Andrew Geddes Bain, the famous road maker and explorer, set up a camp at Tweerivieren in the southern Kalahari, at the confluence of the Auob and Nossop Rivers, preparatory to taking a group of Bushmen to the Empire Exhibition in Johannesburg later that year. Bain, a "failed farmer and publicist of bushman causes," had a long history of involvement with Bushman affairs at the peripheries of science, including acting as local guide to the quasi-scientific Denver Africa Expedition of 1925. His ostensible purpose in taking the Bushmen to the Empire Exhibition was to pressure the Union government to create a Bushman reserve, as a way of "saving the Bushmen from extinction". Bain drew people to his camp "by enticing them with game". This was followed by a "sorting out process" aimed at extracting "the best specimens for study and exhibition" (Rassool and Hayes 2002: 140, 133).

From the beginning, the Bushmen were subject to intense forms of scrutiny and control. This combined a kind of improvised scientificity, with the updating and modernization of a set of practices in relation to the Khoekhoen and San with a long history in the discourse of the Cape. In July 1936, a University of the Witwatersrand Expedition arrived at Tweerivieren, under the direction of the physical anthropologist Raymond Dart. This was unusual, even unprecedented, in that it involved five full professors from a range of disciplines (in addition to Dart, there were the linguists C. M. Doke and L. F. Maingard, the musicologist P. R.

Kirby, and I. D. MacCrone). With the arrival of the University of the Witwatersrand Expedition, the Bushmen were made to wear "little cardboard dogtags", with their measurements and identifying characteristics. These were added to incrementally as they passed through the hands of the different professors. A medical laboratory was set up in a large, grass-walled enclosure at the centre for the camp. Here individuals were checked for illness or disease, and it was here that physical anthropological and anthropometric studies were conducted. Raymond Dart and his assistant, John Maingard, the professor's son, took detailed physical measurements of the Bushmen, collecting information on facial form, "constitution", and features, bodily habitus and stature, skin and eye colour, hair distribution, the limbs, and "mammae". Close attention was paid to the external genetalia in both men and women, and to evidence of "steatopygy" (Dart 1937b).

A speculative interest in the external genetalia of women, in particular, had been a long running feature of travellers' accounts to the Cape, and a subtext to public displays of "Bushmen" and "Hottentots". This was mainstreamed as part of medical discourse in a paper published by James Drury and Matthew Drennan on "The Pudendal Parts of the South African Bush Race" in 1926 (Drury and Drennan 1926). Dart elaborated on this research at Tweerivieren and produced a typology of Bushman groups based, in part, on the size and shape of the labia minora (in women) and the disposition of the penis (in men). These features were also deduced as indicators of racial "purity". From the site of the grass-walled enclosure, individuals passed to the face-casting section. Bushman subjects were placed on a long table with reeds inserted into their nostrils to allow them to breathe: "An application of damp plaster of Paris was applied to cover [the] face, allowed to dry, and then removed along with facial hair" (Rassool and Hayes 2002). Photography was a central component of the physical anthropological studies conducted at Tweerivieren. James van Buskirk, a member of the expedition, was responsible for a series of anthropometric studies of adult and child, female and male "types". These, together with detailed studies of individual body parts, form an important part of the report on Tweerivieren published in two issues of the journal *Bantu Studies* (Dart 1937a, 1937b; Doke 1936a, 1936b; Kirby 1936). Publicity was an important element of the self-styled "laboratory in the desert". Van Buskirk, who also acted as the official publicist of the expedition, sent regular reports "by a special camel patrol furnished through the courtesy of the Desert Police" (Rassool and Hayes 2002).

IN THE PUBLIC EYE

In September 1936, seventy of the Tweerivieren Bushmen were taken to the university research farm at Frankenwald outside Johannesburg. It was from here that groups daily made the journey to be exhibited at the reconstructed "Bushman Camp" at the Empire Exhibition in Milner Park. Organized to celebrate the fiftieth anniversary of the founding of the city of Johannesburg, the Exhibition was part of a genre of spectacular public exhibitions that had sprung up in the wake of the Great Exhibition of 1851 in the Crystal Palace. It was designed to present the modern face of the Union and its place in the Dominion and included pavilions representing Canada, Australia, and New Zealand, as well as a number of British colonies in Africa

(Gordon 1999). The largest structure was the South African government's four-acre model farm, featuring the world's largest rock garden. The "Bushman Camp" was located in a corner, to the right of the entrance. It featured a number of grass shelters and an open, sandy area for dancing. It was "one of the sensations of the exhibition", rivalled only by a replica of the Victoria Falls, which reportedly used more than 2,000 gallons of water per minute (Gordon 1999: 267). The "Bushman Camp" drew more than half a million viewers, including a record 7,692 in a single day.

A typical show began with a talk by Bain over the public address system. Spectators could purchase an illustrated brochure, which feature an introduction by "Kalahari Bain", and numerous photographs. Visitors were also encouraged to take their own photographs, as a way of capturing the experience. Early in 1937, Bain took fifty-three members of the group to Cape Town. In addition to being displayed in the Rosebank Showgrounds, their itinerary included a symbolic march on Parliament as part of the campaign to create a Bushman Reserve. It also included "an interesting scientific experiment" in which one of the senior women from the group, /Khanako, and four members of her family were induced to pose in the Bushman cast room of the South African Museum, so that as "living Bushmen" they could be compared with the casts made earlier by the renowned modeller James Drury (Rassool and Hayes 2002: 141).

Ciraj Rassool and Patricia Hayes, on whose account I have relied, focus their interest in these events around the life and fate of /Khanako. Begun as an exercise in "biographical rehumanisation", their study develops into something more far-reaching: a searching indictment of the legitimization of forms of racial science and their institutionalisation in the South African academy, as well as a meditation on the violence of ways of looking and of knowing. The events of 1936–1937 looked backward and forward: backward to an embedded set of practices and ideas in the discourse of the Cape, and forward to the growth and mainstreaming of Bushman Studies and Kalahari Studies through the 1950s and 1960s, under the auspices of a range of disciplines (anthropology, archaeology, linguistics, musicology, anatomy). Rassool and Hayes argue that these events constituted a key convergence between science and spectacle. There were two features of the science that emerged. The first was a focus on racial purity, often in the face of "potentially interesting data hinting at massive hybridity in a highly fluid region" (Rassool and Hayes 2002: 137). For example, Dart records but does not develop the information that /Khanako had five daughters, "No. 51, female, /keri-/keri and No. 7, Marta, young women, her daughters by a bushman booi, No. 6 female, klein /khanako (or klein /ganaku) and No. 9 female, kuskai, young girls, her daughters by an unnamed Hottentot, and No. 8 female lena, her daughter by an unnamed European" (Dart 1937a: 162).

This selective focus on "pure specimens" reinforced an image of the Bushmen as a people apart, rather than being a group knitted into society at a complexly changing colonial frontier. A second, and related, feature of the discourse was a salvage paradigm, or "paradigm of preservation", which increasingly informed public and scientific responses to the Bushmen.

WHAT MR GOODWIN SAW AT THE SHOWGROUNDS

Goodwin's photographs of the Tweerivieren Bushmen are contained in six envelopes of prints in Box 98 of the Goodwin Collection. None of the photographs are captioned, although one of the envelopes has "Bushman wizard?" written on an inside flap. The box also includes the original role of negatives from which the prints were made, so that it becomes possible to reconstruct the order in which the photographs were taken. In the spatial rendering of the Bushman display at the Rosebank Showgrounds, it becomes possible to reconstruct Goodwin's walk-path, as he moved among the groups of Bushmen, pausing here and there to snap off a photograph.

The Bushmen were loosely arranged in an open area close to the public stands. Unlike the "Bushman Camp" at the Empire Exhibition, they were exhibited without the benefit of supporting props. Neither was there a clear demarcation of space. The Bushmen stood in groups – a line of men, several groups of women, lone figures, a group of children playing – with the spectators arranged in a half-circle around them. The men and women wore loin cloths or short skirts, but little else. Many had what appear to be an improvised set of accessories. Some of the men wore leg-rattles crossed over their chests like bandoliers. Several wore elaborate headdresses. In some of the photographs, onlookers are visible in the background. Their formally dressed figures contrast with the near-nakedness of the Bushmen; in fact, the distinction between clothed and unclothed figures was one of the features that marked off the observers from the observed in the improvised exhibitionary space.

In some of the early photographs an attempt has been made at an anthropometric front-and-sides approach, but this is quickly abandoned. Most seem simply to record impressions. Goodwin gets in close: a single figure or a row of faces fills the frame. In one image, the heads of a group of women have been cropped, so that they appear as a line of torsos (one woman holds a child to her breast). The photographs are black and white and have a grainy quality. The effect is to aestheticize the scene and to impart to it an atmospheric quality, a kind of stillness. The figures loom out of the surrounding background, frozen in a set of characteristic poses. For the most part, they look at the camera. Their expressions are open but unreadable. This is, after all, an intensely photographed and scrutinised group of persons, certainly one of the most photographed groups of the period. There must be literally thousands of private collections of photographs of the Tweerivieren Bushmen, in addition to their scientific and media representations. Gordon notes that Bain's Bushman displays "set the standard of the emergent current 'tradition' of Bushman displays in South Africa" (Gordon 1999: 266). They also constituted a key moment in a local history of looking, an intense scopic regard, in many cases mediated by the camera and by processes of photographic representation and reproduction. It is possible that there was some form of interaction between Goodwin and his subjects. In some photographs a group of men appear to have been arranged in a straggling line. Many photographs repeat themselves. Groups and individuals appear again and again. A group of women is singled out for particular attention. In fact, in the sequence of photographs, Goodwin is returning to this same group again and again, as he traces his path among the Bushmen.

The profusion here is the profusion of skin, of surface. What can it mean, this proliferation of bodies and parts of bodies – breasts, arms, legs? Persons and parts of persons are photographed and rephotographed, image piled on image. Is this an exercise in compiling information, and if so, what is the nature of this information? Is there a narrative organisation to these images, besides the narrative of Goodwin's own restless movement? Is it hoped that a single, overarching meaning will emerge through repetition, through the adding of ever more detail? If so, this hope is frustrated as meaning is submerged, overwhelmed by sensory impressions and "data". There is at once an excess of impressionistic detail and a paucity of interpretation. Meanings fly off in all directions. Is that a twinkle in "Old Abraham's" eye? Can it be that he is enjoying this accumulated attention? Or is it another privation, a further indignity, in a life of hardship and privation (as signified by his furrowed brow)? A young woman has painted her face with markings intended to signify the onset of menstruation and womanhood. Here is the beginning of narrative, a message of sorts. Yet she appears with painted face over all the weeks and months of her exhibition. Is this another accessory, part of Bain's patter? Do the markings signify anything beyond themselves ("markings intended to signify the onset of menstruation and womanhood")?

The woman with the painted face is young and nubile. She is foregrounded in Goodwin's photographs, as she is in many of the media images of the group. Is this the basis of her appeal? Or rather, in the ambiguous, layered nature of the encounter, what part does this play in her appeal, and in what terms do the different protagonists – the observer and the observed, the photographer and the photographed – know this, describe this to themselves? Can Goodwin say what it is that he saw at the showgrounds? Ultimately, it appears that he is defeated by the open-ended nature of the encounter, by its lack of a convincing meta-narrative. As an encounter in which terms slip out of control, it cannot be "uncreated". Instead, he consigns it to the layered depths of the archive, as a set of uncaptioned images, kept without commentary.

The events around the Tweerivieren Bushmen constitute a significant convergence of science and spectacle. Goodwin's own encounter with them was a hybrid moment, snatching images for science in the midst of a public spectacle. We might imagine this scene of encounter from two perspectives. First, from the perspective of the Bushmen: a figure separates itself out from the crowd. He is carrying a camera, into the viewfinder of which he peers. He steps in close, first to one group, then to another. Sometimes he offers direction, but mostly he just moves among the people, taking photographs. Second, we imagine the scene from the perspective of the crowd of onlookers. One of its number steps forward and moves among the Bushmen, taking photographs. To the choreography of the spectacle – the dancing figures, the children playing, the groups of men and women – is added a new element, a figure with a camera, weaving among the Bushmen, clicking away.

Showing, Telling, Looking

There is an ambiguous play of showing and not showing, exhibiting and withholding, which is deeply a part of the events around the Tweerivieren Bushmen. Dart's report on the University of the Witwatersrand Expedition published in *Bantu Studies* includes more than ninety plates made up of van Buskirk's photographs. A small number of these, the ones dealing with male and female genetalia and steatopygia, were withheld from general circulation and made available in loose leaf only to scientists and research libraries. Reprinted editions of the journal include some but not all of these plates. Rassool and Hayes write of their own struggle to evolve critically accountable forms of practice in relation to the images of /Khanako. When they first presented their paper at a "Gender and Colonialism" conference at the University of the Western Cape in 1997, they made the decision not to show the images. In the resultant debate over "censorship", some of their colleagues argued that the sources should be "quoted", even if visible, so that the readers and audiences could "judge for themselves". In the published version of the paper, they include some of the images of /Khanako, writing, "we must take full responsibility for the new circuits of representation which we have generated in our own academic genre" (Rassool and Hayes 2002: 154).

On the one hand, this ambivalent play of showing and not showing is an admission of uneasiness about the kinds of practices and forms of representation that might legitimately go under the heading of science. On the other hand, it is part of a deeper ambivalence around looking, seeing, and being seen, and the terms under which this takes place. This extended to the motivation behind ethnographic displays-in-life like the Bushman Camp. In preparing for the Empire Exhibition, Bain had to defend himself against charges that the Bushmen were being displayed for purposes of profit and entertainment. The elaborately choreographed science of Tweerivieren was itself part of an attempt to offset such criticism.

Staged as spectacle, the bodies of the Tweerivieren Bushmen invited looking – and not just any looking, but free and uninhibited looking, looking without consequences. They were subject to intense forms of contemplation and "hyperfocalization". To what end did this focussed looking take place? The answer is likely to be complex (information, entertainment, pleasure, desire, data). Part of the point of the exercise was that the Bushmen were available for exhibition in this way; that they could be subjected to certain kinds of looking. Another part of the point of the exhibition-in-life was its repeatability and profusion. What counted was not the specific instance but the general condition, and a specific category within this general condition, the type. The staging of these various encounters specifically excluded the possibility of dialogic interaction and what follows from it, interiority and individuality. The conclusion that this demanded from those who looked was that the nature of things is revealed in their surface aspect. States of mind, forms of culture, ways of being – all are read off from appearances.

As the characteristic artefact of these encounters, the photograph condenses and perfects this objectification. It decisively removes the possibility of dialogue. All is surface, and not just any surface, but the detailed, mimetic surface of the photographic print. At the same time that it suggests an array of possible meanings, it offers its own surface as being indexical of a kind of truth. This is the source of its power, and the nature of its "second life". Each viewing of the image restages the original drama of looking and being seen – not as an event in life but, as it were, through association, through replaying the tropes and ideas that clustered around the original encounter (primitiveness, blackness, sexuality, Otherness, fascination and denial, desire, and fear). At the same time, it recalls the violently objectifying nature of the act. In an interview conducted long after the fact, Ouma /Una Rooi, one of the survivors of the 1936 Kalahari anthropometric research, described some of the photographs as the product of *'n kamera wat verkrag* (a camera that rapes; Rassool and Hayes 2002: 123).

Set in these terms, the question of reprinting the images of the Tweerivieren Bushmen is not supplementary to the telling of the tale but central to it. Neither is this a decision about evidence and "sources". Rather, it raises a set of issues that strike at the foundations of knowledge and a politics of representation. What happens if we decline the invitation in the image? What happens if we refuse to replay these mini-dramas of looking and being seen, these occasions of violent objectification and the banal science that frames them? What if we treat these encounters not as phenomena of surfaces, but of depths? What if we use these photographs as opportunities for asking questions? Every act of looking is predicated on the seeing subject, the one who looks and the one who is seen. These images are not for reproducing, not here, not now, not by me.

LIVING AND DEAD BUSHMEN

The photographs from Oakhurst Cave form a coda to the images of the Tweerivieren Bushmen. Images of another encounter – this time not with the living but with the dead – they invite us to reflect on the different modalities of the archive (the public archive, the hidden archive, the official archive, the illicit archive). The photographs from Oakhurst Cave are semipublic. A carefully edited selection of photographs was published in the extensive report on the Oakhurst Cave excavation (Goodwin 1937). The unpublished photographs attest to the more impromptu aspects of the excavation, but even in the published selection, there is something unsettling, something that is in excess of their purpose. Meant to demonstrate the methodical nature of the excavation and to give information about the disposition of the dead, they also speak of other things: the intimacy of death and interment, the poignancy of the grave, and about care of the dead, and its corollary, grieving and loss on the part of the living.

Oakhurst Cave is a large and productive site on the southern Cape coast, remarkable for the number of burials found there and the richness of the associated material culture. The farm Oakhurst lies east of the town of George, inland from the coastal lakes that characterise the region. It was owned at the time by R. E. Dumbleton, a farmer with some experience of excavation. He reported finding a rock shelter "in an enclosed valley on the farm, containing undisturbed deposits of unknown depth" (Goodwin 1937: 229). Oakhurst Cave is about 4 miles from the ocean and stands about 20 feet above the Klein Keurbooms stream. It faces east and is cut into the southern corner of a high overhanging cliff of sandstone. At the time of its excavation, the shelter was approached by an old elephant path leading down, from the 300-foot peneplain above, through dense forest.

It was probably Goodwin's most extensive and ambitious excavation. He returned to Oakhurst Cave for six field seasons over the course of three years. He had made his name in his 20s as a laboratory practitioner and stone tool analyst. Oakhurst Cave was intended to establish his reputation as a fieldwork practitioner. The extended report on Oakhurst Cave published in the *Transactions of the Royal Society of South Africa* is a model of timely reportage. Goodwin was its principal author, with sections by J. F. Schofield on the pottery, and M. R. Drennan on the skeletal remains (Drennan 1937a, 1937b; Schofield 1937). Mary Nicol, later Mary Leakey (described in the report as "a European prehistorian," p. 244), visited the shelter and excavated "Grave XVII". She also commented favourably on Goodwin's field methods. The idea of method was important to Goodwin. Ten years after the publication of the Oakhurst Cave report, he published *Method in Prehistory* (Goodwin 1945), the first manual on archaeology written for local conditions.

Goodwin's move to install method in the practice of prehistory was part of the modernization of the discipline. He was also reacting against comparatively widespread practices of casual excavation and exhumation. These ranged from trophy hunting to more self-consciously scientific, but often no less casual, harvestings of material. Drennan confirms this in the second part of his report on Oakhurst Cave, on "The Children of the Cave Dwellers", when he notes that it is rare that "such a good series of infant skeletons" should be retrieved from excavation and made available for physical anthropological study. This is because of the delicate nature of the remains. The skull bones are "as thin as paper in certain regions". He writes: "As a result the casual collector usually passes them by in favour of less delicate trophies" (Drennan 1937b: 281).

Goodwin reports that the "greatest care" was taken in excavating "skeletons". Each took an average of twelve hours, using a small bricklayer's trowel and a rubber-mounted distemper brush. This careful practice made it possible to recover "grave furniture", including ostrich eggshells, arrow points and linkshafts, stone implements, grindstones, tortoise shells containing pigment, ochre, ostrich eggshell beads, marine shells, and bored stones. Many of the bodies are foetally flexed. Some lie on beds of sea grass (*Zostera capensis*), material "used as bedding, both by the living and the dead" (Goodwin 1937: 238). Indeed, the dead mirror the living, whose sleeping hollows lie just above them.

The photographs from Oakhurst Cave occupy a number of folders in the Goodwin Collection. Some are mounted on card and annotated. A number are reprinted in large format, six by eight inch black-and-white prints. It was Goodwin's practice with the better-preserved graves to take photographs at regular intervals during the excavation, in some cases as close as ten minutes apart. Meant to indicate order, method, and control, to the contemporary eye there is something more haphazard about the progress that they detail. Sections are cut roughly, rootlets emerge and spread their tendrils, a scatter of tools is left lying about, a skull is rolled out of context and lies gape-jawed on the deposit. The photographs chosen for publication are the most diagrammatic. They show more complete exposure, fewer signs of the work of exhumation. Yet even in these images meanings threaten to overwhelm their purpose, as our responses move in unintended directions (horror, curiosity, sympathy, interest). The intention was that these remains should be proudly captured for science; instead, they excite pity.

Like the ambiguous encounter with the Tweerivieren Bushmen, the riskiness of the act of exhumation and its attendant documentary project is impressed on us by these images. The nature of the revealed material is profuse and threatens to outrun attempts to impose order and meaning. In contrast, what emerges in the written report is thin, attenuated, a mixture of empiricism and what might be called "bare description". Here, chosen more or less at random, is a description of Grave III: "Buried beneath a horizontal white sealing layer at a depth of 48 inches. Fully flexed, lying on right side, facing south, head to east. The entire skeleton was intact and undisturbed.... Smithfield B or C" (Goodwin 1937: 248). Of the opening of Grave VII, he writes, "The skeleton proved to be that of a child of about seven years. Most of the skull was broken. The body was flexed and lay on its right side, facing east, head to the south. A number of shells of Donax serra lay along the spinal column. A girdle consisting of a single strand of ostrich eggshell beads was strung round the waist. Red ochre was present on the skull and the neighbouring bones" (Goodwin 1937: 252). Drennan's reports consist of diagrams of the skulls and tables of measurements. Much of the discussion is taken up with the vexed question of assigning the remains to a "tribe" or "race". Although they resemble "modern Hottentots", he decides that they are better described as part of a "Wilton race" or "pre-Bushman type" (in his tables he describes them as an "Oakhurst tribe").

As a set of representative objects, the photographs from Oakhurst Cave – these images of the remains of the newly exhumed dead, bodies bared for bare description – textualize the experience of exhumation in ways that allow for a more complex response. Our inescapable impression is of the sanctity and intimacy of the grave site and the violence of this act of exposure. Can we talk of pornographies of death and desire? Is there an erotics of exhumation and display at work here, in these tales of living and dead Bushmen (as in a set of practices articulated by a logic of desire)? At what point do we pass beyond the limits of representation, or is there no limit to the pursuit of information and the requirement that all shall be bared, all shall be uncovered?

The Archive, the Photograph, and the Grave

The archive, the photograph, and the grave; each is threaded through by a thematics of death and desire. They are also the characteristic sites for the set of encounters that I have described here. They become sites of emergence of particular kinds of knowledge; as such, they double and repeat one another. The resurfacing of the photograph from the intimate depths of the archive mirrors the act of exhumation. The ghostliness of the grave is repeated in the archive, a site replete with traces, where we simultaneously confront the presence of the past and its irreducible absence. Haunted sites, sites of objectification, intimacy, and violence – they deliver up the disappearing past as bone/light/text. The different modalities of these traces speak to the inner workings of the discipline: the archive, home of the declarative voice of text, site of emergence of a particular kind of knowledge; the grave, sign of an assertive presence, site of fugitive knowledges; the photograph, brimming over with meanings, as intimate as a voice whispered in the ear and as enigmatic as the bone in the grave.

Archaeological imaginaries track between these exemplary sites, just as they track between the living body and the body in the grave. This becomes the basis for an alternative dream topography that imagines the South African landscape as a network of graves, a landscape of sacred sites and sites of interment. A landscape of depths, it also has a surface aspect, as a landscape of traces. The hermeneutic eye of the archaeologist scans this landscape for signs of habitation and past life and is able to interpret the traces left in stone and bone.

Tenderly interred in life, the bodies of the buried dead are exhumed "with the greatest care" by the archaeologist. The sweeping actions of the rubber-mounted distemper brush mirror, in reverse, the actions of the hand that patted the soil home. Bared by excavation, the bodies are subject to a different regime of care and to the logic of the archive. They are numbered, accessioned, boxed, shelved, catalogued. Their reanimation takes place within the strict limits of this logic.

Ultimately, we are confronted with the surprising nature of the exhumed dead. The grave is a place to which the dead of Oakhurst Cave have been assigned to place them beyond the reach of the living, yet here they are among us: partial, decayed, fossilized, articulated, scattered. In the world of their reemergence, their death figures as a double death. They are individually dead (dead to themselves and others), but they also represent a way of life that is dead and in the past – fossil bones and fossil people. This image of death-in-life haunts the Bushmen of these various accounts. It amounts to a status, a way of being, so that we might talk of an ontology of death-in-life. This is true of "Bain's Bushmen", explicitly framed as "living fossils", who had constantly to confront their being as death-in-life (in the encounter with the ghostly "life casts", in the way in which parts of their bodies were externalized as *momento mori*, not least in the act of photography itself). This status of death-in-life continues into the present, in a chain of literal and figurative deaths. Gordon writes of his first visit to Tsumkwe, the capital of the apartheid-inspired Bushman "homeland": "What I saw there on my brief three-day visit was profoundly disturbing. I had never been in a place where one could literally smell death and decay" (Gordon 1992: 3).

In Goodwin's own practice, the living Bushmen of the Rosebank Showgrounds are doubled by the dead Bushmen of Oakhurst Cave, just as the dense semiosis of his photographs is doubled by the "bare description" of his archaeological reports. Is this bare description, this language shorn of imagination, the truth of these encounters? Does it capture their meaning? Perhaps, in fairness, we can say that it captures a kind of truth, a possible meaning, even as we leave the door open for other ways of rendering the truth and meaning of these encounters, in life, in death, and in imagination.

REFERENCES

Dart, R. A. 1937a. "The Hut Distribution Genealogy and Homogeneity of the /?Auni-=Khomani Bushmen." *Bantu Studies* 11:157–174.

———. 1937b. "The Physical Characters of the /?Auni-=Khomani Bushmen." *Bantu Studies* 11:175–235.

Doke, C. M. 1936a. "Games, Plays and Dances of the =Khomani Bushmen." *Bantu Studies* 10:461–471.

————. 1936b. "An Outline of =Khomani Bushman Phonetics." *Bantu Studies* 10:433–461.

Drennan, M. R. 1937a. "The Cave Dwellers (Archaeology of the Oakhurst Shelter, George)." *Transaction of the Royal Society of South Africa* 25:259–280.

————. 1937b. "The Children of the Cave-Dwellers (Archaeology of the Oakhurst Shelter, George)." *Transaction of the Royal Society of South Africa* 25:281–284.

Drury, J., and M. R. Drennan. 1926. "The Pudendal Parts of the South African Bush Race." *Medical Journal of South Africa* 22:113–117.

Goodwin, A. J. H. 1937. "Archaeology of Oakhurst Shelter, George." *Transactions of the Royal Society of South Africa* 25:229–324.

————. 1945. *Method in Prehistory: An Introduction to the Discipline of Prehistoric Archaeology with Special Reference to South African Conditions.* Cape Town: The South African Archaeological Society.

————, and P. van Riet Lowe. 1929. *The Stone Age Cultures of South Africa.* Cape Town: Trustees of the South African Museum.

Gordon, R. J. 1992. *The Bushman Myth; The Making of a Namibian Underclass.* Boulder, CO: Westview Press

————. 1999. " 'Bain's Bushmen': Scenes at the Empire Exhibition, 1936," in Lindfors, B. (ed.), *Africans on Stage; Studies in Ethnological Show Business.* Bloomington: Indiana University Press, pp. 266–289.

Kirby, P. R. 1936. "The Musical Practices of the /?Auni and =Khomani Bushmen." *Bantu Studies* 10:373–432.

Rassool, C., and P. Hayes. 2002. "Science and the Spectacle: /Khanako's South Africa, 1936–1937," in Woodward, W., P. Hayes, and G. Minkley (eds.), *Deep Histories: Gender and Colonialism in Southern Africa.* New York: Rodopi, pp. 117–161.

Schofield, J. F. 1937. "The Pottery (Archaeology of the Oakhurst Shelter, George)." *Transaction of the Royal Society of South Africa* 25:295–302.

Shepherd, N. 2002. "Disciplining Archaeology: The Invention of South African Prehistory, 1923–1953." *Kronos* 28:127–145.

————. 2003. "When the hand that holds the trowel is black . . . ." Disciplinary practices of self-representation and the issue of 'native' labour in archaeology." *Journal of Social Archaeology* 3:334–352.

EIGHTEEN

OBSTINATE THINGS

Mary Weismantel

"Sexual silences" in archaeology: when Barb Voss and Eleanor Casella invited me to write on this provocative topic, I responded immediately. I planned to write a paper on the multiple silences that surround certain pre-Columbian ceramics I call the Moche "sex pots": drinking vessels shaped like human genitalia and bottles about a foot high, bearing small figures engaged in a variety of sex acts (Figure 18.2). They are part of a large corpus of fine ceramics produced on the North Coast of Peru during the first millennium CE (Figure 18.1).[1] Perhaps one hundred thousand Moche ceramics are still in existence, scattered in museums and private collections across the globe; some hundreds of these are sex pots. Almost all of them lack provenience, the product of centuries of looting.

Potentially, the Moche sex pots have a lot to offer. For scholars of sexuality, this is a rare corpus of sexually explicit art made by Native Americans. For archaeologists, Moche may mark one of the few times and places in world history where a state developed independently; it is unquestionably a period of intensifying inequality and the consolidation of elite control. These grave goods from elite tombs could provide insights into the ideological shift that underwrote that critical transformation.

That is their promise – but can it be realized? Once pregnant with meaning, now the pots seem silenced by history: ripped out of the ground by looters, sold to wealthy collectors, encased behind glass in museums, gawked at by uncomprehending strangers. They are silent partly because they are so old; objects of similar antiquity from other places, such as Great Britain, are equally enigmatic (e.g., Orton et al. 2008). As Native American material objects, they have also been subjected to additional, deliberate, violent forms of erasure, as part of the process of conquest and colonial domination.

In the modern period, acts of explicit colonial violence, such as religiously inspired iconoclasm, are infrequent; however, neocolonial scholarship imposes its own kinds of silence. Some writers use these artifacts to articulate their own vision of sexuality and history, oblivious to what the pots actually say. Other scholars find themselves unable to hazard any interpretation whatsoever of something so alien and so are effectively silenced by their encounter with the pots. Indeed, some researchers maintain that works of art without historical or cultural context are simply unreadable. Archaeologists, in particular, are pessimistic about what can be learned from looted

FIGURE 18.1. Map of South America showing the location of the Moche.

artifacts: as Hodder and Hutson assert, an object without a known context is "entirely mute" (2003: 3–4).

As it turns out, this is not entirely a story about silence, however. The more time I spent with actual Moche ceramics in museum collections, the more I became aware that the pots evince a stubborn insistence on communication – albeit on their own terms, which were rather different from what I expected. These experiences changed my perception of the pots as colonized objects; they also transformed my research practices and my understanding of the relationship among colonialism, sexuality, and archaeology.

It is easy for scholars studying the relationship between Europeans and their colonial subjects to assume a comfortably superior position, from which we tut-tut over the iniquities of the past. However, when the artifact in question was created before European conquest, the relationship between the enlightened researcher and the oppressed subject of study is inverted: it is we, not them, who are colonized. Moche ceramics, which were already more than seven hundred years old when Pizarro first arrived in South America, express a Native American subjectivity completely free

FIGURE 18.2. This beautiful drinking vessel now graces the entrance to the Larco Herrera Museum in Lima, Peru. When it was photographed in 1954 by Alfred Kinsey's colleague William Dellenbeck, it was in the private collection of Rafael Larco Herrera. Photograph from the collections of *The Kinsey Institute for Research in Sex, Gender, and Reproduction, Inc.* Reproduced with permission.

of European influence. Their modern silence does not inhere in the objects themselves or in their histories: it originates in ourselves, in our collective intellectual history. It is not so much that the pots are mute as that we are deaf.

Whether we are aware of it or not, and regardless of our personal, family, or genetic history, all researchers working today make use of an intellectual tradition forged through European colonialism, which produces a bias toward the written text that can become crippling when we face the products of nonliterate societies. Our difficulty in "reading" these artifacts might best be described as a kind of inherited learning disability, one that blinds us to some rather obvious aspects of the things we study. Like other cognitive impairments, this one can be overcome with patience and effort; the first and most difficult step is simply to become aware of the problem.

This chapter, then, is not so much about silence as it is about different forms of speech – and our ability to hear them. The first part surveys the accumulated silences that surround Moche ceramics; the second part gives the pots a chance to talk back, and argues that archaeology, because of its focus on material objects from the precolonial past, offers a means to decolonize our scholarship by decentering logocentric forms of analysis and incorporating multiple techniques of interaction between the researcher and the object of study.

By paying close attention to the interactive capacities of objects created by past societies, we can achieve some partial awareness of the sensorial and embodied worlds of the past in all their material specificity. We can thus gain some knowledge not only of Moche bodies, but also of the political economy that motivated the production of those bodies and the material culture that formed, constrained, delighted, and moved them.

PART ONE: THE POTS AS COLONIZED SUBJECTS

I was working with the pots in a dusty storeroom of a small museum. Unlike larger institutions that monitor visiting researchers closely, in this friendly place, they left me to my own devices – and led me into temptation. This museum had several examples of the famous South American whistling effigy pots (Figure 18.3), *and I wanted to play them.*

It was not just idle interest; I was trying to develop an approach to Moche ceramics that would incorporate the study of form, as well as iconography. I had noticed many unstudied details, such as hidden holes that allow liquid to trickle out of a figure's mouth, or a row of perforations on a penis that made it into a little flute; but restrictive museum policies limiting the ways that objects can be handled prevented me from finding out more.

Here was my chance. Hesitantly, I began by blowing lightly across the mouth of the pot without actually touching it – like blowing on an empty soda bottle. The result was electrifying – so much so that I almost dropped the pot. Despite my caution, the volume of sound was incredible. I froze, certain that a guard somewhere in the building would come running. No one did, but I still felt like a criminal. The phrase that immediately popped into my head was, "Rape whistle. It sounds like a rape whistle."[2]

The phrase captured how loud the sound seemed in the empty storeroom; later, I reflected that it might be apt in another sense as well. Literal and metaphorical rapes are a cornerstone of colonial relations; like women who decide to "take back the night," the pot had acted like a colonized body no longer content to suffer in silence.

Colonialism, modernity, sexuality: taken together, these well-worn topics of modern scholarship outline a tragic history of forcible silences, enforced by sexual violence. *Colonialism* takes as its goal the production or imposition of modernity in places where it is categorically absent (Trouillot 2002): this is the laborious task undertaken by the emissaries of European colonialism and their neocolonial offspring – military officers, missionaries, and development workers.

The invention of *modernity*, Foucault told us, is also the invention of *sexuality* – a peculiar regime of speech and silence in which sex is simultaneously silenced and yet produced as a domain of incessant, obsessive discursive activity (Foucault 1990). The same might be said of Native Americans: before colonialism and modernity, indigenous people did not know themselves as Indians and did not "have" "cultures"; a succession of colonial and neocolonial regimes invented the Indian even as they violently and literally obliterated as many indigenous people and "cultures" as they could find (Deloria 1969: 1–2).

FIGURE 18.3. A whistling pot. Collection of the San Diego Museum of Man. Photograph by the author.

Where these two processes of suppression and invention of Indians and sex intersect, the result is a curious inversion. In real life, indigenous sexualities have been produced, coerced, forcibly initiated, and violently suppressed. Yet against this proliferation of actual violence, the ideological production of Indians has perversely depended on an absence: the constant erasure of indigenous people as sexual beings. Or more accurately, indigenous sexualities have not been erased so much as taken away from their possessors and given to White men. I had written about this process in my ethnographic work (Weismantel 2001), and I was surprised to encounter it again, in another form, in the neo-colonial life of the Moche pots.

It started with a comment. When I mentioned to Peruvian male scholars that I was studying the *huacos eróticos*, as the sex pots are known in Peru, they frequently replied, "Oh, I own one of those." The speaker's expression on these occasions was humorous, and rather dismissive. Sometimes there were additional details: the pot sat on a shelf in his office (an appropriately manly place, out of the way of wives and children), and he was not sure, but it was probably a fake.

These conversations made me uncomfortable, but I was slow to figure out why. Maybe it was the gender politics: owning something pornographic is a man's prerogative, and enhances his masculinity. Or the insinuation of cultural capital: this guy displayed "erotic" art on a shelf, rather than hiding a "dirty" magazine in a drawer (and not some tacky fake marketed to tourists, either, but a piece so well made that it just might be real –a possibility subtly raised by the "probably" in "probably a fake").

Ultimately, however, it is the racial undertones that make the reference to "ownership" unsavory. Such discursive gambits are double-edged, reinforcing racial inequality in the present even as they valorize an imagined native past (de la Cadena 2000). When the image in question is a non-White body with exposed genitals, the lighthearted claim to ownership suggests possession of something more than an artifact: on the professor's shelf sits a tiny little Indian whose sexual capacities have been appropriated for his entertainment.

The coup de grace is glossing the *huaco* as unimportant – an amusing little thing, easy to dismiss. It is a successful tactic: talking about it, I feel like the humorless feminist who can not take a joke. However, the claim to triviality matters: twentieth-century artists and intellectuals worked hard to legitimize pre-Columbian and contemporary Native American art by placing it in museums and galleries, but the production of cheap tourist knockoffs and the attitudes of "serious" collectors continue to undermine their efforts.

Although the history of collecting Moche ceramics can be read as colonizing males appropriating colonized bodies, this is one of those places where the objects begin to talk back. Having a naked woman on your shelf, especially one who is being penetrated, sounds pretty racy – until you look at a few Moche pots. The feminine figures on the ubiquitous fakes may please the modern heterosexual eye with their curvaceous, enticing bodies, and pretty faces; not so the women on real Moche pots, who have thick bodies, flat chests, and no butts. Their faces frown ferociously, their lips clamped shut just like the warriors on other pots. They take a matter-of-fact approach to having sex, too, grasping their own thighs firmly in their hands and prying them open, ready for action. As they do so, they sometimes raise one hand in a clenched fist.

If you pay attention to the naked woman on the shelf, then, you realize she is not playing along; rather than acting the passive victim, she looks more like she is mooning us. The pots exhibit the same stubborn independence in other contexts: they are no more compliant toward those who want them to be icons of sexual liberation than when asked to be cute and pretty. Throughout their modern history, they have proved too slippery to be held within any ideological straightjacket, from Catholic attempts at total suppression to the sexological studies of Alfred Kinsey to the claims made by twenty-first-century gay researchers.

The Moche period came to an end after 850 CE, but its legacy shaped the North Coast for centuries to come. The wealthy and powerful kingdom of Chimu built on Moche economic, political, and social institutions[3] and enjoyed the fruits of the same skilled artisanal traditions – including ceramics with sexual themes. After the fall of Tawantinsuyu to the Pizarro brothers in 1532, however, the sex pots were gone for good. Catholic persecution of idolators made it fatally dangerous to make or own a sexually explicit image, and European-inspired ceramic technologies and styles displaced the older ones.

If there were no new sex pots being made, though, the old ones soon began to re-emerge. The Spanish "mined" the lavishly appointed tombs of the Moche elite for gold and treasure (Ramirez 1996); fine pre-Columbian ceramics, often misidentified as Asian in origin, were in circulation in the global art market as early as the eighteenth century. (Further evidence that cultural difference has not rendered these works of art completely incomprehensible: objects created as luxury goods for Moche elites were recognized as such – and coveted – centuries later, by other elites in faraway places.) Moche ceramics entered ever-expanding circuits of exchange that ultimately included Madrid, Berlin, London, Havana, Buenos Aires, New York, Chicago, Los Angeles, Tokyo, and Tel Aviv.

The looting has never stopped. A Google search of the term "Moche" yields objects of varying quality and dubious provenance, offered by sources ranging from fly-by-night operations to prestigious auction houses such as Sotheby's and Christie's. Although archaeologists detest its destructive effects, the history of collecting is closely intertwined with that of archaeology itself. Rafael Larco Hoyle, one of the great Peruvian archaeologists of the early and mid-twentieth century, was an avid, lifelong collector of Moche ceramics (Figure 18.4). He was born into a class of well-to-do landowners on the North Coast who owned lucrative sugarcane haciendas and expressed their regional identity through private collections of local archaeological finds.

Larco inherited a fine collection, added to it throughout his lifetime, and left it to the people of Peru when he died. His status as both collector and excavator is troubling to modern archaeologists; scientific researcher by day, he encouraged the clandestine nocturnal looting of sites and the production of fakes by buying whole pots from local people with a voracious enthusiasm. Like the Spanish before him, he was, in effect, "mining" the land for its natural and cultural resources, and he did so using the labor of men who were born, lived, and died on land owned by the Larco family – a scenario as neo-feudal as Thomas Jefferson digging up Indian sites on "his" land with the labor of African-descended slaves.

This is only one side of the coin, however. It was Larco whose frankly appreciative descriptions of the Moche sex pots established them as legitimate subjects of scientific study – and opened the door to a new perspective on them as visible traces of a premodern sexual freedom. Larco is widely admired among Peruvian anthropologists as a founding father, but his interest in the "erotic" ceramics is often erroneously dismissed as an amusing personal peccadillo. This is a mistake. For Latin American intellectuals of his generation, archaeology was an explicitly anticolonialist science, the handmaiden of the modernist project of creating new

American nations. It offered new, non-European founding mythologies, and a scientific means to rebut the prejudices of the past. Larco's dedication to publishing and displaying the "erotic" themes in Moche art was informed by the modern scientific ideas of his day, and especially by his relationship with American "sexologist" Alfred Kinsey (Weismantel 2008).

For Kinsey, the Moche pots were initially very exciting: they "portray every conceivable thing," he enthused. "This completely discounts any theory that the so-called perversions are a development of our modern civilization' (Kinsey, 1947, quoted in Gathorne-Hardy 1998: 412). Yet although Kinsey traveled to Peru at Larco's invitation, their planned collaboration never materialized. Some of the reasons were personal, but they also stemmed from Kinsey's unabashed cultural prejudices, which made the Peruvian materials seem only marginally important. Then, too, there were methodological limitations: Moche archaeology was in its infancy, and with so little known about the society that produced them, the pots were simply enigmatic.

However, as I have suggested elsewhere (Weismantel 2008), Kinsey's silence may have other causes. Once in Peru and confronted with the totality of Moche ceramic art, he must have seen that it did not represent the prelapsarian sexual utopia he envisioned. Moche potters portrayed the mutilation and dismemberment of naked prisoners with as much delight as scenes of mutually pleasurable sex or solitary masturbation. This raised the uncomfortable issue of sexual violence – one that Kinsey had carefully avoided in crafting his sex-positive message in the politically charged landscape of the United States. Having sidestepped it at home, he was unlikely to embrace it abroad.

In the mid-twentieth century, researchers like Larco and Kinsey needed to prove that the Moche sex pots were apt subjects for scientific study, and they hoped that they would reveal an ancient attitude toward sex that was tolerant but not perverse – by the standards of the mid-twentieth century. In this, they were disappointed; by modern standards, the pots display a kind of polymorphous perversity that only Kinsey's nemesis Freud could embrace.

Today, the pots are once again being used as evidence in a political struggle over sex: Peruvian activists and scholars deploy the Moche to combat denunciations of the struggle for gay rights as a foreign import. As they rightly claim, ancient representations of male–male sex and of androgynous figures that may represent a "third sex" demonstrate the existence of a non-heteronormative sexual landscape completely indigenous to Peru. Nevertheless, the actually existing corpus of Moche sex pots overwhelmingly portray male–female couplings; overenthusiastic claims to the contrary can only be supported through inaccurate copies, blurry photos, and selective descriptions.

At various times, then, Peruvians and outsiders have found liberation in the exuberant diversity of sex acts depicted by the ancient Moche; but today as in the past, the Moche sex pots can only be used to achieve modern political ends if they are deployed selectively. The sex pots are equally resistant to every attempt to fit them into modern sexual categories: close familiarity with the corpus undermines attempts to read them as either heternormative or homosexual, benign or sadistic, repressive or liberatory, as we understand these terms today.

FIGURE 18.4. Rafael Larco Herrera, Alfred Kinsey, and Paul Gebhard in Lima, Peru, 1954. Photograph from the collections of *The Kinsey Institute for Research in Sex, Gender, and Reproduction, Inc.* Reproduced with permission.

This is the best thing about the Moche sex pots. Their most radical potential is not their ability to confirm or justify our beliefs, no matter how liberatory – rather, it is in their steadfast refusal to do so. More than anything else, it is their obstinate insistence that they are not what we think they are that makes them worth listening to – not only because of what it can tell us about the past but because it makes them active participants in the present. Rather than passive receptacles of our visions of sexual and social life, they speak to us about things we do not know in an idiom we must struggle to understand.

FIGURE 18.5. A "rocker" pot depicting a frog and a feline in the missionary position. Collection of the Field Museum of Natural History, Chicago. Photograph by the author.

PART TWO: FROM READING TO PLAYING

One of the first Moche ceramics I saw up close was an unusually large female effigy at the Field Museum (Figure 18.6). It had a rather ferocious face, an enormous protruding vulva, and an unmistakable clitoris. This pot grabbed my attention; but like other researchers before me, I felt silenced by a figure at once graphically explicit and entirely ambiguous. In the months that followed, I avoided her frowning face, and took smaller, more manageable pots down from their shelves to study. But her presence weighed on my mind; that large, unreadable body motivated my search for methodologies better suited to three-dimensional modeled figures. And when I finally took her off the shelf, my interaction with her pushed my thinking further still.

Most of the pots at the Field Museum sat on open shelves, but this one, like quite a few of the other sex pots, was strapped into an elaborate Styrofoam contraption. Not because they were more fragile, as I initially supposed, but because they had rounded bottoms instead of a flat, stable base. This in itself made me think more about the form of most Moche pots: a flat bottom is made to rest on a flat surface, such as a shelf or niche. Combined with their size and the scale of the designs, this facilitates an intimate but disengaged viewing experience. I could pick these pots up, turn them around to see the whole design, then set them down again, step back and contemplate them at my leisure.

In contrast, the pots in the Styrofoam straitjackets invited other kinds of interactions. I liked the pair of copulating animals – a frog atop a feline – who could be set in motion with the touch of a finger, rocking back and forth as though in the throes of sex (Figure 18.5). Although it wouldn't sit still, this pot was made to be set on a flat surface and looked at: first you set it in motion, then sit back and watch the fun. When I took down the big female effigy, which I had mentally christened "Big Mama Cocha," I planned to set her on a table too, so that I

FIGURE 18.6. The "Mama Cocha" still wearing some of her Styrofoam armature. Collection of the Field Museum of Natural History, Chicago. Photograph by the author.

could photograph her. But when I unstrapped her from her elaborate supports, I found that to be almost impossible. Unlike the animals, her ungainly body had no center of gravity that I could discover; I would try to let go, and then grab her again for fear she would fall.

What followed was ludicrous. Too large to hold at arm's length, and too unstable to release, I found that no matter how I approached her, we ended up locked in a close embrace.

This experience of being allowed to hold but not see only made sense to me later, when I turned my attention from bottles to drinking vessels. Most of the elite funerary vessels are stirrup-spout bottles, but a small subset are bowls, which my ethnographic work predisposed me to think of as drinking vessels like the moncaguas *used today in lowland South America* (Weismantel 2009). *One subset of the Moche bowls is the* cochas: *open, concave bowls with an internal convex layer in the shape of a supine woman with an open vulva, which serves as the opening to a hidden interior chamber. If filled with an opaque liquid such as the traditional South American beer known as* chicha, *this whole apparatus would be hidden from the drinker until (s)he had already begun drinking – and realized that the liquid flowing into his or her mouth was gushing out of the Mama's vulva.*

I had unthinkingly labeled the big pot a cocha; but was it? It was surely too big to drink out of, and it was not a bowl. What made it like the other cochas was the open vulva, designed to release liquid into a human mouth. I had not given enough thought to how this pot functioned as a vessel – perhaps intimidated by that enormous spout, which did indeed make her the mother of all cochas.

Armed with the idea of the pot as a vessel, I returned to the Field Museum to grapple with it again. This time I thought not just about holding it up to observe and photograph but instead about drinking. What if someone offered her to me full of beer and said, "Drink"? It would be less an invitation than a challenge – reminiscent of some of the drinking vessels used in Classical Greek symposia, where an audience of one's peers watched in amused anticipation as a drinker struggled to drink from a bowl that was unstable and prone to tip and spill – and that sometimes had ribald paintings on its interior, or even a handle in the shape of a phallus (Lissarrgue 1990).

Suddenly her form made sense – a crazy kind of sense. If I thought about drinking from this pot, instead of *looking at it, I could see that it was indeed possible to cradle her bulky form, with her head in my hands and her feet resting on my upper arms. It felt so comfortable that I was sure this was the intended position – but what I saw was alarming. The open spout was now positioned directly in front of my mouth, so that with the slightest tilt, liquid would come pouring out. And what a drink! Without being able to actually put liquid inside the container, I couldn't be completely sure, but this would almost certainly be a big gushing flow. Furthermore, it looked as though the clay clitoris at the spout's top would impinge upon the flow, perhaps causing it to spurt as it leapt toward my mouth.*

This was a lot to handle – practically and intellectually. Fluids gushing from a vulva hardly seemed like the substance of scholarly discourse, at least in archaeology – and yet I did not want to let my new "finding" go. Once again a Moche pot had pushed the envelope in our relationship, shoving me into a physical intimacy I wasn't sure I wanted, and urging me to write about it in graphic terms that might open me to ridicule. Larco (1965) called these kinds of drinking vessel/sex pots "joke pots"; it looked like this particular pot had found one more butt for its ancient humor.

My interactions with the Mama Cocha contain a particular methodological message, which may be called an injunction to abandon *reading* for *playing*. Our difficulties in reading these objects says something about their long history as colonized subjects – but it also speaks to our own inadequacies as readers, or perhaps about the inadequacy of the idea of reading as a metaphor for the study of precolonial things. Historians of colonialism have perfected techniques for studying literate societies, as well as for using ethnohistoric documents derived from colonial contexts. The subtle, supple techniques they have developed are invaluable, but they are also part of the phenomenon they are studying: it was an intrinsic aspect of colonial domination to carefully maintain particular forms of literacy as defining features of racial, class, national, and gender privilege. Using the tools of colonial domination to develop a critical study of colonialism has been fruitful, but it may inadvertently silence the colonized voices to which it seeks to give voice. Not all objects submit to being read.

European colonialism and EuroAmerican neo-colonialism privileged particular forms of communication, and even particular sensory experiences, over others, and made literacy (and the power to withhold it) into a central theme of colonial history. As a European American child, I was an uncritical adherent to this ideology, utterly captivated by the magic and power of reading. It was only in middle age that I received a different kind of education – and it came from precapitalist, non-European things like the Mama Cocha. So far, what I have gotten from the pots is mostly an *un*learning that has moved me away from texts and toward thinking about more embodied forms of communication.

This might sound like a plea to abandon the disciplined skepticism of the scientist in favor of a form of poetic license, in which sensual enjoyment of a work of art is seen as providing a direct conduit to past emotional and sensory landscapes. This could not be further from what I have in mind. Instead, I am calling for an approach that might be best described as historical materialist. It is materialist in its attention to the things that humans made and that, once produced, became part of the social and material environment that in turn shaped them. It is historicist because it rejects any appeal to a putatively universal set of physical and emotional responses and insists instead on the radical particularity of the experience of embodiment and the deployment of the senses within a specific historical and cultural context. It asserts, with Marx (1932), that "the forming of the five senses is a labor of the entire history of the world down to the present" – that is, that far from immersing us in a universal, ahistorical or biologically driven aspect of the human experience, closer attention to sensory data will teach us a greater appreciation of the difference between the present and the past.

This is a familiar message to scholars of sexuality, who take it as a basic premise that even the most physical and intimate of human acts are shaped by history, culture, and language. Yet although theorists in the field repeatedly invoke the idea of materiality, theirs is a curiously disembodied materialism, reliant on textually derived metaphors (cf. Braidotti 2002; Butler 1993; Foucault 1990). The body is envisioned as a thing of surfaces – a blank canvas, an empty slate. A lot is missing in this picture: a visceral, organic image of physiological processes – respiratory, circulatory, digestive; a conceptualization of interactions between the body and the world, such as penetration, ingestion, and excretion, as necessary prerequisites for continued life, as well as an understanding of how these processes and interactions might be modeled, experienced, understood, or altered within particular social contexts. The spout-shaped vulva of the Mama Cocha seems like a far more powerful and accurate representation of living in a culturally produced body than is the metaphor of bodies written on or even, as Grosz (1995) would have it, tattooed.

These pots, which take the form of bodies full of liquid, with orifices built to interact with a human mouth in very particular (and forceful) ways, have something definite to say about the body – and it is a message very much in keeping with the life and times of their makers, and quite alien to our own. In the European tradition, images of liquid gushing out of orifices embody the antithesis of order: Rabelaisian exuberance, Bakhtinian excess. In contrast, the imposition of social and political restrictions, or of a moral order, is strongly associated with the control of bodily functions. This imagery serves misogynist ends when male bodies are represented as sealed off and therefore clean, whereas females are dirty and leaky. Another familiar opposition is that between pornography, a realm of scopophilic hedonism where everything can be seen and no act has reproductive consequences, and the family, where sex acts and sex organs are veiled in secrecy and are defined as solely reproductive. The Moche sex pots are works of sexually explicit art made expressly to be left in family tombs, including the tombs of women and small children; yet they depict – maybe even demand – bodily flows. In short, they make nonsense of the oppositions between family life and promiscuity, closed and open systems, morality and hedonism that we thought we knew.

The social universe where the Moche sex pots made sense was one in which abundant flows of liquid were legitimate sources of both pleasure and power (Weismantel 2004). Archaeological surveys of the region reveal the expansion of a vast system of irrigation canals in the Moche period that opened up large new areas of fertile agricultural land and underwrote an economic, political, and social transformation (Billman 2002). Thus, the imagery of flowing liquid evoked a nested set of powerful images: water itself, ever-precious in an arid land; rivers pouring down steep slopes from ice-capped mountains to the sea; agricultural fecundity blessed by ancestral power; the strong bodies of workers marshaled to dig trenches and lay stone; and the rivers of beer leaders kept flowing to reward them for their labors.

These images of ecological and economic abundance, and of abundant flows of beer and pleasure, would have resonated for every member of Moche society. Yet the sex pots, which circulated among its most privileged members, were also about the restriction of these flows within socially sanctioned channels. The bodies depicted on these pots, marked with the insignia of rank and privilege, are not ordinary bodies. Nor are their exuberant corporeal flows unlimited: they pass on bodily fluids only to one another. Thus, rather than Rabelasian flows of excess that defy the social order, what we have here are mighty but controlled flows: a representation of bodies and bodily experience that carefully supports the existing political and social order.[4]

Limitations of space prevent me from further exploring the dense symbolism of the Moche sex pots here; I introduce it only to demonstrate the potential of using an embodied methodology that takes historical materialism as its foundation. Although some phenomenological approaches in archaeology may utilize "a somewhat gauzy view of 'meaning' limited to the cosmic and the transcendent" (Smith 2003: 67), attention to interactions between bodies and material objects can be an enormously productive line of inquiry for studying issues of political and economic relations and social inequality. Certainly researchers have found it to be a rich source for understanding the lived experience of class difference (Bourdieu 1984). Through the interactions of elite flesh and finely modeled clay, the Moche sex pots helped form a class of people who could control a rapidly expanding economy and enjoy the fruits of its labor.

This brief encounter with the Mama Cocha illustrates the potential strengths of a research methodology that allows us to play with the things we study. Combining traditional, textually derived methods such as iconographic analysis with a consideration of tactile, aural, and haptic forms of sensory perception in addition to the visual, we may be able to arrive at a multidimensional reading of objects, meanings, and social histories that are otherwise opaque to us and offer a glimpse into sensory and bodily worlds quite unlike our own.

CONCLUSIONS

My experiences with the Moche sex pots suggest that one thing archaeology can bring to the study of colonialism is an interrogation of the hoary question of resistance. Material objects resist our efforts to muffle them or to speak too facilely about them, and they do so in particular ways. They do so, first of all, merely by continuing to exist: unlike so many Native American bodies, peoples, and things that no longer exist except in memory, hundreds of Moche sex pots remain as things in the world, and rather forcefully so.

Precolonial objects have been part of our lives in the Americas from the beginning of colonial times to the present and thus have been a constant presence in our conversations about ourselves. Sexually charged or powerfully gendered images from the ancient Americas, such as the Aztec Coatlicue who inspired Chicana writer Gloria Anzaldúa (1987), have been very much part of ongoing pan-American conversations about what it means to have sex, or to have a sex. The Moche sex pots have been a persistent presence in Peruvian culture throughout that nation's modern history. One might have expected them to vanish with their makers at the end of the Moche period, especially given that they were buried in tombs and so seem intended to disappear from sight. Yet people keep digging them up, and the very multiplicity of meanings claimed for them testifies to their participation in modern as well as ancient history. They are part of the present – and of the future: as things in the world, they contain within themselves the possibility of interactions and communications that have not yet happened.

One such possibility is their contribution to archaeological understanding of the pre-Columbian past. The sex pots can provide important insights into the expanding power of elites on the North Coast during one of the most dynamic periods of political development in the ancient Americas. The sexual imagery on these ceramics concerns more than issues of the body, reproduction, and death. It also speaks to the political and economic questions that have been of greatest interest to Moche archaeologists: warfare and imperial expansion; the ritual torture and execution of prisoners; and elite strategies to maintain social and political dominance through the control of key resources such as water and irrigated land.

The study of these ancient things also has the potential to enrich our understanding of colonialism, and perhaps to alter our own scholarly practice. No one alive today can see the pots as they were seen before Pizarro: our vision has been colonized for five hundred years. However, colonization is always a partial and incomplete process; like Native American material culture in general, these vessels are neither completely mute nor entirely pliable in what they can be made to say. (One can lie about them, of course, misrepresent or simply misunderstand them – but this is just as true when we interact with, or speak of, other living people of our own culture and race, as it is of these obstinate objects.)

Their history is that of other colonized subjects. No longer able to circulate in the social world they once knew and subjected to acts of violence both actual and symbolic, they have nonetheless survived, and occasionally managed to say a few things that are not precisely what their colonial interlocutors hoped to hear. Like other encounters across colonial divides, our meeting with the Moche pots startles us both because they are strange, and because they are not: the sexuality they embody is not our own, and yet in their form and imagery, they speak knowingly, physically, and directly to our bodies. In their exuberant physicality and insistent willingness to interact with human bodies – whether those of the first millennium or the beginning of the third – they remind us that our own capacity to speak to one another is not limited to words.

My goal in this project is to develop a methodology based on playing with and learning from the pots and thus to allow these obstinate objects to teach us something of what their makers knew about sex, about themselves, and about their social world. It is a utopian project: to the extent that we could learn something about the Native American past on its own terms, that achievement would in turn transform our understanding of the Pan-American present. So, too, might the process of learning itself, for it would surely involve a radical decolonization of our own scholarly practice.

NOTES

1. On Moche art and archaeology, see Alva and Donnan 1993; Bawden 1996; Bourget and Jones 2008; Pillsbury 2001; Shimada 1994; Uceda and Mújica 1993. On Moche ceramics, see Castillo 1989; Donnan 1992, 1978; Hill 2000. On the sex pots, see Bourget 2006; Bregh 1993; Gebhard 1970; Gero 2003; Kaufmann-Doig 1979; Larco Hoyle 1965; Weismantel 2004.

2. Largely forgotten today except in misogynist humor, the rape whistle is a curious artifact of the women's movement in the United States. As part of a patchwork nationwide effort to encourage women to fight back against rape, some activists distributed extremely loud whistles to women, with instructions to blow on them if attacked.

3. This is a very simplified summary of a complex chronology, which involved regional rivalries and periods of highland intervention before the rise of Chimu.

4. These meanings are further enhanced if we look at the resonances between the form of the ceramics and their archaeological context in tombs. Archaeological and ethnohistoric evidence from this and later periods suggests that a cult of ancestor worship centered on elite tombs was central to the political ideology through which irrigated systems and the agricultural wealth they produced were maintained and controlled. The tombs where the sex pots were placed were nodes of cultural power.

REFERENCES

Alva, Walter, and Christopher Donnan. 1993. *Royal Tombs of Sipán*. Los Angeles: Fowler Museum of Natural History.

Anzaldúa, Gloria. 2007. *Borderlands/La Frontera: The New Mestiza*. San Francisco: Aunt Lute Books, 3rd edition.

Bawden, Garth. 1996. *The Moche*. Oxford: Blackwell.

Billman, Brian. 2002. "Irrigation and the Origins of the Southern Moche State on the North Coast of Peru." *Latin American Antiquity* 13:371–400.

Bourdieu, Pierre. 1984. *Distinction: A Social Critique of the Judgement of Taste* (Richard Nice, trans.). Cambridge: Harvard University Press.

Bourget, Steve. 2006. *Death and Sacrifice in Moche Religion and Visual Culture*. Austin: University of Texas Press.

———, and Kimberly L. Jones, eds. 2006. *The Art and Archaeology of the Moche: Andean Society of the Peruvian North Coast*. Austin: University of Texas Press.

Braidotti, Rosi. 2002. *Metamorphoses: Towards a Materialist Theory of Becoming (Short Introductions)*. London: Polity.

Bregh, Susan E. 1993. "Death and Renewal in Moche Phallic-Spouted Vessels." *RES* 24:78–94.

Butler, Judith. 1990. *Bodies That Matter: On the Discursive Limits of "Sex."* New York: Routledge.

Castillo, Luis Jaime. 1989. *Personajes míticos, escenas y narraciones en la iconografía mochica.* Lima: Pontificia Universidad Católica del Peru.

De la Cadena, Marisol. 2000. *Indigenous Mestizos: The Politics of Race and Culture in Cuzco, Peru, 1919–1991.* Chapel Hill, NC: Duke University Press.

Deloria, Vine Jr. 1998. *Custer Died for Your Sins.* Norman: University of Oklahoma Press. (2nd edition).

Donnan, Christopher. 1992. *Ceramics of Ancient Peru.* Los Angeles: Fowler Museum of Cultural History, University of California, Los Angeles.

————. 1978. *Moche Art of Peru.* Los Angeles: Museum of Cultural History, University of California, Los Angeles.

Foucault, Michel. 1990. *The History of Sexuality: An Introduction, Volume 1.* New York: Random House [English translation, 1978].

Gathorne-Hardy, Jonathan. 1998. *Sex the Measure of All Things: A Life of Alfred C. Kinsey.* Bloomington: Indiana University Press.

Gebhard, Paul. 1970. "Sexual Motifs in Prehistoric Peruvian Ceramics," in Bowie, Theodore, et al. (eds.), *Studies in Erotic Art.* New York: Basic Books. pp. 104–144.

Gero, Joan. 2003. "Sex Pots of Ancient Peru: Post-Gender Reflections," in Anfinest, Nils, and Terje Oestigaard (eds.), *Global Perspectives on Prehistory: A Conference in Honor of Randi Haaland's Contribution to Archaeology.* British Archaeological Reports, International Series. Oxford: Archaeopress.

Grosz, Elizabeth. 1995. *Space, Time, and Perversion: The Politics of Bodies.* Sydney: Allen and Unwin.

Hill, Erica. 2000. "The Embodied Sacrifice." *Cambridge Archaeological Journal* 10(2):317–326.

Hodder, Ian, and Scott Hutson. 2003. *Reading the Past: Current Approaches to Interpretation in Archaeology.* Cambridge: Cambridge University Press.

Kaufmann-Doig, Federico. 1979. *Sexual Behavior in Ancient Peru.* Lima: Kompaktos.

Larco Hoyle, Rafael. 1965. *Checcan.* Geneva: Nagel.

Lissarrague, Francois. 1990. *The Aesthetics of the Greek Banquet: Images of Wine and Ritual* (Andrew Szegedy-Maszak, trans.). Princeton, NJ: Princeton University Press.

Marx, Karl. 1932. "Private Property and Communism". From the Third Manuscript of the *Economic and Philosophic Manuscripts of 1844.* Online version of the book published by Progress Publishers, Moscow, 1959; Transcribed by Andy Blunden in 2000, and corrected by Matthew Carmody in 2009. Martin Mulligan, translator. http://www.marxists.org/archive/marx/works/1844/manuscripts [accessed 21 May, 2011].

Orton, Fred, Ian Wood, and Clare Lees. 2008. *Fragments of History.* Manchester, England: Manchester University Press.

Pillsbury, Joanne, ed. 2001. *Moche Art and Archaeology in Ancient Peru.* Studies in the History of Art 63. Center for Advanced Study in the Visual Arts Symposium Papers XL. Washington, DC: National Gallery of Art.

Ramirez, Susan. 1996. *The World Upside Down: Cross-Cultural Contact and Conflict in Sixteenth-Century Peru.* Stanford, CA: Stanford University Press.

Shimada, Izumi. 1994. *Pampa Grande and the Mochica Culture.* Austin: University of Texas Press.

Schmidt, Robert, and Barb Voss, eds. 2000. *The Archaeologies of Sexuality.* New York: Routledge.

Smith, Adam T. 2003. *The Political Landscape: Constellations of Authority in Early Complex Polities.* Berkeley: University of Chicago Press.

Trouillot, Michel-Rolph. 2002. "The Otherwise Modern: Caribbean Lessons from the Savage Slot," in *Critically Modern: Alternatives, Alterities, Anthropologies.* Bloomington: Indiana University Press, pp. 220–237.

Uceda, Santiago, and Elias Mújica, eds. 1993. *Moche: Propuestas y Perspectives.* Trujillo, Peru: Universidad National de La Libertad.

Weismantel, Mary. 2009. "Have a Drink: Beer and History in the Andes," in Jennings, Justin, and Brenda Bowser, (eds.), *Drink, Power, and Society in the Andes.* University Press of Florida.

_____. 2008. *The Silence of Kinsey.* Invited lecture, Department of Anthropology, University of Chicago.

_____. 2004. "Moche Sex Pots: Reproduction and Temporality in Ancient South America." *American Anthropologist* 106(3):495–505.

_____. 2001. *Cholas and Pishtacos: Stories of Race and Sex in the Andes.* Chicago: University of Chicago Press.

CONCLUSION

NINETEEN

SEXUALITY AND MATERIALITY

The Challenge of Method

Martin Hall

SEXUAL EFFECTS

Sexuality's particular quality is to be both intensely private, personal, and sensory and also public and definitive of the structures of social and economic organization, everywhere. As such, sexuality may leave no material trace and may be denied or disguised in written records, persisting only in the ephemera of memory. But at the same time, sexual norms or prohibitions may shape assemblages of artifacts, the organization of domestic space, the design and construction of institutional buildings, and the layout of cities and landscapes. This play between the personal and sensory and the public and material is a rich and provocative theme that runs through all the chapters in this book.

Developing an archaeology of sexuality – one of the ambitions of the project that resulted in this collection of essays – requires that the particular duality of the private–sensory and the public–material is made explicit and more general. As with all disciplines, archaeology is what archaeologists do. If there is to be an archaeology of sexuality, there needs to be attention to "method," to the hermeneutical processes that move backward and forward between conceptualization and evidence, progressively building up our understanding of the world.

My objective here is to use the rich and varied material in this set of essays to draw out some of these methodological strands. This takes the form of an extended dialogue with Casella and Voss's framing introduction, and with Voss's opening essay, "Sexual Effects: Postcolonial and Queer Perspectives on the Archaeology of Sexuality and Empire." After drawing out some key themes, I make the case for an emerging methodology along a set of overlapping vectors. Taken in combination, these interpretive vectors constitute a significant advance in our understanding of how sexuality is embrocaded in colony and empire, and the ways in which materiality is central to an archaeological interpretation of sexuality. By using some of my own work on sexual effects at the Dutch and British colonial Cape of Good Hope as a foil, I suggest a schema for a rounded methodology for an archaeology of sexuality.

In her opening chapter, Voss emphasizes the need to build a bridge between two bodies of scholarship. The first is the gathering interest in the sexual politics of empire. Coming from feminist and postcolonial scholarship, this work has focused in particular on the European empires of the nineteenth and twentieth centuries, and the ways in which they were organized and functioned. The second strand is the growing momentum of interest in the archaeology of colonialism, and a heightened awareness of the discipline's own origins in the processes of colonialism. These maturing interests have resulted in valuable explorations of creolization, ethnogenesis, hybridity, and syncretism – themes that, in turn, point toward what Voss calls "the intimate entanglements produced through colonial encounters." This broader platform of work on empire, colony and reflexive practice provides a firm foundation for an archaeology of sexuality, of "sexual effects."

Understanding the effects of sexuality within the organizational forms of empire or colony (or, for that matter, within any form of social organization) requires that, a priori, normative assumptions are suspended and interrogated. This is particularly so with sexuality, as Voss emphasizes. Just as the "reflexive turn" of critical archaeologies of colonialism require archaeologists to be aware of their own potential role in colonial processes, so a critical archaeology of sexuality must be enabled by an awareness of the influence of the archaeologist's sexual preferences and assumptions about sexual normality. In particular, there can be no assumption that the processes of colonization and imperialism are invariably heterosexual, or that the expressions of sexuality are inevitably confined to private and domestic spaces. Sexuality, in other words, is "a culturally contingent formation."

CONTESTING ASSUMPTIONS, RECENTERING GENDER AND SEXUALITY

In bringing together these essays, Voss and Casella are clear that, as an archaeological project, materiality will form a strong, unifying thread, noting that these varied studies "all fundamentally consider how an interrogation of *materiality* itself illuminates the embodied, objectified, spatial, reproductive, and sensual dynamics of these new social interactions" (Casella and Voss, Chapter 1, this volume). In exploring the methodologies that enable these studies of material sexuality, I have found it useful to separate out four strands. The first of these challenges assumptions that the heterosexual way is the only way, offering new, and often provocative, explanations of archaeological evidence. The second dimension abandons assumptions of scale, the taken-for-granted that sexuality is to be found only in the privacy of confined and restricted spaces. Third, and building on the ruins of assumptions of heterosexuality and domesticity, authors in this collection seek, in varied ways, to locate sexuality at the core of colonial and imperial processes. Fourth is the persistence of violence, coercion, and persecution – the forces that aid and abet assumptions of heterosexuality and patriarchy in the first place.

Five essays in this collection together illustrate the Pandora's Box of possibilities that emerge if assumptions of heterosexual normality are suspended and interrogated. Their combined effect is the more powerful because of their range in space and time: the Mediterranean, South America, Australia, Africa; from the first century BCE until a century or so ago.

Kay Tarble de Scaramelli, Mireia López-Bertran, and Mary Weismantel each take a new look at conventionalized parts of the broad archaeological narrative, where many would probably assume that the primary dimensions of interpretation have been settled for some time. In reexamining manifestations of Spanish imperialism along the Orinoco frontier, Tarble de Scaramelli notes the general heterosexual and patriarchal set of assumptions that White European men simply overran submissive and feminized indigenous communities – "dark, untamed, virgin territory." These assumptions serve to mask the creative roles of indigenous women in negotiation, resistance, and the *mestizaje* process. And once the assumed dominance of patriarchy and heterosexuality is removed, the evidence points to other possibilities: "under the colonial regime some indigenous women were empowered by their productive capacities both in the biological and agricultural realms and sought to negotiate social mobility through conversion to Catholicism, commodity production for personal economic gain, and, in some circumstances, sexual favors, concubinage, or marriage outside of their birth community" (Tarble de Scaramelli, Chapter 9, this volume).

Similarly, Weismantel takes a new look at those Peruvian ceramics with exaggerated genitalia and sexuality – the Moche "sex pots." These have long been assigned to an uncritical category of pornographic amusement, a lazy assumption facilitated by the tendency of male archaeologists to collect and display them as risqué possessions. Abandoning these long-standing assumptions frees Weismantel to explore new interpretations of the sex pots' role and mode of use. López-Bertran is also interested in clay figurines, in her case from the Punic town of Eivissa in about 600 BCE. Like Tarble de Scaramelli and Weismantel, López-Bertran's essay shows the interpretative possibilities that become evident once stultifying, normative, assumptions about sexuality and gender are set aside.

In contrast, Eleanor Casella and Lindsay Weiss have opened up areas of archaeological inquiry beyond the traditional boundaries of the discipline. Although this means that they have fewer long-cherished archaeological assumptions to dismantle, they still need to clear away the consequences of heterosexual interpretations of colony and empire. Casella's interests are in gender and sexuality in Australia's nineteenth-century penal system and the dynamics of domination and resistance by women caught up in this quintessentially Victorian system of colonization and patriarchal morality. Her point of entry into this system of interpretation is an ambiguity that disturbed those who designed and justified transportation and incarceration – the question of children born to convict women. These prison children were both innocents and evidence of their mothers' illicit sexuality. Casella shows how prison design and structure became "ambiguous theatres of conflict" within the British penal colonies. Her argument is that, by means of the built environment, the colonial bureaucracy tried to cleanse its convict subjects of their sexuality and restore its power as a surrogate paternal authority. By turning heterosexual dominance into the subject of inquiry rather than the assumption in interpretation, Casella throws new light on the well-trodden ground of control, punishment, and the Foucauldian panopticon.

Weiss's essay is concerned with forms of control and resistance a little later in the nineteenth century and on the South African Diamond Fields. Although half a hemisphere away from Australia by sea, South Africa was of course part of the same imperial project and was shaped by similar normative assumptions, often carried by administrators who saw colonial service on both continents. Not surprisingly, then, the conventional landscape of the Diamond Fields has been portrayed as overwhelmingly patriarchal and heterosexual – communities of tough and ruthless men, served and serviced by subordinate women. Weiss's work shows how this ideology was made tangible through domestic accoutrements such as fine tablewares, imported over many miles of rough roads to give the semblance of domesticity in the incongruous setting of a hastily constructed bush camp. Later, as the colonial foothold is strengthened, these structures of domesticity are given more substance through the bungalowed villages built for Diamond Field administrators, each a ground plan for heterosexual normality. But, as Weiss shows, this carefully constructed mythology is blown apart by the custom of same-sex mine marriages that emerged in the segregated barracks for male laborers in South Africa's mine compounds. Here, older and younger men formed emotional and sexual bonds, moving seamlessly from homosocial relationships to heterosexual bonds when their terms of servitude were up. Again, close study of the evidence, unshackled from a priori assumptions, shows just how misleading generally held assumptions of a heterosexual world order can be.

Abandoning assumptions of a normative heterosexuality, then, frees interpretation from the confines of closed domestic spaces. In turn, this opens up the possibilities of sexual effects that are manifested at a range of scales. Three studies in this volume show how this can work at, respectively, the scale of the settlement, the urban quarter, and the city as a whole. By opening up scale in this way, an archaeology of sexuality can take on board a vast new array of material evidence.

Mgoli is a complex of buildings on a nineteenth-century Zanzibar slave plantation and one of the Omani colonial footholds on the East African coastlands. Although the main, five-roomed stone structure was clearly the primary residence of the plantation owner, Sarah Croucher (Chapter 5) develops a compelling argument that a second building, forming the opposite side of a compound, was occupied by a woman held in concubinage to the plantation owner. This architectural interpretation is supported by the excavated artifact assemblages, complementing both documentary evidence and oral traditions on the island. Croucher's archaeology challenges normative assumptions about both the layout of Islamic colonial households and the roles of women and their opportunities for achieving social position and power. Concubines, Croucher shows, were trained to use their sexuality to advance their opportunities and to overcome some aspects of servitude.

San Jose's nineteenth-century Market Street precinct is a case study for sexual effects at a larger scale, with two city blocks serving as home for some 1,000 Chinese immigrants from the early 1860s until a catastrophic fire in 1887 (Voss, Chapter 11). Here, as with Chinese immigration generally in the nineteenth-century United States, sexuality was controlled and directed by legislation. Severe restrictions on female immigration created all-male shared households within the Market Street precinct and split families, with wives remaining in China's Guangdong province. As with the all-male barracks within South Africa's mine compounds, these local conditions of colonialism shaped consequent social and economic structures that are essential to interpreting the archaeological traces, whether these are building structures, spaces, or artifact assemblages. As with women living as concubines in contemporary Zanzibar, Chinese men in San Jose's Market Street precinct fashioned specific and creative ways of ameliorating the conditions of their servitude.

New Orleans ratchets up the scale of sexual effects to the city itself: "New Orleans as a feminine figure is remarkably vivid and persistent, and of a particular character. New Orleans is not simply feminine; the city is imagined as a sexually experienced woman wise in the ways of commerce. Sometimes she is the welcoming, aged courtesan. Other times she is a tragic, fallen figure" (Dawdy, Chapter 16). Shannon Dawdy's chapter explores the ways in which this cityscape became both gendered and sexualized. She focuses on the New Orleans district of Storyville, famed from 1897 until 1917, when it attracted the full force of the U.S. Navy's moral opprobrium. Again, the key to this interpretation is freedom from assumptions of heterosexual, domestic normality. Dawdy shows how the combination of a stable and growing class of propertied, free women and an influx of large numbers of unattached male travelers of all classes created an urban economy dominated by the demand for sexual services. This, in turn, shaped the physical structure of the city and the utilization of its buildings, and the attendant urban mythology that lived on for decades despite, or perhaps because of, the Navy's prurience.

Once the assumption of domestic heterosexuality is knocked off its interpretative pedestal through close studies such as these, the valency of sexuality and gender must be seen as closer to heart of colonialism and empire. Essays in this volume demonstrate this for the Phoenician world, Brazil, Honduras, and colonial Louisiana; there can be little doubt that these cases could, and will, be matched by many more.

Ana Delgado and Meritxell Ferrer compare two Phoenician colonial settings, the southern Iberian Peninsula and western Sicily, between the eighth and sixth centuries BCE. Artifact assemblages from Cerro del Villar, close to modern-day Malaga, provide evidence of ethnically mixed domestic groups, an interpretation that is supported by foodways and funerary practices. Delgado and Ferrer argue that domestic groups combining women of indigenous, colonial, and mestiza origins represent distinctive gender relations shaped by Phoenician colonialism in ways that have not been adequately appreciated. Pedro Funari and Aline de Carvalho make a similar point in the very different context of Palmares, an inland settlement of runaway slaves in seventeenth-century Brazil. Funari and de Carvalho track the historiography of Palmares and its shaping influences. These interpretations have invariably been shaped by a normative heterosexuality, and none is satisfactory; Funari and de Carvalho make the case for looking to polyandry as the organizational keystone of Brazil's history as colony, and in empire.

Russell Sheptak, Kira Blaisdell-Sloan, and Rosemary Joyce's reexamination of the evidence for gender in colonial Honduras shows how both archaeological and documentary evidence point to changing concepts of masculinity as central to the nature of the interaction between indigenous communities and the Spanish Empire. Excavations at the town of Ticamaya tracked how the position of militarized young men changed within the community as their cohorts gained in importance in the face of the Spanish military threat. This was reflected in artifact sets such as arrow points and urban defensive structures. Parallel documentary evidence, read in the context of the archaeological data, revealed the complexity of identities and gender relations at the frontier.

Diana DiPaolo Loren has a similar set of questions for Colonial Louisiana. Here, the indigenous community was the Natchez and the colonial power French, rather than Spanish. Nonetheless, the centrality of gender and sexuality in the confusing, turbulent world of the frontier places the interpretation of the Grand Village of the Natchez in the same frame as Honduran Ticamaya. Loren explores the paradox that intermarriage between native women and French men was permitted to allow for the growth of the colonial population; at the same time, historical documents authored by government officials and missionaries resound with anxieties regarding the impact of interracial intimate relations on French subjects. The ambiguity that this paradox generated is expressed in the materiality of these intimate sexual relationships, in the dress and body adornment of Natchez women, and in the desire that this engendered in French men:

> Glass beads were the materialization of intimate relations with the French, relations that that had reshaped their community and sense of self. . . . To wear glass beads was to transform the body, to physically embody new understandings of self that were actualized through their intimate associations with the French. The French did not share these same fashions of adorning the body with glass beads; it was too far from what sumptuary laws dictated regarding how they held and performed their bodies. These sartorial differences were at the heart of the creation for the desire for Natchez bodies, beaded, adorned, resonating in seductive ways that were strongly heard in colonial narratives. (Loren, Chapter 7)

It is also clear that the sexual effects of colony and empire can have indirect consequences, well away from any frontier of direct interaction. This is well demonstrated by Kathleen Hull's work in epidemiology (Chapter 8). Her case study shows that the Awahnichi experienced substantial disease-induced population decline approximately fifty years before face-to-face engagement with nonnative people in their traditional territory in the Yosemite region of California's Sierra Nevada. It provides perspective on choices made by native people in more traditional colonial settings and the potential consequences of forced change in such practices within institutional colonial contexts in other times or places.

The theme of violence, coercion, and persecution runs through many of the chapters in this volume: Casella's exploration of the institutionalized violence and repression directed against woman and children in convict-era Australia, itself part of a wider colonial society predicated on violence; Weiss's documentation of the racial and sexual oppression of early segregated labor practices in colonial South Africa; Croucher on the gendered repression of Omani colonialism and the ways in which women were obliged to use their sexuality to carve out small zones of personal autonomy; Voss's labor regimes, many of which were based on coercion or designed as instruments of wide-scale repression; Sheptak, Blaisdell-Sloan, and Joyce and the sexual repression and violence of Spanish colonialism in Honduras, essential to the survival of the dominant invaders; and Funari and de Carvalho's review of the historiography of Palmares, forged in the violence of enslavement, resistance, and conquest – persecution that continues in homophobic attacks and the repression of open discussion of sexual effects in contemporary Brazil.

Three case studies can serve to demonstrate the range of gendered violence and coercion at the heart of colonial and imperial projects. The male gladiator is an icon of gendered violence. Renata Garraffoni uses the archaeology of epigraphs to reexamine the standard interpretation of gladiatorial identity. Her interest is in understanding the complexity of the gladiator's position in the nexus of gender, sexuality, and violence. This method – and evidence – frees the interpreter from the views of the elites whose views dominate the conventional textual sources. The gladiators' tombstones, erected by their wives or friends to commemorate their deaths, provide evidence of the complexity of human relations in the Roman past. Garraffoni argues that a gendered approach to the tombstones can help us to rethink some aspects of the gladiators' daily lives from a different point of view.

In contrast with the raw violence of spectacle is the coolly considered psychological violence of the female prison, which Eleanor Casella shows was designed and built with the clear purpose of ensuring that women could hear their children playing while being denied any contact with them. Because the prisoners' work area was accessed by passing the wooden fenced children's area and internally separated from it by a thin brick wall, convict women had to work all day to the sound of the Nurseries. "Allowed no official contact with their infants, these women inhabited an institutional landscape designed to engender a painful yearning for the affectionate bonds of motherhood" (Casella, Chapter 3).

Then there is the violence of representation and interpretation and the use of monuments and records to obliterate or distort the historical record and to buttress a patriarchal reading of the past. This is exemplified in Patricia Rubertone's essay on monumentalization in New England. Rubertone argues that the monumental oversights that underrepresented native women were one of the many ways colonialism attempted to shape their lives. Their underrepresentation in monuments marginalized their influential roles as community leaders and cultural nurturers. Such symbolic violence was intended to divorce them from the landscape by imposing gendered behaviors that discouraged their movements in public space.

TOWARD A METHODOLOGY OF SEXUAL EFFECTS

How can these insights, interpretations, and exemplars be welded together as a working methodology for an archaeology of sexuality? The cases in this volume, with their geographic and chronological span, provide a good opportunity for a thought experiment. By treating this set of assemblages as a set, organized along appropriate vectors, the underlying methodologies that they share become apparent. Equally important, key limitations also become clear, pointing to the further development that will be required to delimit a complete methodology for identifying and studying sexual effects in archaeology.

There are twenty-four distinct assemblages that span the chapters in this volume, ranging from collections of ceramics to the layout of buildings in urban spaces. Most are conventional archaeological sources, some less so. Each is defined and described in Table 19.1, which also references the chapter that provides the full description and context of the evidence.

Table 19.1. Archaeological assemblages, by chapter

Assemblage	Chapter	Description
Ross Prison children's toys	3	Anticipated assemblage of children's toys in area of building designated as a nursery
Ross Prison design	3	Architectural design and excavated layout of prison buildings
Half-Way House assemblage	4	Mixed assemblage from residential area, including ceramics, glassware, and faunal remains
South African mine barracks	4	Design of mine barracks, contemporary documents, and oral accounts of gifts and domestic belongings
South African overseer village	4	Architectural design of model village, spatial layout of settlement, and individual house designs
Zanzibar compound	5	Residential compound, including house of plantation owner, other buildings and spaces
Zanzibar woman's assemblage	5	Assemblage of personal belongings, including women's jewelry
Eivissa figurines	6	Collection of clay figurines from domestic settings and funerary contexts
Natchez dress and adornment	7	Documentary and archaeological evidence for personal adornment, including glass beads
Awahnichi site distribution	8	Distribution and density of archaeological sites across the landscape
Orinoco ceramics	9	Indigenous and imported ceramics from mission assemblages
Ticamaya arrow points	10	Obsidian arrow points excavated from household settings
Ticamaya fortifications	10	Modifications to buildings within settlement to provide for improved fortification
Spanish colonial documents	10	Contemporary accounts of the frontier by military forces
Presidio of San Francisco	11	Excavated assemblages from living areas within fortified military area
Market Street in San Jose	11	Design of building and spaces across a set of city blocks
Phoenician households	12	Domestic assemblages and food remains from households
Gladiators' epigraphs	13	Sets of engraved tombstones with brief epigraphs in memory of deceased
New England monuments	14	Monuments erected to memorialize indigenous communities in colonized landscapes
Palmares	15	Archaeological assemblages, architectural evidence, and documentary sources for settlement
New Orleans	16	Archaeological assemblages and contemporary accounts of city
Tweerivieren Bushmen	17	Anthropometric records and body casts of sample of indigenous people
Goodwin's photographs	17	Archival collection of photographic negatives and prints of indigenous people
Moche sex pots	18	Collection representative of tradition of anthropomorphic clay figurines and vessels

As Voss points out in her introductory essay to this volume, the cultural contingency of sexuality challenges the value of any comparative analysis that assumes a normative stability; having deconstructed assumptions of heterosexuality, and of sexual effects as confined to private and contained spaces, it would hardly be appropriate to impose an alternative fixed framework. This means that comparison is better based on characteristics of instability, on vectors, understood as directions of movement.

One such vector is the movement from the normative to the transgressive. This is to recognize that sexuality ranges from the intensely personal to the overtly public and is closely related to asymmetries of power. It acknowledges the play between desire and repression and connects with widely used analytical concepts, such as the distinction between public and hidden transcripts and between domination and resistance. An example of a stridently normative statement from this collection of evidence is the design of the overseers' village on South Africa's nineteenth-century Diamond Fields, telling all the world that heterosexual domesticity was the essence of civilized order. An example of transgression is the illicit desire that Natchez women's dress provoked in French colonists. Other cases can be arranged in intermediate positions along the normative–transgressive vector.

A second vector is the degree of tangibility of the expression of sexual effects, ranging from enduring and deliberately conspicuous expressions (such as the fortifications at Ticamaya or the monuments in the New England landscape) to manifestations that may be sensory and without material or verbal traces. Because materiality is at the heart of archaeological method, understanding the dynamics of this vector is central to the concept of an archaeology of sexuality: "Sexuality is understood as the most material and bodily realm of social life yet simultaneously is considered to be ephemeral and immaterial, leaving little lasting trace. Archaeologists studying sexuality must grapple with this paradoxical formulation as we seek to interpret the material traces of the archaeological record" (Voss, Chapter 2).

These two vectors can be expressed as intersecting axes (Figure 19.1). This, in turn, creates four quadrants, each of which anticipates different kinds of expressions of sexual effects. The most widely understood, from an archaeological perspective, is the lower right quadrant; material expressions of the dominant order. Work in this area, of course, has a long tradition that embraces a range of theoretical positions. The lower left quadrant – intangible statements of the dominant order – is also well understood, but more from other disciplinary perspectives such as history and anthropology. Here, the methodological challenge is to work across the disciplinary boundaries to ensure rounded interpretations. The more difficult areas of work are in the upper two quadrants, understanding material and immaterial expressions of transgression, ranging from challenges to the dominant order through to closed and interpersonal sexual effects that may leave no material trace.

In turn, this organizational framework can be used to arrange the twenty-four data sets of interest here (Figure 19.2). Not surprisingly, most fall into the familiar quadrant of material expressions of normative conventions and behaviors. The design of the Ross Prison and of the South African overseer village are assertive, highly visible statements of patriarchal control. San Jose's Market Street and the monumentalized New England landscape are equally visible but, perhaps, more

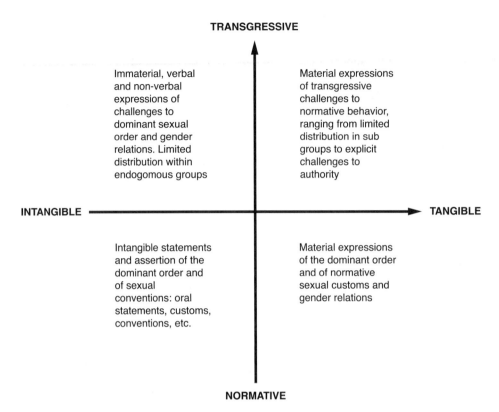

FIGURE 19.1. Grid One: vectors (directions of movement) in an archaeology of sexual effects.

contestable, whereas Tacimaya arrow points and fortifications and Awahhnichi site distributions are clearly normative but less tangible. The New Orleans cityscape and Moche sex pots are material expressions that function close to the boundary between the normative and the transgressive.

There is also a good representation of material expressions of the transgressive. The limit cases here are the South African mine barracks and Palmares. The former combined sexual homosocial relationships, expressed in just-tangible gift exchanges as expressions of commitment and affection, with the participants' ability to move seamlessly into heterosexual household arrangements as circumstances changed. Palmares has challenged Brazilian and colonial normative assumptions since the seventeenth century and continues to do so today.

The paucity of cases that fall in the upper left and lower left quadrants reflect the "paradoxical formulation" at the heart of an archaeology of sexual effects, and therefore the key methodological challenge for an archaeology of sexuality. Sexuality may operate, simultaneously, at the sensory and interpersonal level and in the public and explicit domain: illicit sexual relationships between women in the Ross Prison (Casella 2000) and the use of penal architecture to impose a moral order; homosocial and sexual partnerships in the mine barracks and ideals of Victorian heterosexual domesticity in the bosses' village. Even the most normative assertions of required gender relations and sexual behavior may be intangible – for example, order of preference in ceremonial processions, bodily gestures, and oral expressions

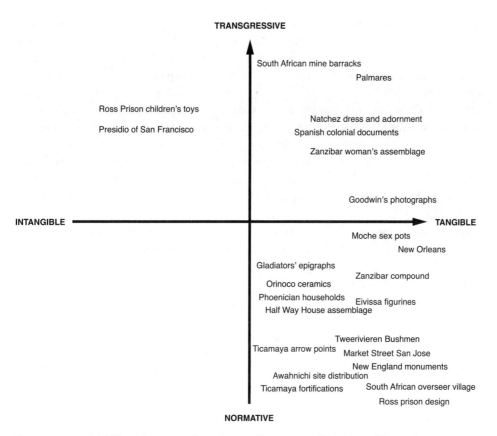

FIGURE 19.2. Grid Two: data sets plotted according to tangible–intangible and normative–transgressive vectors.

of respect and authority. Although the limits of materiality are a problem for many areas of archaeological interpretation, they are a particular difficulty for an archaeology of sexuality that aspires, as do the contributions to this volume, to understand the continuities between intimate and public expressions and behaviors.

How can this set of cases be "stretched" to achieve a methodological suite that covers the full extent of both vectors and that can operate in all four quadrants that their intersection creates? My own work looking for the role of race, gender, and the subaltern expressions of slaves and the underclass at the Dutch and British Cape of Good Hope serves as a point of departure for bringing this methodological suite together.

A Dutch East India Company outpost was established at the Cape in 1652, and soon became the basis for a colony that pushed steadily inland. British forces captured the Cape in 1795; the Cape became a British colony in 1806 and remained so throughout the nineteenth century. The economy was underpinned by slavery from the early years of Dutch settlement through until emancipation in 1838. Of relevance here are the ways in which archaeological, architectural, and documentary sources can be used to understand both the ways in which colonial control worked as a system of dominance and the forms of expression and resistance of subalterns, whether slaves or underclass (Hall 2000).

In exploring this, I found Stallybrass and White's development of Bakhtin's classic concept of carnival particularly helpful. Stallybrass and White show how dominant statements – assertive building designs, monuments, or elite artifact sets – contain a "consciousness" of the unseen statements of those whom they dominated and suppressed (Hall 1992: 392): "a recurrent pattern emerges: the 'top' attempts to reject and eliminate the 'bottom' for reasons of prestige and status, only to discover, not only that it is in some way frequently dependent on the low-Other but also that the top includes the low symbolically, as a primary eroticized constituent of its own fantasy life. The result is a mobile, conflictual fusion of power, fear and desire in the construction of subjectivity: a psychological dependence upon precisely those Others which are being rigorously opposed and excluded at the social level" (Stallybrass and White 1986: 5).

Three dimensions of the traces of Dutch and British colonialism at the Cape show how the "low-Other" can be discerned across both categories of material evidence and scale.

In 1791, in the closing years of the Dutch East India Company administration, one Philip Anhuyzer bought a property in Barrack Street, Cape Town, which he owned and occupied until his death in 1829. Over these four decades, a rich accumulation of domestic debris built up in the house's courtyard well. On his death, a standard probate record of Anhuyzer's possessions was drawn up and lodged in the government archive. Comparison of the archaeological assemblage and the probate record revealed suggestive discrepancies: "the list of personal possessions from Layer Three of the well reveals men (military badge, cane, shoes) but also women (hairpin, brooch, small bells, shoes, thimbles, cotton reels, a doll and a doll's tea service). The probate record, on the other hand, is an overwhelmingly masculine document. The image that emerges from the list of personal possessions is of Philip Anhuyzer himself: perhaps suffering from gout (the crutches), sword and pistol beside him while reading his bible and occasionally peering at his silver watch through his spectacles. His wife, Cecilia van der Kaap, is excluded from the image, and his slave laborer, housemaid and cook are only in the list because they were Anhuyzer's property. Similarly with the underclass. In both the probate record and the street directories, Anhuyzer, his house and his possessions are almost as one. But the assemblage from Layer Three of the well hints at other presences: the common soldiers who left behind buttons and a uniform badge and the servants and slaves who lived off mutton stew and snoek" (Hall et al. 1990: 83).

Anhuyzer's townhouse, in common with others in the street, had a symmetrical façade, probably with baroque-style ornamentation (it is captured, in altered form, in an early photograph). This style was characteristic of the Cape manor house of the eighteenth century and is celebrated today as the "Cape Dutch" architecture of the colonial countryside. Conventional interpretations of this form of building have been of a male-dominated world, with little evidence of either women or the slaves who, by the end of the eighteenth century, accounted for some two-thirds of the population of Cape Town: "the image of the benign patriarch, sitting at ease beneath the oaks, in front of his whitewashed façade, smoking his long clay pipe and contemplating civilization against the barbaric chaos of Africa" (Hall 1994: 1). This representation, however, disguised "the webs of consanguinity and conjugality" that tied these gabled buildings together into a tight set (Hall 1994: 2). Once assumptions of patriarchy were abandoned in favor of the dynamics of race, class and gender, new connections become apparent. A close reexamination of deeds and other records of ownership in the archive revealed that, rather than being commercial transactions between unrelated men, eighteenth-century Cape farms, enabled by slave labor, were linked to just eight dominant families through female ties: "the emerging elite of the colonial countryside formed webs of economic and social relationships around connections between women who were marked out by their claim to racial purity and superiority...a gendered segment within a burgeoning gentry class, these women facilitated capital accumulation and carried the identity of difference from the transgressive miscegenation that was an inevitable consequence of the expanding colonial frontier. The gables themselves can be read as a metaphor of fecundity contained within the discipline of order" (Hall 1994: 3).

The concept of containing disorderly conditions such as fecundity within symmetrical structures extended to the founding cityscape of Cape Town, as with comparable town layouts in the Netherlands, Dutch Manhattan, the Dutch West India Company base in Brazil, and colonial Indonesia (Hall 2000). Street plans linked men to other men and were described in this way in contemporary travelers' accounts. The urban grid structured and directed formal processions and sumptuary declarations of male status, such as elaborate funeral processions. In contrast, elite women were contained within houses, churches, and other acceptable venues for public display. What becomes evident through immersion in this evidence, whether archaeological, architectural, or documentary, is the repetition of these assertions of order; the overdetermination in the insistence on geometry and symmetry, status, order, and movement in the correct sequence. Behind this, however, is a constant presence of fear and violence: violent arguments between men over the seating of their wives in church; punishments for breaking sumptuary codes; public punishments and execution for those challenging the Dutch East India Company's regulations; the fear of slaves "running amuck"; the constant terror of unseen runaways and renegades descending from the vastness of Table Mountain and setting fire to the town by night (Hall 1997, 2000).

These instances – at the scale of assemblage, household, and cityscape – reveal the "bumps, dents and bruises in the patriarchal façade; signs that can be used in extrapolating past relations of gender" (Hall 1997: 227–228). The consciousness of the "low-Other" is evident in absences and inconsistencies (the contrast between Anhuyzer's probate record and the revealing rubbish in his backyard well), in ambiguities and misrepresentations (of the patriarchal Cape countryside, disguising the key role of women in differentiating race and class), and in repetition and overdetermination (the insistence on geometry and order in the layout and ceremonials of the cityscape, seeking to drown out the fear of disorder, violence, and imminent destruction). These are "points of vulnerability, places where the heavy, muffling shrouds of domination become unstitched, the point of disappearance of the subaltern, the aporia" (Hall 1999: 193).

Returning now to the cases in this collection – and testing them for traces of the "low-Other" through hints of absences and inconsistencies, ambiguities and misrepresentations, and repetition and overdetermination – reveals some intriguing bumps, dents, and bruises in their heterosexual and patriarchal façades (Figure 19.3). These can be organized against the two largely empty quadrants, defined by intangible expressions of normative orders and by intangible expressions of transgressive sexual effects.

Voss and Casella, in their respective considerations of the San Francisco Presidio and the Nursery area of the Ross women's prison, consider the implications of absences in the archaeological record. At the Presidio, there was no artifactual trace of indigenous communities in the inner areas, despite the high likelihood that such people worked for, and interacted with, the Spanish in these areas. At the Ross Prison, there was no material trace of children, despite the clear designation of the area in the documentary record (and in contrast with sites such as the Half-Way House Hotel; Weiss, Chapter 4). This leads Casella to ask whether, in prison conditions, artifacts could have other uses and meanings, and, therefore, whether large, metal serving spoons found in the Nursery Ward could have been toys rather than food utensils: "as objects that could be bounced, banged, sucked – but crucially, not swallowed – perhaps these kitchen implements served as 'toys' for the infant and toddler residents of the Nurseries? Ultimately, the invisibility of childhood within this excavated assemblage raises questions on the nature of a carceral childhood, where the absences themselves created a unique spatial cartography of power." Reading artifacts in this way is to move beyond the standard, utilitarian functionalism of archaeology (pots are for preparing food, spoons are for eating) and to interpret material things as "subaltern objects" that acquire their meaning from the relationships of dominance and subservience in their particular contexts.

Once the possibilities inherent in archaeological collections are opened up in this way, other suggestive ambiguities become evident. As Rubertone shows, the monumentalized New England landscape did not result in the simple closure on the question of indigenous history and claims to identity that had been hoped for, and a transgressive undercurrent of resistance, a "hidden transcript" in James Scott's (1992) terms, was nurtured in the shadow of the monuments. This recalls my own argument that the patriarchal façades of the manor houses that monumentalized the South African colonial landscape nurtured their "shadow" in the networks of women that perpetuated elite connections and the slaves who enabled the economy.

Freeing artifacts from the constraints of direct interpretations, as well as using context and other forms of evidence to tease out ambiguities, inconsistencies, and contradictions, opens up further possibilities in other cases in this collection. Croucher touches the surface of the complex relationships between women living and working in the compound at Mgoli; the four wives of Abdalla bin Jabir, and the non-Arab concubine living across the inner courtyard in her separate building: "daily practices in the space between the stone house and the Trench C house would have engaged relationships between women who had children of equal status, who performed the same daily tasks, and who had access to the same material wealth. What separated them most may have been the manner in which they participated in sexual relationships with the same man – for a concubine, these practices may have run the gamut from open seduction of the master, partly for her own pleasure, in the 'private' space to the rear of the main stone house, to deeply coercive sexual acts

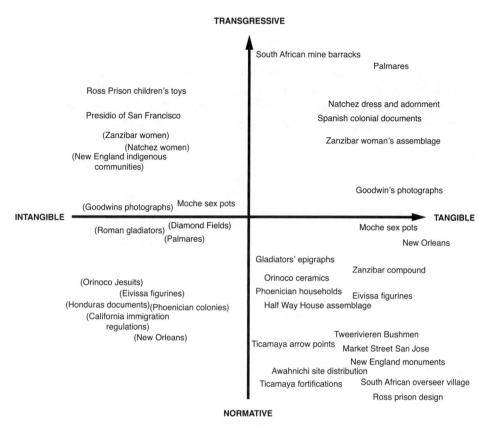

FIGURE 19.3. Grid Three: intangible expressions of normative order and transgressive sexual effects.

between a man and a woman he had enslaved" (Croucher, Chapter 5). This suggests, in turn, the overdetermination of personal adornment, and the sexual effects of the jewelry associated with concubinage at the site. Similarly with the complex relations between Natchez women and French men on the banks of the Mississippi River: "Anxieties regarding fear and desire seep from numerous archival accounts, with most accounts agreeing on the notion that the bodies of Natchez men, women, and children were visually, spiritually, and sexually different from their own" (Loren, Chapter 7). Many of these French men were subservient to the rigors of colonial order and discipline and would have been caught in a complex set of intersections of race, gender, and class. As with the metal spoons in the Ross Prison Nursery and the concubine's jewelry at Mgoli, the glass beads that adorned Natchez bodies would have had an excess of meaning that far surpassed their utilitarian value.

Transgressive sexual effects are, by their nature, less evident in any form of record than intangible expressions of normative expectations and behaviors, and so it follows that, once we recognize the valencies of ambiguities, contradictions, and overdetermination, the wider possibilities of the normative domain will become apparent. Again, the cases in this collection demonstrate this wider potential well.

Sheptak, Blaisdell-Sloan, and Joyce's study of Spanish colonial Honduras shows the value in tracking between documents and the material records. In this case, sexuality is a highly visible structuring principle because, they suggest, of the legal ruling required when children were born as a result of sexual liaisons between colonizers and indigenous people. Although the material record has left collective traces – the obsidian arrowheads left by anonymous young men, the new fortifications raised by unidentified villagers – the documents often name people whose actions or circumstances require reporting or some kind of action. This leaves open intriguing, and still unexplored, possibilities in understanding the intangible significations of the dominant order at the Spanish colonial frontier. For example, what of the "Christian Spanish woman" from Sevilla, mentioned in a report from the field in August 1535, whose husband had been killed in an earlier military action and who had been taken as a wife by an indigenous leader resisting colonization? As Sheptak, Blaisdell-Sloan, and Joyce (Chapter 10) note, the recurrent theme of the "captive woman" invoked "ideas of kinship, shame, and honor. They were strategic, if violent, means by which new societies were forged." Recognition of the ways in which people were distributed across colonial and imperial landscapes in ways such as these extends considerably the reach of interpretation of normative sexual effects.

Looking more deeply at both the evidence from the Orinoco frontier and at turn-of-the-century New Orleans shows, in a similar fashion, how the wider plays of then-normative sexual effects can be extrapolated. Tarble de Scaramelli (Chapter 9) notes a common interest between Jesuit priests seeking to embed colonial control and indigenous women adjusting to the needs of the new order:

> under the colonial regime some indigenous women were empowered by their productive capacities both in the biological and agricultural realms and sought to negotiate social mobility through conversion to Catholicism, commodity production for personal economic gain, and, in some circumstances, sexual favors, concubinage, or marriage outside of their birth community. . . . by gaining the confidence of the women and children, the Jesuits attempted to overcome some of the resistance to the mission regime and, at the same time, undermine the traditional forms of status and political power. It appears that some of the women used these circumstances to their benefit, in a strategy to gain social mobility in the mission context.

Dawdy (Chapter 16) shows that the role of women was equally complex in the changing nature of New Orleans, with women gaining control of key properties ahead of the city's reputation for its sexuality: "New Orleans went from being a gendered *space* to a sexualized *place*". . . . The businesswomen of New Orleans facilitated masculine consumption and the production of a homosocial landscape. Men experienced the city together, as men."

These subtleties of interpretation allow the exploration of the full vector of tangibility across varying forms of normative practices. A number of other cases can be extended in similar ways: Punic Eivissa (the meaning of the linkage among procreation, death, and cremation at a time of significant social and economic change); Phoenician colonies in Iberia and western Sicily (the linkage between domestic routines and concepts of eternity through funerary rituals); California (the overdetermination in the continual regulation of sexual behavior via legislation). Incorporating the consciousness of other meanings that extend beyond the immediate reading of material culture provides a key contribution to a fuller methodology of sexual effects.

Always interesting are those cases that fall on the boundary, in this instance between intangible expressions of normative and transgressive sexual effects. Both the residents of the Diamond Fields' model Victorian village and Goodwin's use of photography a generation later have this quality. Shepherd's interpretation of Goodwin's state of mind can serve for both: "Can we talk of pornographies of death and desire? Is there an erotics of exhumation and display at work here, in these tales of living and dead Bushmen (as in a set of practices articulated by a logic of desire)? At what point do we pass beyond the limits of representation, or is there no limit to the pursuit of information and the requirement that all shall be bared, all shall be uncovered?" (Shepherd, Chapter 17). This is the patriarchal colonial gaze, implicated with desire for the Black native body that was eventually to provoke preventative legislation in apartheid South Africa's Immorality Act of 1950.

The Moche sex pots, the lives of Roman gladiators, and Palmares straddle this boundary. Were the sex pots expressions of a dominant order, or were they defiant challenges to assumptions of sexual privileges? "One of the first Moche ceramics I saw up close was an unusually large female effigy at the Field Museum. It had a rather ferocious face, an enormous protruding vulva, and an unmistakable clitoris. This pot grabbed my attention; but like other researchers before me, I felt silenced by a figure at once graphically explicit and entirely ambiguous" (Weismantel, Chapter 18). How did Roman gladiators reconcile the requirements of playing the archetype of masculinity in the imminence of death with the affectionate relationships indicated by some of their epigraphs? How can we best understand the complex and often contradictory responses that knowledge of Palmares has always provoked, and continues to provoke today?

Conclusion: Resolving the Paradox

The methodological schema that I have outlined here is one of several potential ways of addressing the challenges in developing a fuller approach to the archaeology of sexual effects. But what any schema must do to be helpful is to resolve the paradox with which I opened this chapter: the quality of being at once intensely private, personal, and sensory and also public and definitive of the structures of social and economic organization. A review of the cases used across the range of projects that constitute the chapters in this book shows that they are successful in cutting free of the assumptions of a standard and universal heterosexual world and in mapping and probing different normative and tangible expressions of sexual orders. They are, however, less adroit in finding transgressive sexual effects and, particularly, less tangible expressions of sexuality and gender. I have suggested that this problem can be overcome – and the paradox resolved – by looking for the expression of the "low-Other" that is contained within the dominant expression, the "mobile, conflictual fusion of power, fear and desire in the construction of subjectivity" that is evoked so powerfully in Stallybrass and White's (1986) seminal paper.

My final mapping of the contents of this volume against the two vectors of the normative–transgressive and the tangible–intangible summarizes the ways in which I have stretched the cases in this book to suggest the presence of the "low-Other" (my extrapolations are shown in parentheses in Figure 19.3). As described in this chapter, each extrapolation contributes to the richness of our understanding of sexual effects and demonstrates the vitality and potential of this area of archaeological enquiry.

REFERENCES

Casella, E. C. 2000. "'Doing Trade': A Sexual Economy of 19th Century Australian Female Convict Prisons." *World Archaeology* 32(2):209–221.

Hall, M. 1992. "Small Things and the Mobile, Conflictual Fusion of Power, Fear and Desire," in Yentsch, Anne, and Mary Beaudry (eds.), *The Art and Mystery of Historical Archaeology: Essays in Honor of James Deetz.* Boca Raton, FL: CRC Press, pp. 373–399.

———. 1994. "The Secret Lives of Houses: Women and Gables in the Eighteenth Century Cape. *Social Dynamics* 20(1):1–48.

———. 1997. "Patriarchal Facades: The Ambivalences of Gender in the Archaeology of Colonialism," in Wadley, Lynn (ed.), *Our Gendered Past: Archaeological Studies of Gender in Southern Africa.* Johannesburg, South Africa: Witwatersrand University Press, pp. 221–236.

———. 1999. "Subaltern Voices? Finding the Spaces between Things and Words," in Funari, Pedro Paulo, Sian Jones, and Martin Hall (eds.), *Writing from the Edge: Historical Archaeology.* London, Routledge: 93–203.

———. 2000. *Archaeology and the Modern World: Colonial Transcripts in South Africa and the Chesapeake.* London and New York: Routledge.

———, D. Halkett, J. Klose, and G. Ritchie. 1990. "The Barrack Street Well: Images of a Cape Town Household in the Nineteenth Century." *South African Archaeological Bulletin* 45:73–92.

Scott, J. 1992. *Domination and the Arts of Resistance.* New Haven, CT: Yale University Press.

Stallybrass, P., and A. White 1986. *The Politics and Poetics of Transgression.* Ithaca, NY: Cornell University Press.

INDEX